SECRET HISTORY

WORLD WAR II

JOHN TOWNSEND

W
FRANKLIN WATTS
LONDON•SYDNEY

First published in 2010 by Franklin Watts

Copyright © 2010 Arcturus Publishing Limited

Franklin Watts
338 Euston Road
London NW1 3BH

Franklin Watts Australia
Level 17/207 Kent Street, Sydney, NSW 2000

Produced by Arcturus Publishing Limited,
26/27 Bickels Yard, 151–153 Bermondsey Street,
London SE1 3HA

The right of John Townsend to be identified
as the author of this work has been asserted
by him in accordance with the Copyright,
Designs and Patents Act 1988.

Series concept: Alex Woolf
Editor and picture researcher: Alex Woolf
Designer: Tall Tree

A CIP catalogue record for this book is available from
the British Library.

Dewey Decimal Classification Number: 940.5'485

ISBN 978 0 7496 8231 6

Printed in China

Franklin Watts is a division of Hachette Children's
Books, an Hachette Livre UK company.
www.hachettelivre.co.uk

SL000975EN

Picture credits:
Corbis: cover *top left* (Melbourne Brindle/Swim Ink 2,
LLC), cover *right* (Bettmann), 9 *both* (Bettmann), 10
(Bettmann), 11 (Bettmann), 18 (Bettmann), 19
(Bettmann), 20 (Bettmann), 22 (Bettmann), 23
(Bettmann), 26 (Sion Touhig/Sygma), 27 (Bettmann), 29
(Bettmann), 30 (EPA), 31 (Hulton-Deutsch Collection),
34 (Swim Ink 2, LLC), 37 (Bettmann), 38 (Hulton-
Deutsch Collection), 39 (Bettmann), 41 (Wolfgang
Kaehler).
Getty Images: 6 (Heinrich Hoffmann/Time & Life
Pictures), 7 (Lawrence Thornton/Hulton Archive), 12
(Keystone/Hulton Archive), 13 (Keystone/Hulton
Archive), 14 (Keystone/Hulton Archive), 15
(Keystone/Hulton Archive), 16 (Central Press/Hulton
Archive), 17 (Keystone/Hulton Archive), 21 (Fox
Photos/Hulton Archive), 28 (MPI/Hulton Archive), 32
(Keystone/Hulton Archive), 35 (Kurt Hutton/Picture
Post), 36 (Galerie Bilderwelt/Hulton Archive), 42
(William Vandivert/Time & Life Pictures), 43 (Bentley
Archive/Popperfoto).
NHPA: 25 (Donald Mammoser).
Rex Features: 33 (Action Press), 40 (Everett Collection).
Shutterstock: *spy camera* cover (alphacell), 24
(Sebastian Knight).

Cover pictures: *top left*: US poster from 1942; *bottom
left*: World War II-era spy camera; *right*: Serbian spy
Dusko Popov (1912–1981), who worked for MI5 in
World War II.

Spread head pictures are all from Shutterstock: 6:
World War II American M24 tank (Len Green); 8, 12:
World War II-era spy camera (alphacell); 10, 18, 26,
28, 34: headphones (Dmitry Naumov); 14: World
War II German MP40 submachine gun (Olemac); 16,
38: barbed wire (Nikita Rogul); 20, 22, 24: bomb
(fckncg); 30, 42: World War II pistol (Wyatt Rivard);
32, 40: shovel (mmaxer); 36: megaphone (MilousSK).

Every attempt has been made to clear copyright.
Should there be any inadvertent omission, please apply
to the publisher for rectification.

CONTENTS

A GLOBAL CONFLICT

World War II was fought between the 'Axis' countries (including Germany, Japan and Italy) and the Allies (including the United States, Britain, France and the Soviet Union). It lasted from 1939 to 1945 and involved 61 countries and three-quarters of the world's population. Over 25 million members of the armed forces died in the war, as well as a similar number of civilians.

The German leader Adolf Hitler (1889–1945) walks up steps lined with swastika banners at a Nazi rally in 1934.

THE WAR BEGINS

World War II began when Germany, under Adolf Hitler, invaded Poland in September 1939, the latest in a series of aggressive moves by Germany against its neighbours. In response, Britain and France declared war on Germany. Italy, under Benito Mussolini, allied itself with Hitler. By mid-1940 Germany was in control of most of Western Europe.

ADOLF HITLER

Adolf Hitler and his Nazi Party took power in Germany in 1933. Hitler promised to make Germany great again but he also had secret plans to expand German territory. He wanted to create a powerful empire that would dominate Europe and western Asia. Hitler was also a racist. He planned to enslave or get rid of peoples he thought were inferior or not 'racially pure'.

The surprise attack by Japanese bombers on the US naval base at Pearl Harbor, Hawaii, took the war to a new scale.

THE WIDENING CONFLICT

In June 1941, Germany unexpectedly invaded the Soviet Union, with whom it had earlier formed a pact. In December 1941, Japan attacked the US naval port of Pearl Harbor, bringing the United States into the conflict. The war was now global in scale.

Until mid-1942, the Axis powers won most of the battles. However, from this time, the tide of the war turned steadily against them, thanks mainly to the vast resources of the United States and Soviet Union. The war finally ended in August 1945.

WAR OF SECRETS

World War II was not just about big battles involving guns, tanks and bombs. There was also another, secret conflict going on. Both the Axis and the Allied nations made great efforts to keep information hidden from the other side, and to uncover enemy plans. They engaged in secret operations, plots and missions to wrongfoot the enemy or take them by surprise.

IN THEIR OWN WORDS

This was a secret war, whose battles were lost or won unknown to the public; and only with difficulty is it comprehended, even now, by those outside the small high scientific circles concerned. No such warfare had ever been waged by mortal men.

Winston Churchill, *The Second World War*, Vol 2, p381

SEEKING SECRETS

During World War II, many spies worked behind enemy lines trying to discover secrets. Spying was dangerous work. Those who got caught risked being tortured and shot. Even those who didn't get caught had a hard time finding accurate information, let alone getting it back home safely. Nevertheless, many people in World War II were prepared to take the risk and become spies.

GERMAN SPY IN ENGLAND

German spy Josef Jakobs parachuted into England in January 1941. However, the Home Guard saw him land and arrested him. He had forged identity papers. He also had a radio transmitter for sending secrets back to Germany.

Jakobs was interrogated in the hope that he could be made to change sides and spy for Britain. But he was a committed Nazi and refused. He was taken to a cell in the Tower of London and later shot. Jakobs was one of 15 German spies executed in Britain during World War II.

DOUBLE CROSS

MI5, the British government agency responsible for homeland security and counterintelligence, set up a secret detection centre in England. Here German spies were interrogated and made to reveal their own secrets. Some were trained to become double agents and sent back to Germany to find Nazi secrets. This operation was code-named Double Cross, or 'XX'.

Not all spying took place on the ground. World War II saw the first 'spies in the sky' when powerful cameras were used over enemy territory.

GERMAN SPY IN LONDON

Tyler Kent was a clerk working in the US Embassy in London at the beginning of the war. He was actually a spy who stole hundreds of secret documents and passed important information to Germany. His spying was soon discovered and he was sent to prison for seven years.

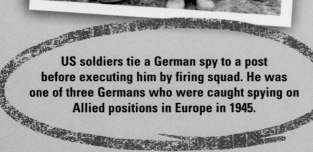

US soldiers tie a German spy to a post before executing him by firing squad. He was one of three Germans who were caught spying on Allied positions in Europe in 1945.

SOVIET SPY IN JAPAN

Probably the most skilful and successful spy in World War II was Richard Sorge. Sorge was a German citizen who spied for the Soviet Union. He spent the war in Tokyo where he posed as a newspaper reporter while sending secrets back to Moscow.

Sorge became friendly with the German ambassador, so he could spy on Germany as well as Japan. He discovered that the Germans were planning to invade the Soviet Union on 22 June 1941. The Soviets, who had a pact with Germany, simply didn't believe Sorge's message and the invasion took them by surprise. In late 1941, the Japanese arrested Sorge, and he was hanged.

DOUBLE AGENTS

Some agents were spies for one country while pretending to spy for another. These 'double agents' may have been previously loyal agents who were 'turned' by the enemy, usually by being threatened with execution. Alternatively, they may have become genuinely disillusioned with their own government and so decided to swap sides. Either way, they ran the risk of being shot for treason.

Josef Klein was a German spy working in the United States. A double agent named William Sebold informed the FBI of Klein's activities. Klein was arrested and imprisoned for espionage.

SPYING FOR THE ENEMY

Some Germans were so appalled by their Nazi leaders that they decided to help the enemy. A few worked secretly for an anti-Nazi organization in Switzerland called the Lucy Spy Ring.

One of these double agents was Rudolf Roessler who managed to pass German secrets to the Soviet Union (an ally of Britain and France from 1941). Some of these secrets were details of planned operations by German forces on the Eastern Front. Roessler's intelligence helped Soviet forces to counter German offensives more effectively.

AGENT ZIGZAG

Eddie Chapman was one of Britain's double agents. At the start of World War II, he worked for the German Secret Service. Although he was a prized Nazi agent, he was really spying secretly for Britain. He was known as Agent Zigzag.

HITLER'S SECRETS SMUGGLED TO AMERICA

Fritz Kolbe was an officer in Hitler's Foreign Ministry. He hated the Nazis so much that he copied around 2,600 secret documents and sent them to the head of the US Office of Strategic Services (OSS) in Switzerland. He didn't even want the United States to pay him for his work.

He was later described by the CIA (the successor to the OSS) as one of the most important spies of the war. The information he provided included descriptions of the following:

- German plans to counter the D-Day landings

- the V-1 and V-2 rocket programmes (see pages 20–21)

- details of the Messerschmitt Me 262 jet fighter

- Japanese plans in South-East Asia

THE OSS

The United States' Office of Strategic Services (OSS) was founded by President Roosevelt in 1942. The OSS collected secrets about countries at war with the United States. In total a team of 16,000 US agents worked behind enemy lines. At the end of the war, the OSS became the CIA (Central Intelligence Agency).

WOMEN SPIES

Some of the most daring spies of World War II were women. Female spies were sometimes dropped by parachute into occupied Europe. They went as part of the Special Operations Executive (SOE), set up by the British government in 1940. By disguising themselves as peasant women, the spies would not attract suspicion and were often able to observe enemy operations and send home vital information. But they faced serious risks.

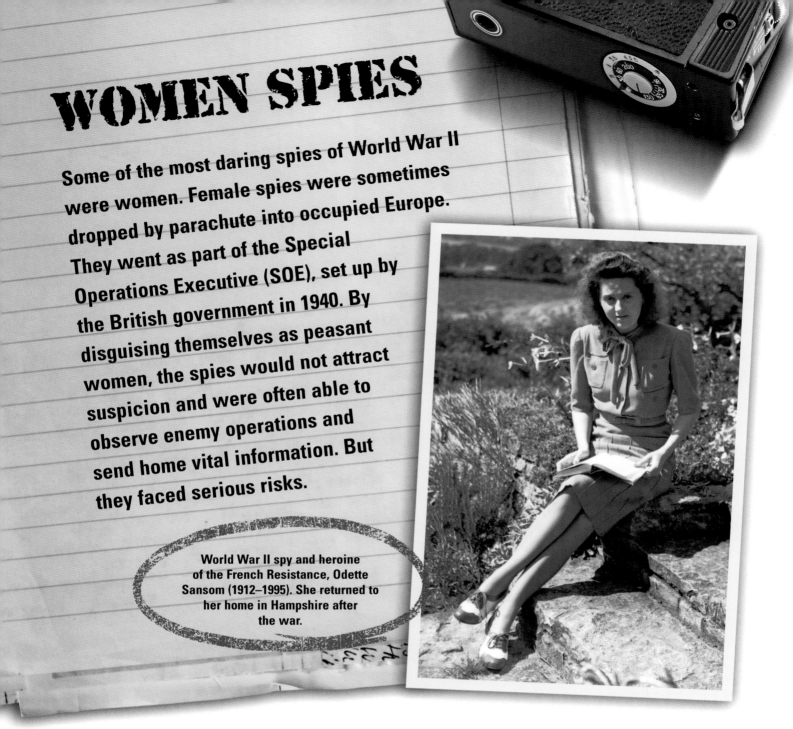

World War II spy and heroine of the French Resistance, Odette Sansom (1912–1995). She returned to her home in Hampshire after the war.

ODETTE SANSOM

Odette Brailly was born in France and moved to England when she married Roy Sansom. Odette became an SOE agent and went to France in 1942 as a radio operator. In 1943 she was caught and tortured by the Gestapo (the Nazi secret police), who pulled out all her toenails to make her talk. She refused to give them any information and was condemned to death and sent to Ravensbrück concentration camp. Remarkably she survived and, after the war, she was awarded the George Cross for bravery.

VIOLETTE SZABO

Violette Bushell was born to a French mother and English father and grew up in London. She married a soldier, Etienne Szabo, who was killed in battle in 1941. This prompted her to join the SOE. She was parachuted into France in 1944 and led a French Resistance group on secret raids sabotaging bridges. She sent back radio reports giving the locations of armament factories, which the Allies could bomb. She was eventually caught and tortured by the Gestapo. Violette was executed by firing squad. After her death, she was awarded the George Cross.

IN THEIR OWN WORDS

Shortly after Violette Szabo's execution, a London newspaper described how she tried to avoid capture:

... she was surrounded by the Gestapo in a house in the south west of France. Resistance appeared hopeless but Madame Szabo, seizing a Sten-gun and as much ammunition as she could carry, barricaded herself in part of the house and, exchanging shot for shot with the enemy, killed or wounded several of them. By constant movement, she avoided being cornered and fought until she dropped exhausted.

Violette Szabo was just 23 years old when she was executed. Her four-year-old daughter was presented with Violette's George Cross medal in 1946.

NOOR INAYAT KHAN

Noor Inayat Khan was a British SOE agent of Indian descent. She was the first female radio operator sent into Nazi-occupied France. Noor was betrayed by a Frenchwoman and arrested. Because she kept copies of her secret signals the Germans were able to use Noor's radio to trick London into sending new agents – into the hands of the waiting Gestapo. Noor refused to reveal information under torture and was shot. She was awarded the George Cross.

THE FRENCH RESISTANCE

In the countries under Nazi occupation, everyone had to obey their new rulers or risk arrest – or worse. Many brave people tried to fight back against the occupiers. They joined secret organizations that carried out ambushes and acts of sabotage against the Nazis. France, in particular, had many secret resistance groups.

A group of Maquisards receive instructions before a raid. Many Maquisards received the Order of the Liberation, a medal awarded to heroes of the French Resistance during World War II.

THE MAQUIS

In France, many of the groups that were determined to resist the invaders hid in the forests and the countryside. They began to organize themselves into a resistance movement called the Maquis – a name for the bushes they used when hiding from the Germans.

As the Maquis groups grew, they led attacks on German forces. They aided the escape of Jews, communists and others who the Gestapo were determined to hunt down. Maquisards also helped many of the spies working secretly in France. When British and US pilots were shot down over France, the Maquis helped them return to Britain.

OPERATION JEDBURGH

British and US secret agents parachuted into France to support the work of the French Resistance. They ran sabotage missions against the Germans, helped by local Maquis groups. The 'Jeds' as they were called (they trained in the town of Jedburgh in Scotland) were sometimes caught and tortured.

Telephone operators helped members of the Maquis, who used a special code to report the movements of German forces in France.

REVENGE

Allied forces invaded Normandy in June 1944 (D-Day) and Provence in August. Before these attacks, the Allies transmitted coded messages to the French Resistance asking them to target German garrisons. These undercover attacks greatly helped the rapid Allied advance through France.

However, there was a cost. In revenge for the French attacks, the Nazis hanged 120 men in Tulle. A German major also ordered the execution of more than 600 men, women and children before setting fire to a village. Despite this, the French Resistance continued their dangerous work until the end of the war.

GILBERT RENAULT

A famous secret agent of the French Resistance was Gilbert Renault, known as Colonel Rémy. He passed Nazi secrets to Britain, which helped the Allied forces prepare for their invasion of France. Awarded the Order of the Liberation medal in 1942, he was on the Gestapo's 'wanted list' but was never captured.

SECRET POLICE

Heinrich Himmler (1900–1945) was head of the SS. His goal was to kill all the Jews in Europe.

Dictators can only rule with the help of a large and powerful secret police force to hunt down, imprison or kill opponents of their regime. Hitler's secret state police was called the Gestapo and its ruthless methods spread fear wherever the Nazis went. The Gestapo was founded in 1933 by Hermann Goering and was later led by Heinrich Himmler.

THE GESTAPO

During World War II, the Gestapo followed the advancing German army as part of the SS, Hitler's vast army of henchmen and bodyguards. Once German rule was established, the Gestapo would round up those they regarded as enemies, including communists, Jews and anyone who resisted Nazi rule. Thousands were imprisoned or shot without trial.

IN THEIR OWN WORDS

Pastor Harald Sandbaek, a leader of the Danish resistance, describes being tortured by the Gestapo in October 1944:

I declared that I had no more to say, after which those devils handed me over to the torturers. They half dragged and half carried me up to the attic of the college, took off all my clothes and put on new handcuffs. To these a string was attached which could be tightened and caused insufferable pain. I was thrown on a bed and whipped with a leather dog whip.

Quoted in Spartacus Educational:
www.spartacus.schoolnet.co.uk/GERgestapo.htm

The Gestapo used brutal methods such as electric shocks, beatings or near-drowning in bathtubs filled with ice-cold water to make people confess their secrets. They had about 45,000 members but had another 160,000 agents and informers. People in occupied Europe had to be careful not to say or do anything that might arouse suspicion in case someone reported them to the Gestapo.

ITALY'S SECRET POLICE

The secret police in Mussolini's Italy was called the OVRA. Though hated by many, the OVRA was not as ruthless as the Gestapo. One method they used to stop troublemakers was to tie them to a tree and make them drink castor oil before forcing them to eat a live toad.

JAPAN'S SECRET POLICE

In World War II, Japan's military police were the Kempeitai. Their job was to maintain security in the Japanese homeland and in the many Japanese prisoner of war camps scattered around South-East Asia. The Kempeitai was notorious for its brutality and frequent use of torture against prisoners and civilians suspected of crimes against the state.

17

SECRET WEAPONS: INVISIBLE WAVES

During World War II, each side competed to develop weapons and equipment that would give them a decisive advantage over their enemies. Large teams of top scientists were recruited to come up with ever more deadly weapons – many of them quite bizarre.

This station on Britain's east coast was part of the world's first radar system. It was used during World War II to detect incoming enemy aircraft.

RADIO WAVES

Radar (Radio Detection and Ranging) was a new technique for working out the position and movement of an object by measuring radio waves reflected from its surface. Radar was first developed in Britain in the 1930s and the British government soon realized the technology had military applications.

Radar played a vital role during the Battle of Britain (July–October 1940). A chain of radar stations along the English coast gave early warning of German aircraft crossing the English Channel

MINIATURE RADAR

By 1940 radar technology had advanced to a point where very small objects could be detected from long distances. Small radar antennae on Allied bombers greatly improved the accuracy of bombing raids on German cities. Aircraft could now detect objects as small as a submarine periscope, allowing ships or bombers to attack and destroy previously undetectable German submarines.

Radar operators on board ships could pick up vital information, as on this aircraft carrier in the Pacific during strikes against Japan.

and North Sea. This gave the RAF time to send up fighter planes to attack the approaching bombers.

BATTLE OF THE BEAMS

German aircraft used radio signals to locate targets in Britain for night bombing. They beamed two radio signals to form a cross above a target. The bomber pilots would fly along one beam and as soon as they picked up the other signal, they dropped their bombs. This resulted in accurate bombing, causing great damage to British cities, factories and military installations.

The British fought back by transmitting other radio signals to confuse the pilots. The Germans had to develop a different system of radio signals to direct its bombers. The British used spies and interrogated captured German pilots to find out how this worked. They were then able to beam yet more radio signals at advancing aircraft, causing them to miss their targets.

R V JONES

Reginald Victor (R V) Jones was a British scientist who played a crucial role in the Battle of the Beams. On Jones's advice, the British began to counter the German radio signals with their own. Jones also suggested that pieces of metal foil falling through the air would create radar echoes and confuse the enemy. These falling clouds of foil became known as 'chaff'.

SECRET WEAPONS: HITLER'S MISSILES

By 1941 Nazi leaders were becoming concerned about the rising losses of German planes and pilots on air raids over British cities. They were determined to reduce their losses, so German scientists began secret work to develop long-range pilotless rocket bombs.

DOODLEBUGS

The first version of the pilotless rocket bomb was completed in mid-1942. However, in tests it kept crashing and it took a further two years before it was ready for use. The missile, known as the V-1, carried an 850 kg warhead and was powered by a jet engine. It travelled at 560 kph and had a range of 240 km. Nearly 10,000 of these 'doodlebugs' were fired at Britain from northern France, killing over 6,000 people.

THE FIRST MODERN ROCKET

In September 1944 a V-2 rocket was fired at London. These missiles, built by the Nazis using slave labour, were powered by liquid fuel and provided the model for

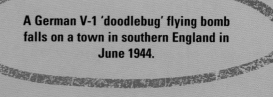

A German V-1 'doodlebug' flying bomb falls on a town in southern England in June 1944.

all future rockets. The V-2 had a 980 kg warhead and a speed of 4,000 kph. Their mobile launchpads made it difficult for Allied bombers to detect and destroy them before they were in the air. Over 3,000 were launched at various Allied targets, killing over 7,000 civilians.

THE V-3 CANNON

The Germans also developed the V-3, an underground cannon, capable of firing shells at London from giant bunkers in northern France. The V-3 would have been able to fire 300 shells an hour at a speed of 1,500 metres per second. But the project was abandoned when Allied troops captured it after D-Day.

The German V-2 long-range missile was the forerunner of modern space rockets.

MIRACLE WEAPONS

At the end of World War II, US special intelligence units searched German factories to find Hitler's secret weapons plans. They found designs for many advanced weapons, from a gun that could shoot a stream of metal at 8,000 metres per second to an orbiting solar mirror gun. Hitler had hoped that these *Wunderwaffen* ('miracle weapons') would stop the advancing Allies in their tracks – but he ran out of time.

IN THEIR OWN WORDS

After the war, aeronautical engineer Roy Fedden led a fact-finding tour of secret Nazi research facilities on behalf of the British government. He reported:

I have seen enough of their designs and production plans to realize that if they [the Germans] had managed to prolong the war some months longer, we would have been confronted with a set of entirely new and deadly developments in air warfare.

Quoted on www.burlingtonnews.net/hitlersufo.html

21

SECRET WEAPONS: THE BOMB

From 1942 US scientists worked in secret to create a bomb so powerful it could end the war. The bomb's explosive power would come through the release of energy stored within atoms. Fear that the Germans would master the technology first drove the scientists on.

American scientist Robert Oppenheimer, leader of the Manhattan Project, views the remains of the steel tower, which melted in the intense heat where the first atomic bomb was tested.

SPLITTING THE ATOM

In the early 20th century, the great physicist Albert Einstein (1879–1955) showed that matter could be turned into energy. To do this scientists had to split apart the basic building blocks of matter – atoms. At the centre of every atom is a cluster of particles called the nucleus. Splitting the nucleus could release tremendous amounts of energy – known as nuclear energy.

Thousands of people were involved in the 'Manhattan Project' to build the bomb.

IN THEIR OWN WORDS

In August 1939 Albert Einstein wrote to the US president Franklin Roosevelt about the possibility of making a massive 'atom bomb':

A single bomb of this type, carried by boat or exploded in a port, might very well destroy the whole port together with some of the surrounding territory.

From *My Silent War* by Kim Philby (MacGibbon & Kee, 1968)

A mushroom cloud towers more than six kilometres above Nagasaki, following the nuclear attack by the United States. The heat on the ground reached about 3,000 degrees Celsius.

CHAIN REACTION

Scientists call splitting the atom 'nuclear fission'. The scientists of the Manhattan Project aimed to create a fission chain reaction. When one atom was split, the particles given off would split the nuclei of other atoms, which would split still others. The chain reaction could only be achieved by using certain rare forms of radioactive elements such as uranium and plutonium. *Radioactive* means they emit energy in the form of streams of particles.

On 16 July 1945, after three years' research, they succeeded in producing the world's first nuclear explosion. It was equivalent to 19,000 tonnes of TNT and it threw into the sky a mushroom-shaped cloud of vapour and debris.

HIROSHIMA AND NAGASAKI

Soon afterwards, the United States used nuclear bombs for the first time as weapons of war. Victory was imminent in the United States' war against Japan, but the Japanese refused to surrender and an invasion looked like the only solution. This was likely to cost the lives of hundreds of thousands of soldiers and civilians.

The US government decided instead to drop nuclear bombs on two Japanese cities to convince the Japanese to surrender. 'Little Boy' was dropped on Hiroshima on 6 August 1945, levelling two-thirds of the city and killing about 200,000. Three days later 'Fat Man' was dropped on Nagasaki. Japan surrendered on 2 September, ending World War II.

SECRET WEAPONS: RISKY AND RIDICULOUS

Not all secret weapons in World War II used the latest science and technology. Some were simply bizarre and not very friendly to animals.

DUMMY LOGS

The British came up with a secret container for carrying grenades – a pretend log! The plaster logs were used for smuggling ammunition into enemy territory. Sealed containers were built into the logs, which were carefully made to look very real. The only danger was if someone tried to burn one on a log fire!

ANTI-TANK DOGS

The Soviet Union trained dogs to carry bombs on their backs and to run under enemy tanks. As the dog slid under a tank, a lever sticking up from the dog's back would switch on the bomb. The enemy tank, as well as the dog, would be destroyed.

The Soviet dog-trainers kept the dogs hungry and taught them to run under tanks to find food. But there was a problem. In their training, the dogs were fed under Soviet tanks, not German tanks, which looked different. So during

battles, the dogs tended to run under the Soviet tanks and blow *them* up! However, in one battle, dogs were reported to have destroyed 12 German tanks.

BAT BOMBS

An American dentist came up with an idea for getting back at Japan for bombing Pearl Harbor. He suggested strapping small firebombs to thousands of bats and dropping them over Japan. The bats would roost inside buildings during the day, and then timers would ignite the bombs. Thousands of Japanese buildings would be destroyed. That was the theory!

The US Navy carried out tests with thousands of bats. In one episode during testing, a colony of bats with bombs escaped and roosted under a fuel tank at a US air base in New Mexico. The resulting fire caused extensive damage. The project was dropped soon afterwards.

EXPLODING RATS

It was Britain's Special Operations Executive that came up with the idea. Why not, they suggested, use dead rats packed with explosives to blow up the enemy's boilers? The idea was to leave 'rat bombs' on piles of coal. When they were shovelled into the boiler along with the coal, the heat would detonate the bombs. In fact, the rat bombs were never used. The Germans discovered the first batch and the secret was out!

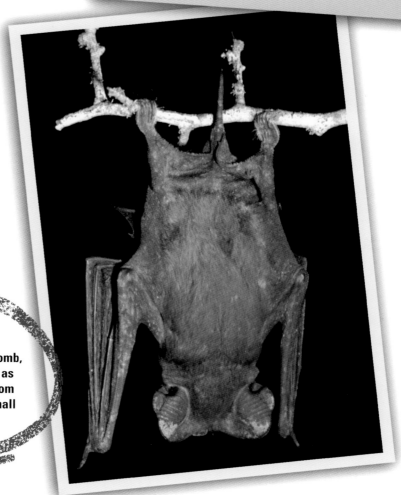

Mexican free-tailed bats such as this one were to be used in the proposed bat bombs. The inventor of the bomb, Dr Lytle Adams, predicted they would be as effective but less devastating than the atom bomb. They would cause thousands of small fires across the target city, yet little loss of life.

CODES AND CODE-BREAKERS

In wartime, governments and armed forces must often share secret information about plans and operations. The challenge is to keep these communications secret from the enemy. This is usually done by putting confidential information into code, making it meaningless to anyone without a code-breaker.

The Enigma machine contained many cogs and wheels, which could be set in different ways. Each setting produced a unique set of coded letters.

ENIGMA

In World War II, the Germans used a very advanced code machine called Enigma. The machine encoded all communications sent from military headquarters to outposts in occupied Europe. Enigma used a series of rotating wheels to scramble messages into meaningless text. It contained billions of possible combinations, so if you didn't

CODES IN TOOTHPASTE

Spies had to find ways of carrying and hiding secret codes. That could mean stitching paper into clothes or hiding messages inside everyday objects. Toothpaste tubes were often used. The top would be filled with toothpaste, but underneath there would be a space to hide a message.

know the Enigma setting, the message was impossible to work out. To make things even harder, the code's settings were changed every day.

CRACKING THE CODE

At the start of the war, the British set up a team of expert code-breakers to try and crack the Enigma code. They were based at 'Station X' in Bletchley Park, Buckinghamshire. The initial team of four had risen to around 3,500 by the end of 1942, and around 9,000 by January 1945.

The Germans, with their orderly way of doing things, actually helped the code-breakers, as coded messages would often start with the words 'To the Group'. Such repeated phrases were known as cribs and were a great help in cracking other parts of the code. The code-breakers were also helped by the fact that no letter could be coded as itself, reducing the number of possible settings for Enigma. Using these clues, the code-breakers succeeded in cracking the code on many occasions.

CODE TALKERS

In the Pacific War between the United States and Japan, the US Marines frequently used Native Americans to send secret messages by radio or telephone. While ordinary codes can be broken fairly quickly, codes based on a unique language must be studied for a long time before being understood. The Japanese never cracked the spoken code. US commanders claim the United States would never have won the Battle of Iwo Jima without the help of the 'code talkers'.

Two US Marine 'code talkers' use their native Navajo language to send a radio signal during a battle in the Pacific War.

SECRET INTELLIGENCE

The information decoded by the Allies at Bletchley Park and elsewhere was known as Ultra. The Allies were able to use Ultra to prepare for or evade enemy attacks and to launch attacks of their own. This secret intelligence undoubtedly helped the Allies win the war.

THE WAR IN EUROPE

Ultra provided the British with information about Operation Sealion, the planned German invasion of Britain. It also helped the British during the Battle of Britain, guiding them on how best to deploy the fighter planes of the RAF.

Just after the D-Day landings, decoded signals between Hitler and his generals helped Allied forces in Europe. The messages revealed when German reserve forces might be committed to battle.

BATTLE OF THE ATLANTIC

Perhaps the greatest triumph of the Bletchley Park code-breakers was cracking Naval Enigma, the code used by the German U-Boats (submarines) in the North Atlantic. The U-boats were sinking large numbers of Allied ships, threatening vital supplies to Britain.

A secret map of 1941 with details of Operation Sealion, the planned invasion of Britain by the Germans.

D-DAY DECEPTIONS

The Allied invasion of Europe was a huge undertaking that somehow had to be kept secret from the Germans. Much effort went into deception activities so that the Germans would not know the exact timing and location of the landings. These involved the use of dummy tanks, fake ships and elaborate troop movements. Ultra intelligence reassured the Allies that these deceptions were working.

Just after this German U-boat surfaced, it was sunk by US bombers as a result of decoded secret intelligence.

The decoded messages enabled the Allies to work out the routes of U-boat patrols, and ships could then be re-routed to evade them. Historians estimate that cracking Germany's Naval Enigma shortened the war by more than a year.

COVERING THEIR TRACKS

A key challenge for the Allies was to ensure that Germans did not find out that their codes had been broken. Otherwise the Germans might use even more complex codes. The Allies therefore took care to cover their tracks. For example, before an attack on a ship, they would send out a scout plane, making sure the Germans spotted it. The Germans would then think it was the plane and not a code-breaker that was responsible for the attack that followed.

'CONGRATULATIONS, MR X'

The Allies were able to decode messages sent by the Germans detailing the course of ships carrying supplies from Europe to troops in North Africa. When a convoy of ships from Naples in Italy was attacked and sunk by Allied aircraft, the Germans grew suspicious. So Allied commanders sent a message to a spy in Naples congratulating him on his excellent work. As planned, the Germans intercepted this message and believed it. The spy, however, did not exist.

29

SECRET PLOTS

By mid-1943 the tide of the war had turned against Germany. Some officers in the German army privately began to question Hitler's judgement. They regarded him as the person responsible for the disaster facing their country. They held secret meetings to decide what to do. They knew that if word got out about their plots, they would be killed, along with their families.

GETTING RID OF HITLER

The plotters believed that assassinating Hitler was the only way to save Germany. A new government could then be formed and a peace negotiated with the western Allies in time to prevent Germany from being invaded by the Soviet Union.

OPERATION VALKYRIE

The most serious plot to kill Hitler was called Operation Valkyrie and it took place on 20 July 1944. On that date, Hitler met with senior army officers at his Wolf's Lair military headquarters on the Eastern Front. One of the officers in attendance was Claus von Stauffenberg, a leading member of the plot. He came to the meeting with a time bomb in his briefcase.

Claus von Stauffenberg (1907–1944) was a supporter of Hitler at the start of the war. He is now remembered as a tragic hero who could have shortened the war if his plot had succeeded.

PLOTS AGAINST HITLER

There were several attempts to kill Hitler. In 1943 a bomb was placed on an aeroplane with Hitler on board, but it failed to go off. A few days later, a suicide bomber tried to kill Hitler at an exhibition of captured Soviet weapons – but the dictator left the exhibition early. Other attempts were made using grenades and guns, but luck favoured Hitler every time.

Adolf Hitler shows Italian dictator Benito Mussolini his damaged Wolf's Lair headquarters after the bomb blast that nearly killed him on 20 July 1944.

He placed the briefcase under the conference table. After a few minutes, he made an excuse and left the room. Soon afterwards, the bomb detonated. The room was demolished and four people were killed. Hitler, however, was shielded from the blast by a thick table leg, and he survived with only minor injuries.

THE PLOTTERS' FATE

Stauffenberg and the other plotters believed Hitler was dead and they prepared to take over the government in Berlin. Meanwhile, Hitler quickly ordered that Stauffenberg be shot by a firing squad. Eight of the other plotters were also executed. Their hangings were filmed and shown to Hitler.

THE PLOT TO KILL CHURCHILL

In 1943 the Germans managed to obtain details of the route to be taken by British prime minister Winston Churchill on a flight home from Egypt. The plane would stop at Algiers and Gibraltar on its way to London. Four Nazi assassins were sent to North Africa with orders to kill him when his plane landed there. However, code-breakers at Bletchley Park learned of the plot, so Churchill changed his flight plan.

ESCAPES

Many people spent the war imprisoned by the enemy. These included thousands of ordinary civilians in Japanese-controlled South-East Asia, as well as captured soldiers, airmen and political opponents in Nazi-occupied Europe. Some prisoners of war (POWs) decided to risk all and try to escape. Failure usually meant death, so any escape attempt required immense courage, careful planning and great secrecy.

Captured RAF officers at Stalag Luft III lay the foundations for a new hut. From here 76 POWs made a break for freedom, inspiring the war film *The Great Escape*.

STALAG LUFT III

One of the most famous escapes of World War II was the mass break-out of Allied POWs from the German prison camp Stalag Luft III in Poland. The Nazis considered the camp escape-proof. However, the prisoners had other ideas and decided to tunnel their way out. They built three tunnels, nine metres deep and

THE ONLY GERMAN TO ESCAPE

Franz von Werra (1914–1941) was a German fighter pilot who was shot down over England. He was captured and sent to a prison in Canada. He managed to escape from there and crossed the United States to Mexico. On his return to Germany, Hitler awarded him a medal. Seven months later, Werra's aircraft disappeared over the North Sea. His body was never recovered.

Colditz Castle in Germany was a high-security prisoner-of-war camp for officers who had escaped from other POW camps. Over 300 escape attempts were made during the war and 30 POWs succeeded in getting back to their home countries.

over 100 metres long. Out of odd bits of equipment they fashioned pumps to feed air to the tunnellers and rail-car systems for removing sand from the tunnels. They even installed electric lighting.

TUNNELLING TO FREEDOM

Somehow, the prisoners at Stalag Luft III managed to keep their operation secret. When German guards eventually discovered one of the tunnels, the operation appeared doomed. But another of the tunnels was completed soon afterwards and on 24 March 1944, 76 prisoners escaped. However, only three of them managed to evade recapture and get back home.

RAID AT LOS BAÑOS

There were few escape attempts from Japanese POW camps because of the high security and brutality of the regimes there. However, US and Filipino forces did launch a spectacular raid on a Japanese camp at Los Baños in the Philippines. The raid took place on 23 February 1945. It relied on stealth, speed and surprise and was an outstanding success, resulting in the liberation of over 2,000 POWs and internees. When they found out what had happened, the Japanese soldiers turned their anger on the local population, killing some 1,500 men, women and children.

KEEPING QUIET

Life was tough for civilians on the home front during World War II. Many lived in fear of air raids and had to cope with shortages of food and other essentials. Children were often evacuated to places in the countryside, far from their parents. People also had to live in a world of secrets.

LIMITED NEWS

Unlike today, the news media gave very few details of important events. It was considered safer and better for everyone if no one knew exactly what was going on.

CARELESS TALK...

Civilians were told to be careful about passing on information to anyone. Posters warned people not to gossip, as 'careless talk costs lives'. Servicemen and women

Posters warning of the danger of 'saying too much' were probably exaggerated, but they helped to make the public aware of security matters and feel they were part of the war effort.

REMOVING NAMES

In 1939, while the threat of a Nazi invasion hung over Britain, the government ordered signposts across the country to be painted over or removed. They wanted to make it harder for invading forces to find their way around. They also feared that low-flying German aircraft would be able to navigate by seeing place names. Railway station names were taken down and everyone was warned not to give strangers directions in case they were enemies or spies.

This posed photo from 1943 aimed to show the British public how to spot a Nazi spy in a pub. Conditions in Germany were apparently so bad by this time that the coat of the 'spy' (on the left) would be worn and thin, the buttons broken and the shoulders unpadded.

were forbidden to tell their families what they were doing and where, just in case the enemy found out. Letters to and from loved ones serving on the front were censored and any sensitive information was removed. The motto was 'secrets save lives'.

HIDING BAD NEWS

During World War II, governments wanted to keep bad news hidden because they feared its effects on national morale. Censorship was used to hide the truth from citizens as much as to hide it from the enemy.

THE ROHNA

In 1943 a German missile sank the British troopship *Rohna* off the coast of Algeria. The death toll was 1,138, including 1,015 American troops – the greatest loss of forces at sea in US history. It was also the first successful attack on a ship at sea by a German missile. To keep the news of Germany's new weapon secret and to stop public panic, the US government kept quiet about the tragedy.

PROPAGANDA

In wartime, all governments try to put out messages that help build support for the war effort and maintain morale. This is called propaganda. In World War II, governments used the latest mass media, such as radio and cinema newsreels, to ensure their propaganda reached as many people as possible. Propaganda often hides or distorts the truth; sometimes it is deliberately false.

PUBLIC ENLIGHTENMENT

Most propaganda in Nazi Germany was produced by the Ministry for Public Enlightenment and Propaganda, run by Josef Goebbels, who once said, 'If you tell a lie, tell a big one'. The ministry controlled all the country's media outlets. It fed the German people a constant diet of messages through speeches, posters, newspapers, radio broadcasts and cinema newsreels.

Germans were continually reminded of their country's on-going struggle against their enemies, especially the communists and the Jews. They were told of the greatness of German achievements.

This German propaganda poster from World War II intended to raise public morale with the message 'Ein Kampf, ein Sieg!' – One fight, one victory!

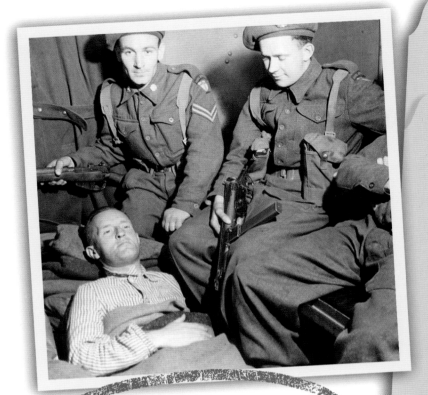

British forces arrest William Joyce, the most famous of the Lord Haw-Haws, in Germany at the end of the war. He was hanged for treason in 1946.

US PROPAGANDA

When World War II began, most US citizens were firmly against their country becoming involved. US government propaganda focused on convincing people that German and Japanese aggression was a threat to the United States. After the Japanese attack on the US naval base at Pearl Harbor in December 1941, the public no longer needed convincing of this. Propaganda then turned to encouraging people to increase production and conserve resources for the war effort.

The British were described as cowards and Americans as gangsters. German workers were urged to increase their productivity to help with the war effort.

LORD HAW-HAW

Germany even broadcast radio messages in English aimed at people in Britain and the United States. The announcer was known as 'Lord Haw-Haw'. Several announcers were used, but the most famous was an American called William Joyce. Lord Haw-Haw gave discouraging reports of high Allied losses and called on the British to surrender.

IN THEIR OWN WORDS

Winston Churchill, Britain's wartime prime minister, was famous for his stirring speeches to the nation on the radio. He helped to raise spirits and give hope. Even so, he admitted that lies were sometimes necessary to protect the truth. He said:

In wartime, truth is so precious that she should always be attended by a bodyguard of lies.

37

DEADLY SECRETS

The worst of all World War II's secrets remained mostly hidden until the war was nearly over. Many people knew about the labour camps to which thousands of Jews and others were sent. Rumours spread about the bad conditions there, but it was only when the first camps were liberated in late 1944 that the world began to learn the full horror of the Holocaust: the Nazi attempt to exterminate the Jews of occupied Europe.

As early as 1933, the Nazis began their anti-Jewish campaign in Germany, preventing the public from using Jewish shops.

HATRED OF JEWS

This mass murder of around six million Jews and the attempt to wipe out Jewish culture in Europe had its roots long before World War II. Hitler's Nazi Party blamed the Jews for all of Germany's problems, including the Great Depression. When they came to power in 1933, the Nazis brought in anti-Jewish laws, and Jews became increasingly isolated from German life. Attacks on Jews increased.

IN THEIR OWN WORDS

Lilli Kopecky, a Jew from Slovakia who survived Auschwitz (one of the death camps), later wrote:

I recall a Dutch Jew asking angrily, 'Where is my wife? Where are my children?' The Jews in the barracks said to him, 'Look at the chimney [of the crematorium]. They are up there.' But the Dutch Jew cursed them.... This is the greatest strength of the whole crime, its unbelievability.

Quoted in Martin Gilbert, *Never Again* (HarperCollins, 2000)

THE FINAL SOLUTION

When the war began, SS troops followed the German army into conquered territories. They isolated Jewish communities in ghettos. In the Soviet Union, they killed them. In 1941 Nazi leaders decided on the 'final solution to the Jewish question'. They ordered the building of death camps.

Jews from all over Europe were sent by cattle train to these camps. On arrival, elderly people and children were exterminated in gas chambers and their bodies were burned. The rest were used as slave labour and worked to death. In all, seven out of every ten Jews living in Europe were murdered in the Holocaust.

LEAVING EVIDENCE

Some Jewish prisoners tried to leave evidence of the Holocaust in case people later found it hard to believe it had happened. At one camp a buried note was found after the war. It said:

Dear finder, search everywhere, in every inch of soil. Dozens of documents are buried under it…. Great quantities of teeth are also buried here. It was we … who expressly have strewn them all over the terrain … so that the world should find material traces of the millions of murdered people.

Quoted in Martin Gilbert, *Never Again* (HarperCollins, 2000)

A German woman is overcome as she walks past the bodies of some 800 slave workers murdered by SS guards. The bodies were laid here by the post-war government, so that local people could view the work of their Nazi leaders.

SECRET HIDING PLACES

As the Nazis rounded up Jews across Europe and sent them to the camps, many families went into hiding. Some went into forests; others hid in cellars or secret spaces inside buildings. They all feared the knock on the door in the middle of the night from the Gestapo.

ANNE FRANK

One of the million Jewish children who died in the Holocaust was a German girl called Anne Frank. She and her family moved to Amsterdam, Holland, when the Nazis came to power in 1933. After the Nazi occupation of Holland in 1940, life became increasingly dangerous, and in 1942 they went into hiding.

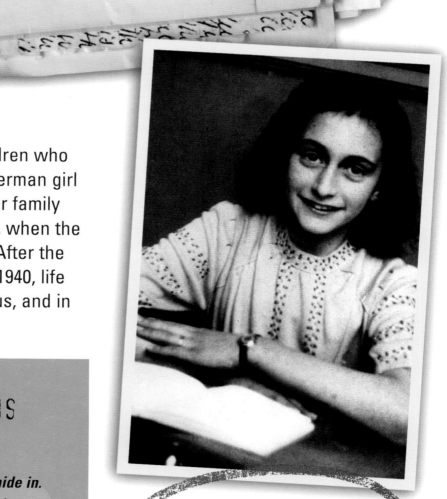

Anne Frank was born on 12 June 1929 and went into hiding when she was 13. She died at the age of 15.

IN THEIR OWN WORDS

In her diary, Anne Frank wrote:

The Annex is an ideal place to hide in. It may be damp and lopsided, but there's probably not a more comfortable hiding place in all of Amsterdam.

11 July 1942

In August 1944 someone reported their presence there to the Gestapo and they were arrested. Anne and her sister Margot were sent to Belsen Camp. They both died there of typhus in March 1945 just a few weeks before British troops arrived to liberate the camp. Otto Frank, Anne's father, survived the war and arranged for her diary to be published. Today her book has been printed in many languages and studied in schools around the world. Hers is the lasting voice of all who died in the Holocaust.

Anne wrote in her diary: 'Now our Secret Annex has truly become secret…. Mr Kugler thought it would be better to have a bookcase built in front of the entrance to our hiding place. It swings out on its hinges and opens like a door.'

For the next two years they lived in a secret annex of an office, which they shared with another family. Anne's father's friends smuggled food to them, at great risk to themselves. Anne kept a record of her life in the annex in a diary. She wrote about her experiences in hiding, her fears and hopes.

BRONIA BEKER

Bronia Beker was a Jewish girl from Kosowa, Poland. When the Germans invaded in 1941, two of Bronia's brothers, along with many other Jewish men, were taken to a forest and shot. The rest of Bronia's family dug a large cave in the ground where they hid. The Nazis found the cave's ventilation pipes and blocked them up. By the time a friend discovered them, the whole family was dead apart from Bronia. She went into hiding on a farm and managed to survive the war.

FINAL SECRETS

As Allied forces closed in on Berlin, Hitler refused to surrender. Instead, he and his most trusted officers and staff retreated to his bunker – a secret complex of underground rooms beneath the city. His last weeks were spent there and have since become the subject of rumour and mystery.

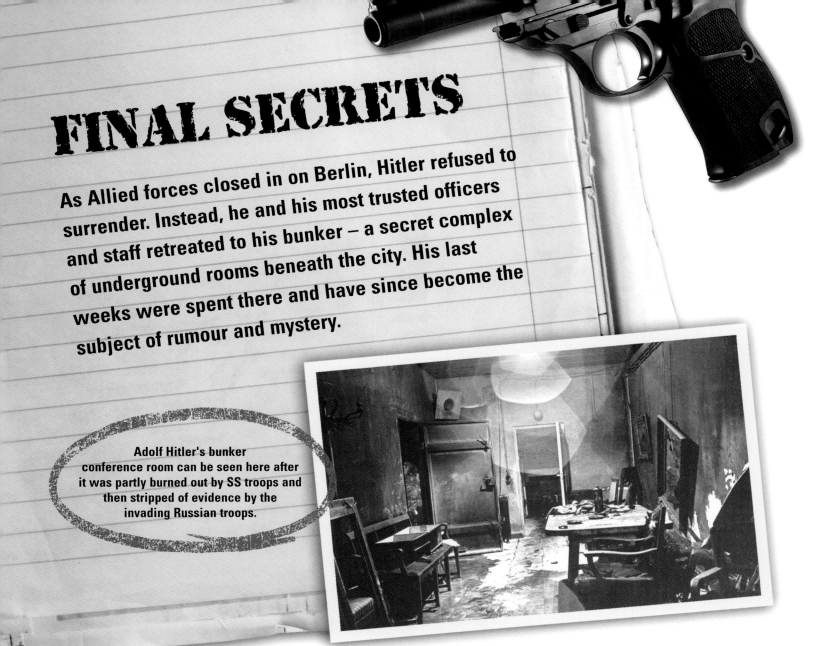

Adolf Hitler's bunker conference room can be seen here after it was partly burned out by SS troops and then stripped of evidence by the invading Russian troops.

HITLER'S FATE

Rumours spread after the war that Hitler had escaped the bunker and survived. The mystery was fuelled by the lack of a body and the secrecy of the Soviet authorities following their capture of East Berlin. However, the accepted view now is that Hitler committed suicide in his bunker.

IN THEIR OWN WORDS

On 20 April 1945, Josef Goebbels toasted Hitler on his 56th birthday. He said:

It is on this beautiful day that we celebrate the Führer's birthday and thank him for he is the only reason why Germany is still alive today.

Ten days later, Hitler was dead and the war in Europe was over.

Major Bernd von Freytag-Loringhoven, a witness to Hitler's last days, later reported that the Führer had become like a sick, old man. By this time he had lost all grasp of military reality, issuing orders for counter-attacks against Allied forces that had no chance of being carried out. He flew into frequent rages, believing he had been betrayed by his generals and his closest colleagues.

Only at the very end did Hitler realize his fate and accept that the Third Reich, which he once said would last 1,000 years, was doomed. On 29 April he married his long-time companion Eva Braun. The following day, with Soviet forces just 500 metres from the bunker entrance, he committed suicide.

WHAT HAPPENED TO HIS BODY?

According to the accepted version of events, Hitler and his wife swallowed cyanide pills before he shot himself. Their bodies were then taken to a small garden at ground level and set alight. A Russian museum has exhibited a fragment of bone, which they claim is all that remains of Hitler's skull, but the final resting place of his ashes remains a mystery.

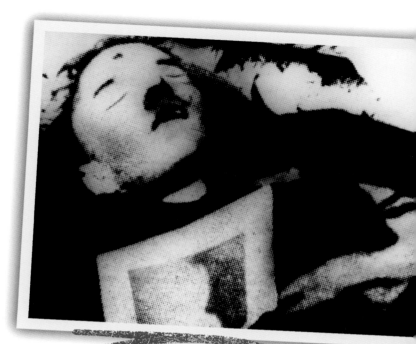

In 1964 this picture was found, apparently taken by a member of Hitler's staff. It supposedly shows Hitler's corpse in his underground bunker.

ESCAPED NAZIS

After the war, many leading Nazis were tried for war crimes at Nuremberg, Germany. However, many more fled Europe and found refuge in Spain, Argentina, Chile, Paraguay and Brazil. Nazi hunters such as Simon Wiesenthal tried to bring former Nazis accused of war crimes to justice. In a few cases, such as Sebastian Wiemann and Adolf Eichmann, they succeeded. However, many other notorious figures have never been found.

TIMELINE

1 September 1939 Germany invades Poland, sparking World War II.

15 August 1941 Josef Jakobs, the German spy, is shot by firing squad at the Tower of London.

18 October 1941 Richard Sorge, the Soviet spy, is arrested in Tokyo.

7 December 1941 Japan attacks Pearl Harbor. The United States enters the war.

20 January 1942 The Wannsee Conference confirms plans for the mass murder of Jews.

13 June 1942 The Office of Strategic Services (OSS), a US intelligence agency, is founded.

December 1942 Eddie Chapman – Agent Zigzag – German spy, offers his services to MI5.

16 April 1943 SOE operative Odette Sansom is arrested and imprisoned.

26 November 1943 HMT *Rohna* is sunk with the loss of over 1,000 lives. The news is kept secret.

24 March 1944 76 Allied prisoners escape from the German prison camp Stalag Luft III.

6 June 1944 Operation Jedburgh: British and US spies arrive in France to help the Resistance.

10 June 1944 SOE agent Violette Szabo is captured by German troops.

20 July 1944 Operation Valkyrie: the attempt to kill Hitler at his Wolf's Lair headquarters fails.

4 August 1944 Anne Frank and her family are discovered and arrested.

7 September 1944 The first V-2 is fired – at Paris. The following day, a V-2 hits London.

30 April 1945 Hitler commits suicide in his bunker. Two days later, Germany surrenders.

2 September 1945 Japan surrenders and World War II comes to an end.

GLOSSARY

Allies The military and political alliance that fought the Axis powers in World War II, including the United States, Britain and the Soviet Union.

atom The smallest portion into which an element can be divided and still retain its properties.

Axis The military and political alliance of Germany, Italy and Japan that fought the Allies in World War II.

cinema newsreels Short news and documentary films shown in cinemas that were popular during the first half of the 20th century.

concentration camp A prison camp used for confining political prisoners, foreign nationals or civilians during wartime.

crematorium A building containing a furnace where bodies are burned.

cyanide A very poisonous chemical that can kill in minutes.

D-Day 6 June 1944, the day Allied forces landed in northern France to begin the liberation of occupied Europe in World War II.

Führer The title given to Adolf Hitler, meaning 'leader' or 'guide' in German.

George Cross The highest gallantry award in the UK for civilians or military personnel for actions not on the battlefield.

Gestapo The secret police of Nazi Germany. *Gestapo* is a contraction of *Geheime Staatspolizei*: Secret State Police.

ghetto An area of a city lived in by a minority group, whether by choice or because they are forced to.

Home Guard A defence organization of volunteers in the UK during World War II.

intelligence Information, often secret, about an enemy's forces and plans.

internee A civilian who is confined in a prison or concentration camp during a war.

Kempeitai The military police of the Imperial Japanese Army from 1881 to 1945.

Nazi Party The extreme nationalist and racist party that ruled Germany from 1933 to 1945.

nucleus The central part of an atom, consisting of protons and neutrons.

nuclear fission The splitting of the nucleus of an atom.

OVRA The Organization for Vigilance and Repression of Anti-Fascism was the secret police of Italy from 1927 until 1945.

propaganda Information and publicity put out by a government to promote a policy, idea or cause.

radioactive Describes an element that emits energy in the form of streams of particles, due to the decaying of its unstable atoms.

RAF Britain's Royal Air Force

Soviet Union A state encompassing Russia and other nearby countries, which existed from 1922 to 1991.

Special Operations Executive (SOE) A British organization of World War II responsible for organizing and encouraging espionage and sabotage in occupied Europe.

SS Schutzstaffel, or defence squadron, was a powerful armed force in Nazi Germany known for its brutality.

Third Reich The rule of the Nazi Party in Germany between 1933 and 1945.

treason The crime of attempting to overthrow or harm the government of one's country.

typhus A severe disease and high fever, spread especially by body lice.

U-boat A German military submarine, especially one used during World Wars I and II.

FURTHER INFORMATION

BOOKS
At Home in World War II: Propaganda by Stewart Ross (Evans Brothers, 2004)

Code Talker: A Novel about the Navajo Marines of World War II by Joseph Bruchac (Puffin Books, 2006)

The Diary of a Young Girl by Anne Frank (Reissue edition: Penguin, 2007)

Spies and Spying: Super Spies of World War II by Kate Walker and Elaine Argaet (Smart Apple Media, 2003)

Stories from World War II: Ultra Hush-Hush: Espionage and Special Missions by Stephen Shapiro and Tina Forrester (Annick Press, 2005)

World War II Spies by Tim O'Shei (Edge Books, 2008)

WEBSITES
www.annefrank.org

www.historylearningsite.co.uk/WORLD%20WAR%20TWO.htm

www.iwm.org.uk

www.spartacus.schoolnet.co.uk/2WWsecret.htm

INDEX

Page numbers in **bold** refer to pictures.

BIOMECHANICS
IN CLINIC AND RESEARCH

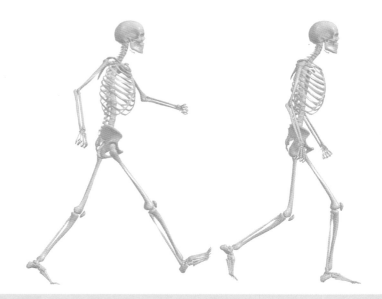

For Jackie, Imogen and Joe

For Elsevier:
Commissioning Editor: Robert Edwards
Development Editor: Rebecca Gleave
Project Manager: Elouise Ball
Cover Designer: Stewart Larking
Designer: Steven Stave
Illustration Manager: Bruce Hogarth
Illustrator: Antbits

BIOMECHANICS
IN CLINIC AND RESEARCH
www.biomechanicsonline.com

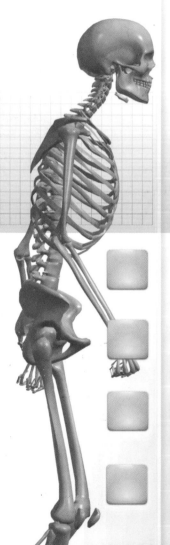

Use your unique PIN to log on to your complete, fully interactive online course…

together with this book, it takes you all the way from the basic ideas through to postgraduate-level concepts and the clinical interpretation of data.

Full of animations to show how the theory works

Fantastic library of quizzes to test what you've learnt

Many additional graphics explain the basic science

47 lessons parallel the structure of this book

CHURCHILL LIVINGSTONE

Log on and start learning NOW!
v.biomechanicsonline.com

www.biomechanicsonline.com

DELIVERS
BIOMECHANICS IN CLINIC AND RESEARCH
ONLINE AND MORE!

Thank you for purchasing **Biomechanics in Clinic and Research.**

Your purchase entitles you to free online access to **www.biomechanicsonline.com**

- ■ **Full of animations to show how the theory works**
- ■ **Fantastic library of quizzes to test what you've learnt**
- ■ **Many additional graphics explain the basic science**
- ■ **47 lessons parallel the structure of this book**

How to register

1. Scratch off the sticker below to reveal your unique PIN code

2. Connect to the internet and go to
www.biomechanicsonline.com
for simple instructions on how to register – you'll need your PIN code and e-mail address to register

Important note: Your purchase of *Biomechanics in Clinic and Research* entitles you to access the website until the next edition is published, or until the current edition is no longer offered for sale by Elsevier, whichever occurs first. If the next edition is published less than a year after your purchase, you will be entitled to online access for 1 year from your date of purchase. Elsevier reserves the right to offer a suitable replacement product (such as a downloadable or CD-ROM-based electronic version) should online access to the website be discontinued.

Note

Book cannot be returned once panel is scratched off

Scratch off the sticker with care!

Scratch off Below
Richards

BCR6GB56YG78

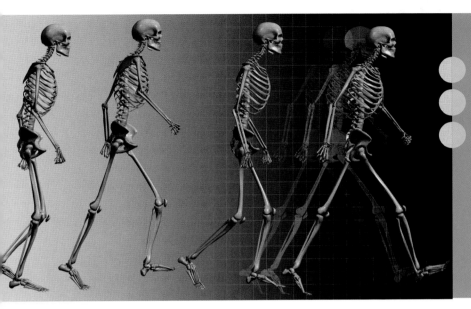

BIOMECHANICS
IN CLINIC AND RESEARCH

An interactive teaching and learning course

JIM RICHARDS BEng, MSc, PhD
Professor of Biomechanics
Department of Allied Health Professions
Faculty of Health
University of Central Lancashire
Preston, UK

Edinburgh London New York Oxford Philadelphia St Louis Sydney Toronto 2008

First published 2008

ISBN 978-0-443-10170-0

British Library Cataloguing in Publication Data
A catalogue record for this book is available from the British Library

Library of Congress Cataloging in Publication Data
A catalog record for this book is available from the Library of Congress

Knowledge and best practice in this field are constantly changing. As new research and experience broaden our knowledge, changes in practice, treatment and drug therapy may become necessary or appropriate. Readers are advised to check the most current information provided (i) on procedures featured or (ii) by the manufacturer of each product to be administered, to verify the recommended dose or formula, the method and duration of administration, and contraindications. It is the responsibility of the practitioner, relying on their own experience and knowledge of the patient, to make diagnoses, to determine dosages and the best treatment for each individual patient, and to take all appropriate safety precautions. To the fullest extent of the law, neither the publisher nor the editors assumes any liability for any injury and/or damage.

The Publisher

Contents

Contributors

Jim Richards PhD MA GDPhys MCSP

Professor of Biomechanics, Department of Allied Health Professions, Faculty of Health, University of Central Lancashire, Preston, UK

Jim Richards worked for 10 years as a Senior Lecturer at the University of Salford, and has taught biomechanics to prosthetists/orthotists, podiatrist, physiotherapists and sports therapists. Jim Richards was appointed Professor in Biomechanics in the Department of Allied Health Professions at the University of Central Lancashire in 2004. Professor Richards has considerable experience in conducting clinical research. This includes much work on clinical application of biomechanics, the development of new assessment tools for chronic disease, conservative and surgical management of orthopaedic and neurological conditions, and development of evidence-based approaches for improving clinical management and rehabilitation. The focus of Professor Richards' work is to encourage inter-professional research and to develop direct parallels with research to the 'real world' of allied health work. Professor Richards is also a visiting Professor to the Department of Orthopaedics and Traumatology at the University of Perugia, and holds Honorary Research Fellowships at several hospitals. Professor Richards has authored many research papers and has contributed to a number of textbooks, including *Tidy's Physiotherapy* (2003).

Sarah Jane Hobbs PhD PGCertHE BEng(Hons)

Senior Lecturer, Department of Technology, University of Central Lancashire, Preston, UK

Sarah Jane Hobbs has worked as a Senior Lecturer in the Department of Technology at the University of Central Lancashire since 2000 and has recently been awarded a PhD in equine biomechanics. Dr Hobbs has held several positions within both the equine and technology industries, and has considerable experience with the application of technology in the measurement and assessment of human and animal biomechanics. Dr Hobbs is becoming well known in the field of equine biomechanics and has had a number of invited presentations around the world.

James Selfe PhD, MA, GDPhys, MCSP

Professor of Physiotherapy, Department of Allied Health Professions, University of Central Lancashire, Preston, UK

James Selfe worked for 9 years at the University of Bradford and has taught many health care professions at both undergraduate and postgraduate level. James Selfe moved to the University of Central Lancashire in 2003 and was appointed Professor of Physiotherapy in 2006 and is Co-research Lead with Professor Richards of the Research Centre in the Department of Allied Health Professions at University of Central Lancashire. Professor Selfe has also recently developed, and leads, the Chartered Society for Physiotherapy Regional Research Hub for Cumbria and Lancashire. Professor Selfe has considerable clinical and research experience and is the author of many research papers and given many invited talks on patellofemoral pain and the scientific bases of assessments and movements used in clinical practice. Professor Selfe has also recently published a new text book *'Red Flags: A guide to identifying serious pathology of the spine'* with Churchill Livingstone, Elsevier.

Dominic Thewlis BSc

Department of Allied Health Professions, University of Central Lancashire, Preston, UK

Dominic Thewlis works as a research fellow in the Department of Allied Health Professions at the University of Central Lancashire. Dominic has been, and is currently, involved with delivering courses on applied and clinical biomechanics. The focus of Dominic's research is currently in three main areas: orthopaedic biomechanics, the use of biomechanical measures in public health, and biomechanical methods and modelling. Dominic's specific interests are the biomechanics of total joint replacement, the biomechanics of conservative management techniques, movement strategies associated with various groups and optimization of modelling methods.

Introduction

Over the years many clinicians have commented about the increase in the need for what is described as Evidence Based Practice or Evidenced Based Medicine. The users' guides to evidence-based medicine (Journal of the American Medical Association, 1992), states that;

- The understanding of basic mechanisms of disease are **not** sufficient guides for clinical practice alone.
- Systematically recorded observations and reproducible measurements are needed to study the effectiveness of clinical practice.

The two main problems in physical therapy are: the reproducibility of measurements of effectiveness and the clinical relevance of the measures made. So the questions that need to be asked of biomechanics are:

- Can biomechanics offer new and sensitive measures of assessment?
- Can biomechanics assess the effectiveness of different treatments?
- Can biomechanics offer immediate, informed, and direct feedback to clinical practice?

This book covers the concepts and theory necessary to understand the nature of biomechanical measurements, and the methods available to collect, analyse, and interpret biomechanical data in a clinically meaningful way. This includes: the mathematical and mechanical concepts necessary for the understanding of the musculoskeletal system and the interpretation of biomechanical measurements, the variety of methods available for biomechanical measurement, and the biomechanics of conservative management of musculoskeletal and neurological pathologies.

This book also covers the biomechanics of orthoses from both an orthotist's and a podiatrist's perspective, and the biomechanics of common movement tasks used in clinical assessment. This therefore should allow undergraduate and postgraduate allied health professionals to advance their biomechanical knowledge and understanding in a way relevant to both training and clinical practice.

A substantial interactive web-based virtual learning environment and teaching resource runs parallel with this book. The virtual learning environment contains 48 lessons all relating to the material covered in the paper text book. This also includes many interactive questions to help the learner determine the level of their understanding as they proceed.

This "course" has been designed to take a minimum of 15 hours of self-directed learning to complete.

The virtual learning environment is highly illustrated and contains animations which describe the mathematical and mechanical concepts needed to understand biomechanics. The virtual learning environment also contains links with many 3D animations that play in a downloadable viewer allowing the user to view movement data from every possible angle. These animations demonstrate the theory covered, and allow the user to control animations of the various clinical case studies included in the text.

In addition there is a library of online interactive quizzes to test your knowledge and understanding of the material covered in the different chapters. This provides a stream of online information on biomechanics in a modular format for teaching and learning, and builds understanding and application of biomechanics at a steady pace.

The virtual learning environment has a structured approach that is designed to act as a companion to undergraduate and postgraduate courses featuring clinical biomechanics. This structure also allows the lecturer to plan their teaching in relation to specific learning outcomes, and aims to help both lesson delivery and the development of structured courses.

Chapter 1 covers the basic mathematics and mechanics needed to understand the much more complicated problem of the mechanics of the human body. This chapter shows how problems may be broken down into separate parts. The techniques covered in the chapter aim to make the more advanced biomechanical problems covered later much easier to solve.

Chapter 2 considers the use of mathematics and mechanics techniques in relation to the musculoskeletal system in more detail. With these techniques and the study of the properties of the body segments, the joint moments, muscle forces, and joint reaction forces in upper limb and lower limb will be considered.

Chapter 3 considers the use of Ground Reaction Forces as functional measure and the consideration of the nature of various measures that may be drawn from them. This covers Ground Reaction forces during postural sway, walking and different running styles.

Chapter 4 covers the basic methods of gait assessment through to the description and discussion of the involvement of the three-dimensional movement of the foot, ankle, knee, hip and pelvis in the function of walking in individuals who are pain and pathology free.

Chapter 5 covers the concepts of linear and angular work energy and power and how these can be determined from force data, and demonstrates the concept of how angular work and power can be used to analyse the action of muscles during gait.

Chapter 6 covers the concept of inverse dynamics. This includes the nature of Radius of Gyration and Internal Torque. Examples of how the dynamic joint moments and forces may be found and the consequences of not considering dynamic force are also covered.

Chapter 7 covers the measurement of Force and Pressure. This includes the different methods of assessing force and pressure and the identification of measurements commonly used in research and clinical assessment.

Chapter 8 covers the measurement of movement. This includes the different methods of assessing movement, the processes required to collect and analyse movement data, and the consideration of possible errors.

Chapter 9 covers different marker sets that can be used in movement analysis. This includes both modelling of the lower limb and foot. The nature of six degrees of freedom measurement is considered and the associated errors encountered when considering different coordinate systems.

Chapter 10 covers the methods commonly used to assess muscle function and physiological cost. This includes the use of EMG, Isokinetic and isometric testing, and physiological measurement. This chapter also covers common measurements that may be found and how these can relate to different aspects of muscle function and physiological cost.

Chapter 11 covers the biomechanics of orthotic management of the lower limb. This includes the theoretical mechanics of indirect and direct orthotic management and clinical case study data of the use of the devices covered.

Chapter 12 covers the biomechanics of common movement tasks used in clinical assessment of the lower limb. This includes step and stair ascent and descent, sit to stand, timed up and go, gait initiation, and squats and dips.

I owe an enormous debt of gratitude to all my colleagues and students past and present. Particularly I wish to thank my main contributors Dominic Thewlis and James Selfe for their tireless work and contributions. I would also like to thank Sarah Jane Hobbs, Department of Technology, UCLan; and John Burston, Podiatrist from Barnsley Primary Care Trust, who have assisted with valuable comments and contributions.

Acknowledgements

I owe an enormous debt of gratitude to all my colleagues and students past and present. Particularly I wish to thank my main contributors Dominic Thewlis and James Selfe for their tireless work and contributions. I would also like to thank Sarah Jane Hobbs, Department of Technology, University of Central Lancashire and John Burston, Podiatrist from Barnsley Primary Care Trust, who have assisted with valuable comments and contributions.

Glossary of Terms

ambulation   Walking

angular displacement   The rotational component of a body's motion

angular velocity   The rate of change of angular displacement

anterior   The front of the body or a part facing toward the front

anthropometry   The study of proportions and properties of body segments

biomechanics   The study of mechanical laws and their application to living organisms, especially the human body and its movement

cadence   The number of steps taken over a period of time, usually steps per minute

centre of mass   The midpoint or centre of the mass of a body or object

centroid   The two-dimensional coordinates of the centre of an area

coplanar   Lying or acting in the same plane

coronal plane   Frame of reference for the body – viewed from the front (see frontal plane)

direct linear transformation (dlt)   The common mathematical approach to constructing the three-dimensional location of an object from multiple two-dimensional images

dorsiflexion   To flex backward, as in the upward bending of the fingers, wrist, foot, or toes

double support   The stance phase of one limb overlaps the stance phase of the contralateral limb creating a period during which both feet are in contact with the ground

electrogoniometer   A device for measuring changes in joint angle over time using either a potentiometer or strain gauge wire

E_m Energy expenditure per metre (J/kg/m)

EMG or electromyography   The study of the electrical activity of muscles and muscle groups

E_s Instantaneous energy of any body segment

E_w Energy expenditure per minute (J/kg/min)

extension   A movement which increases the angle between two connecting bones

filtering   The process of manipulating the frequencies of a signal through analogue or digital processing

flexion   A movement which decreases the angle between two connecting bones

force platform   A device for measuring the forces acting beneath the feet during walking

frontal plane   Frame of reference for the body – viewed from the front

g   Acceleration due to gravity

gait   The manner of walking

gait analysis   The study of locomotion of humans and animals

global frame of reference   A set of orthogonal axes, one of which is parallel with the field of gravity

ground reaction force   The reaction force as a result of the body hitting or resting on the ground

habituation   Becoming accustomed

hemiplegia   Paralysis of one side of the body

h_s Height of the centre of mass above the datum

instantaneous power   Power at a particular moment in time

I_s Moment of inertia about the proximal joint

kinematics   The study of the motion of the body without regard to the forces acting to produce the motion

kinetic energy   The energy associated with motion, both angular and linear

kinetics   The study of the forces that produce, stop, or modify motions of the body

k_s Radius of gyration of body segment

linear displacement   Distance moved in a particular direction

linear velocity   Speed at which an object is moving in a particular direction

loading response   Period immediately following the initial contact of the foot

mid stance   The period from the lift of the contralateral foot from the ground to a position in which the body is directly over the stance foot

mid swing   This is the period of swing phase immediately following maximum knee flexion to the time when the tibia is in a vertical position

moment of inertia   The rotational inertial properties of an object

motion or movement analysis   A technique of recording and studying movement patterns of animals and objects

m_s Segment mass

non-collinear   Points that do not lie in a straight line

obliquity plantarflexion   The downward bending of the foot or toes

posterior   The back of the body or a part placed in the back of the body

potential energy   The energy associated with the vertical position of the centre of mass of an object

preswing The period immediately before the lifting off of the stance foot

pronation To rotate the foot by abduction and eversion so that the inner edge of the sole bears the body's weight

radius of gyration This is a fictitious distribution of the mass around the centre of mass

range of motion The angular excursion through which a limb moves

rehabilitation Restoring a patient or a body part to normal or near normal after a disease or injury

relative velocity A measure of velocity in terms of the height of the individual. The units reported are statures/s

r_s Position of the centre of mass from the proximal joint

sagittal plane Frame of reference for the body – viewed from the side

single support The period during the gait cycle when one foot is in contact with the ground

spatial Distance

stance phase The period when a foot is contact with the ground

step length Distance between two consecutive heel strikes

step time Time between two consecutive heel strikes

stride length Distance between two consecutive heel strikes by the same foot

stride time Time between two consecutive heel strikes by the same foot

supination To rotate the foot by adduction and inversion so that the outer edge of the sole bears the body's weight

swing phase Period when a foot is not in contact with the ground

temporal Timing

total support The total time the body is supported by one leg during one complete gait cycle

translation Movement in a particular direction

transverse Frame of reference for the body – viewed from above

v_s absolute velocity of the centre of mass

walk mat and walkway A device to measure the temporal and spatial parameters of gait

$\dot{x}, \dot{y}$ and $\dot{z}$ Linear velocities in the x, y, and z directions

ω_s Absolute angular velocity of segment

Forewords

Biomechanics is an area that has grown exponentially over the last two decades. A plethora of textbooks on the subject of biomechanics has appeared in the literature. Many books within the field of biomechanics suffer from a lack of in-depth detail on the clinical application of biomechanics and fail to elaborate on extrapolating the theory into clinical actions. The authors have written a textbook and an associated online course that not only reflect the basic but also the applied biomechanical principles. This book and online material has been designed around addressing issues within the clinical biomechanical arena.

Chapter 1 describes the basic principles of mathematics and mechanics in terms that are applicable to the human body. In Chapter 2 the application of techniques covered in Chapter 1 are specifically aimed at the musculoskeletal system. The chapter highlights the application of forces, moments and muscles to lower limb muscle activity. Chapter 3 considers measurement derived from ground reaction forces in running and walking. Lower limb motion is described in Chapter 4 and techniques describing the movements of the ankle, midfoot and rearfoot are described. The authors remind us of the importance of the foot as being described either as a single segment or as multiple segments, which has clinical implications working within this field. Work, energy and power are described in Chapter 5.

The concepts of inverse dynamics and the effect on the calculation of dynamic joint movements and forces are described in Chapter 6. The reader is given the opportunity to explore simple to advanced models and the effects the different methods have on moments and power calculations. Chapter 7 describes the different methods to collate and analyse force data. The reader is given the opportunity to review examples of moment calculations using a piezoelectric platform. A section on force platform configurations allows the reader to consider the position of force platform and cameras to ensure that steady-state gait is achieved. The section on measuring pressure explores some of the issues relating to the number of systems currently available on the market.

The analysis of movement described in Chapter 8 focuses on the array of equipment available to measure gait parameters. The conceptualization of three-dimensional joints in motion is excellently described using either a single or multiple cameras to reconstruct two or three-dimensional movement data.

The role of anatomical models and marker sets is considered in Chapter 9 with the reader given an opportunity to review the different marker methods. This section on foot models draws on new research evidence. Specific emphasis is illustrated on models for the multiple segment foot. Recent literature has highlighted the issues and concerns with foot modelling and the current textbook gives an insight to the complexity of modelling the foot. However, the importance of foot modelling will be invaluable to clinicians who assess the foot and lower limb and undertake therapeutic interventions that include foot orthoses and footwear.

Chapter 10 explores different methods of assessing muscle function and physiological costs, and distinguish what information can be drawn from their use. Methods of recording EMG in both the upper and lower limb give an opportunity to the reader to draw upon the clinical uses. A particular interest to clinicians is the section on EMG biofeedback and its clinical benefits. Chapter 11 considers the impact of orthotic management on the lower limb. The biomechanics of various types of orthoses ranging from knee orthoses to foot orthoses gives the reader an opportunity to analyse the impact of forces using orthotic interventions. The introduction of lateral wedging in medial compartment osteoarthritis is a relatively new area of research and the section reflects on the biomechanical principles.

The final chapter highlights the biomechanical aspects of common movement tasks used in clinical assessment of the lower limb. Previous textbooks focus on walking or running. This chapter focuses on different complex functional tasks such as stair walking, timed-up-and-go-test and sit-to-stand activities. From a clinical perspective this chapter demonstrates theoretical biomechanical principles of movement tasks being applied into clinical setting.

The online course, a functional version of the textbook, is a key and unique feature. There are opportunities for the reader to interact with the textbook by utilizing an excellent online programme. The programme involves animated skeletons of normal and pathological gait as well as clearly illustrated diagrams of biomechanical principles. The text is simply explained and follows a logical sequence from basic mechanics to the evaluation of interventions such as lower limb orthoses. A feature of the online course is the use of summary boxes and a summation from the author of important biomechanical features.

Biomechanics in Clinic and Research impacts knowledge successfully on the underpinning theory with an emphasis on clinical practice. It is the act of using biomechanical principles in a clinical setting that informs and reinforces the knowledge and understanding of its concepts. Jim Richards and his co-authors have years of experience in teaching biomechanics in both the academic and clinical arenas. The textbook and online course are very well written in a clear and concise manner. There are many excellent illustrations and problem-solving activities. Current evidence is cited for additional reading for those who wish to study the material in more depth. This textbook will be an invaluable resource to clinicians, researchers and students with an interest in clinical biomechanics and should be recommended as core material.

Professor Keith Rome
Auckland, New Zealand
2008

I was destined to have a career in biomechanics. I trained as an engineer, but spent much of my time refining my athletic skills paddling a canoe. A chance visit to Simon Fraser University to meet a friend resulted in my attending a lecture on the biomechanics of sport. This fusion of my fancies (a confluence of engineering principles and human movement) was revealed and within days I was a volunteer in the biomechanics laboratory. Twenty five years later with a PhD and several post-doctoral fellowships in hand I am now the director of research at C-Motion Inc., a company dedicated to the development of biomechanical analysis software.

As the person responsible for helping people use our software, I am in an ideal position to recognize and identify the challenges of teaching biomechanical concepts related to 3D motion capture data. The author of this book, Dr. Jim Richards, was one of the early adopters of our software, and a more inquisitive and questioning customer would be hard to find. He attended one of the first Visual3D training seminars that I ever gave and dominated the presentation with challenging and enlightening questions. His queries that day reflected his general commitment to probing the core premises and capabilities of biomechanics. At the same time, he champions what appears to be a mantra and cause similar to mine: the relevance of biomechanics to clinical diagnosis and rehabilitation. It is with great pleasure that I contribute the foreword to, and wholeheartedly recommend the reading of, Jim's book.

The book focuses on the analysis of lower limb mechanics (gait and posture) and, most importantly from my perspective, gives a yeoman's effort to present a 'soup to nuts' description that ranges from data collection and quality assurance, to data interpretation. All of these topics are, moreover, mingled interestingly within an historical context. While their application is directed at lower limb mechanics, the principles described are sound and readily transferable to many different biomechanical applications.

There are no definitive recipes for 3D Motion capture and the biomechanical analysis of movement. This text is unique in making the reader aware that the experimenter actually has a choice in where to place the 3D markers. With this attitude the text debunks the classical notion that there is a rote method of marker placement, data interpretation, and reporting that is suitable for all gestures. The appropriate placement of markers is crucial to the successful tracking of the pose of a segment/model by most 3D motion capture systems. For example, pathological movements may obscure markers from cameras. Furthermore, in order to elucidate functional limitations, some pathological movements may require custom models.

The concepts described throughout the text are presented at a methodical, controlled pace that reads as a novel for the mathematically inclined, but that also, because of the illustrations and accessible examples, shouldn't be daunting to the mathematical novice. Jim takes the user on a journey of analyzing and interpreting gait and posture from simple statics to dynamics. Textbooks often leave the reader unsure why they should bother taking the trouble to extend their analyses from static to dynamics; this text, however, demonstrates the differences between the methods for interpreting gait using examples that compare statics and dynamics directly.

Another impressive aspect of the book is that, while the mechanics is clearly defined, the representation of the mechanics for clinical description is also presented carefully. For example, I receive many questions about the representation of a joint angle, and while this is a relatively simple concept in theory, it actually presents a challenge because clinical descriptions of joint motions are variable and dependent on the joint and context. Impressively, this text does not shy away from the challenge of this topic and explores the problem through examples, followed by careful recommendations.

The adjunct web site dedicated to this text book parallels the content of the text and is straightforward to navigate. To those of us reliant on visual clues to decipher textual descriptions and static images the animations of the data and analyses in the text book aid in enlightenment. To allow deeper exploration of the examples, many have been made available on the website as extra animations rotatable in three dimensions, accessible through a free Visual3D reader.

Finally, though quantitative assessment should be a foundation for medical diagnosis, the complexity of the motor system, linking coordination, strength, balance, and sensory processing makes it inherently difficult to quantify and daunting for students to learn. Thankfully, however, this book and website are now accessible and adeptly tackle the issue of quantifying and interpreting the physical performance of a task.

There are many textbooks on biomechanics, but few do as much justice to the fundamental issues of marker placement, data quality assurance, and data presentation as this text does. This text addresses many of the fundamental questions that I am asked repeatedly, and represents an excellent primer to our software. Moreover, one of the most relevant examples in the text actually combines two of my greatest pleasures (biomechanics and beer), and so, finally, I commend Jim for finding a way to squeeze an example on the mechanics of drinking a beer into his instructive text!

Scott Selbie
2008

Maths and Mechanics

Jim Richards

This chapter covers the basic mathematics and mechanics needed to understand the much more complicated problem of the mechanics of the human body. This chapter illustrates how problems may be broken down into separate parts and shows the techniques used for the more advanced biomechanical problems covered later.

Chapter 1: Aim

To consider and describe the maths and mechanics necessary to build and understand more complex biomechanical concepts.

Chapter 1: Objectives

- To describe how vectors can be resolved
- To explain how Newton's laws relate to the human body
- To explain the difference between mass and weight
- To explain what is meant by a turning moment.

1.1 Maths

The nature of biomechanics means that this section is absolutely essential. This section covers the basic mathematics necessary to understand the majority of the calculations in this book, although the problems themselves may get a lot harder, the basic principles remain consistent throughout. Many clinicians have difficulties with the maths element of biomechanics due to its abstract nature, so I have presented this material with reference to anatomy and clinical assessment throughout.

1.1.1 Trigonometry

Trigonometry is absolutely essential in the understanding of how things move and the effect on objects of forces. For instance, if we want to measure how the knee moves and what forces are acting on it while it is moving we will need trigonometry to find this out. The challenging part of biomechanics is working out what it all means after we have carried out all the calculations, but trigonometry is a vital albeit first step. Most, if not all, movement-analysis systems will work this out for you, but these are useful skills for understanding what is going on which can in turn help understanding of patient assessment. The next sections will cover Pythagorean theorem, and tan, sine and cosine by considering body parts rather than triangles to try to illustrate this point.

Pythagorean theorem

Pythagoras was alive from 560 to 480 BC. It was Pythagoras who first discovered that in a right-angled triangle, the square of the hypotenuse is equal to the sum of the squares of the other two sides. This only works for right-angled triangles (where one of the internal angles is 90°).

Interestingly, no matter how complex we go with biomechanics we can get away with considering most things in terms of right-angled triangles. This is mostly due to the way we divide up the body into three planes, which are at 90° to one another (or orthogonal, if we wish to use the scientific term). These three planes are better known as sagittal, coronal and transverse, but the useful thing from the mathematical point of view is that whichever anatomical plane we are looking at we will have a 90° angle present. This is good news, because triangle problems with a 90° angle are a lot easier to solve, mind you everything is relative!

So hopefully you are now convinced that triangles are important for biomechanics and we will now look at the Pythagorean theorem. If we now consider the position and angle of the femur: the length of the femur depends on the positions of the proximal and distal ends of the bone, the femoral epicondyles (A) at the knee and the head of the femur at the hip (C).

Pythagorean theorem states that the square of the hypotenuse is equal to the sum of the squares of the other two sides. The hypotenuse is the longest side in any right-angled triangle, where the remaining two sides make up the 90° angle (Fig. 1.1).

$$AC^2 = AB^2 + BC^2$$

where AB is the horizontal distance between the knee and hip joints, BC is the vertical distance between the knee and hip joints, and AC is the hypotenuse or length of the femur.

Movement analysis systems will often tell us the position of the ends of a body segment in x and y coordinates. If we consider that we know the lengths of the horizontal and vertical sides, AB = 20 cm and BC = 50 cm, we can use Pythagorean theorem to find the length of the femur or AC.

So:

$$AC^2 = AB^2 + BC^2$$

$$AC^2 = 20^2 + 50^2$$

$$AC^2 = 400 + 2500$$

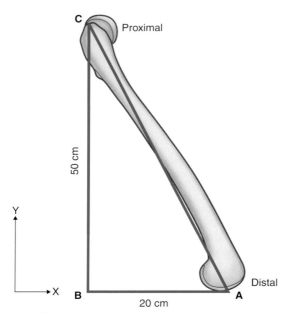

Figure 1.1   Pythagorean theorem

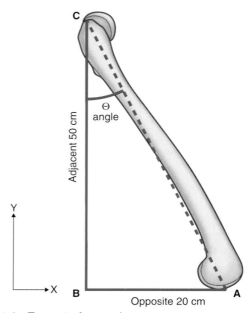

Figure 1.2   Tangent of an angle

$$AC^2 = 2900$$

$$AC = \sqrt{2900} = 53.85\,cm$$

Therefore, the length of the femur is 53.85 cm.

It is very important to note that the length of the femur, or hypotenuse, is the longest side of the triangle. This will always be true, if you work out the hypotenuse to be shorter than either of the other two sides then you have probably got a little mixed up with the equation.

So if we know any two sides of a right-angled triangle, the third side can be found. Or, to consider the femur, if we know the horizontal and vertical positions of the knee and hip joints, we can work out the length of the femur. Although for most people this is not terribly exciting, without this we would know little about mechanics, and even less about biomechanics.

What are tan, sine and cosine?

The best way of thinking about tan, sine and cosine is as ratios of the different sides of a triangle. In the UK we often describe the steepness of a hill in terms of how far up we go in relation to how far along we go, e.g. a 1 in 4 hill means we go up 1 m for every 4 m we go along, this tells us something about the steepness of slope of the hill.

This is fine until we try to relate this to an angle in degrees as we can't really express a hip flexion angle meaningfully in these terms. At this point tan, sine and cosine come to our rescue; these convert the ratios between the different sides into an angle in degrees. Now at this point I could go into a lot of detail about how tan, sine and cosine work, BUT we want to know how to use tan, sine and cosine, not prove where they come from and why they work! The best way to convert these ratios into angles in degrees is using any scientific calculator, alternatively if you are 'electronically challenged' and do not have a scientific calculator, you could use tables that will do the same job.

Students note: When solving these with a scientific calculator you will need to use the sin, cos, tan buttons when you know the angle. If you are trying to find the angle from a ratio you will need to use the $\sin^{-1}$, $\cos^{-1}$ and $\tan^{-1}$, you may have to use a second function key to get to these.

The tangent of an angle

In a right-angled triangle the ratios of the sides of the triangle determine the angles within the triangle and visa versa (Fig. 1.2).

$$\text{The tangent of angle } \theta \ (\tan \theta) = \frac{\text{Opposite side}}{\text{Adjacent side}}$$

An important aspect of biomechanics is the calculation of body segment angles in the different planes from knowing the location of the proximal and distal ends on the body segment. Now this can get quite complex when we look at three dimensions (x,y,z), but for the moment we will focus on two dimensions (x,y). If we consider the femur again with the same measurements as before we know the lengths AB and BC are 20 cm and 50 cm respectively. One of the things we may need to find out is the thigh angle θ from the vertical (which in this example is thigh flexing forwards). The most important thing about working out angles is naming the sides. If a side is opposite the angle we call it the 'opposite side', if it is next to the angle it is the 'adjacent side'.

Students note: Now at this point you could say there are two sides next to the angle; however, the longest one will always be the hypotenuse, which we are not considering in our angle calculations just yet.

$$\tan \theta = \frac{\text{Opposite side}}{\text{Adjacent side}}$$

$$\tan \theta = \frac{20}{50}$$

$$\tan \theta = 0.4$$

So we have found tan θ, we now need to find the angle θ in degrees. To do this we simply move the tan function over the equals sign, which then becomes tan⁻¹. Then it is a simple matter of putting the number in the calculator.

$$\theta = \tan^{-1} 0.4$$

$$\theta = 21.8°$$

So the thigh flexion angle is 21.8°.

In this way, if we know the length of the side opposite to the angle and the side adjacent to the angle we can find the thigh segment angle θ. Likewise, if we know the angle θ and length of the opposite side we can find the length of the adjacent side.

The sine and cosine of an angle

Two other ratios also exist between the sides of a right-angled triangle and the angles of the triangle. These are sine and cosine, which are commonly written sin and cos. Sine and cosine work in much the same way as tan; however, they use the hypotenuse and the opposite and adjacent sides respectively (Fig. 1.3).

$$\text{The sine of angle } \theta \, (\sin \theta) = \frac{\text{Opposite side}}{\text{Hypotenuse}}$$

$$\text{The cosine of angle } \theta \, (\cos \theta) = \frac{\text{Adjacent side}}{\text{Hypotenuse}}$$

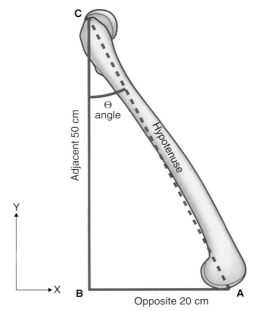

Figure 1.3　Sine and cosine of an angle

Sine

If we look at sine first, and consider that we know the thigh angle θ is 21.8°, and we know the opposite side is 20 cm, but say we need to find the length of the femur using only this information:

$$\sin \theta = \frac{\text{Opposite side}}{\text{Hypotenuse}}$$

$$\sin 21.8 = \frac{20}{\text{Hypotenuse}}$$

$$0.3714 = \frac{20}{\text{Hypotenuse}}$$

We now move the hypotenuse to the other side of the equation, where instead of dividing, it then multiplies:

$$0.3714 \times \text{Hypotenuse} = 20$$

$$\text{Hypotenuse} = \frac{20}{0.3714}$$

$$\text{Hypotenuse} = 53.85 \, \text{cm}$$

(which is the same length for the femur as before, not surprisingly).

Cosine

So now for cosine, in this example we will consider the hypotenuse and the adjacent side to find the thigh segment angle. We now know the hypotenuse is 53.85 cm, and the adjacent is 50 cm, how do we find the angle, θ?

$$\cos \theta = \frac{\text{Adjacent side}}{\text{Hypotenuse}}$$

$$\cos \theta = \frac{50}{53.85}$$

$$\cos \theta = 0.9285$$

$$\theta = \cos^{-1} 0.9285$$

$$\theta = 21.8°$$

Again this is the same value of the thigh flexion angle we calculated before. This demonstrates that the different ratios can be used interchangeably depending on what information about a particular triangle you are given. So there is often more than one way to tackle a particular problem.

A summary of sine, cosine and tangent

A quick summary of the ratios of the sides of right angle triangles and a possible memory aid is the word SOHCAHTOA:

Sin θ = Opposite/Hypotenuse
Cos θ = Adjacent/Hypotenuse
Tan θ = Opposite/Adjacent

With this information if we know the length of one side and one angle of a right-angle triangle, we can find the length of all the other sides and their angles.

Within biomechanics it is possible to use only right-angle triangles. With the tools above it is possible to solve almost all the trigonometry necessary for biomechanical assessment.

1.1.2 Vectors

What is a vector

Vectors have both magnitude (i.e. size) and direction. All vectors can be described in terms of components in the vertical and horizontal directions, or described by a resultant effect acting at a particular angle (Fig. 1.4).

One vector that we will be considering throughout this book is that of the force on the foot from the ground, or ground reaction force, which we will consider in much more detail later. Figure 1.4 shows the horizontal and vertical components of this force and the overall effect, the resultant, of these components. Other examples of vectors include displacement, velocity and acceleration.

Vectors may be worked out in exactly the same way as shown above with right-angled triangles, the only difference being the terminology.

The resultant

This is the combination effect of all the vectors. In the previous example the resultant is the overall force acting from the ground. This in essence is just a hypotenuse and can be found using Pythagoras' theorem, or with sine, cosine and tangent depending on what information is provided.

The component

The components of the resultant act at 90° from one another, these are equivalent to the opposite and adjacent sides of a right-angle triangle. These components act along a coordinate system or frame of reference, which in this case is vertical and horizontal to the ground. So if we always consider the horizontal and vertical 'effects' we will always create a right-angle triangle, which we can solve using the methods covered earlier.

Adding and subtracting vectors

In practical biomechanical problems, the segments or limbs which are analysed will usually be subjected to a number of forces acting in various directions. Often, we will wish to 'add' these forces together to determine their overall effect. The simplest example is where the vectors are acting along the chosen frame of reference. Figure 1.5 shows the different forces acting and the resultant effect.

If all the vectors involved act along the same line they can be added algebraically, that is forces acting in one direction are regarded as positive, whilst those acting in the opposite direction are regarded as negative. The example below shows forces pushing left and right, and up and down, with the overall effect (Fig. 1.5). Do not worry about the units N (newton) just yet!

Resolving

Vectors may act in many different directions as well as magnitudes; this is particularly true when we consider the forces acting around the joints of the body. When vectors do act in different directions it is still possible to break these down and find the overall effect if we follow a set of steps no matter how complex the problem looks.

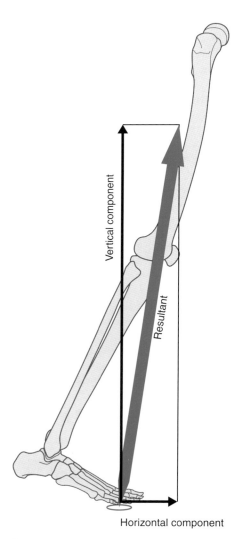

Figure 1.4   Vector diagram

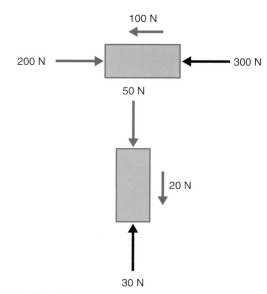

Figure 1.5   Resolving

The key to successfully looking at complex systems of vectors is 'resolving'. Resolving is the term used for finding the component vectors from a resultant vector or visa versa, which once again takes us back to right-angled triangles.

1.1.2(vi) Guidelines for solving vector problems

When considering vector problems we need to first decide on a sensible frame of reference or coordinate system. Frames of reference may be:

1. The vertical and horizontal direction relative to the ground
2. The planes of the human body, e.g. sagittal, coronal or transverse
3. Along a body segment and at 90° to it.

To calculate and understand the overall effect of all the vectors we must relate each vector to the same sensible frame of reference. When dealing with the human body this can be either in the vertical or horizontal directions to the sensible frame of reference.

We often have problems where we have vectors acting at an angle to the chosen frame of reference. I sometimes refer to this as acting at a 'funny angle', i.e. the vector does not line up with the frame of reference. If this is the case the vector at the 'funny angle' can be 'resolved' horizontally and vertically along the sensible frame of reference, or, to put it another way, the vector at the funny angle, the hypotenuse, can be split into the opposite and adjacent sides of a right-angled triangle. The opposite and adjacent sides will be the component vectors acting in each of the directions of your reference system.

Similarly, if we have the horizontal and vertical components (the opposite and adjacent sides) we can find the resultant (the hypotenuse) using Pythagoras. Then use sine or cosine to find the angle at which the resultant acts.

A simple vector problem

This problem deals with the forces we have during push off when walking. At this point we will not concern ourselves with what this means or the nature of the units. The aspect we need to focus on is that we have a vector of magnitude 1000 N acting at an angle of 80°. Although we will be using the units for force, N (newton), we don't at this time need to worry about what this actually means.

The question that needs answering is this: what are the magnitudes of the horizontal and vertical components of this resultant force during push off?

Before we do anything we have to decide on a sensible frame of reference. In this case this is quite straight forward, with the vertical and horizontal to the ground making most sense. We should now draw a box around the ends of the vector at the 'funny angle', i.e. the vector that does not line up with vertical and horizontal to the ground. Do not be distracted by the rest of the anatomy, although this matters as the force has an effect on the anatomy, we need to ignore it for the moment and just focus on the vector. We now need to consider what the vertical and horizontal components look like, their magnitude and where they originate from.

The magnitudes of the components will be the lengths of the vertical and horizontal size of the box we have drawn around the vector. All components must originate from the same point, i.e. the tails of the arrows representing the resultant, horizontal and vertical components should all converge on the same point, which in this example is under the metatarsal heads of the foot (Fig. 1.6).

We now have our sensible frame of reference and can visualize the horizontal and vertical components. Now, and only now, are we ready to consider calculating the magnitudes of the horizontal and vertical components; this is what we sometimes refer to as a laboratory or global coordinate system. This may seem like overkill, but without being able to visualize we are likely to make mistakes on more complex problems.

So on to the easy part: the maths! In Figure 1.6 we now have two identical right-angle triangles. For the triangle below we know one of the internal angles. Now all we need to do is to identify the hypotenuse, and the opposite and adjacent sides of the triangle, and use sine and cosine to find the horizontal and vertical components (Fig. 1.6).

$$\text{The cosine of the angle} = \frac{\text{Adjacent side}}{\text{Hypotenuse}}$$

$$\cos 80 = \frac{\text{Adjacent side}}{1000}$$

$$1000 \cos 80 = \text{Adjacent side}$$

$$173.6 = \text{Adjacent side}$$

Horizontal component = 173.6 N

$$\text{The sine of the angle} = \frac{\text{Opposite side}}{\text{Hypotenuse}}$$

$$\sin 80 = \frac{\text{Opposite side}}{1000}$$

$$1000 \sin 80 = \text{Opposite side}$$

$$984.8 = \text{Opposite side}$$

Vertical component = 984.8 N

To put this in a functional context, this means that a force of 984.85 N is pushing up, whereas 173.6 N is pushing, or propelling the body forwards. But there will be much more on this later.

A more difficult vector problem

This problem deals with the muscle forces acting around the hip joint. The two muscle groups we are considering here are the hip adductors and abductors, the anatomical insertions here being a rough illustration only.

The question is: what force is acting along the femur and what force is pushing the femur into the hip joint?

Again we are going to first consider a sensible frame of reference. However, in this case we want to know what is happening in reference to the femur which will be different to the horizontal and vertical in relation to the ground we used in the previous example. This is because the femur is not aligned perfectly to the vertical. This is what we sometimes call a local or segment coordinate system (Fig. 1.7), as before we will be using the unit for force, N (newton).

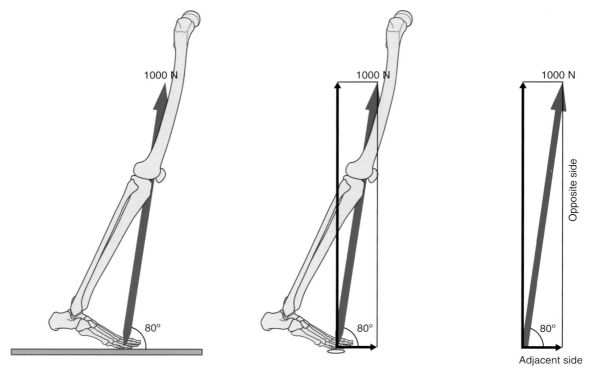

Figure 1.6   Resolving vectors. A simple vector problem.

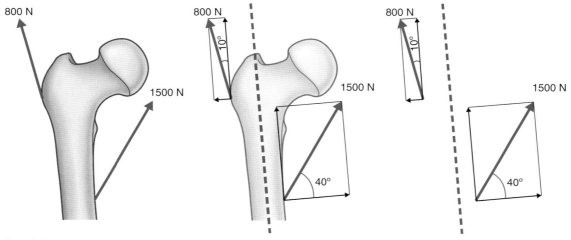

Figure 1.7   Resolving vectors. A more difficult vector problem.

Once we have drawn on this frame of reference we then need to draw boxes around the ends of each of the muscle force vectors making sure that the components align with this frame of reference. As before we are going to ignore the femur itself and focus on the vectors and their frame of reference only, once we have solved the problem we will then relate it back to the anatomy.

Next we will consider each muscle separately and work out the components along the long axis of the femur and at 90° to the femur (our sensible frame of reference in this case). If we consider first the hip adductors (Fig. 1.7).

The force along the long axis of the femur is the opposite side to the angle of 40°. Therefore:

$$\text{The sine of the angle} = \frac{\text{Opposite side}}{\text{Hypotenuse}}$$

$$\sin 40 = \frac{\text{Opposite side}}{1500}$$

$$1500 \sin 40 = \text{Opposite side}$$

$$964.2 = \text{Opposite side}$$

Long axis component = 964.2 N

The force along the axis at 90 degrees to the femur is the adjacent side to the angle of 40°. Therefore:

The cosine of the angle = $\dfrac{\text{Adjacent side}}{\text{Hypotenuse}}$

$\cos 40 = \dfrac{\text{Adjacent side}}{1500}$

$1500 \cos 40 = \text{Adjacent side}$

$1149 = \text{Adjacent side}$

Component at 90° to the femur = 1149 N

If we now consider the hip abductors (Fig. 1.7).

The force along the long axis of the femur is the adjacent side to the angle of 10°. Therefore:

The cosine of the angle = $\dfrac{\text{Adjacent side}}{\text{Hypotenuse}}$

$\cos 10 = \dfrac{\text{Adjacent side}}{800}$

$800 \cos 10 = \text{Adjacent side}$

$787.8 = \text{Adjacent side}$

Long axis component = 787.8 N

The force along the axis at 90° to the femur is the opposite side to the angle of 10°. Therefore:

The sine of the angle = $\dfrac{\text{Opposite side}}{\text{Hypotenuse}}$

$\sin 10 = \dfrac{\text{Opposite side}}{800}$

$800 \sin 10 = \text{Opposite side}$

$138.9 = \text{Opposite side}$

Component at 90° to the femur = 138.9 N

If we now combine what we have found from both muscles.

Total force along the axis of the femur = 964.2 + 787.8
Total force along the axis of the femur = 1752 N
Total force at 90° to the long axis of the femur = 1149 − 138.9
Total force at 90° to the long axis of the femur = 1010.1 N

We have now simplified the problem as all the forces are either acting along the axis of the femur or at 90° to the long axis (Fig. 1.8). We can now add the forces acting along the axis and at 90° to the long axis of the femur. To do this we need some simple rules:

- All forces acting up are positive and all forces acting down are negative.
- All forces acting to the right are positive and all forces acting to the left are negative.

The above problem can be taken one step further as these forces must be balanced with the joint forces (Fig. 1.9).

This is the beginning of solving quite complex biomechanical problems, which we have achieved by breaking the problem up into more simple parts. We will deal with both muscle and joint forces in far more detail in Chapter 2: Forces, moments and muscles.

1.2 Mechanics

1.2.1 Units – system international

We have already started to consider different units, such as cm and N. The system of units we use for measurement is the system international (SI), which was devised in 1960. It defined a system of units to be used universally. The system of measurement units was based on the MKS (meter-kilometer-second) system. These and only these units should be used when working out problems, do not use pounds and feet! If you do not use SI units in your calculations then problems become a lot harder to solve, and you don't want that do you?

Some of the common SI units that are used in biomechanics are given below. Many of these units have a close relationship with one another which aims to make problems easier to solve (Table 1.1).

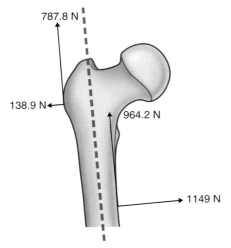

Figure 1.8   Forces along and at 90° to the long axis

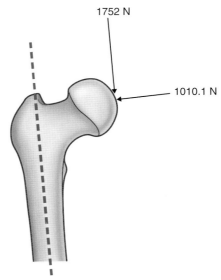

Figure 1.9   Joint forces

Table 1.1   Units

Quantity	Name of base	SI unit symbol
Length	Metre	m
Mass	Kilogram	kg
Time	Second	s
Area	Square metre	m^2
Volume	Cubic metre	m^3
Velocity	Metre per second	m/s
Acceleration	Metre per second squared	m/s^2
Force	Newton	N
Pressure	Pascal	N/m^2
Energy	Joule	J
Power	Watt	W

Table 1.2   Indices

Multiplication factor	Prefix symbol
1 000 000 000	10^9 giga G
1 000 000	10^6 mega M
1000	10^3 kilo k
100	10^2 hecto h
10	10^1 deka da
0.1	10^{-1} deci d
0.01	10^{-2} centi c
0.001	10^{-3} milli m
0.000 001	10^{-6} micro μ
0.000 000 001	10^{-9} pico p

1.2.2 Indices

Indices are a way of expressing very large or very small numbers without including lots of zeros (Table 1.2). For example 100 000 m may be written as 100 km, and a pressure of 10 000 000 Pascals may be written as 10 MPa. This can be very useful in biomechanics, in particular for pressure measurement when the values can be very large.

1.2.3 Forces

The fundamental concepts of mechanics include the study of forces, movement and moments. Forces make things move, stop things moving, or make things change shape. They can either push or pull. In the SI system of units, forces are measured in newton (N). Force is a vector quantity; therefore, all forces have two characteristics, magnitude and direction, which both need to be stated in order to describe the force fully. A good place to start considering the effect of forces is with the laws formulated by Newton.

1.2.4 Newton's laws of motion

Isaac Newton (1642–1727) in 1687 published a three volume work 'Philosophiae Naturalis Principia Mathematica', which

was published first in Latin, revised in 1713 and 1726, and, interestingly, was not translated into English until 1729, after his death. In this epic work he dealt with many of the concepts in physics including the 'inverse square' law of gravity and the three laws of motion, which we will now consider, although somewhat abridged from the original.

Newton's first law

'Every object in a state of uniform motion tends to remain in that state of motion unless an external force is applied to it.'

This law states that if an object is at rest it will stay at rest; and if it is moving with a constant speed in a straight line it will continue to do so, as long as no external force acts on it, i.e. if an object is not experiencing the action of an external force it will either keep moving or not move at all.

This law expresses the concept of inertia. The inertia of a body can be described as being its reluctance to start moving, or stop moving once it has started. In fact the state of being at total rest or constant velocity never happens in animals, as there is always some movement which means a continually changing velocity. Even if we consider a runner at a perceived constant speed, there will in fact be significant changes in vertical and horizontal velocities of the whole body and the individual body segments.

Newton's first law of motion was an important first statement which highlighted the nature of an object travelling in a frictionless environment at a constant speed; this also set the scene for the remaining two laws of motion.

Newton's second law

'The relationship between an object's mass(m), its acceleration(a) and the applied force (F) is F = ma. The direction of the force vector is the same as the direction of the acceleration vector.'

This law states that the rate of change of velocity (acceleration) is directly proportional to the applied, external, force acting on the body and takes place in the direction of the force. Therefore, forces can either cause an acceleration or deceleration of an object. **Acceleration** is usually defined as being positive and **deceleration** as being negative.

F = ma

F = Applied force (N)

m = Mass of the body (kg)

a = Acceleration of the body (m/s^2)

One way to think about this is to consider what would happen if you put a mouse on a skateboard and gave it a push, a single external force. The skateboard and mouse would accelerate off quickly while you were pushing, or providing a force (F) as the mass (m) is small. Now consider exchanging the mouse for a large dog and you provided the same force during the push. Clearly the dog would accelerate at a much slower rate; this is due to its larger mass. So for the same force two different accelerations would be attained due to the different masses of animal by the relationship of a = F/m.

This law also raises an interesting point about external forces in biomechanics, where we often have many external forces acting at any one time. Therefore to work out how an object is going to move we need to consider **all the forces** acting. This can make some problems very difficult to solve.

Newton' third law

'For every action there is an equal and opposite reaction.'

This law states that if a body A exerts a force on a body B, then B exerts an equal and opposite directed force on A. This does not mean the forces cancel each other out because they act on two different bodies. For example, a runner exerts a force on the ground and receives a reaction force that drives him up and forward. This is known as a **ground reaction force** or **GRF**, which we will be considering in greater detail throughout this book.

1.2.5 Mass and weight

So what is mass?

Mass is the amount of matter an object contains, or to put it another way the number of atoms that make up your body. This will not change unless the physical properties of the object are changed, e.g. you change the amount of matter you contain by growing, dieting or losing a body part. One extreme example of demonstrating this is going into orbit or going to the moon, although you may well become weightless, or much reduce your weight, you still contain the same amount of matter. Therefore, the dieting group 'weight watchers' is in fact incorrectly named and 'mass watchers' would be more correct, as the thing which is being changed is the amount of matter, or mass of the body.

So what is weight?

Weight is an attractive force we have with whichever planet or celestial body we happen to be on or near. In fact this attractive force is present between all objects; however, unless the mass of one of the objects is very large, the effects are very hard to observe. This force depends on both the mass of the object and the acceleration acting on it, e.g. gravity. Weight is often interpreted as being the force acting beneath our feet, e.g. bathroom scales measure this force, although they very rarely use the correct units, which are newton.

So can we change our weight? A good way to lose weight is to stand in a lift and press the down button. You will lose weight, i.e. the force beneath your feet will reduce as the lift accelerates downwards. Unfortunately when the lift comes to a stop you will gain weight again as the lift decelerates downwards. This is of course not really true, as what we are doing is temporarily changing the conditions with the additional acceleration of the lift as well as the acceleration due to gravity.

Another example of the difference between mass and weight is to consider astronauts. When they are in space they are weightless, this does not mean they have gone on an amazing diet, but it does mean that there is little or no acceleration acting on them, so any force acing on them is zero.

So weight is a force which is dependent on the mass of the object and the acceleration due to gravity. This brings us back to Newton's second law of motion, F=ma, but with weight as the force and the acceleration being the acceleration due to gravity.

Force = Mass × Acceleration

Weight = Mass × Acceleration due to gravity

Weight = mg

Acceleration due to gravity

Wherever you are on planet Earth there is an acceleration due to gravity acting on you. So where does this acceleration due to gravity come from? Once again we look to Newton who found what is called the inverse square law.

$$F = \frac{G\,M\,m}{r^2}$$

where: F = force, G = universal gravitational constant = $6.67300 \times 10^{-11}\,Nm^2/kg^2$, M = mass of object 1, m = mass of object 2 and r = the distance away from the centre of the objects.

F is the attractive force between any two objects, so the greater the mass the objects contain, the larger the attractive force between the objects. So the larger the body the more attractive it is!

So let's now consider my attractive force with the Earth, or weight.

The mass of the Earth is approximately 5.9742×10^{24} kg, the radius of the Earth is approximately 6375 km and my current mass is 70 kg.

$$F \text{ or weight} = \frac{6.67300 \times 10^{-11} \times 5.9742 \times 10^{24} \times 70}{6\,375\,000^2}$$

This gives a weight = 686.65 N

So this gives me an attractive force with the Earth of 686.65 N, this is my current weight in newton. Now if we relate this back to Newton's second law of motion we will find a much easier way of doing this:

F = m a

686.65 = 70 × a

$\frac{686.65}{70}$ = a

a = 9.81 m/s²

So the attractive force between each of us and the Earth produces an acceleration due to gravity (g) of 9.81 m/s², which is the accepted value and is only subject to very small geographic variations over the surface of the Earth. For the purposes of rough calculations this is often rounded up to 10 m/s². However, to get the best possible accuracy 9.81 m/s² should be used; therefore, I will be using 9.81 m/s² in this book.

Weight = mass × gravity

or

Weight = mg

1.2.6 Static equilibrium

The concept of static equilibrium is of great importance in biomechanics as it allows us to calculate forces that are unknown. Newton's first law tells us that there is no resultant force acting if the body is at rest, i.e. the forces balance.

Therefore if an object is at rest, the sum of the forces on the object, in any direction, must be zero. So when we resolve in a horizontal and vertical direction the resultant force must be zero.

If we consider someone standing still, they will have a reaction force from the ground under each foot. This will have a vertical component, but there will also be a small horizontal medial (directed towards the middle) component under each foot, as the feet are wider apart than the width of the pelvis. However, these horizontal forces will in fact act against one another and cancel out in the same way described in the section on vectors, as they act on the same object, in this case a person. The other force we need to consider is the weight acting down, this will be equal and opposite to the vertical component of the reaction forces acting under the feet. So the sum of the forces in the vertical and horizontal will be zero, indicating that the person is indeed standing still (Fig. 1.10).

1.2.7 Free body analysis

Free body analysis is a technique of looking at and simplifying a problem. We have already seen an example of this in the section on vectors.

If we consider two people having a tug of war, both pulling a rope (Fig. 1.11). For each person we need to identify all the forces. In this example we have the tension in the rope, which is pulling each person towards the centre, a resultant force pushing up beneath the feet, and the weight of each individual acting down. Once we have drawn these then consider how these are acting in relation to a sensible frame of reference, and if the forces do not align with this frame of reference they will need to be resolved vertically and horizontally. This breaking down of a problem and drawing the system of forces is called a free body diagram (Fig. 1.12).

Once we have drawn this diagram we can then start to think about the forces and solving the problem, which in this case is to find: a) the tension in the rope and b) the mass of the person. Assuming that the two people are the same weight and height, that they are in identical positions and that they are in static equilibrium, the resultant force beneath the feet is 900 N and the angle of the force acting to the vertical is 30° (Fig. 1.13).

Resolving

First we must resolve the force of 900 N so that it is in the sensible frame of reference, which in this case is horizontal and vertical to the ground.

Horizontally

$$\sin 30 = \frac{\text{Horizontal component (opposite)}}{\text{Resultant force (hypotenuse)}}$$

$$\sin 30 = \frac{\text{Horizontal component (opposite)}}{900}$$

$$900 \sin 30 = \text{Horizontal component}$$

$$450\,\text{N} = \text{Horizontal component}$$

Tension in the rope = 450 N

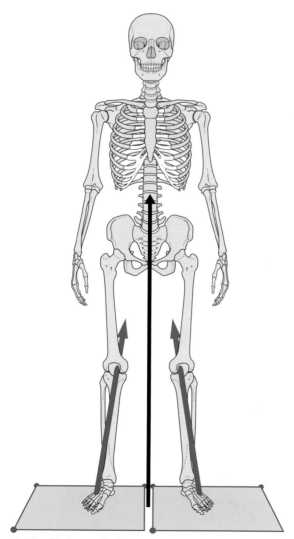

Figure 1.10   Static equilibrium

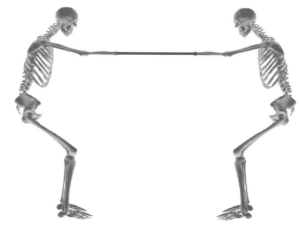

Figure 1.11   Tug of war

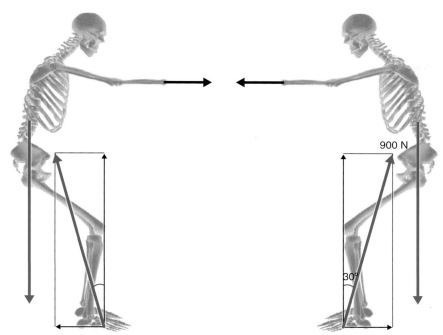

Figure 1.12   Free body analysis

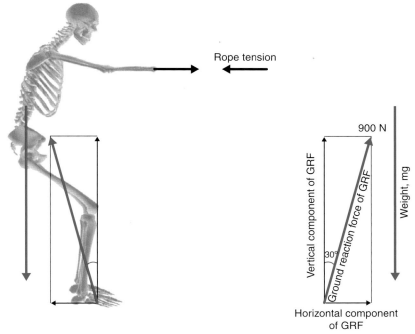

Figure 1.13   Forces during a tug of war

There are no other horizontal forces acting on the person apart from the tension in the rope, therefore, if this is in static equilibrium this force MUST be equal and opposite to this force in the rope from Newton's third law of motion.

Vertically

$$\cos 30 = \frac{\text{Vertical component (adjacent)}}{\text{Resultant force (hypotenuse)}}$$

$$\cos 30 = \frac{\text{Vertical component (adjacent)}}{900}$$

$900 \cos 30 = \text{Vertical component}$

$779.4\,\text{N} = \text{Vertical component}$

Weight of person = $779.4\,\text{N}$

There are no other vertical forces apart from the weight of the person, therefore, if this is in static equilibrium the weight MUST also be equal and opposite to this force from Newton's third law of motion.

But what is the person's mass? If we now consider the concept of mass and weight again.

Weight = Mass × Acceleration due to gravity

779.4 N = Mass × 9.81 m/s²

$$\frac{779.4}{9.81} = \text{Mass}$$

79.45 = Mass

Therefore the mass of the person is 79.45 kg.

1.2.8 Moments and forces

When a force acts on a body away from its pivoting point a turning effect is set up. Consider opening and closing a door. You are in fact creating sufficient force to turn the door on its hinges: the force required to do this multiplied by the distance away from the hinges you are pushing is the moment (Fig. 1.14).

A turning moment is defined as:

M = F × d

where: M = turning moment, F = magnitude of force (how hard you push) and d = distance from the pivot.

Balancing moments

This is very much like working out the unknown forces using static equilibrium. As with static equilibrium we can balance the moments by making the overall effect zero, i.e. the effect of one moment cancels out the effect of another

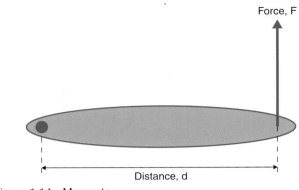

Figure 1.14   Moments

moment. The best way of thinking about this is considering the turning forces on a seesaw (Fig. 1.15).

It is clear that this seesaw will not balance. In fact, a better way of describing this would be that the seesaw would rotate in the clockwise direction. This would have the effect of moving the heavier person down until their feet touched the ground, at which point some of the force would be removed from the seesaw. So it is clear to balance the seesaw we need to move the pivot point closer to the heavier person (Fig. 1.16).

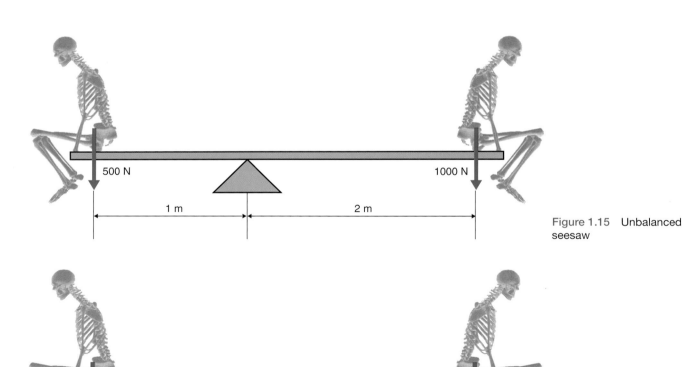

Figure 1.15   Unbalanced seesaw

Figure 1.16   Balanced seesaw

The mathematics behind balancing moments

To solve problems with moments we have to consider what the action of each force would be in turn. To do this we consider if each force will try to rotate the object (in this case a seesaw) in a clockwise or anti-clockwise direction. If it is in a clockwise direction it is considered to be in a positive direction, and if anti-clockwise it is considered to be in a negative direction. So if we consider the mathematics of the example in Figure 1.16:

> The 500 N weight will try to turn the seesaw anticlockwise.
> The 1000 N weight will try to turn the seesaw clockwise.

If the seesaw balances then the sum of the clockwise turning effects and anticlockwise turning effects must be zero. To do this we are going to break the problems down by considering the effect of each force separately, and then consider the overall effect.

So if we consider anticlockwise moments as negative and clockwise as positive:

Moment = Force × Distance to pivot

Moment = −(500 × 2) + (1000 × 1)

Moment = −1000 + 1000

i.e. the moments cancel out and the seesaw is balanced.

Although there seems to be little effect, if we now consider Newton's third law of motion then we do in fact have a third force acting. If we consider the seesaw vertically we have two forces (weights) on either side acting down giving a total force of 1500 N. From Newton's third law of motion there must be an equal and opposite reaction acting up. The only place for this to act is at the pivot; therefore, there must be a force acting up of 1500 N as it is static equilibrium (Fig. 1.17).

These techniques of finding forces and moments are identical to the ones we use to find muscle and joint forces in the body, which will be dealt with in more depth in Chapter 2: Forces, moments and muscles.

1.2.9 Pressure

What is pressure?

Pressure is best thought about as the force acting over an area. If we consider a large force distributed over a very large area the pressure will be relatively small, alternatively if we consider the same force acting over a very small area the pressure will be very high. So pressure is dependent on the force applied and the area over which the force acts.

Pressure has been measured using a variety of units over the course of history, which unfortunately still plague us today. These include: millibars, bars, pascals, kilopascals, megapascals, newtons per square centimetre, newtons per square metre, atmospheres, inches of water, feet of water, mm of water, inches of mercury, mm of mercury, kilograms per cm squared, pounds per square inch (psi), pounds per square foot, tonnes per metre squared, to mention just some of them!

Within biomechanics, thankfully, we are a little more consistent, although there is still a variety that are used including: newton per millimetre square (N/mm^2), newton per centimetre square (N/cm^2), kilograms per millimetre square (kg/mm^2), kilograms per centimetre square (kg/cm^2), pounds per square inch (psi) and millimetres of mecury (mmHg).

Any measurement of pressure involving kilograms is strictly speaking wrong, as this a measure of mass and NOT a measure of force. However, more people are likely to have a conceptual idea of what a kilogram is, which has contributed to its use. The same argument could be made for the use of pounds, even though the Conférence générale des poids et measures (CGPM) agreed over three decades ago in 1971 to maintain the metric standards of the Convention du Mètre nearly 100 years earlier in 1875! The use of different units makes the comparison of clinical data difficult and only makes the calculations harder.

So what units should we use? The SI unit for pressure is pascal (Pa), although in pressure because of the size of the measurements kPa makes more sense, i.e. 1 kPa = 1000 Pa. The unit pascal is named after Blaise Pascal (1623–1662) a French mathematician and physicist. A pascal is the pressure produced when a force of 1 newton is distributed over an area of 1 m^2.

$$\text{Pressure} = \frac{\text{Force (N)}}{\text{Area (m}^2)}$$

Finding pressures when standing

If a subject of weight (force) 700 N stands on a block with a side of 4 cm, then we can find the average pressure beneath the area of the foot in contact with the block:

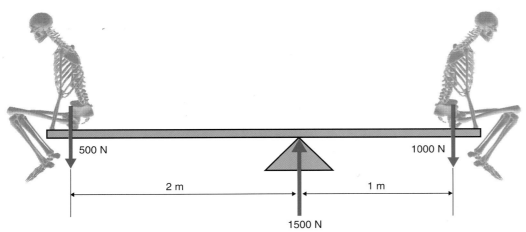

500 N   1000 N

2 m   1 m

1500 N

Figure 1.17 Pivot reaction force

Area = 0.04 × 0.04 = 0.0016 m²

The force beneath the foot will be equal to the weight from Newton's third law. The average pressure between the foot and the block = force/area:

$$\text{Pressure} = \frac{700}{0.0016}$$

$$= 437\,500\,\text{N/m}^2\,(\text{Pa})$$

$$= 437.5\,\text{kN/m}^2\,(\text{kPa})$$

If the subject of weight 700 N now stands on a block with a side of 2 cm, the average pressure beneath the foot will be greater. Again this depends on the area of the foot in contact with the block and the subject's weight.

The area beneath the foot in contact with the block is calculated by:

Area = 0.02 × 0.02 = 0.0004 m²

The average pressure between the foot and the block = force/area:

$$\text{Pressure} = \frac{700}{0.0004}$$

$$= 1\,750\,000\,\text{N/m}^2\,(\text{Pa})$$

$$= 1750\,\text{kN/m}^2\,(\text{kPa})$$

e.g. if an individual stands with flat feet they will have lower pressures on the foot than an individual with arched feet as the area over which the force is distributed is larger.

This only considers the average pressure over the whole foot. However, load will not be evenly distributed over the whole of the base of the foot, but will be concentrated at various points on the foot. The distributions of pressure beneath the foot are extremely important in both pain relief and prevention of tissue breakdown; this will be dealt with in much more detail in Chapter 7: Measurement of force and pressure.

1.2.10 Friction

What causes friction?

We have already talked briefly about friction, or at least the absence of it, when considering Newton's first law of motion. But what is friction and what causes it?

When the two surfaces meet what happens? The surfaces in contact weld together microscopically. Then when the objects continue to move against each other the peaks break off. This process creates a force that tries to resist the motion and this force is what we call the frictional force.

This process also leaves fragments that also resist the movement and wear down the surfaces further; this is known as three body wear, the three bodies being the two opposing surfaces and the fragments themselves. So where there is friction, there is wear and you need look no further than the soles of your shoes.

Static friction

When a body moves or tries to move over a surface it experiences a frictional force. The frictional surfaces act along a common surface, and are in a direction to oppose the movement. If we consider pulling an object along the ground, an unwilling dog or child perhaps, initially the force is small and the object does not move. As the pulling force is increased there reaches a point where the object starts to slide (note: this should not be considered necessarily as good parenting or dog ownership practice).

This indicates that for small values of pulling force the frictional force is equal and opposite, but there is a maximal frictional force that can be brought into play, this is known as the limiting frictional force. When the pulling force is greater than the limiting frictional force the object will accelerate in accordance to Newton's second law. Interestingly, however, once the object starts to move the force required to overcome the friction force reduces slightly.

What does frictional force depend on?

Friction force depends on two main factors; how hard the object is pressing down onto the surface (the normal reaction), and the roughness of the contact between the two surfaces (coefficient of friction).

Coefficient of friction

The frictional force can be shown to be proportional to the normal reaction force by placing increasing loads on a platform and then applying a horizontal force. The force required to move the platform will increase with the loading on the platform. Therefore, we can say as the reaction force increases so does the limiting frictional force. Therefore, as the normal reaction (R) increases the limiting frictional force (F) would also increase. The limiting frictional force will vary depending on the materials the two surfaces are made of. Each combination of materials will have its own coefficient of friction given the symbol μ.

Maximum (limiting) frictional force available

A good way of considering the limiting frictional force is by thinking of two objects of the same shape but different weights. An example would be a mouse and a dog standing on a block. If we try to push the block the coefficient of friction will in fact be the same for both conditions; however, the dog's larger weight will produce a larger reaction force which will mean the amount of frictional force available is much greater than the same block with the mouse.

Maximum frictional force available may be found using the equation below:

Maximum frictional force available = coefficient of friction × normal reaction

$$F = \mu R$$

where:
F = maximum frictional force available,
μ = coefficient of friction
R = normal reaction.

Figure 1.18 shows the frictional force increasing in proportion to the applied force. The object is then pulled along a flat surface at a constant velocity. The frictional force equals the pulling force as the object is neither accelerating nor decelerating.

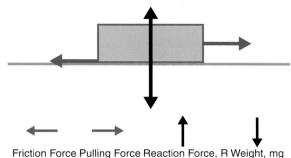

Friction Force Pulling Force Reaction Force, R Weight, mg

Figure 1.18   Frictional force

This horizontal force will have to be equal to or less than the maximum friction force available for each surface. To find the maximum frictional force available we first need to find the 'normal reaction' or 'vertical component' of the ground reaction force.

The sine of the angle $= \dfrac{\text{Opposite side}}{\text{Hypotenuse}}$

$\sin 80 = \dfrac{\text{Opposite side}}{1000}$

$1000 \sin 80 = \text{Opposite side}$

$984.8 = \text{Opposite side}$

Vertical component = 984.8 N

Limiting frictional forces during walking

Limiting frictional forces are extremely important for our stability during walking. If we consider the effect of walking on two different surfaces with different coefficients of friction we can predict whether an individual is likely to slip (Fig. 1.19). So if a person walks in the way shown below (first on a carpet, $\mu = 0.55$, and then on a tiled floor, $\mu = 0.18$) will they slip?

First we have to find the vertical and horizontal components of the ground reaction force.

The cosine of the angle $= \dfrac{\text{Adjacent side}}{\text{Hypotenuse}}$

$\cos 80 = \dfrac{\text{Adjacent side}}{1000}$

$1000 \cos 80 = \text{Adjacent side}$

$173.6 = \text{Adjacent side}$

Horizontal component = 173.6 N

Maximum frictional force available for carpet

The size of the vertical component will determine the amount of friction force available with each coefficient of friction.

Maximum frictional force available = normal reaction × coefficient of friction

$F = \mu R$

Maximum frictional force available for carpet = 0.55 × 984.8 = 541.6 N

The maximum friction force available when walking on carpet is 541.6 N, which is much greater than that of the horizontal force, 173.6 N, therefore the person is quite safe.

Maximum frictional force available for tiled floor

Maximum frictional force available for tiled floor = 0.18 × 984.8 = 177.3 N

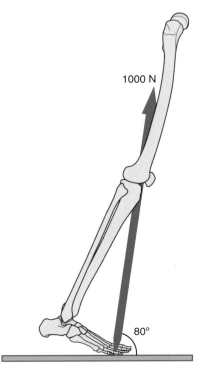
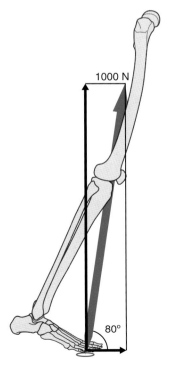

1000 N   1000 N   1000 N

80°   80°   80°

Figure 1.19   Frictional force during walking

The maximum friction force available when walking on the tiled floor is much reduced, 177.3 N, but there is just sufficient frictional force available to support the 173.6 N horizontal force to stop the person slipping. However, any greater horizontal force or any slight reduction in the coefficient of friction will mean the person's foot will slip backwards, as the floor will no longer be able to maintain the anterior frictional force to stop it.

The clinical relevance of friction

Friction affects many aspects of biomechanics, without friction there would be no horizontal forces when we walk. You only have to consider walking on a frozen pond with shoes with no grip, the lack of friction would either not allow us to move at all or make us slip over if we ever did get moving. Much work has been carried out on non-slip surfaces which allow, in theory, the best coefficient of friction with minimum floor wear under all conditions to yield the largest available frictional force to enable us to walk safely.

Friction is also used in many external prostheses, for instance some external prosthetic knee units have a frictional brake, which allows an amputee some knee flexion during stance phase whilst remaining stable. Conversely, internal prosthetic devices (knee and hip replacements) aim to reduce the friction as much as possible, which increases the life of the prosthesis.

Summary: Maths and mechanics

- Vectors are quantities that have magnitude and direction. We can describe these in terms of a value and an angle from a frame of reference. From this their effects can be found along anatomical axes.
- When a body moves it is in a continuous state of acceleration and deceleration. Internal and external forces are continually at work to drive these movements.
- Weight and mass are not the same. Mass is the amount of matter a body contains, whereas weight is a force due to the body's mass and the accelerations acting on it.
- Moments describe turning effects about pivot points. Understanding moments is essential when considering the action of muscles and how they control joint movement.
- Pressure is a measure of the distribution of the force, or pressure, beneath the foot or contact area. Pressure can be used to determine variations in the loading or pressure patterns. High pressures can cause tissue breakdown and injury.
- Frictional forces are always present. Perhaps the most important friction force is between the foot and the ground. Without this force we would not be able to propel or stop ourselves when walking.

Forces, Moments and Muscles

Jim Richards

This chapter considers the use of the techniques covered in Chapter 1 in relation to the musculoskeletal system in more detail. It also considers the properties of the body segments, the joint moments, muscle forces, and joint reaction forces in upper and lower limbs.

Chapter 2: Aim

To relate forces and moments to muscle forces and joint forces.

Chapter 2: Objectives

- To explain the nature of centre of mass and how to find body segment information
- To understand the calculation of moments about joints in static problems
- To understand the calculation of muscle forces in static problems
- To understand the calculation of joint forces in static problems.

2.1 Centre of mass

So what is the centre of mass? The centre of mass is a point on an object where all the mass can be considered to act. The centre of mass of an object does not always coincide with its geometric centre as it is affected by not just the shape of the object, but also the distributions of the den-

sities of material throughout the object. The concept of 'centre of gravity', a term often used interchangeably with centre of mass, was first introduced by the ancient Greek mathematician, physicist and engineer Archimedes. The defining of a single point where all the mass can be considered to act is very useful in mechanics and biomechanics as it allow us to study the force due to an object's position and its response to external forces.

2.1.1 The centre of mass by calculation

The calculation of the position of the centre of mass of an object can be done in a very similar way to that used when considering the moments of the two people on the seesaw. However, on this occasion we have to find the horizontal position of the centre of mass, although we will ignore the weight of the seesaw (Fig. 2.1).

The centre of mass of an object is the point at which its weight acts, and in this case the object is the entire system of the seesaw and the two people. If the object is pivoted about its centre of gravity there would be no turning moment about that point and, therefore, the seesaw would balance. However, in the above example I have neglected to tell you the balance point, as this is the very thing we are trying to find out. So the balance point will be X metres from one end, all we have to do now is find out what X is.

As before, we are going to consider the moment of each side of the seesaw, but now we are going to do this in terms of our unknown value X. As before clockwise moments are considered as positive and anticlockwise moments are considered as negative. So:

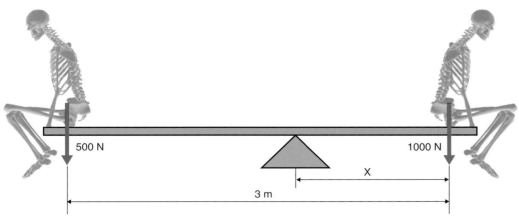

Figure 2.1 Centre of mass by calculation

The moment due to the 1000 N – The moment due to 500 N = 0

1000 X – 500 (3 – X) = 0

1000 X – 1500 + 500 X = 0

1500 X – 1500 = 0

1500 X = 1500

$$X = \frac{1500}{1500}$$

Therefore, X = 1 m

This tells us the exact location of the centre of mass of the object, which is 1 m from the heavier person.

2.1.2 Finding the centre of mass by experiment

The calculation method can be very useful; however, if we have to find the two-dimensional or three-dimensional location of the centre of mass of irregular objects, such as body parts, this technique becomes harder. In these situations we should consider another technique for finding the centre of mass by experiment.

Ankle foot orthosis (AFOs) are ankle supports frequently used in the management of cerebral palsy and stroke. We could find the centre of mass using a computer aid design (CAD) package if we have a precise three-dimensional representation of the device; however, AFOs are often hand made from casts on the subject's foot and ankle, therefore, the best way of finding the centre of mass is to find it experimentally. To do this we need to suspend the object from a location near an edge and drop a plumb line and mark this on the object. We then suspend the object from another location not too close to the first and drop a second plumb line and mark again. The intersection of the two lines will be at the centre of mass. This may then be checked by choosing a third suspension location, which should coincide with the intersection already marked (Fig. 2.2a, b, c).

2.1.3 Centre of mass and stability of the body in different positions

For an object of variable shape, such as the human body, the precise position of the centre of mass will clearly change with the position of the limbs. Different body positions may result in the centre of mass falling inside or outside of the body. During standing, for instance, the centre of mass of an adult lies within the pelvis in front of the upper part of the sacrum, its exact location depending on the build, sex and age of the individual. However, as the person moves the relative position of the body segments move. Figure 2.3 shows how the position of the centre of mass moves during a sit-to-stand task.

The first diagram shows the sagittal plane view just after the person has left the chair. Notice that the force falls behind the foot. If the person were to stop at this point they would fall back onto the chair. The second diagram shows the force is nearer the pelvis and the line of force now falls in the base of support of the feet, if the person were to stop at this point they would now be in a stable crouched position. The third and fourth diagrams show the sagittal and coronal views at the end standing position.

2.2 Anthropometry

2.2.1 Background to anthropometry

The study of muscle and joint forces requires data regarding the length of body segments, mass distributions, centre of mass and the radius of gyration of body segments. Information about human body dimensions was first collected in the late 19th century by Braune and Fischer (1889). Since then more comprehensive studies have been undertaken, most notably by Dempster (1955), Dempster and colleagues (1959), Drillis and Contini (1966), Clauser et al (1969), Chandler (1975), Zatsiorsky and Seluyanov (1983), and de Leva (1996). Some of this information has been obtained from cadavers and some used measured segment volumes in conjunction

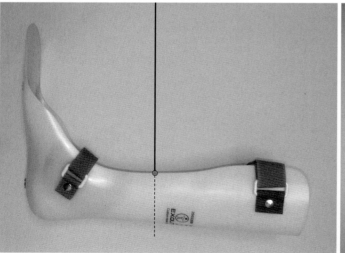

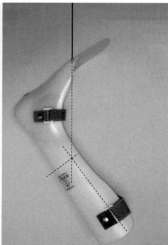

a   b   c

Figure 2.2   (a, b and c) Centre of mass by experimentation

with density tables. Kingma et al (1995) discussed the errors associated with using stereotyped anthropometric data and suggested procedures to optimise the calculation of segment centres of mass and centre of mass of the whole body. A greater degree of accuracy may be achieved by taking measurements of segment lengths and therefore removing some of the errors due to natural variation. To remove all errors associated with these calculations, full anthropometric measurements need to be taken; however, this takes a considerable amount of time and is also open to numerous measurement errors itself.

The work by Dempster in 1955 is still considered by many as the best to work with, and much of the subsequent research into anthropometry has been on adjustments to Dempster's values, rather than new independent work. However, these must be viewed as estimates of segment values as Dempster's report in 1955 only included data from eight cadavers, and Dempster saw some variations between the cadavers. Dempster's report covered many aspects of anthropometry including the design of a mannequin, but most quoted are the values of the mass of body segments, the position of the centres of mass and the moments of inertia. Drillis and Contini (1966) reported the relative segment

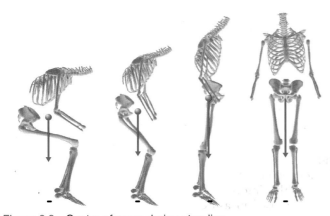

Figure 2.3   Centre of mass during standing

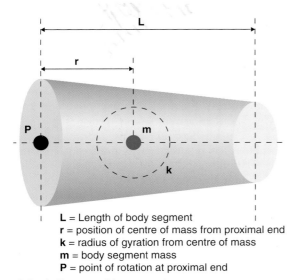

L = Length of body segment
r = position of centre of mass from proximal end
k = radius of gyration from centre of mass
m = body segment mass
P = point of rotation at proximal end

Figure 2.4   Anthropometric parameters

lengths based on the overall body height. From these data we are able to find an estimate of all the physical properties of all body segments using measures of only the subject's mass and height. However, this is open to error due to the natural variation in anatomical proportions. Although we should go to reasonable lengths of reducing any errors, most sources of anthropometric data provide similar results and it is debatable whether the different models produce clinically significant different results.

2.2.2 Common anthropometric parameters

The most common anthropometric measurements used in biomechanics are: segment lengths with respect to body height (L), segment mass with respect to total body mass (m), and the position of centres of mass (r) and radius of gyration (k) with respect to segment length (Fig. 2.4). The relationship between the location of the centre of mass and radius of gyration with segment length varies for different body segments; therefore, we have to use specific values for each body part. The radius of gyration of the body segments only needs to be used when the acceleration and deceleration of the body segments are being considered. For the moment we will consider the body segments to be static, although we will need to consider the radius of gyration later when calculating dynamic moments.

Table 2.1 shows a summary of the data found by Dempster (1955) and Drillis and Contini (1966).

2.2.3 Anthropometric calculations

Anthropometric calculations are quite simple as we work from percentages or ratios of the body segments parameters in relation to height, mass or segment length. Therefore, using Table 2.1 the length, mass, centre of mass and radius of gyration may be found from the person's overall height and weight.

The examples below show calculations of body segment parameter in a person of mass of 80 kg and a height of 1.8 m. Using Table 2.1 the length, mass, centre of mass, and radius of gyration of the different body segments may be found. Below are examples of how we can use this table to find information about the different body segments using only the measures of mass and height.

The mass of a foot from the table is 0.014 of the total body mass. Therefore, the mass of a foot may be found by simply multiplying this by the total body mass:

The mass of a foot = 0.014 × 80

The mass of a foot = 1.12 kg

The length of a body segment can also be found in a similar way. The length of the thigh is 0.245 of the total body height. Therefore, the length of the thigh may be found by simply multiplying this by the height of the person:

The length of the thigh = 0.245 × 1.8

The length of the thigh = 0.441 m

The position of the centre of mass may also be found; however, this depends on the length of the segment and not

Table 2.1 Anthropometrics of body segments

Body segments	Length of segment / body height	Mass of segment / body mass	Centre of mass (CoM) segment length (measured from proximal end)	Radius of gyration segment length (measured about CoM)
Foot	0.152 (length) 0.055 (width)	0.014	0.429	0.475
Shank	0.246	0.045	0.433	0.302
Shank and foot	0.285	0.0595	0.434	0.416
Thigh	0.245	0.096	0.433	0.323
Entire lower extremity	0.72	0.157	0.434	0.326
Upper arm	0.186	0.0265	0.436	0.322
Forearm	0.146	0.0155	0.430	0.303
Hand	0.108	0.006	0.506	0.297
Forearm and hand	0.254	0.0215	0.677*	0.468
Entire upper extremity	0.441	0.0485	0.512	0.368
Head and trunk minus limbs	0.52	0.565	0.604 (from top of head)	0.503
Head and neck	0.182	0.079		0.495

* The position of the centre of mass of the forearm and hand is 0.677 of forearm length **only**.

just the height of the person. Therefore, to find the location of the centre of mass in the forearm from the proximal joint we first have to find the segment length and then the centre of mass:

The length of the forearm = 0.146 × 1.8

The length of the forearm = 0.2628 m

The position of the centre of mass is 0.430 × segment length from the proximal joint. Therefore the position of the centre of mass may be found:

The position of the centre of mass = 0.2628 × 0.430

The position of the centre of mass = 0.113 m from the proximal joint.

Student note: Many movement analysis software packages do not use the person's height to find the centre of mass as they automatically find the length of the body segments by knowing the joint centres and then use this value to determine the position of the centre of mass and radius of gyration. This is considered more accurate as it removes some of the error due to natural variation in relationship between body segment lengths and height.

2.3 Methods of finding moments, muscle and joint forces

2.3.1 How to find forces and moments acting on the musculoskeletal system

We are now going to use the concepts of mechanics and anthropometry to consider the forces and moments acting on the musculoskeletal system in exactly the same way as we did on a seesaw (see Moments and forces).

To find the mechanics of forces and moments we need to know the force or forces acting about a joint and the distance at which they act from the joint. However, in biomechanics the forces seldom act at 90° to body segments. Therefore, we invariably need to **resolve the forces** to find what we need (see Vectors). There are two ways of doing this and both are mathematically correct, these are either:

1. Resolve the component of force at 90° to the body segment,

or

2. Resolve the horizontal and vertical components of the force relative to the ground.

My preference is to use technique 1 for upper limb and upper body (trunk) problems, and technique 2 for simple lower limb problems, which involve ground reaction forces. Although for the more advanced methods covered later a combination of techniques is required.

Each technique can be described in a number of ways but to the uninitiated I break this down into main two steps that can be described in very simple terms: 1) **spot where the triangle is**, 2) **spot where the seesaw is**. In fact the difficulty in biomechanics is not the maths itself, but spotting these two 'more simple' aspects. In other words: **muscle forces** may be considered in the same way as **balancing forces on a seesaw**, **joint forces** may be considered in the same way as the force at the pivot in the middle of the seesaw, and joint and segment angles may be considered as triangles.

When dealing with the seesaw problem earlier we also considered the effect of the forces, and whether they would try to turn in a clockwise or anticlockwise direction. For the examples covered in this book I will be considering clockwise moments as **positive** and **anticlockwise** as **negative**. Other conventions can be used but these do not actually change the findings when considering the effects on the muscles themselves.

Any students who have not got a strong maths background should not become too worried as this section uses exactly the same principles dealt with in Chapter 1. Look back at this section and see how the balancing force and the force on the pivot are found, and how vectors can be resolved.

The techniques below are a simplification, however, they are useful to get an idea of the effect forces have in and around joints. For a more advanced model of joint moments and forces during dynamic activities see Chapter 6: Inverse dynamics theory.

2.3.2 How to find muscle force

To see how we can find the forces in muscles we will consider the forces acting around the elbow joint. The biceps muscle acts at an inclined (funny) angle to the forearm, therefore to work out its effect at the elbow we have to break the force up into two perpendicular components, one horizontal and one vertical to the frame of reference. In this case a sensible frame of reference is along the forearm and at right angles to the forearm; this involves us resolving the force by using sine and cosine. These two components of a muscle are sometimes referred to as **rotary** and **stabilizing** components (Fig. 2.5). These can be found using the equations below, where the angle **A** is the angle between the biceps muscle and the forearm:

Rotary component = Muscle force × sin A

and

Stabilizing component = Muscle force × cos A

The **rotary** component is the force that tries to turn the body segment around the proximal joint (e.g. flexing or extending the joint). The **stabilizing** component is the force that acts along the body segment (e.g. forearm shown below) forcing into, or pulling out of the joint.

The stabilizing component acts through the joint, and therefore has no effect on the joint moments, whereas the

rotary component will produce a moment about the proximal joint. Although only the rotary component has an effect on the muscle forces, both the rotary and stabilizing components have an effect on the joint forces.

2.3.3 How to find the joint force

To find the joint force we need to think back to the seesaw problem, where the force at the pivot was equal to the sum of the two forces acting down. This is the same technique as we will adopt here. However, for joint forces we have to consider the forces acting horizontally and vertically; in fact, if we want a complete picture we need to think about the coronal plane also and not just the sagittal plane dealt with below, although the technique is exactly the same (Fig. 2.6).

There are two main ways we can consider joint forces, either looking at the forces acting horizontally and vertically at the joint, or working out the overall resultant force acting at the joint. There are good points to both methods. The resultant, for instance, gives us the overall force acting on the joint, but this does not necessarily relate the forces in an anatomical frame. Whereas considering the forces in their horizontal and vertical components on a body segment can give information about compressive forces and shear forces acting on a joint.

To find the vertical component of the joint force we need to consider all the forces acting in a vertical direction or at 90° to the body segment. These comprise of the vertical component of the muscle force, the weight of the body segment and the vertical joint force. The sum of all these forces must equal zero, which means if we know two of these forces we can find the third.

As with the vertical forces the sum of all the forces acting in the horizontal direction must equal zero. However, in this example we only have two forces, the horizontal component of the muscle force, and the horizontal joint force.

We can also find the resultant joint force by using the Pythagorean theorem. So to find the resultant joint force we need to use the equation below:

$$\text{Resultant joint force}^2 = \text{Vertical joint force}^2 + \text{Horizontal joint force}^2$$

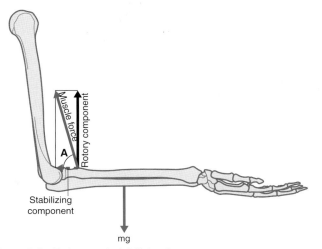

Figure 2.5   Rotary and stabilizing forces

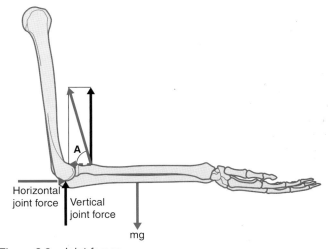

Figure 2.6   Joint forces

Dynamic joint forces

In more dynamic situations this is a simplification as the true forces on the joints are going to also depend on the accelerations and decelerations of the body segments, but perhaps even more significant is the muscle action around the joints. This last point is quite an important one. Although we have a way of calculating the muscle forces in our simplified model in 'How to find the muscle force', this does not consider all the muscles that may be acting, or even the way they might be acting. For example, if we were to stand upright and relax, and were then to tense our muscles in the lower limb, the mechanics may not show any difference between the two situations using the methods above. However, the co-contractions around the joints will, in fact, pull the body segments together into the joints, which will increase the forces experienced by the joint surfaces. One way of improving our modelling of joint forces is by considering muscle tensions and forces in more detail, and using what is sometimes referred to as an EMG (electromyography) assisted model. These factors aside, the techniques described are very useful to get an idea of the nature of the forces acting at joints.

2.4 Joint moments — muscle forces and joint forces in the lower limb

We will now consider some examples of how we can find the joint moments, muscle forces and joint forces during different lower-limb tasks. The two tasks we consider here are a lower-limb squat exercise and walking. In this section we will consider the moments by considering the force and the distance to the joint; for a more advanced method see Chapter 6: Inverse dynamincs theory.

2.4.1 Joint moments during a squat exercise

The squat exercise aims to work the quadriceps; however, we can determine any additional effects this may have about the ankle and hip joints also. To determine the effect we need to know the point of application of the ground reaction force and the position of the ankle, knee and hip joints. If we consider the squat exercise being a fairly slow exercise then there will be little acceleration and deceleration of the body segments and, therefore, we can assume that the problem is not dynamic. If we also assume that the descent is well controlled then the ground reaction force will be acting straight up.

Figure 2.7 shows that the ground reaction force falls in front of the ankle joint, behind the knee joint and through the hip joint. Before we consider the effects on the muscles around the ankle, knee and hip joints we are first going to consider the moments at the ankle knee and hip joints created by the ground reaction force.

If we know the magnitude of the ground reaction force and the horizontal distances from the ground reaction force to the ankle, knee and hip joints we can simply consider effect of the ground reaction force for each joint separately. So for each joint we focus only on the position of the joint and the force acting.

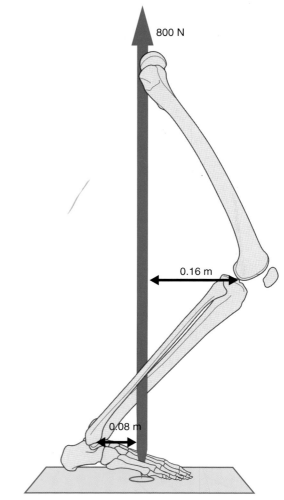

Figure 2.7   Joint moments during a squat exercise

Moments about the ankle joint

If the ankle joint is a horizontal distance of 0.08 m away from a ground reaction force of 800 N all we have to do is consider the force and the joint, and whether the force will try to turn clockwise or anticlockwise. So all we are in fact considering is what effect an 800 N force will have about a pivot shown below. If we consider the pivot is fixed in space, then the 800 N force will try to push up, which will try to turn the distal segment of the joint in an anticlockwise direction, therefore the moment will be considered as a negative moment.

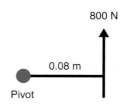

So:

Moment = Force × Distance

Moment about the ankle = –(800 × 0.08)

Moment about the ankle = –64 Nm

The negative sign indicating the effect is to try to turn the distal (foot) segment anticlockwise in relation to the proximal (tibial) segment of the joint.

Moments about the knee joint

The knee joint is at a horizontal distance of 0.16 m away from the ground reaction force of 800 N. Again if we consider the pivot is fixed in space then the 800 N force will try to push up and try to turn the distal segment of the joint in a clockwise direction, as the force is now on the left-hand side of the joint; therefore, the moment will be considered as a positive moment.

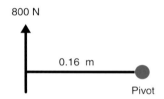

So:

Moment = Force × Distance

Moment about the knee = +(800 × 0.16)

Moment about the knee = 128 Nm

The positive sign indicating the effect is to try to turn the distal (tibial) segment clockwise in relation to the proximal (femoral) segment of the joint.

Moments about the hip joint

Again we are going to consider this in much the same way; however, in this case the 800 N force acts straight through the hip joint. This has the same effect as sitting in the middle of the seesaw, directly over the pivot. In this case no moment is produced as the distance the force acts away from the pivot is in fact zero.

So:

Moment = Force × Distance

Moment about the hip = +(800 × 0)

Moment about the knee = 0 Nm

So what are the effects of these moments on the muscles?

About the ankle joint the ground reaction force had an anticlockwise turning effect, which would try to dorsiflex the ankle joint. This would be commonly referred to as a dorsiflex**ing** moment of 64 Nm. If the subject is holding this position in a stable manner then there must be an equal and opposite balancing clockwise moment of 64 Nm, which is provided internally by the muscles posterior to the ankle joint (calf group) or plantarflexors. Therefore, this is sometimes referred to as a plantarflex**or** moment, as the posterior muscles are responsible for plantarflexing the ankle joint.

Similarly around the knee joint the ground reaction force had a clockwise turning effect, which would try to flex the knee joint. This would be referred to as a flex**ing** moment of 128 Nm. The muscles active holding this position would be the knee extens**ors** (quadriceps), so this is also sometimes referred to as the extensor moment.

With the hip joint there was no moment as the force passed through the hip joint, although in reality there will be stabilizing muscle contractions around the hip joint. These will not be as a result of the ground reaction force but will be more due to the position of the joint.

The concept of flexing/extensor moments and extending/flexor moments can get confusing. Throughout this book I will be referring to the external effect from the ground reaction force on the joint and whether it will produce a flexing or extending effect on the joint **only** and describing the effect on the muscles, rather than describing the moments from the muscles the 'point of view'.

2.4.2 Joint moments in the lower limb during walking

During walking external ground reaction forces act on the lower limb. These are due to the foot hitting or pushing off from the ground and the deceleration/acceleration of the body. Therefore, the ground reaction forces during walking are more complicated than those during the squat as they are not simply going to act upwards. For a more complete analysis the accelerations and deceleration of the body segments should be considered as these will have an effect on the moments about the joints; however, at first we will only consider the effect of the ground reaction force.

Figure 2.8 shows the resultant ground reaction force (thick arrow) seen at foot flat in a normal subject. The resultant ground reaction force can be broken up into two separate components: one in the vertical direction and the other in the horizontal direction.

If the point of application and angle of the ground reaction force and the position of the ankle, knee and hip joints are known, we can calculate the turning moments produced by the ground reaction force about the ankle joint, knee joint and hip joints. From this we can then determine which muscle groups must be acting to support these moments. To do this we are going to use exactly the same steps as with the squat exercise, except the ground reaction force we have to deal with here is acting at an angle. Therefore, the first thing we have to do is to resolve it into its vertical and horizontal components (Fig. 2.8a, b).

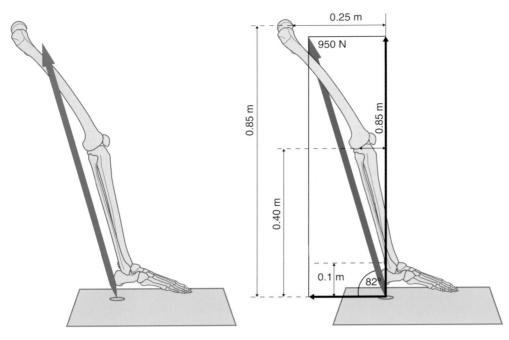

Figure 2.8   (a and b) Joint moments in the lower limb during walking

The ground reaction force, 950 N, is acting at 82° to the horizontal.

Resolving

Horizontal ground reaction force = $950 \times \cos 82$

Vertical ground reaction force = $950 \times \sin 82$

Horizontal ground reaction force = 132.2 N

Vertical ground reaction force = 940.75 N

Once the vertical and horizontal forces have been found we can now consider the action of each component about each joint separately.

Moments about the ankle

The vertical component of the ground reaction force acts straight through the joint, therefore, this will not produce a moment. The horizontal component acts to the right and below the ankle:

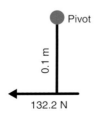

Moment about the ankle = $-940.75 \times 0 + 132.2 \times 0.1$
$$= 13.2 \, \text{Nm}$$

Moments about the knee

The vertical component of the ground reaction force acts in front of the knee joint. The horizontal component acts to the right and below the knee:

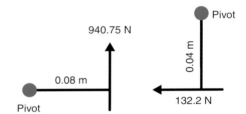

Moment about the knee = $-940.75 \times 0.08 + 132.2 \times 0.4$
$$= 22.38 \, \text{Nm}$$

Moments about the hip

The vertical component of the ground reaction force acts in front of the hip joint. The horizontal component acts to the right and below the hip:

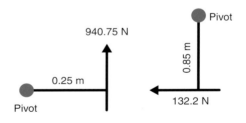

$$M_{hip} = -940.75 \times 0.25 + 132.2 \times 0.85 = -122.82 \, \text{Nm}$$

So what are the effects of these moments on the muscles?

The moment about the ankle joint is a plantarflexing moment, therefore, the muscles in the anterior compartment of the ankle joint must be active (dorsiflexors).

The moment about the knee joint is a flexing moment, therefore, the muscles in the anterior compartment of the knee joint must be active (knee extensors).

The moment about the hip joint is a flexing moment, therefore, the muscles in the posterior compartment of the hip joint must be active (hip extensors).

2.4.3 Muscle forces in lower limb

As in the previous examples we will need to resolve the ground reaction force into its vertical and horizontal components. These component vectors can then be used to find the moments about joints if we know the horizontal and vertical distances from the joint of interest to the vertical and horizontal component forces. However, it is also possible to estimate muscle forces by knowing how far the point of insertion of the muscle is away from the joint and the line of pull of the muscle. The reason I use the term 'estimate' is because we have to make various assumptions, e.g. that we only have one muscle active, and that there is no co-contraction. These are BIG assumptions; however, it is still possible to a gain a useful estimate of muscle forces.

The example below shows a force during push off of 1000 N at an angle to the horizontal of 80° (Fig. 2.9).

Resolving forces

As in the previous example the first step is to resolve the ground reaction force into its horizontal and vertical components.

Vertical component of the GRF = 1000 sin 80°

Vertical component of the GRF = 984.8 N

Horizontal component of the GRF = 1000 cos 80°

Horizontal component of the GRF = 173.6 N

Taking moments

We can now find the moments about the joints. In this case we will just consider the ankle joint:

Moment about the ankle = −984.8 × 0.1 − 173.6 × 0.15

Moment about the ankle = −124.52 Nm

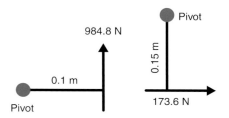

Muscle forces

The moment about the ankle is the external moment that must be supported by an internal moment. This internal moment is produced by the muscle and must be equal and opposite to the external moment. The external moment due to the ground reaction force is acting anticlockwise; therefore, the internal muscle moment will be acting in a clockwise direction, therefore:

Muscle force × Distance to joint centre − 124.52 = 0

Muscle force × 0.04 = 124.52 Nm

Muscle force = $\dfrac{124.52}{0.04}$

Muscle force = 3113 N

2.4.4 Joint forces in lower limb

Joint forces depend on all the forces acting horizontally and vertically around a joint. However, there are variations in the way we can do this. The two techniques relate to whether the muscle forces are included in the calculations or not. Muscle forces can contribute quite significantly to the magnitude of the joint force. Below I have run through the same example, firstly considering the joint force with no muscle force and secondly considering the joint force with the action of a single muscle.

Joint force without muscle forces

If we not only consider the vertical and horizontal components of the ground reaction force as before, but also consider the weight of the distal body segments (in this case just the foot as we are considering the ankle joint) we get the values below. These forces must be equal and opposite to the joint forces, or to put it another way, the sum of all the forces in the vertical and horizontal direction must be zero (Fig. 2.10).

Vertical component of the GRF = 1000 sin 80°

= 984.8 N

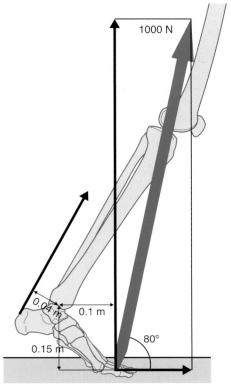

Figure 2.9   Muscle forces in lower limb

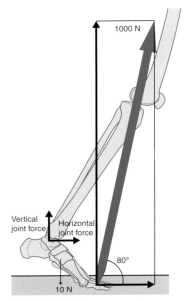

Figure 2.10   Joint force without muscle forces

Weight of the foot = 10 N (approximate value from anthropometry)

Horizontal component of the GRF = 1000 cos 80°

$$= 173.6 \, N$$

If we consider up as positive and down as negative, and right as positive and left as negative we get the equations:

Vertical joint force +984.8 − 10 = 0

Vertical joint force = 10 − 984.8

Vertical joint force = −974.8 N (the negative referring that this acts down, i.e. the force from the tibia onto the ankle joint)

Horizontal joint force +173.6 = 0

Horizontal joint force = −173.6 N (the negative referring that this acts to the left)

From the horizontal and vertical joint forces we can find the resultant joint force:

Resultant joint force^2 = 173.6^2 + 974.8^2

Resultant joint force = 990.1 N

Joint force with muscle forces

In this example we will consider the force acting in the muscles posterior to the ankle joint (calf muscles) found previously. As with the ground reaction force the muscle forces must be resolved vertically and horizontally with respect to the frame of reference. To find the joint force all the vertical and horizontal forces need to be considered separately and balanced with the vertical and horizontal joint forces (Fig. 2.11):

Vertical component of the GRF = 984.8 N

Horizontal component of the GRF = 173.6 N

The force in the muscle is 3113 N from the earlier calculation. However, this is acting at an angle of 30° to the vertical and so has to be resolved into its horizontal and vertical components:

Vertical muscle force = 3113 cos 30

Vertical muscle force = 2695.9 N

Horizontal muscle force = 3113 sin 30

Horizontal muscle force = 1556.5 N

Again if we consider up as positive and down as negative, and right as positive and left as negative we get the equations:

Vertical joint force +984.8 + 2695.9 = 0

Vertical joint force = −984.8 − 2695.9

Vertical joint force = −3680.7 N (the negative referring that this acts down, i.e. the force from the tibia onto the ankle joint)

Please note I have excluded the weight of the foot as I did not include this in the original moment calculations when finding the muscle force. Although strictly speaking this should be included its effect in this particular example is negligible.

Horizontal joint force +173.6 + 1556.5 = 0

Horizontal joint force = −1730.1 N (the negative referring that this acts to the left)

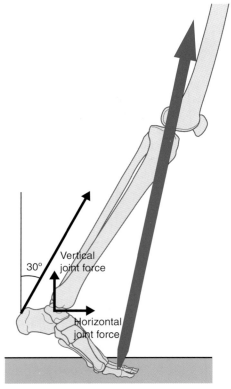

Figure 2.11   Joint force with muscle forces

Again from the horizontal and vertical joint forces we can find the resultant joint force:

$$\text{Resultant joint force}^2 = 1730.1^2 + 3680.7^2$$

$$\text{Resultant joint force} = 4067\,\text{N}$$

So why the difference in methods of finding joint forces?

Clearly the introduction of an additional large muscle force will affect the forces at the joint itself, but why the two methods? In most biomechanical models of the lower limb we use the first method where muscle forces are not considered. This is mainly due to the fact that internal forces in muscles and ligaments are VERY hard to find or estimate accurately. At this point we should consider the work by Paul (1967) who calculated the forces acting at the hip joint and then in 1970 found the effect of walking speed on the force transmitted at the hip and knee joints. Paul calculated the inter-segment forces, i.e. the joint forces, dynamically, but he also considered the forces in both tendinous and ligamentous structures to infer a joint force. This in essence is what was found in the previous example 'Joint force with muscle forces'; except Paul did not just consider one internal force from one muscle, but many forces from many structures, a feat which few have tried to replicate today, let alone with the computing power of the 1960s! Around the same time Rydell (1966) took a more 'direct' approach to finding joint forces during walking. Rydell reported two clinical cases of patients 6 months post total-hip-replacement surgery, where the hip prostheses fitted contained electrical strain gauges. Paul found that the pattern of forces acting at the hip joint varied between 1.7 to 9.2 times body weight during the gait cycle. To put this into perspective a 1000 N person would have a force of more than 9000 N acting on the hip during level walking, or to convert crudely to non-SI units nearly a tonne of force! Rydell found smaller forces of up to 3 times body weight; however, Rydell's subjects had undergone hip-replacement surgery and had significantly reduced stride lengths compared to Paul's subjects.

So if Paul could do this why don't we do it now! The simple answer is that in most biomechanical studies the forces at the joints are not necessarily the primary research outcome measures; therefore, we do not consider the internal forces in the tendinous and ligamentous structures. More often we consider the external moments that are balanced with the internal moments the muscles provide, rather than estimating the muscle forces themselves. Interestingly though, by not including the muscle forces the moment calculations are still correct, as all the internal forces and moments of the muscles are influenced directly from the external forces and moments, i.e. the ground reaction force and the weight of the body segments are balanced by the internal structures.

It should be noted, though, that the action of the forces at joints is still extremely important in many musculoskeletal conditions, and models do exist that consider the forces in muscles and their effects on joint forces (Fig. 2.12).

Table 2.2 shows a summary of previously published work where the joint forces have been estimated using such models.

2.4.5 The effect of the weight of the segments on moment calculations

In the lower-limb examples covered here we have only considered the effect of the ground reaction forces as an external force. However, the weight of the segments themselves will also have an effect. In simple calculations this is often ignored in lower-limb problems as the ground-reaction force will have the largest effect due to its magnitude, the weight of the segments is also frequently ignored as it does make the problems a little harder to solve!

By including the weight of the segments the accuracy of the calculations will be improved, however, it should be noted that even if we do include the segment weights this still does not consider all the forces involved when the body starts to accelerate and decelerate. To assess the effect of all the 'dynamic' forces we need to consider the topic of inertia (from Newton's second law of motion) in a lot more detail, the effect of the inclusion and exclusion of the different 'dynamic' forces is covered in Chapter 6: Inverse dynamics theory.

2.5 Calculation of moments, muscle and joint forces in the upper limb

One only has to do a quick search of the biomechanics literature to realize the majority of the attention has been on the lower limb and pelvis, with some attention to the spine and even less on the upper limb. Although the upper limb is not often in contact with the ground, this does not mean it is not subjected to significant forces.

The examples covered in this section relate to normal situations for the upper limb. In upper limb problems we cannot ignore the weight of the body segments as these have a far more substantial effect as the other external forces are much smaller compared with the effect of the ground reaction force on the lower limb, unless we are doing a handstand of course! In each of the examples the weight of the body segments, muscle forces and joint forces are considered.

2.5.1 Moments, muscle and joint forces while holding a pint of beer

The lower limb examples so far have all involved the effect of the ground reaction forces. The biomechanics of drinking

Table 2.2 Joint loading

	Joint	Loading
Taylor et al. 2004	Hip	2.4 × BW compressive
	Tibiofemoral	3.1 × BW compressive
	Tibiofemoral	0.6 × BW shear
Anderson and Pandy 1999	Hip	4.0 × BW
	Tibiofemoral	2.7 × BW
	Ankle	6.0 × BW
Komistek et al 1998 Walking 1 ms⁻¹	Hip	1.9 – 2.6 × BW
	Tibiofemoral	1.7 – 2.3 × BW
	Patellofemoral	0.2 – 0.4 × BW
Seedhom 1979	Patellofemoral	0.6 × BW
Reilly and Martens 1972	Patellofemoral	0.5 × BW

BW: bodyweight.

beer may not be the most clinically important topic in this book; however, the same concepts used here are transferable to many upper-limb activities. In the example of drinking a pint of beer (we will deal with SI units shortly) we have to consider the weight of a pint of beer, the weight of the forearm and hand, the length and position of the centre of mass of the forearm and hand, any inclination of the forearm, the point of insertion of the muscle and the line of action of the muscle. To make this slightly easier at first we will consider that the forearm is held in a static horizontal position, not much good for drinking, but one step at a time.

The weight of a pint of beer

If we assume a pint is roughly 0.568 l and specific gravity of well brewed beer is 1000 kg/m^3, then the mass of a pint of beer is 0.568 kg. If we also add on the mass of the glass 0.25 kg then the mass comes to 0.818 kg, a weight of 8.02 N.

The anthropometry

If the person holding the glass is 1.7 m tall with a mass of 70 kg, then the length of the forearm and hand, the weight of the forearm and hand and the position of centre of mass of the forearm and hand may be found using anthropometry. The mass of the forearm and hand is 0.0215 × body mass, the length of the forearm and hand is 0.254 × height, and the centre of mass of the forearm and hand is 0.677 × forearm length. Therefore:

Mass of the forearm and hand = 0.0215 × 70
Mass of the forearm and hand = 1.5265 kg
                  or weight = mg
                  = 14.975 N

The length of the forearm and hand = 0.254 × 1.7
                  = 0.4318 m

The length of the forearm = 0.146 × 1.7 = 0.2482 m

The centre of mass of the forearm and hand
= 0.677 × 0.2482 = 0.168 m

These calculations assume the hand is fully extended and not gripping the glass; however, this will serve as a simple estimate of the forces involved (Fig. 2.13).

Moments about the elbow

The moments about the elbow joint = (Weight of forearm × centre of mass) + (Weight of beer × Length of forearm)

Moment about the elbow joint
= (14.975 × 0.168) + (8.02 × 0.4318)

Moment about the elbow joint = 2.526 + 3.463

Moment about the elbow joint = 5.989 Nm

2.5.2 Finding the force in the muscle

If the muscle is inclined to the forearm at 80° and the muscle insertion point is 0.06 m away from the elbow joint how can we find the muscle force?

The muscle must provide an equal and opposite turning moment to support the weight of the arm and the weight

of the beer. However, the muscle is inclined to the forearm so the muscle force needs to be resolved so that it is perpendicular to the forearm.

If the muscle force is given the symbol m_f the vertical component (or rotary component) of it will be m_f sin 80.

As the muscle produces an equal and opposite turning moment the clockwise component must equal the anticlockwise component, i.e. the muscle must provide an equal and opposite moment to the moment about the elbow joint. Therefore:

$$m_f \sin 80 \times 0.06 = 5.989$$

$$m_f = \frac{5.989}{(\sin 80 \times 0.06)}$$

$$m_f = 101.36 \, N$$

It should be noted that the muscle force is significantly larger than both the weight of the forearm (14.975 N) and the weight of the beer (8.02 N). The close proximity of the muscle insertion point to the elbow joint requires a comparably large muscle force to balance the external moment.

2.5.3 Finding the joint force

To find the joint force we once again have to consider the forces in the vertical and horizontal directions to a frame of reference. The best frame of reference for this example would be along and at 90° to the forearm. The forces at 90° to the forearm comprise of the weight of the beer, the weight of the forearm, the vertical component of the muscle force and the joint force (Fig. 2.14):

Weight of beer + Weight of forearm − m_f sin 80 + Vertical joint force = 0

8.02 + 14.975 − 101.36 sin 80 + Vertical joint force = 0

Vertical joint force = −8.02 − 14.975 + 99.82

Vertical joint force = 76.825 N

The forces along the forearm comprise of the horizontal component of the muscle force and the joint force:

Horizontal joint force −101.36 cos 80 = 0

Horizontal joint force = 17.60 N

These horizontal and vertical components are along and at 90° to the segment. Using this frame of reference the horizontal force will relate to the stabilizing or compressive force on the joint and the vertical will relate to the rotary component. However, as in previous examples we could also find the resultant joint force using the Pythagorean theorem:

Resultant joint force^2 = 76.825^2 + 17.60^2

Resultant joint force = 78.815 N

2.5.4 Moments and forces about the elbow joint while holding a 20 kg weight

Now we will use the same method to find the forces acting when holding a much larger object of mass 20 kg, with the forearm inclined down by 30° to the horizontal (Fig. 2.15).

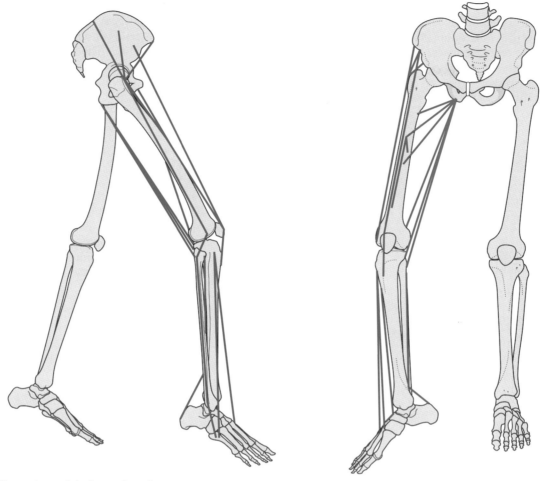

Figure 2.12   Dynamic model of muscle actions

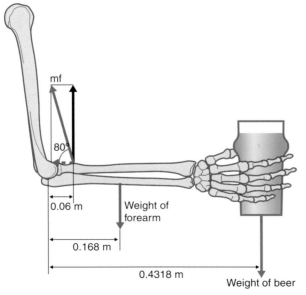

Figure 2.13   Moments while holding a pint of beer

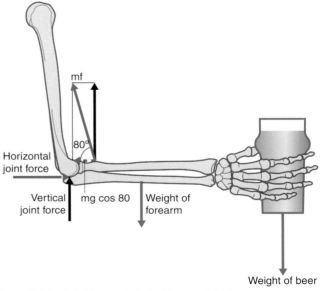

Figure 2.14   Joint force while holding a pint of beer

External moments

To find the moments about the elbow we need to find out the length and the centre of mass of the forearm and hand, and the position of the centre of mass, all of which may be found from anthropometry:

$$\begin{aligned} \text{Mass of the forearm and hand} &= 0.0215 \times 70 \\ &= 1.5265 \text{ kg, or} \\ \text{Weight} &= mg \\ &= 14.975 \text{ N} \end{aligned}$$

$$\begin{aligned} \text{The length of the forearm and hand} &= 0.254 \times 1.7 \\ &= 0.4318 \text{ m} \end{aligned}$$

$$\text{The length of the forearm} = 0.146 \times 1.7 = 0.2482 \text{ m}$$

$$\begin{aligned} \text{The centre of mass of the forearm} &= 0.677 \times 0.2482 \\ &= 0.168 \text{ m} \end{aligned}$$

The forces causing external moments are the weight of the body segment and the weight of the 20 kg mass (Fig. 2.16):

The moments about the elbow joint = (weight of forearm cos 30 × centre of mass) + (weight cos 30 × length of forearm)

From above the weight of the body segment was 14.975 N. The weight of the 20 kg mass = mg = 20 × 9.81 = 196.2 N:

Moment about the elbow joint
= (14.975 cos 30 × 0.168) + (196.2 cos 30 × 0.4318)

Moment about the elbow joint = 2.179 + 73.369

Moment about the elbow joint = 75.548 Nm

Muscle forces

If the biceps were angled at 50° to the forearm and had the same muscle insertion point as before, 0.06 m, the muscle force may be found. The external moments must be balanced with the internal moments provided by the internal structures, in this case the biceps (Fig. 2.17).

$$\text{Muscle force sin } 50 \times 0.06 = 75.548$$

$$\text{Muscle force} = \frac{75.548}{(\sin 50 \times 0.06)}$$

$$\text{Muscle force} = 1643.68 \text{ N}$$

Joint forces

Because the forearm is inclined at an angle we need to resolve all the forces so that there is a component of the force acting along the segment and a component at 90° to the segment. This is our frame of reference or segment coordinate system. From this we can consider the forces acting at the joint (Fig. 2.18).

Vertical joint force + 1643.68 sin 50 – 14.975 cos 30 – 196.2 cos 30 = 0

Vertical joint force + 1259.13 – 12.97 –169.9 = 0

Vertical joint force = –1076.26 N

Horizontal joint force –1643.68 cos 50 + 14.975 sin 30 + 196.2 sin 30 = 0

Horizontal joint force –1056.54 + 7.4875 + 98.1 = 0

Horizontal joint force = –950.95 N

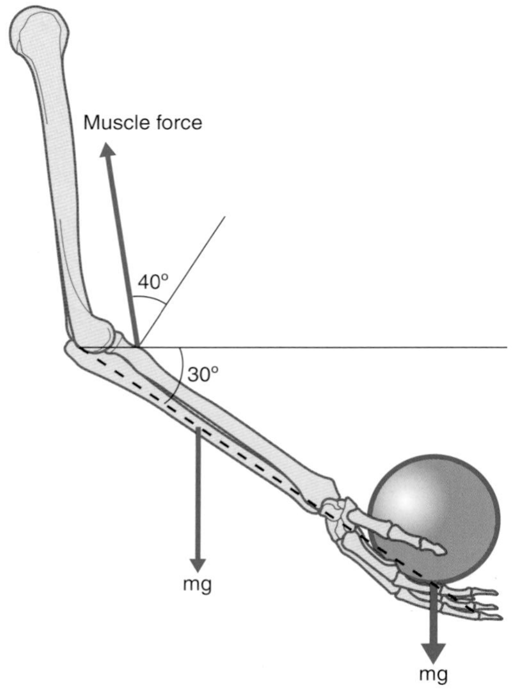

Muscle force

40°

30°

mg

mg

Figure 2.15   Moments and forces about the elbow joint while holding a weight

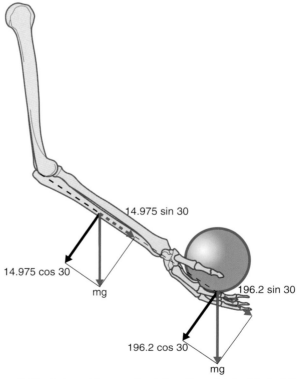

14.975 sin 30

14.975 cos 30

mg

196.2 sin 30

196.2 cos 30

mg

Figure 2.16   External forces about the elbow joint while holding a weight

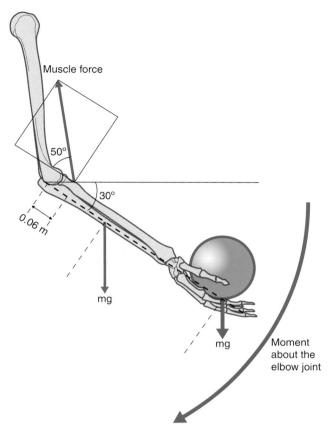

Figure 2.17   Muscle forces about the elbow joint while holding a weight

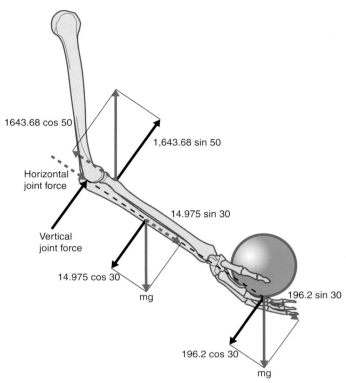

Figure 2.18   Joint forces about the elbow joint while holding a weight

Both these forces can be very useful to know. The vertical force relates to the shearing force across the joint and the horizontal force relates to the compressive joint force or axial force along the forearm. We can also find the overall resultant force acting on the joint, although this will not have any anatomical reference:

Resultant joint force^2 = 1076.26^2 + 950.95^2

Resultant joint force = 1436.19 N

The resultant force on the elbow joint in this example is significantly greater than the person's body weight. Although 20 kg is a fairly large weight it is far from the largest weight that could be held in this manner. In the next section we deal with the concept of what exactly is strength.

2.6 Muscle strength

So far in this chapter we have been looking at moments, muscle forces, and joint forces. However, one way in which we often talk about muscle and joint performance is *strength*. But what exactly *is* strength? The dictionary tells us that strength is the capacity for exertion or endurance or the power to resist force. However, a better way of thinking about *muscle* strength is the amount of force a particular muscle or muscle group can produce. However, when evaluating muscle strength, the measures taken are

not directly measuring the actual strength of the muscle or muscle group. What is usually recorded is the effective moment being produced by the muscle. This is because muscle forces are hard to measure, requiring information about the position of the muscle, position of the body segment, muscle insertion points and the line of pull of the muscle; all of which will be constantly changing during dynamic activities.

Most measures taken in the clinical setting do not go as far as to estimate actual muscle forces. However, there are a number of methods of indirect evaluation. Indirect evaluation of the force produced by a muscle can be influenced, however, by a number of factors. The following section will consider the different permutations of these factors when considering upper limb muscle strength.

These factors include:

- body segment inclination
- load position and size
- muscle insertion
- angle of pull of the muscle
- type of contraction
- speed of contraction.

2.6.1 Changing the effective moment caused by the weight of the limb

The inclination of body segments can have a very large effect on joint moments. The affect of the weight of the forearm in the three positions shown is very different. The maximum moment about the elbow is when the forearm is level; when the forearm is inclined either up or down the moment reduces and when the forearm is vertical there will be no moment about the elbow at all, as the entire weight of the segment will be acting through the joint. It is also important to note the direction of the 'stabilizing' component that acts along the forearm. When the forearm is angled down, the component acting along the forearm will try to pull the forearm away from the upper arm; whereas with the forearm angled up the forearm is pushed into the upper arm, this will have the effect of reducing and increasing the joint force at the elbow respectively (Fig. 2.19a, b, c).

2.6.2 The position and size of the applied load

The position and size of the load applied has an important effect on the moment about the elbow and will, in turn, have a significant effect on the muscle and joint forces. When assessing muscle strength both these factors should be measured and taken into account. If you position a load at the end of a subject's arm to see if he/she can support it, the moment will depend on the size of the load and the subject's limb length (Fig. 2.20).

Both the size of the load and the subject's limb length need to be considered when assessing an individual's muscle performance or strength. For example, if two individuals of different heights and, therefore, different tibial (shank) lengths conducted the same leg raise activity with the same loads the shorter of the two would, in fact, use less muscle force (strength) to lift the same load, assuming the muscle insertion points were not significantly different.

2.6.3 Muscle insertion points

Different muscles will have different insertion points. The position of these insertion points will have a large effect on the muscle force required to support a given turning moment. Figure 2.21a, b shows two examples: a) the muscle insertion point is close to the elbow joint and b) the muscle insertion point is much further away (Fig. 2.21a, b).

For a particular load there will be a larger force in the muscle if its insertion point is close to the joint. Conversely if

there is a maximum force that a muscle group can cope with then larger loads will be able to be carried with the insertion point further away from the joint.

This leads us to an interesting point when we consider weight lifters. Is a weight lifter able to lift a larger load because he or she can support larger muscle forces, or is this due to a difference in the muscle insertion points? If the latter is the case are we actually assessing something different from *strength* (the force in the muscle) with the task?

2.6.4 The effect of the angle of muscle pull

As the body segment moves relative to the ground, so the angle of the muscle moves relative to the body segment. Consider the examples from 2.6.1, but instead of thinking about the moment due to the weight, think about the line of action of the force in relation to the forearm. The maximum moment that the muscle can produce is when the elbow is at 90° as this makes an approximately 90° angle between the muscle and the body segment and, therefore, produces the greatest rotary component from the muscle force. As the elbow joint is moved away from this position, either flexed or extended, the moment that the muscle can produce is reduced as the rotary component of the muscle force acting at 90° to the forearm is reduced. When the forearm is vertical with the elbow fully extended, the muscle would find it much harder to produce a moment as the rotary component will be at its smallest. It is also interesting to note the direction of the 'stabilizing' component of the muscle force when the elbow is flexed. This appears to be pulling the forearm away from the joint and will not provide a compressive stabilizing force into the joint; however, in this position the rotary component will be providing a compressive force into the joint. In reality we will also have a co-contraction from the extensor muscles to stabilize the elbow joint (see Fig. 2.19).

2.6.5 Type of muscle contraction

The type of muscle contraction affects the resistance that can be controlled, held or overcome. The three types of muscle

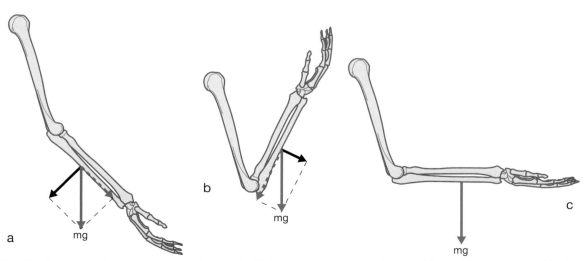

Figure 2.19 Effective moment caused by the weight of the limb: (a) forearm angled down, (b) forearm angled up and (c) forearm horizontal

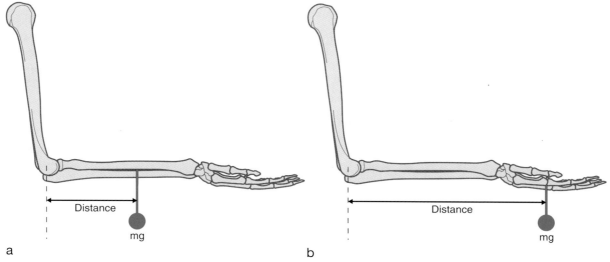

Figure 2.20   Position and size of the applied load

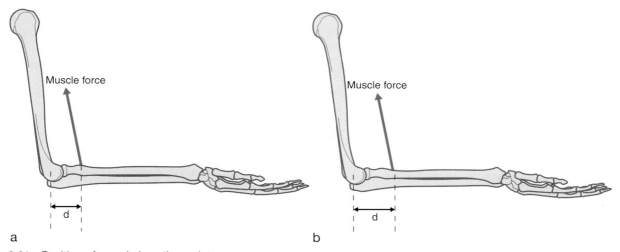

Figure 2.21   Position of muscle insertion point

contraction are isometric, concentric and eccentric. Isometric contractions are stabilizing contractions where the muscle length remains virtually constant. Concentric contractions are where the muscle shortens during the activity. These are generally the weakest muscle contractions, requiring more motor unit recruitment than isometric and eccentric for a particular load. Eccentric contractions are where the muscle lengthens during the activity. These are generally the strongest muscle contractions, requiring less recruitment than isometric and concentric for a particular load.

2.6.6 The effect of the speed of contraction

There are three ways of classifying speed during exercises: isotonic, isokinetic and isometric. Isotonic is when a constant load is applied but the angular velocity of the movement may change, this allows an infinite variation in the rate of contraction of a muscle. Although this is closest to real-life muscle and joint function, the changing speed continually affects the amount of force that a muscle can produce and makes the exact muscle function quite hard to

assess. Isokinetic is when the velocity or angular velocity of the movement is kept constant, but the load may be varied. This setting of the speed of working helps improve our assessment of muscle performance, but the speed or velocity of the joints are being restricted to only one set speed at any one time. Isometric relates to the force varying, but the joint is held in a static position; therefore, muscle length remains the same as no movement occurs. This tells us what static moment may be supported; however, this does not necessarily relate to the moments that can be produced or supported dynamically.

2.6.7 The Oxford scale and muscle strength

The Oxford scale is a common clinical assessment method for muscle strength. The Oxford scale classifies muscle strength, this is categorised using the following criteria:

0 = No contraction
1 = Flicker of a contraction
2 = Active movement with gravity eliminated

3 = Active movement against gravity

4 = Active movement against light resistance

5 = Full functional strength (full range of motion against strong resistance).

The aim of the Oxford scale is to assess the functional ability of an individual. Scores 0–3 give a very useful functional progression by assessing if the individual can support the weight of a limb against gravity; however, care must be taken that the body segments are constantly placed to ensure a consistent and 'correct' effect due to the weight of the body segment, and associated muscle action. Scores 3–5, however, are open to considerable variability as the exact definition of light resistance and strong resistance will vary from clinician to clinician. The position of the applied load on the body segments will be variable and will depend on the length of body segment and the position the clinician chooses to offer the resistance, and also the velocity with which the joint moves. This leads to difficulties in the comparison of assessments using the Oxford scale between clinicians doing the testing and the individuals being tested.

The Oxford scale has come under much criticism; however, it does offer a rough guide for the assessment of muscle strength. One way of improving the concept of the scale is to introduce a degree of measurement to the assessment. This could be as simple as measuring the distance from the resistance to the joint and being consistent in this distance for the testing of a particular joint for all individuals, or bringing in some form of force measurement to assess what force can be produced. This could give a more objective means of assessing change in muscle function through a rehabilitation programme. Objective measurement of muscle function will be considered in far more detail in Chapter 10: Measurement of muscle function and physiological cost.

Summary: Forces, moments and muscles

- Anthropometry allows us to find important information about the proportions of body segments including the mass, weight and the position of the centre of mass.
- The net or overall moments about joints may be found by considering all the forces acting on the distal body segments to a particular joint. Moments can also be used to describe muscle action during different movement tasks.
- By knowing joint moments and the approximate muscle insertion points, useful estimates of the muscle forces may be obtained. It is very important to consider as many of the forces present as possible to ensure a good estimate.
- Joint forces may be found by considering all the forces acting vertically and horizontally, or along and at right angles to the distal body segment. Sometimes these are found by including the estimates of the muscle forces that provide the most useful estimate of the joint forces, although these are often not included when using the inverse dynamics approach, which is considered in Chapter 6.

Ground Reaction Forces, Impulse and Momentum

Jim Richards

Chapter 3

This chapter considers the use of ground reaction forces as functional measure and the consideration of the nature of various measures that may be drawn from them. This covers ground reaction forces during postural sway, walking and different running styles.

Chapter 3: Aim

To consider measurement derived from ground reaction forces in individuals who are pain and pathology free during different functional tasks.

Chapter 3: Objectives

- To describe the nature and use of centre of pressure measurements by considering standing balance
- To interpret vertical, anterior–posterior and medial–lateral forces during walking in relation to function
- To explain how to construct Pedotti or vector diagrams
- To calculate impulse and momentum from ground reaction force data
- To apply the use of impulse and momentum to the ground reaction force during running
- To interpret vertical, anterior–posterior and medial–lateral forces during different running styles.

3.1 Ground reaction forces during standing

Borrelli in 1680 was the first to measure the centre of mass of the body and described how balance is maintained during gait. Borrelli was also the first to consider the effect of ground reaction forces acting about joints.

A ground reaction force is the force that acts on a body as a result of the body resting on the ground or hitting the ground. This relates to Newton's third law of motion, relating to an equal and opposite reaction force, and to the second law of motion relating to deceleration during an impact or acceleration during propulsion.

If we first consider a person standing on the floor without moving, the person will be exerting a force on the floor, but the floor will be exerting an equal and opposite reaction force on the person. This reaction force is known as the ground reaction force (Fig. 3.1).

If the person does not move, the forces under each foot will remain in exactly the same position and will not move. The position on the floor of these ground reaction force vectors is known as the centre of pressure. The term 'centre of pressure' can be misleading as it is not a measure of pressure but a measure of position and refers to the average pressure point beneath the foot or feet. Figure 3.1 shows the two ground reaction force vectors under each foot. Each of these will have a relative position (centre of pressure) under each foot. I have also included a combined force that is a

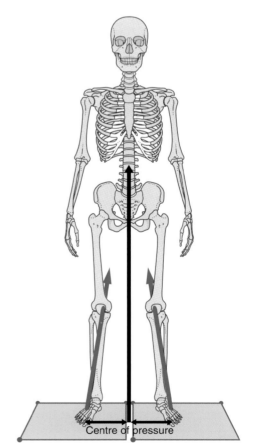

Figure 3.1 Force and centre of pressure during standing

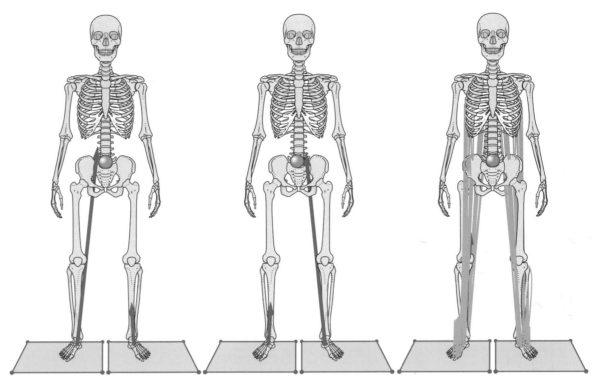

Figure 3.2   Postural sway in the medial–lateral direction

summation of the two forces. The centre of pressure of the combined force is often used to study postural sway, which we will consider next.

In reality we are never completely static and, although we may well be in this position from time to time, we will also be prone to postural sway both in the medial–lateral direction (Fig. 3.2), and the anterior–posterior direction (Fig. 3.3). These figures show an exaggerated postural sway test to illustrate how the forces beneath the feet vary.

During postural sway the ground reaction force will always try to point towards the approximate position of the centre of mass; so the force vector will point inwards in relation to the base of support. If the force vectors point outwards this will produce an acceleration vector away from the centre of mass and the person will become unstable and is, therefore, likely to fall.

The position the force is acting on (centre of pressure) will also move as the person sways from side to side and back to front (Fig. 3.4). The amount of movement of the centre of pressure is often used to quantify dynamic stability during postural sway tests. A common experiment is to look at the amount of movement in the medial–lateral and the anterior–posterior directions with eyes open and eyes shut.

3.2 Ground reaction forces during walking

3.2.1 The vertical force component

The vertical component of the ground reaction force can be split into four sections. Each section may be related to functional events during foot contact and can give us important information about the overall functioning of the lower limb (Fig. 3.5).

Heel strike to 1st peak

This is where the foot strikes the ground and the body decelerates downwards and transfers the loading from the back foot to the front foot during initial double support. The 1st peak should be in the order of 1.2 times the person's body weight.

The first peak relates to the amount of loading the person is putting onto the front foot. In amputee gait, for example, this can relate to the person's confidence in the prosthetic limb, a reduction in the loading relating to poor confidence. A reduced loading could also relate to the presence of any pain and discomfort, poor functional movement of the joints of the lower limb or a slow walking speed.

1st Peak (F1) to trough (F2)

As the body starts to progress the knee extends, raising the centre of mass. As the centre of mass approaches its highest point it is slowing down or decelerating its upwards motion. This has the same effect as going over a humped-backed bridge in a car, as you reach the top of the hump you feel very light, i.e. the contact force is reduced. This deceleration of the body upwards produces a dip or trough in the vertical force pattern with the normal value being in the order of 0.7 times the person's body weight.

The depth of the trough, therefore, relates to how well the person moves over their stance limb, which again could be affected by pain and/or lower limb dysfunction. A high

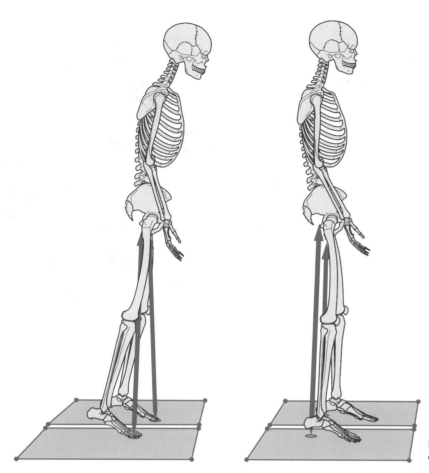

Figure 3.3   Postural sway in the anterior–posterior direction

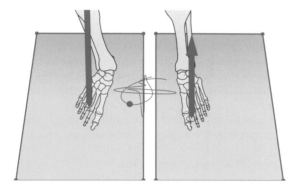

Figure 3.4   Movement of the centre of pressure during postural sway

trough value, or shallow trough, can relate to a poor movement of the body over the stance limb or a slow walking speed. A low or deep trough may be produced by a fast walking speed or large vertical translations of the body during walking. The trough usually occurs at 50% of the stance phase, although this does vary between individuals, and should occur at approximately the same time as the cross-over point of the anterior–posterior force (see Fig. 3.6).

Trough (F2) to 2nd peak (F3)

The centre of mass now falls as the heel lifts and the foot is pushed down and back into the ground by the action of muscles in the posterior compartment of the ankle joint. Both the deceleration downward and propulsion from the foot and ankle complex cause the 2nd peak. The 2nd peak should be in the order of 1.2 times the person's body weight.

The 2nd peak relates to the amount of vertical propulsive force, which drives the person upwards. A low peak relates to a poor ability to push off, whereas a high peak could relate to the person accelerating. Although this is important, this does not tell us about the force that drives the person forwards.

2nd peak (F3) to toe off

The foot is unloaded as the load is transferred to the opposite foot. The time taken to off load from the back foot will relate to the speed of transfer of the weight to the front foot; therefore, the longer the offloading period from the back foot, the lower the first peak during loading on the front foot. When investigating force patterns great care should be taken in considering the forces under both feet as a poor push off and offloading phase may cause changes in the initial loading on the opposite side.

3.2.2 The anterior–posterior force component

As with the vertical forces the anterior–posterior ground reaction forces can also give us important information about the overall functioning of the lower limb. The anterior–posterior component of the ground reaction force during walking may also be split into four sections (Fig. 3.6).

Claw back and heel strike transients

Claw back is an initial anterior force that is not always present during walking. This is caused by the swinging limb hitting the ground with a backwards velocity, thus causing an anterior force as the leg decelerates. Claw back is often exaggerated during marching as the swing limb is driven back to meet the ground. A heel strike transient is a rapidly increasing force due to an impact. Consider walking with and without shoes, with shoes we will have better shock absorption due to the properties of the shoes; however, when shoes are removed a rapid 'transient' force can often be seen as the unprotected heel strikes the ground.

The example below shows a subject with a large heel strike transient force with claw back. In this example the transient force at impact is greater than that of both the loading and propulsive forces. The claw back has the effect of sending the force vector anterior to (in front of) both the knee and hip joint. This person had problems with knee and hip pain; however, with the introduction of heel cushioning, this effect was significantly reduced and the person's pain was alleviated. Although patterns as extreme as this are rare, this pattern demonstrates the nature of transient ground reaction forces and claw back (Fig. 3.7a, b).

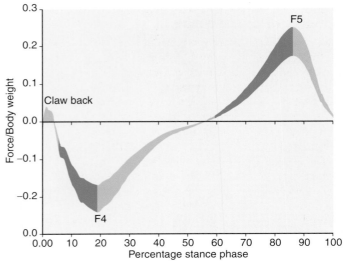

Figure 3.6   Anterior–posterior component of the ground reaction force

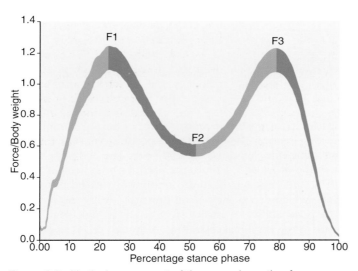

Figure 3.5   Vertical component of the ground reaction force

Heel strike to posterior peak (F4)

After the initial claw back (if present) the heel is in contact with the ground and the body decelerates causing a posterior shear force. Imagine you are walking on a thick carpet, loading your front foot, and suddenly you are transported to an ice rink; your foot would slide forwards. This is because the coefficient of friction between the ice and your foot is very low, whereas the carpet can provide a posterior reaction force that stops your leg from slipping forwards. The posterior peak should normally be in the order of 0.2 times the person's body weight.

As with the vertical ground reaction force, this peak can relate to speed of walking or the person's confidence in loading the front foot, with a reduction in the loading relating to poor confidence. We will also naturally adapt this value depending on the maximum frictional force available, which will depend on the coefficient of friction between our shoes/feet and the surface we are walking on.

Posterior peak to cross over

The posterior component reduces as the body begins to move over the stance limb, reducing the horizontal component of the resultant ground reaction force. At the cross-over point the horizontal force is zero; therefore, the only force acting is that of the vertical ground reaction force. At this point the body is directly positioned above the foot, this is sometimes defined as the point of mid-stance, which is usually at 55% of stance phase, and should also approximately correspond with the trough in the vertical force pattern.

Cross over to anterior peak (F5)

The heel lifts and the foot is pushed down and back into the ground by the action of muscles in the posterior compartment of the ankle joint. This has the effect of producing an anterior component of the ground reaction force that propels the body forwards. As with the other force measurements this is dependent on walking speed; however, the anterior peak should be in the order of 0.2 times the person's body weight. A reduced peak would tell us the person is not propelling the body forwards well no matter what the vertical force pattern may show.

Anterior peak to toe off

This is now the period of terminal double support where the force is now being transferred to the front foot and the anterior force, therefore, reduces. The length of time the force takes to reduce and offload can affect the loading during the next foot contact.

3.2.3 The medial–lateral component of the ground reaction force

The medial–lateral component may be split into two main sections. Initially, at heel strike there is a lateral thrust during loading, during which time the foot is working as a mobile adaptor and generally moving from a supinated position into pronation. After the initial loading the forces push in a medial direction as the body moves over the stance limb. Small lateral forces are often seen during the final push off stage (Fig. 3.8).

The medial–lateral forces are the most variable of the three components, and can be easily affected by footwear and foot orthoses. Normally the maximum medial force is between 0.05 and 0.1 of body weight. The maximum lateral force should generally be less than the maximum medial force. Although the medial–lateral forces can be variable they can have a substantial effect on the loading of the ankle and knee in the coronal plane and should not be ignored when considering the effects of shoe modifications and orthotic management.

3.3 Centre of pressure and force vectors during normal walking

3.3.1 Centre of pressure during walking

The term 'centre of pressure' is the position of the force coming out of the floor, as mentioned before. The centre of pressure can move forward and backward (anterior and posterior) and side to side (medial and lateral) under each foot. Figures show the force appearing under the heel during loading and under the toes during push off (3.9a, b).

The centre of pressure during walking is often presented as: i) a combined medial–lateral and anterior–posterior graph, ii) the anterior–posterior or iii) medial–lateral centre of pressure against time (Fig. 3.10a, b, c). The combined medial–lateral and anterior–posterior graph gives a useful picture of how the force moves from heel to toe and any variations in the medial–lateral of the centre of pressure during this movement. The centre of pressure in the different directions allows the progression and speed of progression to be investigated in more detail (ii and iii).

The centre of pressure in the anterior–posterior direction (ii) shows a smooth steady progression of the force forwards beneath the foot from heel strike until toe off. The centre of pressure in the medial–lateral direction (iii) shows a small amount of movement from medial to lateral. It should be noted that both these movement patterns of the centre of pressure are in relation to the ground and not the anatomy of the foot (Fig. 3.10a, b, c).

One example of centre of pressure is the examination of a subject with an early heel lift. Figure 3.11a shows the vector

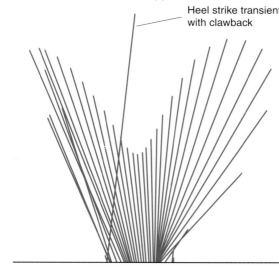

a

b

Figure 3.7   (a and b) Claw back and heel strike transients

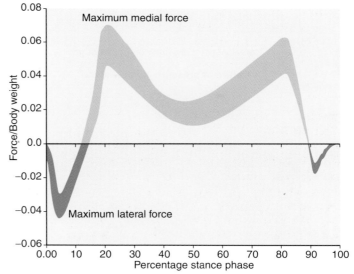

Figure 3.8   Medial–lateral component of the ground reaction force

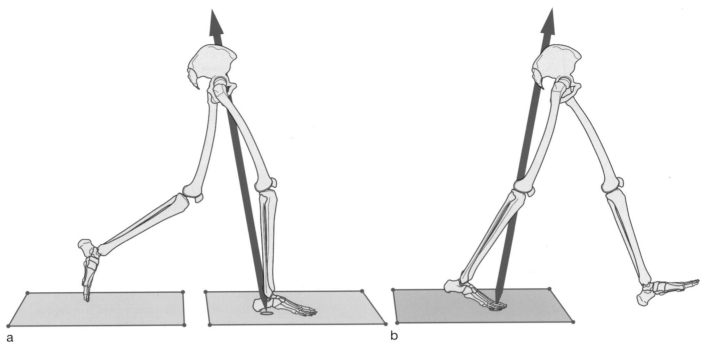

Figure 3.9   Ground reaction force during walking: (a) loading force and (b) push-off force

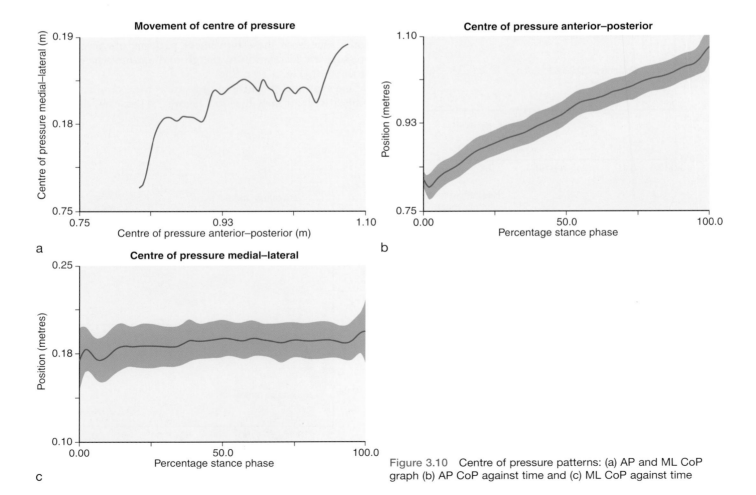

Figure 3.10   Centre of pressure patterns: (a) AP and ML CoP graph (b) AP CoP against time and (c) ML CoP against time

diagram and 3.11b the anterior–posterior centre of pressure against time. This subject showed a pronounced loading pattern 1, coupled with a fast movement of the centre of pressure forwards until it reached the metatarsal heads, as the heel begins an early lift off the ground 2. This dwelling of the force under the metatarsal heads can be seen by a close grouping of the force vectors. The subject then shows a faster final movement of the centre of pressure forwards from the metatarsal heads to the toes during push off 3 (Fig. 3.11a, b).

3.3.2 Resultant ground reaction forces and Pedotti diagrams?

The resultant ground reaction force is made up from three components: vertical, anterior–posterior and medio-lateral. The interaction of the vertical, anterior–posterior and medio–lateral force may be shown with a Pedotti diagram. Figures 3.12a and b show a Pedotti diagram; note how the magnitude and direction of the force changes and how the centre of pressure moves from heel to toe. The Pedotti diagram shows the magnitude of the resultant ground reaction force (Fig. 3.12a, b).

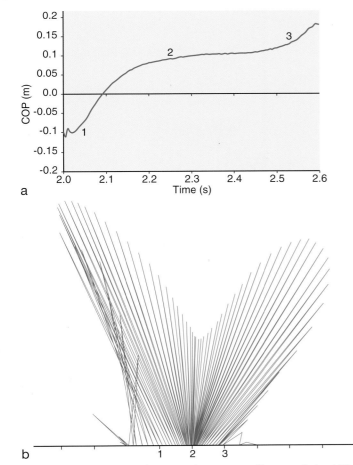

Figure 3.11 Forces and centre of pressure with an early heel lift: (a) anterior–posterior centre of pressure and (b) vector (Pedotti) diagram

The ground reaction force points posterior for the first part of stance phase, the magnitude of the force increases during loading response (deceleration phase), then decreases as the body moves over the stance limb during mid stance. After mid stance the magnitude of the force increases again, but now the force is pointing in an anterior direction during propulsion (acceleration phase).

The Pedotti diagram shows the magnitude of the resultant ground reaction force and is a good way of visualizing the interaction of the forces in different directions with the centre of pressure. However, to determine the magnitude and function of the different aspects of the ground reaction force it is easier to consider each component separately.

3.3.3 Construction of Pedotti diagrams

Pedotti diagrams rely on the information provided by force platforms. To construct a Pedotti diagram we need to know the vertical and horizontal forces, and the position of the centre of pressure in the plane of interest for each moment in time.

As a subject walks the forces during stance phase, moving forward from under the heel to the toe, therefore, the centre of pressure moves from posterior to anterior. As we have seen in the previous sections the vertical and horizontal ground reaction forces are continually changing during stance phase, therefore, changing the direction and magnitude of the resultant ground reaction force.

Figure 3.13a–f shows the vertical, horizontal and resultant ground reaction force components being drawn at heel strike. The centre of pressure then moves forwards and the new vertical, horizontal and resultant ground reaction force components are drawn from the new position. This is repeated throughout stance phase giving a butterfly-like diagram.

3.3.4 How force vectors relate to muscle activity

To estimate the muscle activity, consider which side of the joint the ground reaction force passes, i.e. in front or behind. If the ground reaction force passes in front of the knee joint this will try to extend the knee; therefore, the knee flexors need to be working to support the turning moment produced. This is sometimes referred to as a **flexor moment** (meaning the external moment will try to extend but the body needs to produce an internal flexion moment from the knee flexors). If the ground reaction force passes behind the knee joint this will try to flex the knee; therefore, the knee extensors need to be working to support the turning moment produced. This is sometimes referred to as an **extensor moment** (meaning the external moment will try to flex but the body needs to produce an internal extension moment from the knee extensors). It must be emphasized that, although very useful in observation gait analysis, these can only be used for estimation and do not give precise numerical data.

During swing phase there is no effect due to the ground reaction force. However, muscle activity is still required to overcome the inertial forces due to the acceleration and deceleration of body segments. Moments during the accelerations and decelerations during swing phase can be found using a technique called inverse dynamics, see Chapter 6: Inverse dynamics theory.

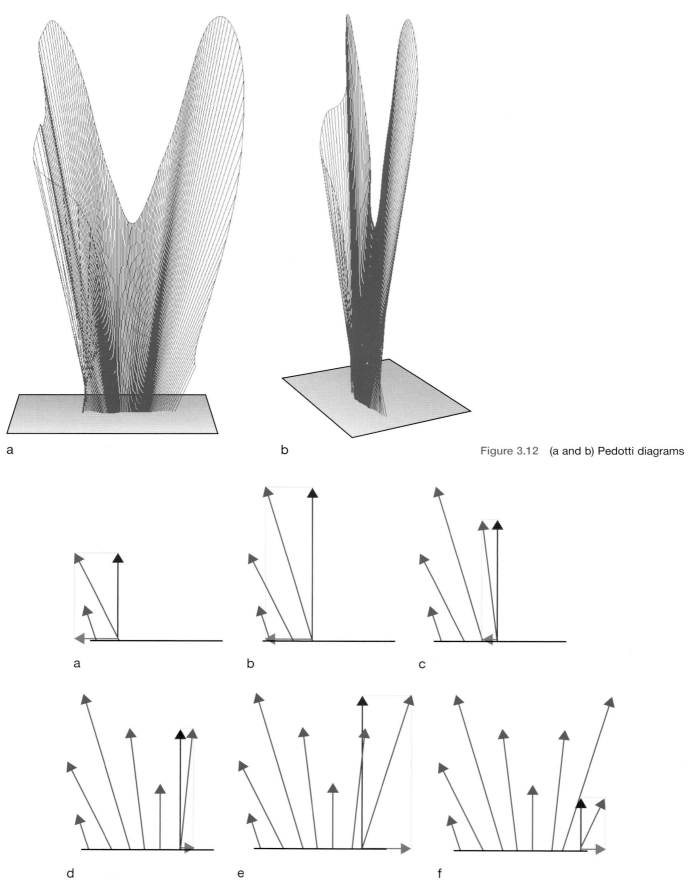

a   b   Figure 3.12   (a and b) Pedotti diagrams

a   b   c

d   e   f

Figure 3.13   (a–f) Construction of Pedotti diagrams

3.4 Impulse and momentum

3.4.1 Impulse

Although force alone is extremely useful as it tells us how big propulsion forces are, it does not tell us all we may need to know about the entire propulsive stage. Impulse and momentum can give us important additional information if we have a force acting over a given time. This can be useful when considering the effect of an impact where we may have rapid changes in velocity over very short periods of time or when considering changes in velocity during propulsion. When considering the concepts of impulse and moments we first need to go back to Newton's second law of motion:

$$F = ma$$

where:

F = Force applied, m = Mass of the object,
a = Acceleration of the object

If we now consider what we mean by acceleration, i.e. a change in velocity over time:

$$Acceleration = \frac{Change\ in\ velocity}{Time}$$

So we could say that:

$$Force = m\frac{change\ in\ velocity}{time}$$

From this we can find the equation for force × time:

Force × time = Ft = mass × change in velocity

Ft = m (final velocity − initial velocity)

This product of both force and time is known as the impulse force or impulse. This tells us that an increase in force or a longer time will give a larger impulse.

Consider the impact or impulse of an object of mass 2 kg as it hits the ground. If the object is travelling at 20 m/s just before it hits the ground and it comes to rest after the impact then the impulse may be found (Fig. 3.14).

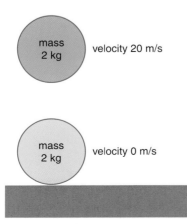

Figure 3.14   Impulse during impact

Ft = m (final velocity − initial velocity)

Ft = 2 (0 − 20)

Ft = −40

But what are the units for impulse? If we consider the right-hand side of the equation:

mass (kg) × velocity (m/s)

Therefore, the units may be written:

kg m/s

But if we now consider the left-hand side of the equation we get:

Ns

These are in fact the same thing as:

$$F(N) = m(kg) \times a(m/s^2)\quad or\quad F(N) = \frac{m\ (kg) \times a\ (m)}{s^2}$$

So:

$$F(N)\ t(s) = \frac{m(kg) \times a(m)}{s}\ or\ F(N)\ t(s) = m(kg) \times v(m/s)$$

However, impulse is usually written with the units **Ns**.

3.4.2 Momentum

So what is momentum? If something is said to have momentum this implies it is hard to stop. A heavy object travelling fast will have a much greater momentum than a light object travelling slowly. This is due to both the mass of the object and the object's velocity. So momentum may be considered as simply the mass of the object multiplied by its velocity.

Momentum = mass × velocity

If we consider impulse again, the impulse is the mass multiplied by the change in velocity, therefore, the impulse tells us about the change in momentum.

Change in momentum = mass × change in velocity

Force × time = Ft = mass × change in velocity

3.4.3 Conservation of momentum

This is mainly of interest when considering the collision of two or more objects. The conservation of momentum states that the total momentum before a collision equals the total momentum after the collision.

3.4.4 Impulse and change in momentum during a sprint start

We have seen above how impulse relates to Newton's second law of motion, but how can we relate this to ground reaction force patterns? A good example is to consider the impulse and change of momentum during a sprint start. Figure 3.15 shows graphs of the vertical and anterior–posterior forces of the back and front feet during a sprint start in an individual who is able to run 100 m in approximately 11 seconds.

Impulse may be written as force × time. This means that the area under a force–time graph must relate to the impulse and, therefore, the change in momentum and velocity. So how large is the change in velocity during the sprint start and what are the contributions of the front and back foot to the total change in momentum? It should be stressed at this point that the data presented below were collected without the use of starting blocks (Fig. 3.15).

From the graphs below the net anterior–posterior impulse from the back foot and the front foot may be found by finding the **area under the force–time graph** or 'integrating' the force–time graph between the start of the movement to the point each foot leave the ground:

The net anterior–posterior impulse for the back foot = 50.6 Ns

The net anterior–posterior impulse for the front foot = 69.5 Ns.

Therefore, the back foot is responsible for 42% of the horizontal acceleration and the front foot is responsible for 58%. The total net anterior–posterior impulse for the sprint start may be found by simply adding these values together:

Total impulse = 50.6 + 69.5 = 120.1 Ns

If the mass of the individual is 62 kg then the change in velocity just during the push-off phase of the sprint start may be found.

Impulse (Ft) = mass × change in velocity

120.1 = 62 × change in velocity

Change in velocity = 1.94 m/s

This is a significant proportion of the average velocity of the total 100 m sprint:

Average velocity of sprint = $\dfrac{100}{11}$

Average velocity of sprint = 9.09 m/s

From the change in velocity occurring over 0.45 s, i.e. the time taken from the start of the movement to the moment the front foot leaves the ground, the acceleration over the start may also be found.

Average acceleration = $\dfrac{\text{change in velocity}}{\text{time}}$

Average acceleration = $\dfrac{1.94 \, \text{m/s}}{0.45 \, \text{s}}$

Average acceleration = 4.3 m/s²

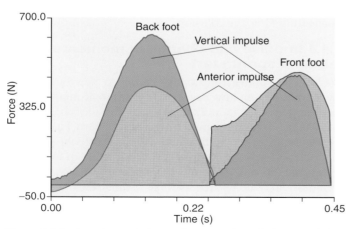

Figure 3.15   Impulse and change in momentum during a sprint start

3.4.5 Protection against the force of impacts

The relationship between the impulse, velocity and forces is very important when considering the mechanics of impacts. If a person jumps or falls, if they can lengthen the time of impact, the magnitude of the force is reduced in proportion. One example of this is bending the knees when landing from a jump. Increasing the time the impact occurs over using joint movement is not always possible, but one solution is to use padding to act as a 'shock absorber', which will also lengthen the time over which the impact is spread. This may be seen in many types of running shoe, which incorporate many different devices and materials that act as shock absorbers.

3.5 Integration and the area beneath data curves

In the previous section we considered the concept of impulse and momentum, which may be found by calculating the area under the force time graph. Integration, or finding the area beneath data curves, can tell us important biomechanical information: the area under a velocity–time graph can tell us the distance travelled, the area under force–distance graphs can tell us about the work done, and the area under force–time graphs can tell us the impulse or change in momentum. However, all these patterns can be extremely complex, so how can we integrate complex data curves?

3.5.1 Integration

Integration is a way of finding the sum of the area under the graph. We can integrate between limits, i.e. choose the starting point and the finishing point between which we can find the area.

The general formula for integration is:

Integral of $X^n = \dfrac{X^{n+1} + c}{n + 1}$

So if a curve had the relationship:

y = x

which can be written x^1 therefore the integral would be:

$\dfrac{1}{2} x^2$

3.5.2 Integration of simple shapes

If we first consider the area, or integral, of simple data curves, these can be found by considering the height and width of simple shapes, such as triangles and rectangles (Fig. 3.16).

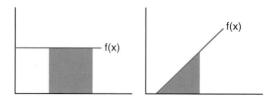

Area = Base × Height   Area = ¹/₂ (Base × Height)

Figure 3.16   Integration of simple shapes: area = base × height area = ¹/₂ (base × height)

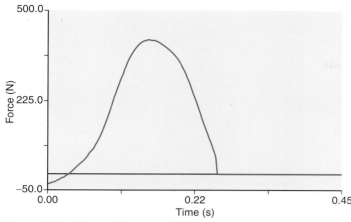

Figure 3.17   Force during a sprint start

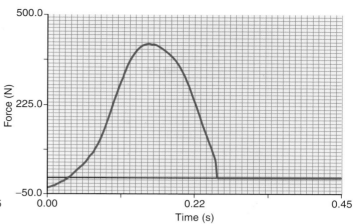

Figure 3.18   Counting the squares to determine area under graph

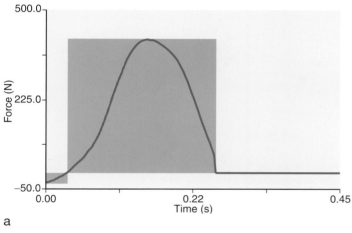

a

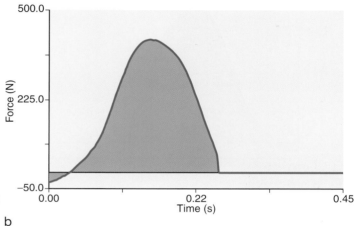

b

Figure 3.19   Bounds for the area: (a) rectangle and (b) actual area

Although this is a useful technique in biomechanics, it is usual that the relationships between parameters are far more complex. To use this technique we also need to know the equation for a data line, in biomechanics this is seldom the case (Fig. 3.17).

In cases such as the force–time graph of the sprint start we need a simple and accurate method of finding the area under the graph that does not require knowing the equation to describe the line.

3.5.3 Counting the squares

One method is to divide the pattern into a series of squares and count them (Fig. 3.18). This is time consuming and is open to errors such as miscounting, and inaccuracy due to the size of the squares, and can give you a headache!

3.5.4 Bounds for the area

When it is not possible to find the area under the curve exactly we need to approximate. One method is to look at the upper bounds of the area, where a rectangle is drawn around the data. When using the technique of drawing the rectangle it is clear that in the case above the rectangle is going to be much greater than the two areas, and will give a considerable error (Fig. 3.19a, b).

3.5.5 The rectangular rule

If we play around with the height of the rectangle we will find one with a height that gives us a completely accurate estimate of the area, but this is not always easy to find. What we need in practice is to obtain a fairly good answer easily.

3.5.6 Trapezium rule

If we consider the graph in Figure 3.17 and draw vertical lines of set width from the horizontal axis until these meet with the data curve, and then draw a line between these two meeting points we create a series of trapeziums. The area of each trapezium may then be found separately (Fig. 3.20a, b, c).

The area of each trapezium may be found by the following equation:

Area = ¹/₂ (height at 1 + height at 2) × width of base

What we are doing is finding the average height of a trapezium and multiplying by the width of the base:

Area = average height of strip × width of strip

The larger the widths of strip the less accurate this method is. The more strips we divide the curve into the greater the accuracy of the estimation of the area under the graph. Figure 3.20c shows 15 strips whereas in Figure 3.20a above we

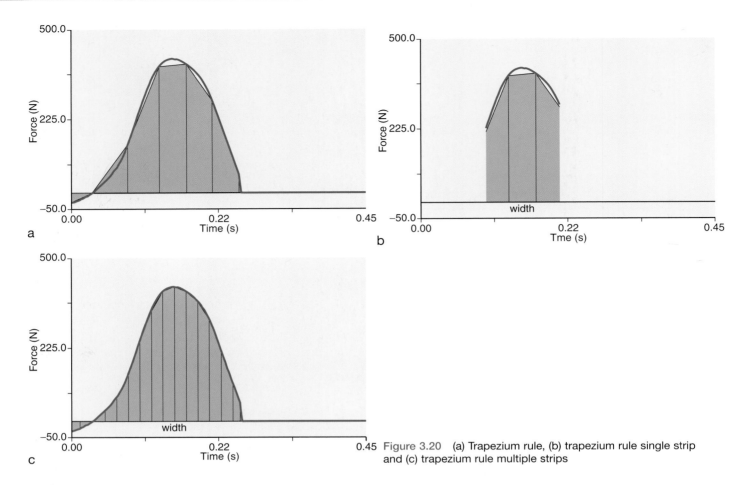

Figure 3.20   (a) Trapezium rule, (b) trapezium rule single strip and (c) trapezium rule multiple strips

considered only 6. This shows that the top of the trapeziums fits much better to the line of the data, although we are still in essence fitting a straight line to a line that is, in fact, curved.

When we use this technique in biomechanics the widths of the strips are the individual frame rates. These particular data were collected at 400 readings per second, with the total time of the data pattern being 0.25 s; therefore, we would normally divide up this pattern into 100 trapeziums. Although this is still 'an estimate' of the area under the curve, it is clear that the error becomes very small indeed.

3.6 Ground reaction force patterns during running

As with walking we can study the forces during any activity where there is either contact or impact with the ground. One activity which demonstrates the concept of impulse and momentum is running as the force acts over a very short period of time. During walking the contact phase is in the order of 0.6 s or 60% of the gait cycle, during running the force acts for approximately 0.25 s or 30% of the gait cycle, although this is open to considerable variation depending on speed.

3.6.1 Vertical forces during running

The vertical forces during running show very little similarity with those for walking. Although the pattern may still loosely

be divided into a loading peak, trough and propulsive peak, the function of each of the different sections is different (Fig. 3.21a, b, c).

Initial rate of loading

The initial rate of loading shows how well the shock from initial contact is being absorbed. This is found by taking two measurements of vertical force and the time that they occur and dividing the change in force by the change in time. If this is a high value then shock absorption is poor, which relates to poor function of the ankle and knee joint and/or poor shock absorbency of the shoes being used. In the graphs in Figure 3.21 we can see that rearfoot strikers have the greatest impact loading rate, followed by midfoot strikers, with forefoot strikers having the lowest rate of loading. This parameter is particularly important for footwear design and any shock-related problems, such as shin splints. The data from the three different types of impact would indicate that different footwear designs and orthotic management are required for the different running styles.

$$\text{Rate of loading} = \frac{\text{change in force during initial loading}}{\text{time taken for that change}}$$

The impact peak

The magnitude of this shows how hard the person is hitting the ground, i.e. the force which is attenuated up the stance limb in the vertical direction during the initial impact. This

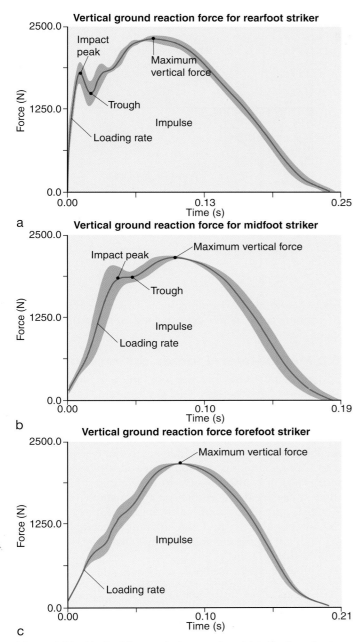

Figure 3.21   Vertical forces during running: (a) typical rearfoot striker, (b) typical midfoot striker and (c) typical forefoot striker

initial loading peak should not exceed the maximum vertical propulsive force. Again the magnitude of this peak relates to the shock absorbency characteristics, in particular the nature of the initial contact, with heel strikers (rearfoot strikers) having the largest and the most discernible peak, followed by the midfoot strikers, with forefoot strikers often with no discernible impact peak.

Trough
This trough does not correspond with the zero crossing in the anterior–posterior forces as it does in walking; however, it does relate to a reduction in force after the initial impact.

The reduction of this force approximates to the ankle moving rapidly into plantarflexion to the foot flat position, this trough is barely discernible in midfoot strikers, and not present during forefoot running due to the fact that the ankle moves into dorsiflexion and not plantarflexion.

Maximum vertical force
The maximum vertical force relates to the deceleration of the body downwards or vertical breaking force. The increase in force is due to the knee controlling the vertical deceleration of the body during the loading phase. This also has the effect of producing an eccentric stretching effect on the knee extensors, which initiates a stretch shorting cycle, which in turn aids propulsion, which starts shortly after the maximum vertical force as the knee starts to extend to propel the body forwards. The maximum vertical force is usually in the region of 2.5 times body weight; however, this is very dependent on the running speed.

3.6.2 Anterior–posterior forces during running
The anterior–posterior forces during running are not dissimilar to those for walking; as with walking, the pattern can be divided up into a period of loading and a period of propulsion (Fig. 3.22a, b, c).

The posterior impact peak
As with the vertical impact peak, this is the magnitude of the force telling us how hard the person is hitting the ground. As with the vertical force this is dictated by the nature of the initial foot contact and the footwear. The graphs (Fig. 3.22) show that rearfoot strikers again produce the largest impact forces with the largest posterior loading rate, although there is some variation between midfoot and forefoot strikers.

Maximum posterior breaking force
This is the maximum posterior force that occurs during the loading or breaking as the body decelerates at impact. The maximum posterior force is usually in the region of 0.4 times body weight; however, as with the vertical loading this is very dependent on the running speed. After the maximum posterior breaking force the force reduces to zero; the crossover point when the force in the sagittal plane acts straight up. As with walking this can be referred to as the point of mid stance; however, in running this usually occurs at slightly less than half the stance time.

Maximum anterior thrusting force
This is the maximum anterior force that occurs during propulsion as the body accelerates forward. During this horizontal propulsion phase the centre of pressure moves forward under the forefoot, which puts the force a greater distance away from the ankle joint. This maximizes the moment about the ankle and the power production and is responsible for the driving of the person forwards (see Chapter 5: Work, energy and power).

Breaking and thrusting impulse
The area under the anterior–posterior force graph, or impulse, can be divided easily into breaking and thrusting impulse,

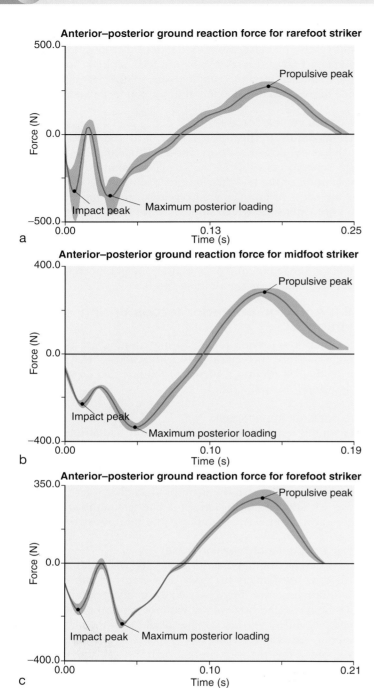

a

b

c

Figure 3.22 Anterior–posterior forces during running: (a) typical rearfoot striker, (b) typical midfoot striker and (c) typical forefoot striker

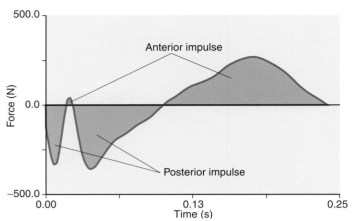

Figure 3.23 The anterior–posterior impulse of rearfoot striker running

check when studying running to ensure the subject is, in fact, running at a steady velocity and not speeding up or slowing down.

3.6.3 Medial–lateral forces during running

The data below show the rearfoot, midfoot and forefoot strikers considered before. The most notable difference is the magnitude of the medial impact force with the rearfoot striker, which is considerably greater than with the midfoot and forefoot strikers (Fig. 3.24a, b, c). The variability of the medial–lateral forces between individuals can be considerable due to varying amounts of pronation and supination during stance phase. It is also possible to have either a lateral or a medial impact peak depending on the position of the foot and which part of the foot makes initial contact. However, it is still possible to find the maximum medial and the maximum lateral forces, and the times that they occur from the force–time graphs.

As with walking, the medial–lateral forces (although variable) can have a substantial effect on the loading and stability of the ankle and knee joints in the coronal plane. These should not be ignored when considering the effects of footwear and orthotic management, which can give clinically significant changes to both the medial and lateral force patterns for an individual (Fig. 3.25a, b).

Summary: Ground reaction forces, impulse and momentum

- The centre of pressure is a single point where the ground reaction force can be considered to act. Centre of pressure can be very useful in assessing the movement of the ground reaction force beneath each foot during walking and the amount of postural sway during standing balance tests.
- The overall effect or resultant of the ground reaction force may be shown using a Pedotti diagram. The components of the ground reaction force may be considered in the vertical, anterior–posterior and medial–lateral planes of the body.

with the breaking impulse being negative and the thrusting impulse positive (Fig. 3.23). The breaking impulse and the thrusting impulse should be the same in magnitude. However, if the person is speeding up the **net impulse** (the sum of the breaking and the thrusting impulse) will be positive, and if the person is slowing down the net impulse will be negative. From the breaking and thrusting impulse the exact deceleration or acceleration of the body may be found (see 3.4 Impulse and momentum). This may be a very useful

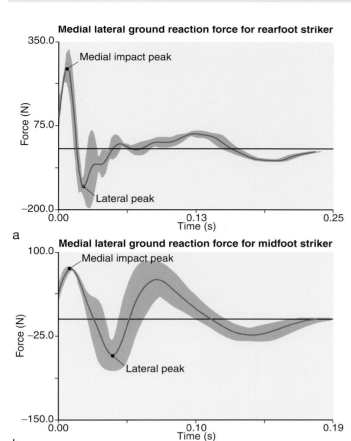

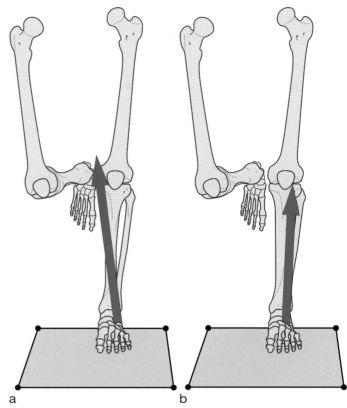

Fig 3.25   (a) Medial loading peak and (b) lateral peak

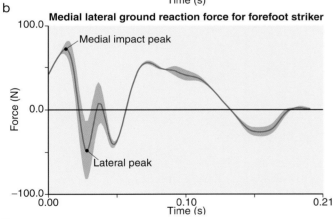

Figure 3.24   Medial–lateral forces during running: (a) typical rearfoot striker, (b) typical midfoot striker and (c) typical forefoot striker

- Separating the ground reaction force into the different body planes yields important information about the loading, propulsion and the stability of the body during different movement tasks.
- Impulse, the area under a force–time graph, corresponds with the change in momentum of an object. This can be useful in determining change in velocity during walking and running and may be used as an assessment of steady state gait.
- Ground reaction forces can be very useful in determining dysfunction during walking and may also be used to determine different running styles.

Motion and Joint Motion

Chapter
4

Jim Richards and Dominic Thewlis

This chapter covers the basic methods of gait assessment through to the description and discussion of the involvement of the three-dimensional movement of the foot, ankle, knee, hip and pelvis during walking in individuals who are pain and pathology free.

Chapter 4: Aim
To consider the function of the movement of the lower limb in individuals who are pain and pathology free.

Chapter 4: Objectives
- To relate simple methods of temporal and spatial parameters of gait to functional assessment of gait
- To recognize and draw the movement patterns of the lower limb and pelvis
- To interpret the movement patterns of the lower limb and pelvis in relation to their functional contribution to walking
- To interpret the different methods of graphing the interaction of the movement of the lower limb and pelvis.

4.1 Movement analysis in clinical research

4.1.1 The early pioneers

The study of human movement can be dated back to Borrelli in 1680. However, it wasn't until the late 19th century with the invention of photography that the analysis of movement was possible. Muybridge and Marey both collected movement data from humans. Marey (1873) was the first to produce a stick figure of human movement, whereas Muybridge produced film footage to consider movement strategies of many activities.

However, the majority of the work has been carried out in the second half of the 20th century. Bresler and Frankel (1950) were the first to carry out a mechanical analysis of walking. Their work included studying joint motion and inertial forces involved during gait. Saunders et al (1953) referred to the major determinants in normal gait and applied these to the assessment of pathological gait. Inman (1966, 1967) and Murray (1967) both published detailed analyses

on the kinematics and conservation of energy during human locomotion, which are frequently referred to today. Inman et al (1981) later published *Human Walking*, a comprehensive textbook on human locomotion. Many of the techniques of collection and analysing human locomotion have been applied to clinical practice and this has lead to more detailed clinical assessment of therapeutic and surgical intervention; one example of which is the assessment of the treatment of cerebral palsy (Sutherland et al 1978, Davids et al 1993, Gage 1994).

4.1.2 Clinical gait analysis

The walking cycle or gait cycle is often studied with respect to foot contact times. One complete gait cycle is defined as the period from initial contact of the foot to the next initial contact of the same foot. The gait cycle may be simply divided into stance and swing phases, where the foot is either in contact with the ground or not. Stance may then be divided into periods of single and double support, i.e. when either one or both feet are in contact with the ground (Murray et al 1964).

The gait cycle can also be studied in more detail, by studying the periods of foot contact and the action and motion of the different body segments separately during the gait cycle. This is commonly known as the study of kinematics. The variables involved with kinematics are foot contact times and distances, linear and angular displacements, velocities and accelerations of body segments. Kinematics is not concerned with the internal and external forces, but with the movement itself.

Brand and Crowninshield (1981) highlighted the distinction between the use of biomechanical techniques to 'diagnose' or 'evaluate' clinical problems. Brand and Crowninshield stated: 'Evaluate, in contrast to diagnose, means to place a value on something. Many medical tests are of this variety and instead of distinguishing diseases, help determine the severity of the disease or evaluate one parameter of the disease. Biomechanical tests at present are of this variety.'

Brand and Crowninshield (1981) gave a guide of six criteria for tools used in patient evaluation:

1. The measured parameter(s) must correlate well with the patient's functional capacity.
2. The measured parameter must not be directly observable and semi quantifiable by the physician or therapist.
3. The measured parameters must clearly distinguish between normal and abnormal.

4. The measurement technique must not significantly alter the performance of the evaluated activity.
5. The measurement must be accurate and reproducible.
6. The results must be communicated in a form which is readily identifiable.

Brand and Crowninshield stated: 'It is clear to us that most methods of assessing gait do not meet all of these criteria. We believe that it is for this reason that they are not widely used.'

Advances in biomechanical assessment in the last 25 years have been considerable. The description of normal gait in terms of movement and forces about joints is now commonplace. The relationship between normal gait patterns and normal function is also well supported in both peer reviewed papers and textbooks (Bruckner 1998, Perry 1992, Rose & Gamble 1994). This allows deviations in gait patterns to be studied in relation to changes in function in subjects with particular pathologies. It is possible for a clinician or physician to subjectively study gait; however, the value and repeatability of this type of assessment is questionable due to poor inter- and intra-tester reliability. For instance, it is impossible for one individual to study, by observation alone, the movement pattern of all the main joints involved during an activity like walking simultaneously. Studying movement patterns requires objective motion analysis which allows information to be gathered simultaneously with known accuracy and reliability. In this way changes in movement patterns due to intervention by physical therapists and surgeons and their effect on function may be assessed unequivocally. Most motion analysis systems now report on the joint kinematics for the individual recorded, and also contain information for the mean for normal on the same graph allowing a direct comparison of the individual's movement pattern in relation to a predefined normal.

Patrick (1991) reviewed the use of movement analysis laboratory investigations in assisting decision making for the physician and clinician. Patrick concluded that the reasons for the use of such facilities not being widespread was due to: the time of analysis being considerable, bioengineers designing systems and presenting results for researchers and not clinicians, and a lack of understanding by physicians and clinicians of applied mechanics and its relevance to assessment of treatment outcome. Since 1991 the movement analysis laboratory has become more widely accepted by physicians, the time needed for analysis is ever decreasing, resulting in new laboratories appearing in the clinical setting.

Winter (1993) reviewed techniques of gait analysis under the title 'Knowledge base for diagnostic gait assessment'. This was a reply to the criticisms from Brand and Crowninshield. Winter gave evidence to show that clinical gait assessments can give a valuable contribution to: diagnostic information to assist surgeons in planning orthopaedic procedures, planning of rehabilitation and in the assessment of prosthetic devices. Winter also demonstrated the use of a generalized strategy and diagnostic checklist developed for all pathologies. This checklist did not focus on a particular pathology, but rather targeted gait problems that may be common to many pathologies. Winter demonstrated the use of such a checklist using five case studies: knee arthroplasty, below knee amputee, cerebral palsy hemiplegia, above knee amputee and patellectomy. The paper concluded by stating that assessment of pathological gait is not an easy task, and can require considerable expense in equipment, software and specialised personnel. Winter also stressed the need for a database of normal data for children, adult and elderly subjects.

A common argument against movement analysis laboratories has been cost. The cost of movement analysis equipment and its potential use in the clinical setting has been reported (Bell et al 1996). A broader question, indeed, could be put to any clinical assessment or treatment that requires the use of technology. One example of this is the relative cost of radiography to movement analysis equipment, which in comparison is modest (Bell et al 1996). Gage (1994) claimed that gait analysis costs are comparable with MRI or CAT scans. Gage also stated that the use of movement analysis, as a detailed form of assessment, may have wider cost benefits and improve clinical services more than first realized. Bell et al (1995) highlighted the use of a holistic approach to motion analysis including muscle performance, joint range of motion, as well as kinematic and kinetic parameters of gait. This holistic approach may be applied to many pathologies to give a detailed assessment of pathology and the subsequent effects of treatment.

4.2 The gait cycle

For normal walking the obvious division is the duration when the foot is in contact with the ground and the period when it is not. These are known as stance phase (approximately 60% of the gait cycle) and swing phase (approximately 40% of the gait cycle) respectively.

The stance phase can be subdivided by specific events (Fig. 4.1a–e): 1) heel strike, 2) foot flat, 3) mid stance, 4) heel off and 5) toe off.

The swing phase can be subdivided into phases (Fig. 4.2a, b, c): 1) early swing, 2) mid swing and 3) late swing.

The simplest way in which we can look at walking patterns is by studying distances and times while the foot is in contact with the ground.

4.2.1 Spatial parameters

To define a subject's walk the spatial parameters of foot contact during gait should be considered (Fig. 4.3). The spatial parameters of foot contact during gait are: step length, stride length, foot angle and base width (Murray et al 1964, 1970, Rigas 1984).

Step length and stride length are defined as the distance between two consecutive initial contacts by different feet and the distance between two consecutive initial contacts by the same foot, respectively. Foot angle is defined as the angle of foot orientation away from the line of progression. Base width is defined as the medial–lateral distance between the centre of each heel during gait (Murray et al 1964, 1970, Rigas 1984). Two other parameters may easily be calculated using this information; these are cadence and average velocity.

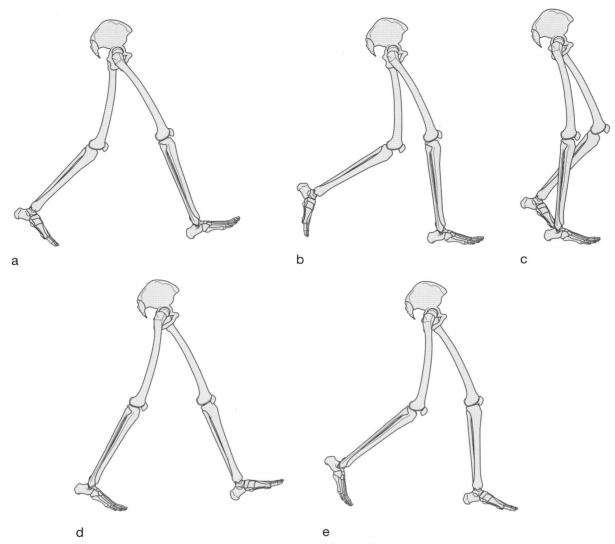

Figure 4.1   Stance phase: (a) heel strike, (b) foot flat, (c) mid stance, (d) heel off then (e) toe off

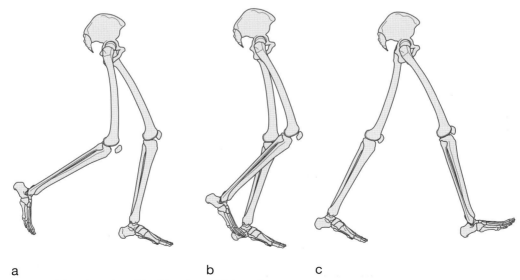

Figure 4.2   Swing phase: (a) early swing, (b) mid swing, (c) late swing

The spatial parameters of foot contact during gait are:

Step length – this is the distance between two consecutive heel strikes.

Stride length – this is the distance between two consecutive heel strikes by the same leg.

Foot angle or angle of gait – this is the angle of foot orientation away from the line of progression.

Base width or base of gait – the medial–lateral distance between the centre of each heel during gait.

4.2.2 Temporal parameters

Foot contact times are important temporal parameters of gait. If the time of each consecutive heel strike and toe off is recorded, then the step and stride time may be calculated. Step time and stride time are defined as the time between two consecutive initial contacts by different legs and the time between two consecutive initial contacts by the same leg; therefore, one complete gait cycle is the same as one stride (Murray et al 1964, 1970, Rigas 1984). However, this is not the only information that can be derived, the single support time and double support time can be found for each leg. Single support time and double support time may be defined as the time when one foot is in contact with the ground and the time when both feet are in contact with the ground respectively. Swing time is the same as single support time on the opposite leg. From this information the symmetry of single support time, double support time and step time can also be found. Foot contact timing and the parameters that can be derived from them are represented in Figure 4.4.

Step time – This is the time between two consecutive heel strikes. This is 50% of the stride time if the person is walking with perfect symmetry between the left and right sides.

Stride time – This can be defined as the time between two consecutive heel strikes by the same leg, one complete gait cycle or 100% of the gait cycle for that limb.

Single support – This is the time over which the body is supported by only one leg, which is approximately 40% of the gait cycle.

Double support – This is the time over which the body is supported by both legs. This comprises two periods, each lasting 10% of the gait cycle.

Swing time – This is the time taken for the leg to swing through while the body is in single support on the other leg. Therefore, this is the same proportion as single support, i.e. 40% of the gait cycle.

Total support – This is the total time the body is supported by one leg during one complete gait cycle. This time is the single support time and the two double support times giving 60% of the gait cycle.

Although the percentages of time spent in single and double support time are useful, they need to be used carefully for clinical assessment as the proportions are very dependent on the speed of walking. The above proportions are for walking at 'normal' speed; as the speed decreases the greater the double support time and the lower the single support time, until we get to the point of zero speed when double support is 100%, i.e. both feet are in contact with the ground all the time and the person is no longer walking!

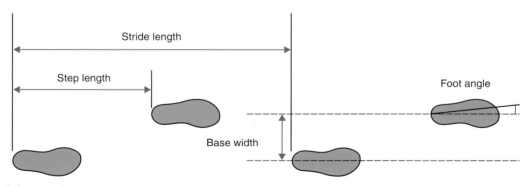

Figure 4.3   Spatial parameters

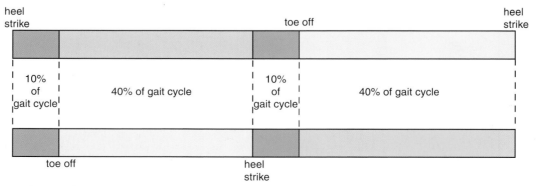

Figure 4.4   Temporal parameters

As the speed increases the double support period decreases until the stance phase and swing phase are nearly equal with very little double support time, this is the transition between race walking to running, where there is no longer any double support time and swing time is greater than stance time.

Other parameters may easily be calculated using this information, these are cadence and velocity. The cadence is the number of steps taken in a given time, usually steps per minute. Velocity may be calculated by the formula below:

$$\text{Cadence} = \text{The number of steps per min}$$

$$\text{Velocity} = \frac{\text{Step length (m)} \times \text{cadence (steps/min)}}{60 \text{ (number of seconds in 1 min)}}$$

Measures of symmetry between the left and right side can also be easily found by dividing the value of a parameter found for the left over that of the right. This can be carried out for all the measures mentioned above:

$$\text{Symmetry of step length} = \frac{\text{Step length for the left}}{\text{Step length for the right}}$$

$$\text{Symmetry of step time} = \frac{\text{Step time for the left}}{\text{Step time for the right}}$$

4.3 Normal movement patterns during gait

Human walking allows a smooth and efficient progression of the body's centre of mass (Inman 1967). To achieve this there are a number of different movements of the joints in the lower limb. The correct functioning of the movement patterns of these joints allows a smooth and energy-efficient progression of the body. The relationship between the movements of the joints of the lower limb is critical, if there is any deviation in the co-ordination of these patterns the energy cost of walking may increase and also the shock absorption at impact and propulsion may not be as effective.

Joint motion patterns commonly reported include: ankle plantar–dorsiflexion, foot rotation, knee flexion–extension, knee valgus–varus, knee rotation, hip flexion extension, hip abduction–adduction, hip rotation, pelvic tilt, pelvic obliquity and pelvic rotation. The movement patterns considered in this chapter include the movement of all the following joints and segments in the sagittal, coronal and transverse planes:

- Ankle joint
- Rearfoot, midfoot and forefoot motion
- Tibial segment
- Knee joint
- Hip joint
- Pelvis.

Additional graphing techniques to show co-ordination between joints are also reviewed, these include:

- Angle–angle diagrams
- Angle versus angular velocity diagrams.

It is also possible to find the energy involved in moving each body segment. More on this can be found in section 5.7: How to find energies involved in moving body segments.

4.3.1 Plantarflexion and dorsiflexion of the ankle joint

The movement of the foot as a whole about the tibia is referred to as ankle joint motion and is the most commonly reported movement pattern of the foot and ankle complex. This overall movement of the foot to the tibia in the sagittal plane is of great importance as it allows shock absorption at heel strike and during stance phase, as well as being vital in the 'push off' or propulsive stage immediately before the toe leaves the ground. During swing phase the motion of the ankle joint allows foot clearance, which can be lacking in some pathological gait patterns and is generally known as drop foot. The range of motion that occurs in walking varies between 20° and 40°, with an average range of motion of 30°. However, this does not tell us how the motion of the ankle varies throughout gait. During gait the ankle has four phases of motion (Fig. 4.5).

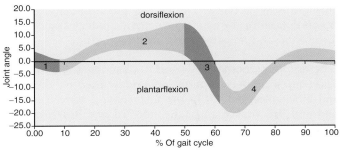

Figure 4.5 Plantarflexion and dorsiflexion of the ankle joint

Phase 1

At initial contact, or heel strike, the ankle joint is in a neutral position; it then plantarflexes to between 3° and 5° until foot flat has been achieved. This is sometimes referred to as 'first rocker' or 'first segment', which refers to the foot pivoting about the heel or calcaneus. During this period the dorsiflexor muscles in the anterior compartment of the foot and ankle are acting eccentrically, controlling the plantarflexion of the foot. This gives the effect of a shock absorber and aids smooth weight acceptance to the lower limb.

Phase 2

At the position of foot flat the ankle then begins to dorsiflex. The foot becomes stationary and the tibia becomes the moving segment, with dorsiflexion reaching a maximum of 10° as the tibia moves over the ankle joint. The time from foot flat to heel lift is referred to as 'second rocker' or 'second segment', which refers to the pivot of the motion now being at the ankle joint with the foot firmly planted on the ground. During this time the plantarflexor muscles are acting eccentrically to control the movement of the tibia forwards.

Phase 3

The heel then begins to lift at the beginning of double support, causing a rapid ankle plantarflexion reaching an average value of 20° at the end of the stance phase at toe off. This is referred to as 'third rocker' or 'third segment' as the pivot point is now under the metatarsal heads. During this time the ankle reaches an angular velocity of 250°/s plantarflexion, which can be associated with power production. This is the propulsive phase of the gait cycle during which the plantar flexor muscles in the posterior compartment of the foot and ankle concentrically contract pushing the foot into plantarflexion and propelling the body forwards. This rapid plantarflexion is responsible for the majority of the power production to propel the body forwards, see section 5.4: The relationship between moments, angular velocity and joint power during normal gait.

Phase 4

During the swing phase the ankle rapidly dorsiflexes (150°/s) to allow the clearance of the foot from the ground. A neutral position (0°) is reached by mid swing, which is maintained during the rest of the swing phase until the next heel strike. This is referred to as the 'fourth segment'. It has been recorded that there is sometimes 3° to 5° of dorsiflexion during the swing phase. During this phase the ankle dorsiflexors concentrically contract to provide foot clearance from the ground and prepare for the next foot strike.

Different terms commonly used to describe ankle motion

There are a number of terms commonly used by clinicians and bioengineers alike. In the text above I have used **1st, 2nd and 3rd rocker** and **1st, 2nd, 3rd and 4th segments**. These terms are also commonly used interchangeably (see Table 4.1).

4.3.2 Movement of the ankle, rearfoot, midfoot and forefoot

The vast majority of studies have considered the foot as a single segment, often defined by the malleoli and the lateral aspect of the metatarsal heads, or the heel and the medial and lateral aspects of the metatarsal heads. However, for decades podiatrists and many other clinicians have been considering the foot in three parts: the forefoot, midfoot and rearfoot (hindfoot).

In this section we will consider the movement of the foot first as a single segment and then we will consider the contribution and interaction between each of the segments (see section 9.6.2 for Models for multiple segment foot). The foot will be considered in three segments: 1) calcaneal, 2) metatarsal and 3) phalangeal segment (Fig. 4.6).

In order to demonstrate the movement that can occur and the differences that exist when considering the foot either as a **single segment** or as **multiple segments**, the data presented shows the differences that may be seen in a single individual walking barefoot. The data show the mean and standard

deviations for five trials. These data should not be used as a normative data set, but should act as a guide to relative movement patterns of the different foot segments.

Foot-to-tibia movement
Sagittal plane (plantarflexion–dorsiflexion)
Tibia-to-foot movement in the sagittal plane is the same as the pattern described in section 4.3.1 Plantar–dorsiflexion of the ankle joint, where the whole foot is defined as a single segments (Fig. 4.7a).

Coronal plane (inversion–eversion)
The coronal plane may be used to describe the inversion–eversion pattern of the foot as a whole. At heel strike the foot lands in an inverted position and moves into eversion during loading. Rapid inversion then takes place just prior to 50% of the gait cycle (Fig. 4.7b). This pattern shows a range of motion of 7°; however, considering the foot as a single segment produces a different pattern of movement when compared to the calcaneal-to-tibial movement. This discrepancy is due to movement between the calcaneal and metatarsal segments.

Transverse plane (internal–external rotation or pronation–supination)
The transverse plane can be used to describe internal–external rotation. The transverse plane movement of the foot to tibia has also been used as a descriptor for pronation–supination (Nester et al 2003). This pattern shows the foot landing in a slightly pronated position and moving quickly into further pronation, this shows slight differences with the work by Nester who showed a slightly supinated position at heel strike. The pronation then reduces and levels off before moving into a supinated position in late stance phase (Fig. 4.7c). It is interesting to note that this pattern, which considers the foot as a single segment, is similar to that of the calcaneal-to-tibial movement, although the range of movement is greater.

Calcaneus-to-tibia movement
When describing the ankle joint we can use the definition of tibia to foot movement; however, this uses a combination of the calcaneal and metatarsal segments to define the distal segment. However, the calcaneal-to-tibia segment movement

Table 4.1	Rocker/segments		
Phase 1	**Phase 2**	**Phase 3**	**Phase 4**
1st rocker	2nd rocker	3rd rocker	Swing phase
Heel rocker	Ankle rocker	Forefoot rocker	Swing phase
1st segment	2nd segment	3rd segment	4th segment
Contact	Midstance	Propulsion	Swing phase

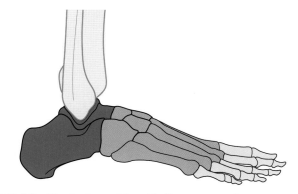

Figure 4.6   The foot considered in three segments

would be more meaningful, in particular when considering the coronal and transverse planes.

Sagittal plane (plantarflexion–dorsiflexion)

The sagittal plane movement shows much the same functional movements during early-to-mid stance as the foot to the tibia. However, the amount of plantarflexion occurring between the calcaneal-to-tibia segments is noticeable less than when the metatarsal segment is included (Fig. 4.8a). This is due to a clear pattern of dorsiflexion and plantarflexion of the metatarsal segment in relation to the calcaneal segment. Therefore, including the metatarsal segment may well give an overall function of the foot; however, it gives a distorted view of 'ankle' plantarflexion.

Coronal plane (inversion–eversion)

At heel strike the foot lands in an everted position and moves into further eversion during loading, this allows midtarsal movement, arch collapse, and a mobile forefoot. The same pattern of rapid inversion seen in the single segment foot model takes place just prior to 50% of the gait cycle; this locks the midtarsal joints creating a rigid lever and a restored arch (Fig. 4.8b). Although the range of motion into further

eversion is less than that seen in the single segment model, this is due to metatarsal-to-calcaneus movement.

Transverse plane (internal–external rotation or pronation–supination)

The transverse plane movement of the calcaneal-to-tibia segment gives much the same pattern of movement as the foot-to-tibial movement, although the range of motion is less. This difference in the range is due to the small amount of movement in the transverse plane between the metatarsal and calcaneal segments (Fig. 4.8c). Therefore, the treatment of the foot as a signal segment (calcaneal and metatarsal segments) appears to give a good indication of the movement pattern of the calcaneus in relation to the tibia.

Metatarsal-to-calcaneus movement
Sagittal plane (plantarflexion–dorsiflexion)

The sagittal plane motion shows metatarsal–calcaneal dorsiflexion during early stance phase, with plantarflexion during late stance phase. This corresponds to the dorsiflexion of the ankle joint as the body moves over the stance limb and plantarflexion during propulsion. This would imply the metatarsal calcaneal movement has a role in both

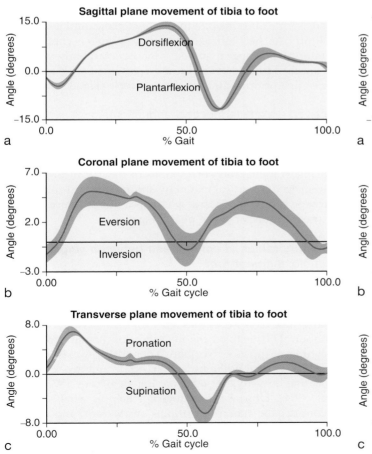

a

b

c

Figure 4.7   (a) Tibia-to-foot movement in the sagittal plane, (b) tibia-to-foot movement in the coronal plane and (c) tibia-to-foot movement in the transverse plane

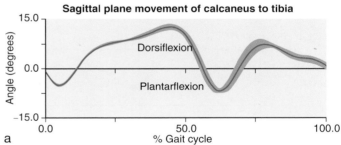

a

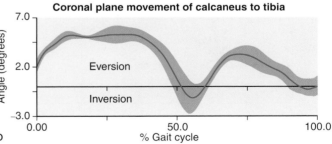

b

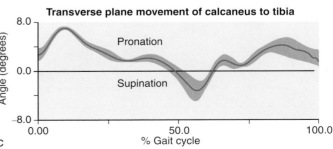

c

Figure 4.8   (a) Calcaneus-to-tibia movement in the sagittal plane, (b) calcaneus-to-tibia movement in the coronal plane and (c) calcaneus-to-tibia movement in the transverse plane

progression of the body over the foot and in the push-off phases (Fig. 4.9a). This involvement causes the discrepancy in the plantarflexion–dorsiflexion pattern between the foot to tibia movement and the calcaneal-to-tibia movement.

Coronal plane (inversion–eversion)

At heel strike the angle between the metatarsal and calcaneal segments is approximately in neutral and moves progressively into a slightly more everted position. The range of movement during stance phase is in the order of 1.5° although it is possible that skin and soft-tissue movement could be responsible (Fig. 4.9b).

Transverse plane (adduction–abduction)

There is a relatively small amount of transverse plane movement between the metatarsal and calcaneal segments; however, this does follow a discernible pattern that is synchronized with the transverse plane movement of the ankle joint. When we consider the foot as a single segment this small amount of movement elevates the value of transverse plane motion. This transverse plane movement equates to adduction–abduction between the metatarsal and calcaneal segments, which would be expected to be small. The movement shows the metatarsal abducting during loading in relation to the calcaneal segment and

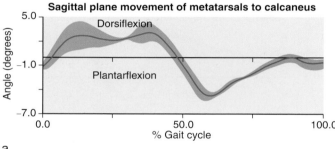

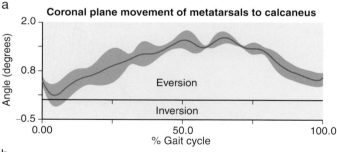

a

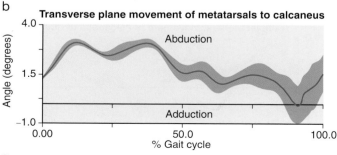

b

c

Figure 4.9 (a) Metatarsal-to-calcaneus movement in the sagittal plane, (b) metatarsal-to-calcaneus movement in the coronal plane and (c) metatarsal-to-calcaneus movement in the transverse plane

then returning to a 'neutral' position during swing phase (Fig. 4.9c).

Metatarsal to phalangeal movement
Sagittal plane (plantarflexion–dorsiflexion)

The sagittal plane movement of the metatarsal–phalangeal joints is perhaps the most notable omission from foot and ankle mechanics in the majority of textbooks and the research literature. At heel strike the metatarsal–phalangeal joints are in a dorsiflexed position and move towards a neutral position as the foot is placed flat on the floor. The metatarsal–phalangeal joints then become progressively more dorsiflexed as the body moves forwards over the foot. At heel off, where the foot pivots on the metatarsal heads at approximately 50% of the gait cycle, the metatarsal–phalangeal joints are forced into rapid dorsiflexion, or extension, just as the ankle starts its rapid plantarflexion during push off. This can be referred to as metatarso-phalangeal dorsiflexion, which will tense the plantar fascia. After toe off the phalanges return to a slightly less dorsiflexed position to aid foot clearance during swing phase (Fig. 4.10a). Although, this movement may not have any function in power generation during push off, it may still be clinically important when considering the stiffness of the forefoot and the effect of foot orthoses designed to control or assist forefoot movement.

Coronal plane (inversion–eversion)

There is little movement in the coronal plane until just before heel off. At heel off an inversion 'twist' occurs at the metatarsal–phalangeal joints, which corresponds with the calcaneal-to-tibial movement, and a pattern of rapid inversion is seen just prior to 50% of the gait cycle (Fig. 4.10b).

Transverse plane (adduction–abduction)

As with the coronal plane there is little movement in the transverse plane until just before heel off. At heel off the 'twist' also creates a rapid abduction movement at the metatarsal–phalangeal joints, this corresponds to the calcaneal-to-tibial movement into a supinated position and restored arch. After toe off the metatarsal–phalangeal joints return to their neutral position for swing phase (Fig. 4.10c).

Summary tables of comparison between single and multiple segment foot
See Tables 4.2a, b, c. Normative data

There are a number of points we need to consider with the data presented here with the single and multi-segment foot. Firstly, these data were collected with the individual walking barefoot. This enabled the identification of the anatomical structures of the foot. Normative data do now exist (Carson et al 2001, MacWilliams et al 2003), and work is now appearing investigating the pathological foot (Woodburn et al 2004). However, this does not help us when we have to consider the action of orthoses on the foot, and whether they restrict or modify the movement patterns between the different foot segments. The model presented above can be applied to footwear, but whether it yields the same data and even the question *should it* yield the same data, as the foot function itself will almost certainly have changed when wearing shoes, has yet to be answered by the research literature.

4.3.3 Movement of the tibial segment

The movement of the tibia segment can give important information on pathological gait patterns. It can be the case, with various pathologies, that the ankle joint motion needs to be restricted with orthotics, due to a lack of muscle power or spasticity. However, if the ankle motion is restricted this

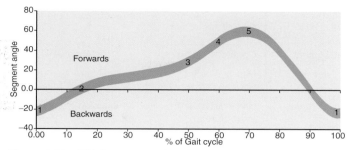

Figure 4.11   Tibial movement in relation to the vertical axis

will restrict the motion of the tibia over the stance limb, making it very hard for the subject to move over the stance limb. In these cases rocker soles are sometimes fitted to the shoes to enable a movement over the stance limb without movement at the ankle joint. If this is the case then we need a measure which will indicate how well the tibia is moving, not in relation to the foot as this motion has been restricted, but in relation to the vertical.

Figure 4.11 shows the tibial movement in relation to the vertical axis. At heel strike (1) the tibia is at its most inclined backwards (the distal joint in front of the proximal joint) at 20°. The tibia then advances quickly past the vertical position (2). The motion then slows as the movement over the stance limb is controlled by eccentric activity of the calf muscles. At heel off (3) the rate of movement increases again, this is in preparation for swing phase. Toe off occurs at (4) where the tibia continues to incline forwards up to 60° to ensure foot clearance (5), this is followed by a quick movement of the tibia forwards for the next heel strike. The point when the tibia is vertical (2) can be used as a reference for the ankle plantar–dorsiflexion pattern. As the tibia passes the vertical position, the foot is in the foot flat position; therefore, the ankle will be in an approximately neutral position, although care must be taken using this for pathological gait patterns.

4.3.4 Motion of the knee joint

During gait the knee joint moves in the sagittal, transverse and coronal planes. However, the majority of the motion of the knee joint is in the sagittal plane, which involves the flexion and extension of the knee joint. However, important functional and pathological movement patterns may be observed when considering both the coronal and transverse planes.

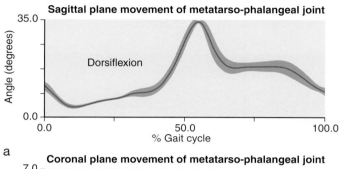

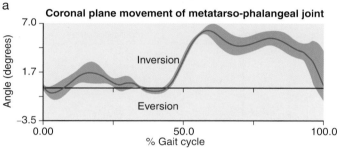

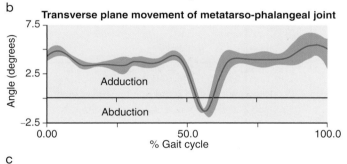

Figure 4.10   (a) Metatarsal-to-phalangeal movement in the sagittal plane, (b) metatarsal-to-phalangeal movement in the coronal plane and (c) metatarsal-to-phalangeal movement in the transverse plane

Table 4.2a Position of segments during gait sagittal plane				
	Gait cycle			
Segment	Contact/loading	Midstance	Propulsion	Swing
Foot	Neutral moving into plantarflexion	Dorsiflexing as leg moves over foot	Plantarflexing as foot pushes off	Dorsiflexed to aid foot clearance
Calcaneal	Neutral moving into plantarflexion	Similar amount of dorsiflexion to single segment	Reduced amount of plantarflexion	Dorsiflexed to aid foot clearance
Metatarsal	Dorsiflexion due to eccentric contraction	Maintains dorsiflexion as forefoot accepts weight	Rapid plantarflexion as heel lifts	Dorsiflexing
Phalangeal	Held in dorsiflexion/ extension	Moves into neutral	Dorsiflexes as heel lifts	Less dorsiflexed position as long extensors aid tibialis anterior

Table 4.2b   Position of segments during gait coronal plane

Segment	Gait cycle			
	Contact/loading	Midstance	Propulsion	Swing
Foot	Hits in inverted position rapidly everting	Maintains everted position	Inverts rapidly as heel lifts	Initially everts then moves towards inversion
Calcaneal	Hits everted and everts further	Eversion maintained	Rapid inversion as heel lifts	Everts before moving towards neutral
Metatarsal	Neutral	Everts a little	Everted	Everted
Phalangeal	Neutral	Neutral	Rapid inversion twist	Initially inverted moves towards neutral

Tables 4.2c   Position of segments during gait transverse plane

Segment	Gait cycle			
	Contact/loading	Midstance	Propulsion	Swing
Foot	Abduction increasing	Abduction reducing	Rapid motion into adduction	Abducting
Calcaneal	Abduction increasing	Abduction reducing	Moves into adduction	Abduction through swing
Metatarsal	Abducting	Abducting	Abduction reduces	To neutral
Phalangeal	Adducted	Adducted	Rapid abduction	Rapid adduction

Motion of the knee joint in the sagittal plane

The flexion and extension of the knee joint is cyclic, and varies between 0° and 70°, although there is some variation in the exact amount of peak flexion occurring. These differences may be related to differences in walking speed, subject individuality, and the landmarks selected to designate limb segment alignments. The knee flexion extension pattern may be divided up into five phases (Fig. 4.12).

At heel strike, or initial contact, the knee should be flexed. However, people's knee posture can vary between slight hyperextension (−2°) to 10° of flexion, with a mean value of 5°.

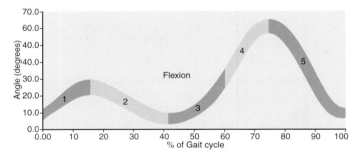

Figure 4.12   Knee joint flexion pattern in sagittal plane

Phase 1

After the initial contact there is a flexion of the knee joint to about 20° when the knee is flexed under maximum weight-bearing load. The knee joint flexes to absorb the loading at a rate of 150–200°/s. This occurs at the same time as the ankle joint plantarflexes, with a net effect of acting as a shock absorber during the loading of the lower limb. During this time the knee extensors are acting eccentrically.

Phase 2

After this first peak of knee flexion the knee joint extends at a rate of 80–100°/s to almost full extension. This relates to a smooth eccentrically controlled movement of the body over the stance limb.

Phase 3

The knee then begins its second period of flexion, which coincides with heel lift. During this second flexion the lower limb is in the propulsive phase of the gait cycle. The knee undergoes a rapid flexion in preparation for swing phase, sometimes referred to as pre-swing.

Phase 4

Toe off occurs when the knee flexion is approximately 40°, at which time the knee is flexing at a rate of 300–350°/s. This flexion, coupled with the ankle dorsiflexion, allows the toe to clear the ground. During initial to mid swing the knee continues to flex to a maximum of 65–70°.

Phase 5

During late swing, the knee undergoes a rapid extension (400–450°/s) to prepare for the second heel strike.

Motion of the knee joint in the coronal plane

The knee angle in the coronal plane has long been an area of debate centred on our ability to truly isolate abduction and adduction. This debate has been very much fuelled by the variance that is evident between individuals and the susceptibility of this plane to the effects of cross talk from other planes. Various authors have attempted to compensate for this; however, in doing so they have used algorithms to artificially minimize the effect. This results in data which are essentially false. It is very rare that you will ever get the same profile for different individuals; however, the standard deviation between individuals will generally be very low.

The most reliable measurements of the coronal plane knee angle have been taken during stance phase. These imply that in normal individuals there will be very little movement besides a slight deformation during loading and the opposite deformation during terminal stance. The direction of this deformation is based on the anatomical alignment of the knee, i.e. adducted or abduction (varus or valgus). Typically we would not expect to see more than 4° of movement during stance (Fig. 4.13). Swing phase is typically where the majority of movement is recorded; however, it is still unclear if this movement is real and due to the laxity of the joint or if it is an artifact due to the change in the orientation of the segment coordinate systems. We will typically see up to 10° of movement during swing phase. If movements that are anatomically impossible appear to be recorded there may be the effects of planar cross talk present or there may be pathology such as osteoarthritis, which can cause a greater deformation during loading.

Motion of the knee joint in the transverse plane

The motion of the knee in the transverse plane is dominated by the motion of the tibia rotating about the femur during both stance and swing phase (Fig. 4.14). This effect has been termed the screw home effect. The screw home movement of the tibia has been documented in a number of publications. One of the first documentations of the movement was identified in Gray's anatomy, where the motion was attributed to length discrepancy between the medial and lateral condyles of the femur. Hallen and Lindahl (1966) conducted a study to investigate the degree of axial rotation and screw home movement in normal knees. This study took 'autopsy specimens' and evaluated the axial rotation of the tibia about the knee at full extension and 160° of extension, 20° of flexion. In addition, measurements were taken that accounted for the natural movement of the tibia during extension (passive extension). Hallen and Lindahl (1966) found 12° of rotation during full extension, 23° of rotation at 160° of extension and 7° of external rotation during passive extension. Andriacchi et al (2005) provide a good clinical explanation of this movement as 'this motion externally rotates the tibia through swing in to stance in order for the tibia and foot to be in the correct alignment at initial contact'. In addition to the joint geometry contribution to screw home, Andriacchi et al (2005) noted that in the Anterior Cruciate Ligament (ACL) deficient knees screw home is reduced, this was attributed to the passive tension developed during terminal stance within the structures of the ACL. Once this tension is released the ACL passively causes the tibia to externally rotate with respect to the knee. It is important to note that it is often assumed that the ACL of a patient suffering from osteoarthritis (OA) is deficient, so the screw home should be also reduced, which supports the findings of Andriacchi et al (2005). This movement essentially involves the passive generation of tension in the ACL during stance due to internal rotation of the foot and tibia. This tension is then released in swing phase, coupled with the discrepancy in condyle length, which results in the external rotation of the tibia.

Knee joint angular velocity in the sagittal plane

Figure 4.15 shows the knee joint angular velocity in the sagittal plane. At heel strike, the knee is already flexing. During the initial loading of the foot the knee flexion peaks at 150–200°/s (1). The knee flexion velocity slows as the knee reaches its initial peak flexion. The thigh then moves over the tibia, this causes an extension velocity of between 80 and 100°/s (2). At 50% of the gait cycle the heel begins to lift and the knee starts flexing again. At toe off the knee is flexing at a rate of 300–350°/s (3), the knee velocity then slows as the knee reaches its maximum flexion. After maximum flexion the knee then starts to extend rapidly at a rate of 400–450°/s (4).

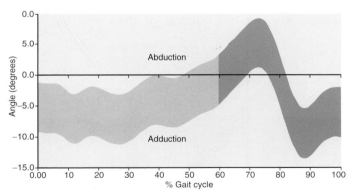

Figure 4.13   The coronal plane motion of the knee

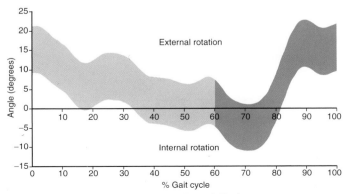

Figure 4.14   Transverse plane motion of the knee

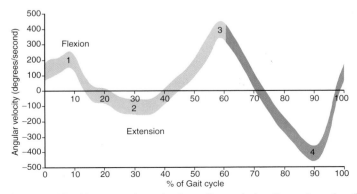

Figure 4.15   Knee angular velocity patterns during the gait cycle

Knee angular velocity has been shown to exhibit more sensitivity than the knee flexion angles and timing parameters alone. This may be explained by the fact that slightly larger ranges in motion occur in slightly lower times. The combination of these two factors causes a significant effect in the knee flexion–extension angular velocities but not of the angle or timing parameters (Richards et al 2003). The idea of velocity being potentially more sensitive than angle and time measures alone reflects that joint angular velocity may be more sensitive to changes in control of joint repositioning rather than the absolute joint position itself (Richards et al 2003).

The use of knee angular velocity has been reflected in other work. Jevsevar et al (1993) studied knee kinematics during walking, stair ascent, descent and arising from a chair in healthy subjects and subjects who had undergone knee arthroplasty. Jevsevar and co-workers studied the range of motion, angular velocity and moments about the knee joint. They reported that sagittal knee range of motion was significantly different between activities, and that knee moments and vertical forces were not significantly different for all activities. However, Jevsevar also found that knee angular velocity measurements showed significant differences between the healthy subjects and subjects who had undergone knee athroplasty. Jevsevar reported that both the flexion and extension velocities during swing phase (unloaded) and stance phase (loaded) in gait were significantly lower in the knee arthroplasty subjects. All the loaded angular velocities were also significantly lower for all activities in the knee arthroplasty subjects with the exception of stair descent. Messier et al (1992) investigated the kinematics of subjects with osteoarthritis of the knee during walking. Messier found that a number of characteristics showed a significant difference between the subjects with OA and normal subjects. These differences included a decrease in the knee range of motion, mean knee angular velocity, and maximum knee extension angular velocity in the subjects with OA. Chou et al (1998) investigated the lower limb kinematics of moving the foot over obstacles of different heights. Chou and co-workers found that knee angular velocity increased as toe–obstacle distance increased, and stated that angular velocity of knee flexion appears to be of primary importance in avoiding obstacle contact. This would indicate that knee angular velocity is important in the control of lower limb tasks.

4.3.5 Motion of the hip joint

Motion of the hip joint in the sagittal plane

During walking the leg flexes forward at the hip joint to take a step and then extends until push off. The hip joint angle is defined as the angle between the pelvis and the thigh segment. The motion of the hip forms an arc starting at heel strike and finishing at toe off (Fig. 4.16a).

Phase 1

After heel strike the hip extends as the body moves over the limb at a rate of 150°/s. Maximum hip extension occurs just after opposite foot strike. The small amount of hip extension can cause confusion as the thigh is well behind the body during late stance phase. This can be explained

quite simply; the hip joint flexion–extension pattern is the angle between the pelvis and the thigh, the pelvis also moves in the sagittal plane, in particular at opposite foot strike the pelvis tilts forwards reducing the angle between pelvis and thigh (hip angle). Some authors have reported no movement into extension at opposite heel strike; however, this discrepancy can, in part, be explained by how the pelvic tilt angle is defined (see Chapter 9 Anatomical models and marker sets).

Phase 2

After maximum hip extension weight is then transferred to the forward limb and the trailing limb begins to flex at the hip. This is the pre-swing period. The toe leaves the ground at 60% of the gait cycle and the hip flexes rapidly at a rate of 200°/s. This can be seen from the increased slope of the angle against time plot below, this rapid flexion progresses the limb forward to take a step. The hip reaches maximum flexion just before the heel strike.

Phase 3

After the maximum hip flexion has been reached there is often a small movement towards extension, i.e. the hip becomes slightly less flexed. This is concerned with the placement of the foot or pre-positioning just prior to heel strike. This is particularly prevalent during marching where the hip flexion is exaggerated.

Thigh angle

Thigh angle has also previously been used in gait assessment. Thigh angle is simply the movement of the thigh segment in relation to the vertical (Fig. 4.16b). This may all seem confusing initially; however, the patterns of thigh and hip flexion

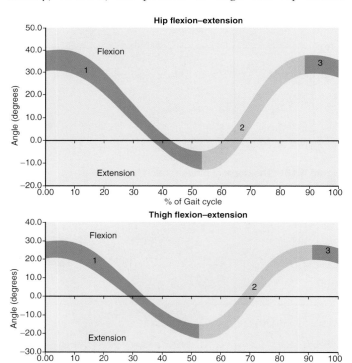

Figure 4.16   (a) Motion of the hip joint in the sagittal plane and (b) motion of the thigh segment in the sagittal plane

extension remain almost the same during normal walking, although the maximum values may move up or down. This is due to the range of the motion of the pelvis in the sagittal plane varys approximately 10° during gait, which accounts for the apparent 10° increase in extension of the thigh angle in comparison to the hip angle.

One parameter always worthy of examination for both thigh and hip angle is the active range of motion, i.e. the difference between the maximum and minimum values; this should be nearly identical whichever system is used and should be in the order of 45° for normal. However, in the study of pathological conditions that have pelvic involvement, the thigh angle should not be considered alone, as this could mask clinically important movement strategies.

Motion of the hip joint in the coronal plane

The movement of the hip in the coronal plane may be described as hip abduction and adduction, abduction referring to a movement away from the centre line of the body, adduction referring to a movement towards the centre line of the body (Fig. 4.17).

Phase 1

At heel strike the hip is in a slightly abducted position. It then moves quickly into adduction as the limb is loaded and the body is supported. This adduction is also due to the dropping down of the pelvis on the contralateral or unsupported limb.

Phase 2

After the initial adduction the hip then moves into abduction as the pelvis then levels out and the body progresses over the

stance limb. The hip reaches maximum abduction shortly after toe off, as the pelvis drops down as the limb is now in swing phase.

Phase 3

The pelvis then levels off again as the limb swings through during mid-to-late swing phase.

The total range of motion is in the order of 15°, with equal amounts of abduction and adduction. This, not surprisingly, produces a very similar movement pattern to the pelvic movement in the coronal plane (see Motion of the pelvis in the coronal plane (pelvic obliquity)).

Motion of the hip joint in the transverse plane

The movement of the hip in the transverse plane, the movement between the femur and the pelvis, may be described as internal and external rotation (Fig. 4.18). At heel strike the hip is in an externally rotated position of approximately 10°, but as the knee flexes and the body starts to move over the stance limb, the hip rotates internally to approximately 5° as the pelvis rotates forwards on the swing side. The peak internal rotation occurs at around opposite heel strike. During late swing phase the hip shows a quick movement back into external rotation. There is a considerable amount of variation in the pattern, which is as much to do with the pelvis positioning as with the femoral rotation itself.

4.3.6 Motion of the pelvis

Motion of the pelvis in the coronal plane (pelvic obliquity)

During early stance phase the contralateral side of the pelvis drops downward in the coronal plane. In normal gait the peak pelvic obliquity occurs just after opposite toe off, which corresponds to early stance phase on the weight-bearing limb (Fig. 4.19). Pelvic obliquity serves two purposes: to allow shock absorption and to allow limb length adjustments. To illustrate the second point when studying above knee amputee gait, the pelvic obliquity does not always follow the normal pattern. As normal control of the knee joint had been lost, foot clearance is ensured by hitching up the contralateral pelvis; in this way pelvic obliquity can be used to shorten the effective limb length when required. However,

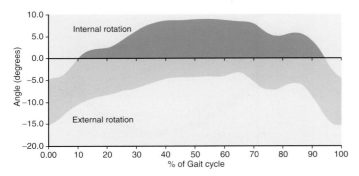

Figure 4.17   Motion of the hip joint in the coronal plane

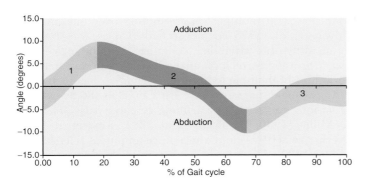

Figure 4.18   Motion of the hip joint in the transverse coronal plane

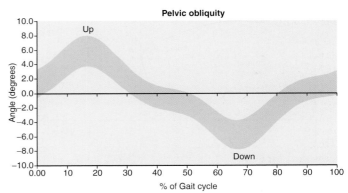

Figure 4.19   Motion of the pelvis in the coronal plane (pelvic obliquity)

this may have energy costs as it increases the excursion of the centre of mass of the entire body, therefore, increasing the work by producing this change in potential energy.

Motion of the pelvis in the transverse plane (pelvic rotation)

During normal level walking the pelvis rotates about a vertical axis alternately to the left and to the right. This rotation is usually about 4° on either side of this central axis, the peak internal rotation occurring at foot strike and the maximal external rotation at opposite foot strike (Fig. 4.20). This rotation effectively lengthens the limb by increasing the step length and prevents excessive drop of the centre of mass of the whole body making the walking pattern more efficient. Pelvic rotation also has the effect of smoothing the vertical excursion of the centre of mass and reducing the impact at foot strike.

4.3.7 Angle–angle diagrams

Angle–angle diagrams are angle diagrams of two joints plotted on the same graph. Grieve (1968) proposed the use of angle–angle diagrams as a simple method of presenting joint angle data in relation to the cyclic nature of each stride or gait cycle. The most popular angle–angle diagram is that of knee flexion–extension versus hip flexion–extension. Knee flexion–extension is plotted on the ordinate (y-axis) and hip flexion–extension on the abscissa (x-axis). This gives a graphical representation of the relationship between the knee flexion–extension and the hip flexion–extension (Fig. 4.21). It should be noted that knee flexion is often considered as negative when drawing knee flexion–extension versus hip flexion–extension angle–angle diagrams.

Distinct parts of the angle–angle plot in Figure 4.21 show the co-ordination between the knee and hip during phases of the gait cycle. The loading response from point 1 to point 2 shows a smooth increase in the knee flexion, with a small amount of movement of the hip in the extension direction; at point 2 the knee is at its maximum flexion during loading response. Point 2 to point 3 shows an equal rate of knee extension to hip extension indicating a smooth advancement of the body of the stance limb, point 3 corresponds to heel lift. From point 3 to point 4 the knee starts its second wave of flexion while the hip starts to flex. Knee flexion then slows and the hip flexion becomes more rapid until point 5, mid swing. After mid swing from point 5 to point 1 the

hip flexion slows and the knee flexion becomes gradually more rapid until heel strike at point 1. In late swing the hip reaches its maximum flexion and begins to move in an extension direction.

This interaction between the knee and the hip joints gives valuable information not only on the co-ordination of the two joints, but also on the smoothness of the transition between the phases of the gait cycle.

Hershler and Milner (1980) discussed the use of visual inspection and quantification of single and multiple loops. Single loops represent a single gait cycle, whereas multiple loops represent many gait cycles. Charteris and Taves (1978) used multiple loop angle–angle diagrams as a measure of the repeatability of knee and hip motion during habituation during treadmill walking, this proved to be a very useful measure for whether a subject had reached a steady state gait pattern. Hershler and Milner (1980) stated that the visual inspection of single loops gives a clinically acceptable representation of the simultaneous movement of two joints. By using this technique various gait patterns may be characterized by the shape of the loop and described with respect to function. Although visual inspection is useful, single angle–angle loops may also be quantified. Parameters that may be obtained from these diagrams included: the ranges of motion of the two joints, the area contained within the loop, the length of the perimeter of the loop, and the position of the centroid of the loop.

Single loop studies are useful; however, they only represent one gait cycle and do not give any information about the repeatability of the movement pattern. To study the repeatability of a gait pattern multiple loops may be studied. These allow a visual impression of the repeatability of the gait pattern. However, multiple loop diagrams can become confusing with multiple traces running over one another. Sidway et al (1995) demonstrated that it was possible to quantify the variability contained within angle–angle diagrams using correlation analysis. The mean and standard deviations of multiple loops are presented in Figure 4.21.

Angle–angle diagrams have been used in the assessment of various gait patterns including cerebral palsy (Hershler & Milner 1980, De Bruin et al 1982, Rine et al 1992, Drezner et al 1994) and above knee amputees (Hershler & Milner 1980). These investigations used electrogoniometers

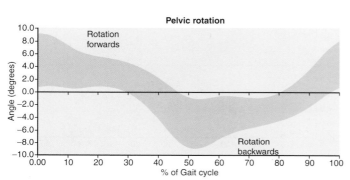

Figure 4.20   Motion of the pelvis in the transverse plane (pelvic rotation)

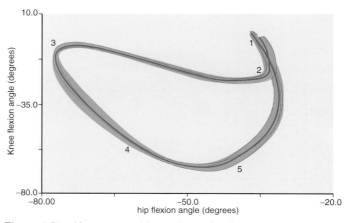

Figure 4.21   Knee versus hip angle–angle diagram

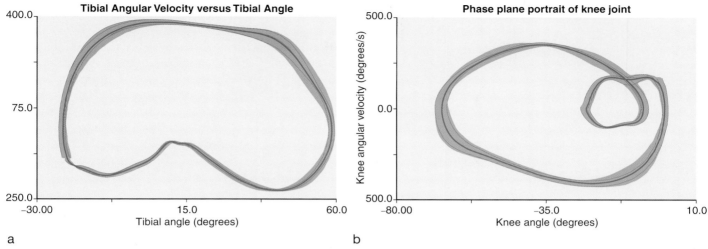

Figure 4.22   (a) Shank angular velocity versus shank angle and (b) phase plane portrait of knee joint

to study the angle–angle patterns for the knee and hip joints, and demonstrated the value of angle–angle diagrams in the description and quantification of gait patterns within clinical assessment.

Hurley et al (1990) used a similar technique to hip versus knee angle–angle plots to study the contralateral limb in below-knee amputee gait. Hurley and co-workers used angle–angle plots of thigh segment angle with leg inclination which the authors felt would give them a better depiction of the action of the lower limbs during walking.

4.3.8 Angle versus angular velocity diagrams (phase plane portraits)

Craik and Oatis (1995) described a technique to show the behaviour of the shank during walking. They isolated two variables that capture the state of the system at any one time and then studied how these change over time, the two variables they selected were shank angular displacement and shank angular velocity (Fig. 4.22a). The choice of variables is considerable within movement analysis and the selection of variables depends, in part, on the questions being asked of the data.

Hurmuzlu et al (1994) stated that standard plots of joint angular displacements against time, although useful, do not provide sufficient information about the dynamics of joints. Hurmuzlu et al described joint angular velocity versus joint angular displacement as 'phase plane portraits' and reported on results from the hip, knee and angle joints during normal walking (Fig. 4.22b). The authors proposed that the use of such plots would give a greater understanding of dynamic changes of joint motion. Hurmuzlu and co-workers went on to use these plots to study the kinematics and dynamic stability of the locomotion of post-polio patients (Hurmuzlu et al 1996).

Sojka et al (1995) used hip versus knee angle–angle graphs and knee angular velocity versus knee angle graphs to assess the knee function in children with cerebral palsy who exhibit genu recurvatum. Sojka and co-workers described the knee angular velocity versus knee angle graphs as knee phase plane

plots. There is little published work using phase plane plots or portraits; however, the use of such plots has been shown to give important information about the co-ordination and control of movement of a particular joint.

Other activities that have been studied using this technique include lifting techniques. Burgess-Limerick et al (1993) studied the co-ordination of joints during lifting. The authors stated 'The use of angular position and velocity information to describe joint movement on a phase plane is advantageous on theoretical grounds because the afferent information available from muscle receptors is effectively in terms of joint position and velocity.'

Summary: Motion and joint motion

- Temporal and spatial parameters of gait relate to the foot contact times and distances, and are two of the simplest measures that can be taken. Despite this they can yield very useful data in clinical assessment and may be used to monitor change during treatment and rehabilitation programmes.
- The movement patterns of all the joints of the lower limb occur in all three planes during walking. Although this makes the clinical assessment of individual patient's gait difficult, it is possible to isolate the different movement patterns of the different joints and describe their movement in relation to function.
- Using new techniques it is now possible to break the foot down into three separate segments. This allows us to consider the movement patterns of each foot segment separately and describe them in relation to function.
- There are several different methods of graphing the movement patterns of the lower limb and pelvis. Angle-versus-time graphs are the most common; however, some, such as angle–angle diagrams, allow the interaction between joints to be described, whereas angle–angular velocity graphs can be used to consider the relationship between joint position and control.

Work, Energy and Power

Chapter 5

Jim Richards

This chapter covers the concepts of linear and angular work energy and power, and how these can be determined from force and movement data. It also demonstrates the concept that angular work and power can be used to analyse the action of muscles during gait.

Chapter 5: Aim
To consider the concepts of work, energy and power, and how these relate to muscle function.

Chapter 5: Objectives
- To explain the differences between angular and linear work and power
- To calculate linear and angular work and power
- To describe how linear power may be found during the vertical jump test
- To explain which factors are important in the assessment of muscle and joint power
- To interpret and explain the interaction between moments, angular velocity and power during gait
- To explain what is meant by body segment energies and how they may be used.

5.1 Linear work, energy and power

5.1.1 Linear work

Work is a product of a force applied to a body and the displacement of the body in the direction of the applied force (Fig. 5.1). This does not refer to the muscular or mental effort. Work is basically a force overcoming a resistance and moving an object through a distance. If, for example, an object is lifted from the floor to the top of a table, work is done in overcoming the downward force of gravity. On the other hand, if a constantly acting force does not produce motion, no work is performed. Holding a book steadily at arm's length, for example, does not involve any work, irrespective of the apparent effort required

Work = Force × Displacement

W = Fs

Units of work

The units of work may be described in terms of the force multiplied by the displacement (newton × m or Nm).

However, work is usually considered in Joule (J). There is an easily defined link between these two units with one Joule of work being equal to a Force of 1 N pushing an object 1 m. Therefore, in this case Nm and Joule may be used interchangeably.

Differences between work and torque

Work is not the same as turning moments even though they both have the same units of Nm. In the case of turning moments the force acts perpendicular to the distance. In the case of work the force acts in the same direction as the displacement.

Work is also done as an object accelerates

From Newton's second law the relationship between an object's mass, its acceleration and the applied force F is F = ma. However, Work = Force × Displacement.

Therefore:

Work = Mass × Acceleration × Displacement

Work = m × a × s

Positive and negative work

Positive work is said to be done when a force acts parallel to the movement in the direction of the movement. Negative work is said to be done when a force acts parallel to the movement in the opposite direction to the movement.

Linear power

Power is the rate of performing work or transferring energy. Work is equal to the force applied to move an object multiplied by the distance the object travels. Power measures how quickly the work is done:

$$\text{Power} = \frac{\text{Work done}}{\text{Time taken}}$$

e.g. suppose a person wants to push a heavy box across a room. To overcome the friction between the bottom of the box and the floor, the person must apply force to the box to keep it moving.

Now suppose the person pushes the box from one end of the room to the other in 10 s, then pushes the box back to its original position in 5 s. In each trip across the room, the force applied and the distance the box is moved is the same, so the work done in each case is the same. But the second time the box is pushed across the room the person has to

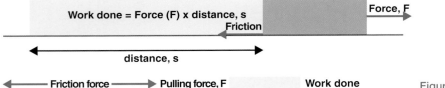

Figure 5.1   Linear work

apply more power than in the first trip because the same amount of work is done in 5 s rather than 10 s.

The units of Power are Joule per Second (J/s) or Watt (W).

5.1.2 Linear energy

While work is done on a body, there is a transfer of energy to the body and so work can be said to be energy in transit. Energy has the same units as work, as the work done produces a change in energy Joule (J). Energy is the capacity of matter to perform work as the result of its motion or its position in relation to forces acting on it. Energy related to position is potential energy and energy associated with motion is known as kinetic energy. If we consider a swinging pendulum, this has a maximum potential energy at the terminal points; at all intermediate positions it has both kinetic and potential energy in varying proportions.

Energy can be transformed, but it cannot be created or destroyed. In the process of transformation either kinetic or potential energy may be lost or gained, but the sum total of the two remains always the same. Examples of this are: if an object suspended from a cord has potential energy due to its position, if the cord is cut then the object will perform work in the process of falling; if a gun is fired the potential (chemical) energy of the gunpowder is transformed into the kinetic energy of the moving projectile. All forms of energy tend to be transformed into heat, which is the most transient form of energy.

5.1.3 Potential energy

This is stored energy possessed by a system as a result of the relative positions of the components of that system. For example, if a ball is held above the ground, the system comprising the ball and the earth has a certain amount of potential energy; lifting the ball higher increases the amount of potential energy the system possesses.

$$PE = Mass \times Gravity \times Height$$

$$PE = mgh$$

Work is needed to give a system potential energy. It takes effort to lift a ball off the ground. The amount of potential energy a system possesses is equal to the work done on the system. Potential energy also can be transformed into other forms of energy. For example, when a ball is held above the ground and released, the potential energy is transformed into kinetic energy.

5.1.4 Kinetic energy

This is energy possessed by an object, resulting from the motion of that object is called kinetic energy. The magnitude

of the kinetic energy depends on both the mass and the speed of the object according to the equation:

$$KE = \frac{1}{2} mv^2$$

The relationships between kinetic and potential energy can be illustrated by the lifting and dropping of an object.

5.2 The relationship between force, impulse and power

5.2.1 The vertical jump test

The vertical jump test, or Sargeant Jump, involves a subject performing a jump from an initially static position. This is usually performed next to a wall, which allows an initial height measurement of the point the fingertips can reach with the feet flat on the ground. The athlete then stands slightly away from the wall, and jumps vertically as high as possible using both arms and legs to assist in projecting the body upwards. At the highest point the subject touches or marks the wall, the difference in distance between the static reach height and the jump height is the score. This score gives a useful indication of the levels of explosive muscular power production of the subject. This is used in activities often described as stretch shortening cycle movements, where muscles are first loading eccentrically to produce a larger concentric power production.

Variations of this test have been used in various sporting activities including: basketball, volleyball, netball and rugby. The vertical jump test has also been used in the understanding of the motor development process and the functional performance in the injured athlete. However, the simple measure of the height jumped does not necessarily tell us all that we need to know about power production. Section 5.6: Joint power during the vertical jump test, shows how the power production from the individual joints may be found during the vertical jump test. But first we will consider what information may be drawn from force platforms alone when performing a vertical jump test to enable objective measurements of performance.

5.2.2 Maximum force at take off and landing

The values for maximum take-off force and landing force may be measured straight from the force–time graph (Fig. 5.2).

5.2.3 Velocity during the jump

The instantaneous velocity of the body during the vertical jump may be identified by finding the area under the

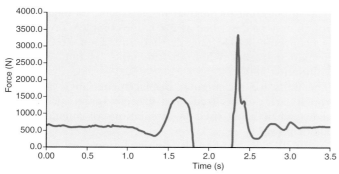

Figure 5.2   Ground reaction forces during vertical jump

force-versus-time graph. The area under the force-versus-time graph gives us the impulse:

Impulse = Mass × Velocity (v)

The area under the force-versus-time graph is found after each time division allowing the instantaneous velocity to be found, see integration. To find the velocity we must first subtract body weight from the original force data. This gives us a force trace that now dips below zero. From:

F = m a

we can say:

$$F = m \frac{(v-u)}{t}$$

So:

Ft = m (v−u)

where u is the initial velocity of the jump (which must be zero as the person has yet to start moving) so:

Ft = m v

We want to find v, and we know the mass because the mass is the body weight divided by 9.81 m/s² so:

$$\frac{Ft}{m} = v$$

So how do we find velocity from these data? We first work out the area of each trapezium for each time slice of the force-versus-time curve. Then to find the velocity we work out a rolling sum of the area under the graph, see section 3.5 integration and the area beneath data curves. This tells us the area under the graph up to a particular time; this will be the instantaneous velocity (Fig. 5.3)!

5.2.4 Calculation of height jumped from force plate data

This may be found by measuring the total time of flight. The time may be measured off the graph (the time when the person is off the ground the force will be zero). The height jumped may also be calculated from the take-off velocity (see above) again using the equations of motion. The instantaneous displacement of the centre of mass of the subject may be found by integrating the velocity:

$$Velocity = \frac{Displacement}{Time}$$

So:

Displacement (s) = Velocity × Time

(or the area under the velocity–time graph – the integral of velocity)

So how can we find displacement from these data?
Again we first work out the area of each trapezium for each time slice of the velocity-versus-time curve. Then to find the displacement we work out a rolling sum of the area under the graph. This tells us the area under the graph up to a particular time; this will be the instantaneous displacement (Fig. 5.4)!

5.2.5 Calculation of power from force plate data

If the instantaneous velocity has been found as in section 5.2.3 and the force is known from the force platform readings, then instantaneous power may also be found:

$$Power = \frac{Work\ done}{Time}$$

However, the work done may be expressed as:

Work = Force × Displacement

Work = F × s

Therefore, power may be express as:

$$Power = \frac{F \times s}{t}$$

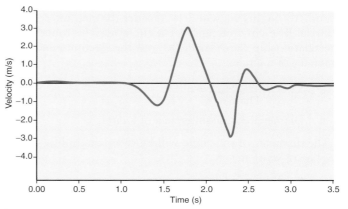

Figure 5.3   Velocity during vertical jump

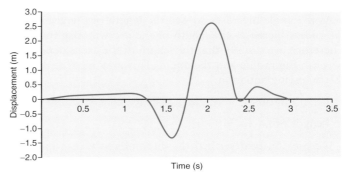

Figure 5.4   Displacement during vertical jump

And velocity may be expressed as:

$$\text{Velocity} = \frac{\text{Displacement}}{\text{Time}}$$

$$\text{Velocity} = \frac{s}{t}$$

Therefore, power may be found by multiplying force and velocity (Fig. 5.5):

$$\text{Power} = F \times v$$

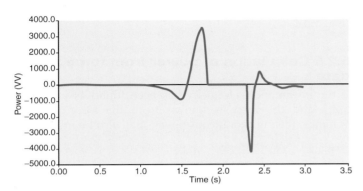

Figure 5.5   Power during vertical jump

5.3 Angular work, energy and power

5.3.1 Angular work

Length of an arc
To find the angular work, the length of an arc must first be found. To do this we will first consider the circumference of a circle. The circumference of a circle may be found from the relationship between Pi (π) and the circumference and diameter of a circle.

$$\pi = \frac{\text{Circumference of a circle}}{\text{Diameter}}$$

$$\pi \times \text{Diameter} = \text{Circumference of a circle}$$

The diameter of the circle will be twice the radius so this may be re-written:

$$2 \times \pi \times \text{Radius} = \text{Circumference}$$

However, the circumference may also be considered as the length of a very large arc. If we consider two arcs with different radii and different angles, these will produce different lengths of arc (Fig. 5.6).

As the angle increases so will the length of the arc and as the radius increases the length of the arc will also increase. Therefore, we can say that the length of the arc is dependent on both the radius and the angle. This may be described by the following equation:

$$\text{Length of an arc} = \text{Angular displacement} \times \text{Radius}$$

$$\text{Length of an arc} = \theta \times r$$

We previously described the circumference of a circle as the length of a very large arc. Where:

$$\text{Circumference} = 2 \times \pi \times \text{Radius}$$

This implies that the angular displacement, or angle moved through may be described as $2 \times \pi$ one complete revolution. π is a constant, 3.1415926......, therefore, $2 \times \pi = 6.2831852$ approximately. But what are the units as one complete revolution is 360°!

The units for the angular displacement (angle travelled through) are radians (rad) and θ needs to be specified in radians when being used in calculations of angular work done or power.

So if 6.2831852 radians is one revolution (360°), then:

$$1 \text{ Radian} = \frac{360}{6.2831852}$$

$$1 \text{ Radian} = 57.295°$$

This is often rounded to 57.3°.

The need to use radians can be demonstrated by considering a leg raise activity. If a subject has a leg length of 1 m, and they move their leg through 90°, how far has their foot moved the length of the arc?

If we use degrees in this calculation:

$$\text{Length of an arc} = \theta \times r$$

$$\text{Length of an arc} = 90 \times 1$$

$$\text{Length of an arc} = 90 \text{ m}$$

This is clearly **not** the case; however, if we consider the angle 90° in radians we get 1.57 radians.

$$\text{Length of an arc} = \theta \times r$$

$$\text{Length of an arc} = 1.57 \times 1$$

$$\text{Length of an arc} = 1.57 \text{ m}$$

This gives us the correct length of arc, or displacement through which the foot is moved. This can **only** be found if we use radians.

Calculation of angular work
The definition for 'work done' as given earlier is:

$$\text{Work} = \text{Force} \times \text{Distance moved}$$

However, when we are considering angular work, the distance moved is the distance the force is moved through an arc, and the length of the arc is $r\,\theta$, therefore (Fig. 5.7):

$$\text{Work} = \text{Force} \times r \times \theta$$

However:

$$\text{Force} \times r = \text{Moment (M)}$$

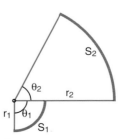

Figure 5.6   Lengths of arc

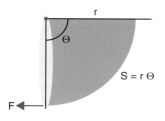

Figure 5.7   Angular work

Therefore:

Work = Moment (M) × θ

Work = M × θ

where θ is in radians (rad).

5.3.2 Angular power

If we consider the definition for power from earlier:

$$Power = \frac{Work\ done}{Time\ taken}$$

$$Power = \frac{Force \times \theta \times r}{t}$$

or

$$Power = \frac{Turning\ moment\ (M) \times \theta}{Time\ taken}$$

$$Power = \frac{M \times \theta}{t}$$

however:

$$\omega = \frac{\theta}{t}$$

so:

$$Power = M\ \omega$$

where ω is in radian/s (rad/s).

Therefore, to study power we need to consider the net moments about a joint and the angular velocity of that joint. Power may be positive and negative. In the following section a positive power relates to power generation and a negative power-to-power absorption.

5.4 The relationship between moments, angular velocity and joint power during normal gait

5.4.1 Joint moments, velocity and power during normal gait

Inverse dynamics combines the study of kinetics and kinematics. This may be used to calculate moments about joints and the angular velocity of joints. Moment calculations are covered in Chapter 2: Forces, moments and muscles; however, these calculations assume that the body segments are not accelerating. If the body segments are

accelerating then the inertial effects have to be taken into consideration in the calculation of turning moments and power about joints (see Chapter 6: Inverse dynamics theory). We will now consider the relationship between joint moments, angular velocity, and the power absorption and generation about the ankle, knee and hip joints during normal walking.

5.4.2 Typical ankle moments during normal gait

At heel strike the ground reaction force passes very close to the ankle joint centre, therefore, producing a very small moment. In some cases this will be behind the ankle joint giving rise to a plantarflexion moment. After heel strike the ground reaction force moves in front of the ankle joint producing a dorsiflexion moment. This increases as the force moves under the metatarsal heads and the force increases during push off (Fig. 5.8).

5.4.3 Typical knee moments during normal gait

At heel strike the ground reaction force initially passes anterior to the knee joint, giving rise to an extension moment. The ground reaction force then quickly passes behind the knee joint causing a flexion moment. After mid stance the force passes in front of the knee again until toe off. During swing phase, the knee also has significant moments due to the acceleration and deceleration of the foot and tibia (Fig. 5.9).

5.4.4 Typical hip moments during normal gait

At heel strike the ground reaction force passes quite far anterior to the hip joint producing a peak flexion moment. After heel strike the ground reaction force still passes anterior to the hip; however, the distance from the force to the hip is much reduced. After mid stance the force passes posterior to the hip giving rise to an extension moment. As with the knee there are significant moments during swing phase due to the acceleration and deceleration of the lower limb (Fig. 5.10).

5.4.5 Joint angular velocity during normal gait

Careful note

Angular velocity may be used to find the power; however, the values below must first be converted into rad/s, i.e. divide by 57.3 (the number of degrees in 1 radian).

5.4.6 Ankle angular velocity

At heel strike the ankle plantarflexes to foot flat, this is controlled by an eccentric contraction of the muscle in the anterior compartment of the ankle joint. After this point the tibia then begins to move over the ankle joint, again this is controlled by an eccentric contraction; however, this time by the posterior compartment. At 50% of the gait cycle the heel begins to lift and the ankle rapidly plantarflexes at up to 250°/s (4.4 rad/s), this is produced by a concentric contraction of the posterior group, and provides propulsion for the body (see power graphs, section 5.4.9) (Fig. 5.11).

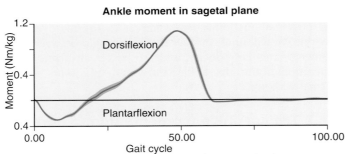

Figure 5.8   Typical ankle moments during normal gait

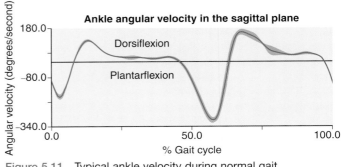

Figure 5.11   Typical ankle velocity during normal gait

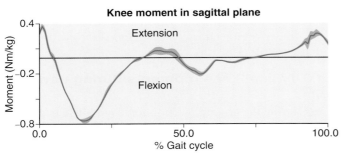

Figure 5.9   Typical knee moments during normal gait

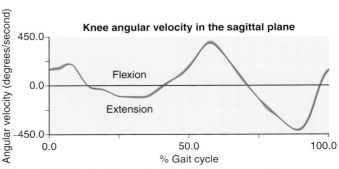

Figure 5.12   Typical knee velocity during normal gait

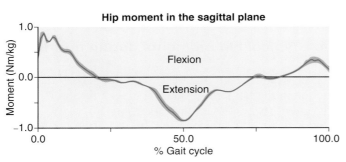

Figure 5.10   Typical hip moments during normal gait

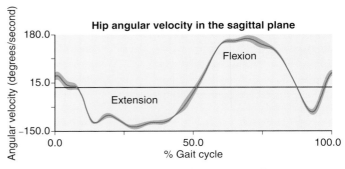

Figure 5.13   Typical hip velocity during normal gait

5.4.7 Knee angular velocity

At heel strike the knee is already flexing. During the initial loading of the foot the knee flexion peaks at 150–200°/s. The knee flexion velocity slows as the knee reaches its initial peak flexion. The thigh now moves over the tibia (at the same time the tibia moves over the ankle joint), this causes an extension velocity of between 80 and 100°/s. At 50% of the gait cycle the heel begins to lift and the knee starts flexing again. At toe off the knee is flexing at a rate of 300–350°/s, after this point the knee velocity slows as the knee reaches its maximum flexion. After the point of maximum knee flexion the knee then starts to extend rapidly at a rate of 400–450°/s (Fig. 5.12).

5.4.8 Hip angular velocity

The hip flexion velocity graph is far simpler. At heel strike the hip is flexed and stationary, it then moves into extension as the body moves over the limb. At 50% of the gait cycle the heel lifts pushing the thigh forwards, which starts the hip flexion velocity. The hip extension velocity is slower than its flexion velocity, this indicates a controlled movement over the stance limb followed by a more rapid flexion velocity to move the leg forwards to take a step (Fig. 5.13).

5.4.9 Joint power during normal gait

The results below are found by combining the joint moments (Nm or Nm/kg) and joint angular velocities (rad/s). Positive values show power generation, negative values show power absorption. It is also sometimes beneficial to consider whether the muscle action is either concentric or eccentric. Concentric activity is associated with power development, whereas eccentric activity is associated with power absorption. These graphs can be hard to interpret, however, if you consider whether the moments are trying to flex or extend and what movements are occurring at each time. The examples below consider the power absorption and generation of the

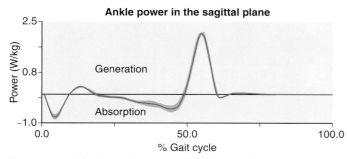

Figure 5.14   Typical ankle power during normal gait

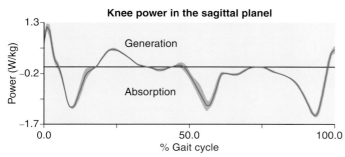

Figure 5.15   Typical knee power during normal gait

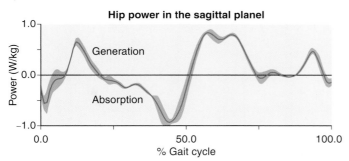

Figure 5.16   Typical hip power during normal gait

5.4.11 Knee power

At heel strike the knee shows power generation, this is due to the ground reaction force being in front of the knee, therefore, producing an extension moment while the knee is flexing. This initial power generation or concentric contraction of the hamstrings ensures that the knee does, indeed, flex at heel strike, rather than moving into a hyper-extended position. After this point the ground reaction force falls behind the knee creating a flexion moment whilst the knee is flexing, therefore, the quadriceps will be working eccentrically to act as a shock absorber. The knee then shows power generation at approximately 20% of the gait cycle. At this point the ground reaction force is behind the knee and, therefore, this relates to the quadriceps acting concentrically pulling the femur over the tibia. As the knee extends the ground reaction force passes through the knee joint producing no moment and, therefore, little or no power is generated or absorbed. It is interesting to note the involvement of the knee during push off at 50–60% of the gait cycle. During this time the ground reaction force falls behind the knee creating a flexion moment, but at this time the knee is flexing and, therefore, power is being absorbed and not generated. So the knee has little or no involvement in the power production during push off (Fig. 5.15).

5.4.12 Hip power

At heel strike the hip shows power absorption at heel strike, this is due to the hip having a small period of flexion velocity coupled with a flexion moment. The hip then extends to start to move the body over the stance limb whilst the moment is still trying to flex the hip; this is achieved by power generation by the hip extensors. At approximately 25% of the gait cycle the moment passes behind the hip changing from a flexion moment to an extension moment; however, the hip is still extending and this relates to power absorption or eccentric control of the hip flexors as the body moves over the stance limb. After 50% of the gait cycle the hip reaches its maximum extended position, after this point there is a rapid power generation during push off. This power generation is due to the ground reaction force creating an extension moment while the hip changes from an extending angular velocity to a flexing angular velocity and, therefore, contributes to power production during push off (Fig. 5.16).

5.5 Motion and power during running

5.5.1 Ankle joint

At foot strike the ankle is in slight dorsiflexion, it then becomes progressively more dorsiflexed and reaches a peak dorsiflexion velocity of 400°/s. During this time the calf muscles are eccentrically contracting and act as a shock absorber. The tibia then moves over the foot and at the same time the ankle undergoes rapid plantar flexion at up to 650°/s; during this time the ankle produces it peak power of 1150 W to maintain forward momentum and to propel the subject forwards and upwards. Therefore the calf muscles concentrically contracting to provide this power to accelerate the subject. During swing the subject dorsiflexes

ankle, knee and hip joints during walking. Power absorption (eccentric activity) is shown as negative and power generation (concentric activity) is positive.

5.4.10 Ankle power

If the ankle has a dorsiflexion velocity and the moment is dorsiflexing about the ankle joint, then the posterior muscles must be working eccentrically and absorbing power. If the ankle has a plantarflexion velocity and a dorsiflexion moment, then the posterior muscles must be working concentrically and, therefore, generating power.

At heel strike there is a plantarflexion moment and angular velocity; therefore, at heel strike there is eccentric power absorption from the dorsiflexors. This is followed by an eccentric power absorption by the plantarflexors as the body moves forwards over the foot. During push off there is a dorsiflexion moment and a plantarflexion velocity; therefore, power is generated by concentric activity of the plantarflexors (Fig. 5.14).

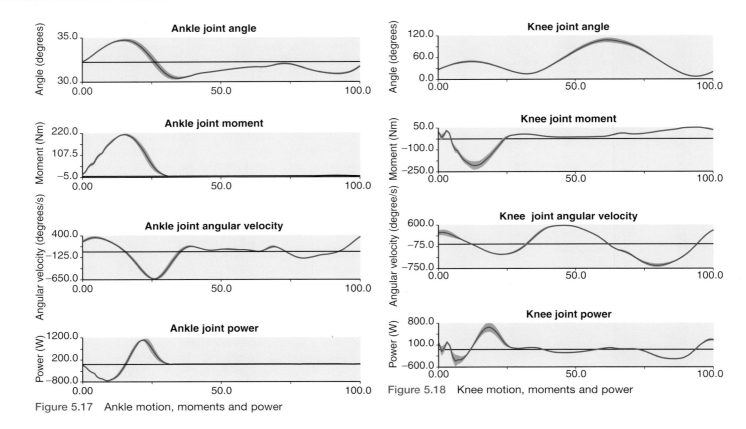

Figure 5.17   Ankle motion, moments and power

Figure 5.18   Knee motion, moments and power

the ankle joint to ensure foot clearance and prepares for the next foot strike (Fig. 5.17).

5.5.2 Knee joint

The knee is flexed at foot strike and then continues to flex to absorb the shock of the impact up to 50°. During this time the knee has a peak power absorption of 500 W. The knee then starts to extend rapidly at up to 550°/s to advance the body over the stance limb and to produce power of up to 700 W. The peak power production of the knee occurs fractionally earlier than that of the ankle and is less than half that produced by the ankle. The knee reaches maximum extension at toe off at 30% of the gait cycle; at this point the knee angular velocity is zero. The knee then flexes rapidly to aid foot clearance up to 110°, this also has the effect of reducing the inertial moment required to accelerate the leg forwards. The knee then extends rapidly to prepare for the next foot strike at 100% of the gait cycle (Fig. 5.18).

5.5.3 Hip joint motion

The hip is flexed at foot strike and moves into extension at 350°/s as the body moves over the stance limb, this also has a significant role in the power production. The peak power production of the hip reaches 450 W, and this occurs earlier than the knee power production, which in turn is fractionally earlier than the ankle power production. This indicates a power delivery mechanism working proximal to distal. After toe off the hip flexes at approximately 400°/s, with a total range of motion of the hip of 45° during swing phase. During swing phase there is still significant power

production to accelerate the limb forwards to the next foot strike (Fig. 5.19).

5.6 Joint power during the vertical jump test

We have previously looked at how power may be found by just studying the ground reaction forces and using the concepts of impulse and momentum. However, this does not tell us the individual contributions of the different joints during the jump. As with walking and jogging we need to consider the moment and velocity pattern of each joint separately.

5.6.1 Preparation and propulsion

The motion of the ankle and knee show the knee and the ankle joint flexing and dorsiflexing as the subject moves into the crouched position. The knee and ankle then rapidly extend and plantarflex together generating the power to take off. During this phase the knee angular velocity is approximately 600°/s, slightly less than that of the ankle joint, which peaks at approximately 700°/s plantarflexion. The knee produces 550 W of power during propulsion similar to that of the ankle at 600 W, with the hip producing the least power with 390 W. The peak power production of the hip occurs fractionally earlier than that of the knee, which in turn is fractionally earlier than the peak ankle power production. This indicates a power delivery mechanism working proximal to distal, which is also seen during running.

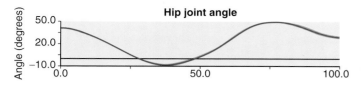

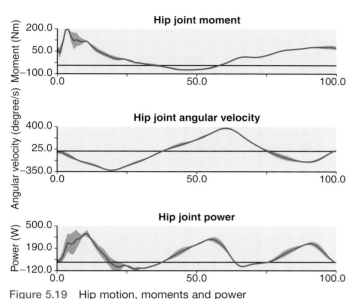

Figure 5.19   Hip motion, moments and power

than the knee angular velocity, in the order of 500°/s. The ankle has the largest power absorption, in the order of 1500 W, more than twice that of the knee at approximately 700 W, and the hip has the smallest power absorption, which is under 200 W (Fig. 5.20a, b).

5.7 How to find energies involved in moving body segments

5.7.1 Body segment energies

The energy of each body segment consists of three components: potential energy, and translational and rotational kinetic energy. Once the anthropometric data have been estimated, and angular and linear displacements and velocities found, the segment energies can be calculated. We will now consider how the different segment energies may be found. This includes:

1. Translational kinetic energy of body segment
2. Rotational kinetic energy of body segment
3. Potential energy of body segment
4. Total energy of body segment.

5.7.2 Calculation of translational kinetic energy

Initially linear displacements and velocities can be found for each joint in the three directions. From this the velocity of the centre of mass of a body segment in a given direction may be found (Fig. 5.21).

5.7.3 Calculation of rotational kinetic energy

If an object rotates with a constant angular velocity (ω) then any position away from the point of rotation will have both a linear and angular velocity, one such position is the radius of gyration, k, (see section 6.2.2). As a result the linear velocity of the radius of gyration, k, may be found by:

5.6.2 Flight

During flight the knee remains slightly flexed and the ankle remains plantarflexed in preparation for landing.

5.6.3 Landing

During landing the knee and ankle undergo rapid flexion and dorsiflexion to absorb the shock of the impact. Again the ankle angular velocity, in the order of 1000°/s, is greater

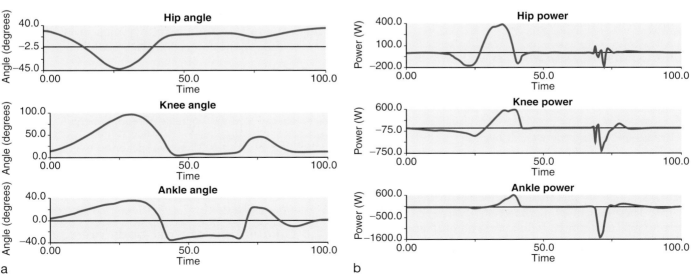

Figure 5.20   (a) Graphs of the movement of the hip, knee and ankle and (b) graphs of the moments and power of the hip, knee and ankle

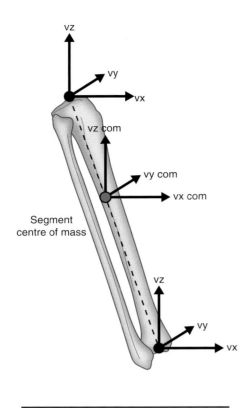

Figure 5.21 Calculation of translational kinetic energy: translational kinetic energy = $\frac{1}{2} m (v_{x\,com}^2 + v_{y\,com}^2 + v_{z\,com}^2)$

Where:

$$v = \omega k$$

linear kinetic energy is given by:

$$\text{Kinetic Energy} = \frac{1}{2} m v^2$$

Therefore:

$$\text{Rotational kinetic energy} = \frac{1}{2} m (\omega k)^2$$

$$\text{Rotational kinetic energy} = \frac{1}{2} m \omega^2 k^2$$

$$I_{com} = mk^2$$

(see Chapter 6)

$$\text{Rotational kinetic energy} = \frac{1}{2} I \omega^2$$

To find the rotational kinetic energies the angular velocities are calculated for each segment in the xy, xz, and yz planes. Figure 5.22 shows the angular velocities in the xy and xz planes. The moment of inertia of the body segment about the proximal end can be found using anthropometry. From this information the rotational kinetic energy can, therefore, be calculated using the equation below (Fig. 5.22a).

$$\text{Rotational kinetic energy} = \frac{1}{2} I (\omega_{xy}^2 + \omega_{xz}^2 + \omega_{yz}^2)$$

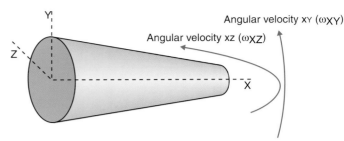

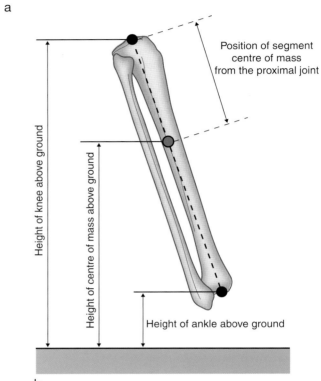

Figure 5.22 (a) Angular velocities in the xy and xz planes and (b) calculation of potential energy = $m g h_{com}$

5.7.4 Calculation of potential energy

The potential energy may be found by finding the location of the centre of mass for a particular segment in relation to a datum in the vertical direction (Fig. 5.22b).

5.7.5 Calculation of total segment energy

The total energy for a given body segment may be calculated from the sum of the translational kinetic energy, rotational kinetic energy, and the segment potential energy.

$$\text{Total energy} = PE + KE_{rotational} + KE_{translational}$$

$$E_{total} = mgh_{com} + \frac{1}{2} I (\omega_{xy}^2 + \omega_{xz}^2 + \omega_{yz}^2)$$
$$+ \frac{1}{2} m (v_x^2 + v_y^2 + v_z^2)$$

5.7.6 Calculation of total body energy and power

Total body energy may simply be found by summing all the total segment energies. The instantaneous body power may be found by finding the rate of change of total body energy.

5.7.7 Body segment energy patterns during normal walking

Segment energies are the mechanical energies involved in the movement of body segments. Cavagna et al (1963) referred to the external work done as that associated with the displacement of the centre of mass of the body. Inman (1966) studied the energy required for human locomotion by considering the ground reaction forces and the kinetic and potential energy of the centre of mass of the body. Inman stated that the centre of gravity of the body rises and falls converting energy from potential to kinetic and back to potential.

Ralston and Lukin (1969) defined 'total external positive work' as work measured by increases in the sum total of the energy levels of the body segments. Ralston and Lukin carried out a study of energy levels of human body segments during level treadmill walking. Ralston and Lukin concluded that the simultaneous measurement of the mechanical energy levels of the principal body segments and the metabolic

expenditure during walking provided a powerful tool for the analysis of human locomotion.

Winter et al (1976) reported further results for the instantaneous energy of body segments during normal walking. This included the total body energy, torso energy and energy of both legs. Winter and co-workers tested normal individuals whilst free walking under laboratory conditions, data were gathered from three strides in five subjects in the sagittal plane, ignoring any movement in the coronal and transverse planes. However, Winter and co-workers did calculate the rotational as well as the translational kinetic energy of each body segment. Pierrynowski et al (1980) also investigated the transfer of mechanical energy within the total body and mechanical efficiency during treadmill walking. Pierrynowski et al (1981) used the same technique to study load carriage using different devices.

The calculation of potential energy differs in different studies. To calculate potential energy a reference height or datum is required, this may either be relative to the ground

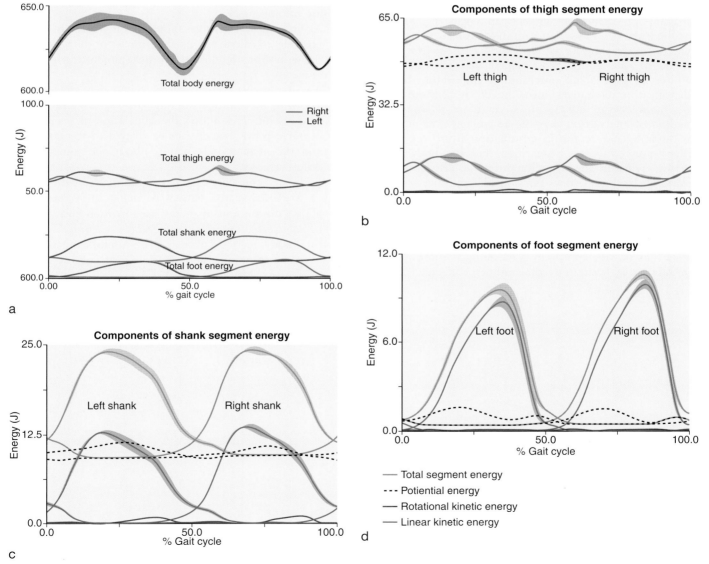

Figure 5.23   (a) Total body segment energy, (b) thigh segment energy, (c) shank segment energy and (d) foot segment energy

(Quanbury et al 1975, Winter et al 1976, Pierrynowski et al 1980) or some other reference height, such as the centre of mass of the body while standing (Ralston & Lukin 1969). Whichever system is used the same pattern of changing energies can be demonstrated. However, the magnitudes of the values will differ.

Winter (1978) reported on the use of energy in the assessment of pathological gait. Winter stated that: 'This technique permits identification of precise sources of high energy cost, locates the period when they occur in the gait cycle, indicates the segment(s) that are responsible and the type of energy involved.' Mansour et al (1982) studied segmental mechanical energy changes of normal and pathological human gait in three dimensions. Subjects included normal individuals and a group of subjects with pathologically impaired gait. In the normal subjects there was a greater exchange between potential and kinetic energy than in pathological gait. The authors also stated that the patterns of energy changed in subjects with pathologically impaired gait, but this varied with the type of pathological disorder. This indicated that body segment energy patterns may give further information as to changes in movement and function of movement in different pathologies (Fig. 5.23a–d).

Olney et al (1986) studied the mechanical energy of walking in ten subjects who had suffered a cerebral vascular accident. The authors commented on the statement by Winter (1978): 'This precision is important: It allows identification of changes in the movement that are required to obtain energy savings. It is therefore a sophisticated method of analysis but has the advantage over many such methods by not requiring information from force plates.' Olney and co-workers identified that the body segment energy approach does have limitations in predicting energy costs. The technique does not consider the energy involved in maintaining a static position by isometric contraction of postural muscles present in slower pathological walking. One muscle group may generate energy at one joint at the same time as it is absorbed at another resulting in metabolic costs that do not appear in a mechanical energy analysis. Despite these limitations the authors concluded that the use of mechanical energy analysis could be valuable in pinpointing specific causes of high energy costs of walking and to assist in determining approaches in treatment. Olney et al (1987) studied the gait of cerebral palsied children with hemiplegia. Olney et al (1989) applied the same technique to the mechanical energy patterns for slow speed walking in normal older adults to determine any differences from slow walking to normal walking speeds.

Other uses of the body segment energy approach include work carried out by Miller and Verstraete (1996) who used the body segment energy approach to calculate the total body energy during gait initiation and determined the number of steps necessary to attain a net mechanical work over one stride of zero to define a steady state gait pattern.

Summary: Work, energy and power

- Work and power depends on the applied force and the distance moved over time. With linear work and power the force and the distance act in a straight line. With angular work and power the force is moved through the arc of movement.

- As linear power involves movement in a straight line it is possible to calculate a useful estimate of the whole body power production during a vertical jump using force data alone.

- Angular power about specific joints may be found by knowing the moments acting and the angular velocity of the joint. This allows the calculation of positive and negative power which can be related to the concentric and eccentric muscle action about the joints during different tasks.

- Body segment energies may be used to assess the amount of work associated with a particular movement. This allows the amount of energy used by each body segment to be assessed separately which may be compared to the total body energy. This can give a useful estimate of the energy expenditure and physiological cost of different movement patterns.

Inverse Dynamics Theory

Jim Richards

This chapter covers the concept of inverse dynamics. This includes the nature of radius of gyration and inertial moments. Examples of how the dynamic joint moments and forces may be found and the consequences of not considering dynamic force are also covered.

Chapter 6: Aim
To consider the concepts of inverse dynamics and the effect on the calculation of dynamic joint moments and forces.

Chapter 6: Objectives
- To explain the differences between the calculation of the I-value for a wheel and a body segment
- To explain why the inertial components need to be found
- To explain what forces and are present and how they can be calculated
- To explain what moments are present and how they can be calculated
- To compare the simple and advanced techniques of finding joint moments and forces.

6.1 Introduction to inverse dynamics

Inverse dynamics combines the study of kinetics and kinematics. This may be used to calculate turning moments about joints and the power absorption–generation about those joints. Moments calculations are covered in Chapter 2: Forces, moments and muscles; however, these calculations assume that the body segments are not accelerating. If the body segments are accelerating then the inertial effects have to be taken into consideration in the calculation of turning moments and power about joints.

6.2 A simple wheel

When the wheel of a car or bike is spun round at a particular angular velocity it will continue spinning forever, providing there is no friction at the bearings. If you try to slow down or speed up the wheel you will need to produce a torque or turning moment with your hands. So far we have considered

an object's mass in terms of the centre of mass, a point where all the mass can be considered to be concentrated (Fig. 6.1a). If this were the case no turning effect would be required to accelerate or decelerate the wheel, i.e. no force would need to be applied.

The above case can clearly not occur as the wheel's mass is not all concentrated at the centre of mass, therefore, there will be a turning moment twisting your arms as you try to accelerate or decelerate the wheel. The wheel's unwillingness to change angular velocity, or deceleration, depends on the distribution of mass around the centre of mass and the mass, m, of the wheel itself. The distribution of mass around the centre of mass of the wheel may be given a value called 'the radius of gyration, k'.

This is a fictitious distribution of the mass around the centre of mass. In the same way the centre of mass assumes that all the object's mass acts at one place for linear motion, the radius of gyration, k, assumes a distribution of the object's mass is a known distance away from the centre of mass for rotational motion. How the radius of gyration is calculated need not concern us here as tables of values for the position of the radius of gyration exist (see Anthropometry in Chapter 2) (Fig. 6.1b).

If the mass is now considered to be concentrated at the radius of gyration then any accelerations of this mass will need to overcome an inertial force (Newton's second law) as the radius of gyration will have a tangential linear acceleration–deceleration. Figure 6.1 shows the inertial force acting at the radius of gyration perpendicular to the radius of the wheel.

6.2.1 Moment of inertia

The wheel has a property called moment of inertia, I, which acts around the centre of mass and depends on the mass of the wheel and the radius of gyration. The moment of inertia describes the wheel's unwillingness to change its angular velocity, ω.

$$I_{com} = m\,k^2$$

where: I_{com} = moment of inertia, m = mass of the object, k = radius of gyration.

Example (part 1)
If a wheel had a mass, m, of 5 kg and a radius of gyration, k, of 0.2 m, then we would have a moment of inertia about its centre of gravity of:

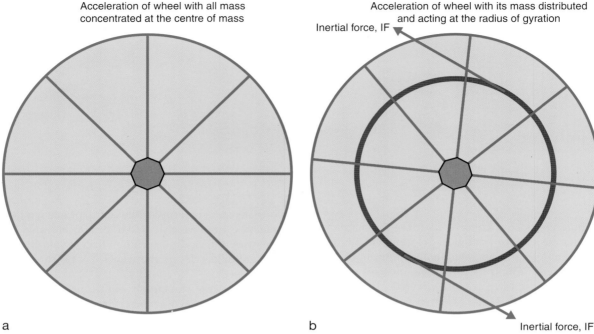

Acceleration of wheel with all mass
concentrated at the centre of mass

Acceleration of wheel with its mass distributed
and acting at the radius of gyration

Inertial force, IF

a

b

Inertial force, IF

Figure 6.1   (a and b) Inertial properties of a wheel

$I_{com} = m\,k^2$

$I_{com} = 5 \times 0.2^2$

$I_{com} = 0.2\,kg/m^2$

As with mass and length, the moment of inertia of an object is fixed and cannot change unless the mass or the dimensions of the object are changed.

6.2.2 Inertial torque or moment

Figure 6.1b shows the inertial forces that have to be overcome if the wheel is to accelerate. These forces are acting at the radius of gyration and will, therefore, produce an inertial torque or moment. This is purely as a result of the change in angular velocity of the wheel. From earlier work we know that:

$M = F \times d$

where: F = the inertial force, **IF**, which depends on the mass, **m**, and the tangential linear acceleration, a; d = the radius of gyration, **k.**

There is a link between linear (tangential) and angular velocity and acceleration. If we consider velocities on the rotating wheel at different positions, for a given constant angular velocity the closer to the centre of the wheel we are the smaller our linear velocity will be, but as we move towards the outer rim of the wheel, or increase the distance from the point of rotation, our linear velocity will increase. The same is true of the relationship between angular acceleration and linear acceleration (Fig. 6.2).

This relationship between the tangential linear velocity and acceleration depends on the magnitude of the angular velocity and acceleration, and the perpendicular distance of

the point being considered away from the point of rotation, **r.** In the example above this is the centre of the wheel; however, this may not always be the case. So the linear velocity and acceleration of a point may be found using the equations below:

$v = \omega\,r$

$a = \alpha\,r$

However, we must be careful as both ω and α MUST be expressed in radian/s and radian/s^2 respectively (see section 5.3.1: Angular work).

So the equation for inertial force becomes:

$IF = mass \times a$

$IF = mass \times \alpha \times k$

As **k** is the distance the mass may be considered to be acting as it is distributed around the centre of mass.

Therefore, the inertial moment must be:

Inertial moment = $IF \times k$

Inertial moment = $mass \times \alpha \times k \times k$

or

Inertial moment = $mass \times \alpha \times k^2$

or

Inertial moment = $mass \times k^2 \times a$

However:

$I_{com} = m\,k^2$

So a simpler way of finding the inertial moment is:

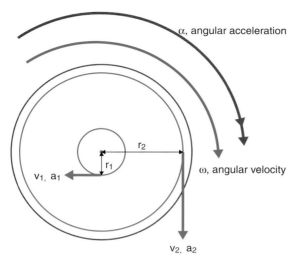

Figure 6.2   Linear and angular velocity and acceleration

Inertial moment = $I_{com}\,\alpha$

Therefore, if the wheel is turning at a constant angular velocity and is then slowed down, or decelerated, it produces a moment that depends on:

1. The distribution of the mass around the centre of mass, k, and the mass, m, of the wheel, which we have called the moment of inertia.
2. The angular acceleration or deceleration of the wheel, α.

The calculation to find the amount of turning moment (inertial torque) derived above is:

$$M = I_{com}\,\alpha$$

where: M = inertia moment as a result of the change in angular velocity, I_{com} = moment of inertia, α = the angular acceleration.

Example (part 2)

So, if a wheel had a mass, m, of 5 kg and a radius of gyration, k, of 0.2 m as before, then it would have a moment of inertia about its centre of gravity of:

$$I_{com} = 0.2\,\text{kg/m}^2$$

If the wheel was initially turning at an angular velocity of 2 rads/s, and was slowed down to 0 rads/s in 1 s, the angular acceleration–deceleration would be:

$$\alpha = 2\ \text{rad/s}^2$$

$$M = I_{com}\,\alpha$$

$$M = 0.2 \times 2$$

$$M = 0.4\,\text{Nm}$$

6.3 Body segments

6.3.1 Rotation about the centre of mass

A wheel turns about its centre of mass, a leg does not. When the point of rotation of an object changes so does its inertial properties (Fig. 6.3).

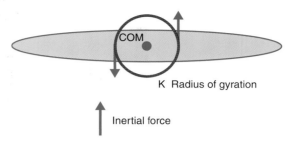

Figure 6.3   Rotation about the centre of mass

If we accelerate a bar about its **centre of mass** to 1 rads/s over a 1 s period, it will produce (or we will have to overcome) an inertial moment and/or unwillingness to change its angular velocity. This will act in the opposite direction to the angular acceleration. We have seen this depends on:

1. the distribution of mass around the centre of mass, k
2. the mass, m, itself
3. the angular acceleration/deceleration.

$$I_{com} = m\,k^2$$

where: I_{com} = moment of inertia, m = mass of the object, k = radius of gyration.

$$M = I_{com}\,\alpha$$

where: M = turning moment as a result of the change in angular velocity, I_{com} = moment of inertia, α = the angular acceleration.

6.3.2 Rotation about one end

If we now rotate the bar about one end, point P, the inertial properties will change. If we consider holding a pool cue at one end and try to rotate it we find it is harder than rotating it about its centre. Therefore, as we accelerate the bar in the two positions to the same angular velocity over the same period of time, a larger resistance would be felt if the bar were rotated about one end. But the only thing that has changed is the distance of the centre of rotation (the point about which you are swinging the bar) to the centre of mass.

In the first case we are rotating the bar about the centre of mass so the distance to the centre of mass is obviously zero, therefore, there will be no tangential linear acceleration of the centre of mass.

However, now we are considering rotating the bar about a point away from the centre of mass, so you now not only have the inertia caused by the distribution of the mass about the centre of mass I_{com}, but also the moment caused by an inertial force at the centre of mass. This inertial force is due to a tangential linear acceleration at the centre of mass, caused by a change in linear velocity of the centre of mass, i.e. an inertial force acting perpendicularly to the bar at the centre of mass as the mass of the bar tries to resist the change in velocity (Fig. 6.4).

If the body segment shown in Figure 6.4 accelerates in a clockwise direction, then there must be an inertial force acting in an opposite anticlockwise direction. As the body segment decelerates the 'acceleration' acts in the opposite

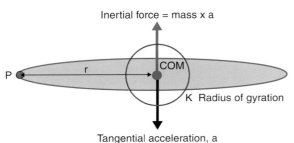

Figure 6.4   Inertial properties when rotation about one end

(clockwise) direction causing the inertial force to also act in the opposite (anticlockwise) direction. In both cases the inertial force will try to resist any change in angular velocity. Figure 6.4 also shows the tangential linear acceleration at the centre of mass, which will always act in the opposite direction to the inertial force. See below:

The inertial force IF = mass (m) × tangential linear acceleration (a)

However, there is a link between linear (tangential) and angular velocity and acceleration:

$v = \omega r$

$a = \alpha r$

So the equation for inertial force becomes:

IF = mass × α × r

where: r = distance from the proximal end to the centre of mass.

This internal force at the centre of mass will produce a moment at the proximal end of the body segment, which can simply be found by force × distance.

M = IF × r   or   M = mass × α × r^2

6.3.3 Total inertial torque

So the total inertial moment can be found by adding:

1. the moment produced by the acceleration of the mass at the radius of gyration, due to rotation about the centre of mass (section 6.3.1)

and

2. the moment produced by the acceleration of the mass at the centre of mass, due to rotation about the proximal end (section 6.3.2).

M = m k^2 α + m r^2 α or   M = (m k^2 + m r^2) α

which can be written:

M = I_{total} α

Therefore, the total moment of inertia or I value when an object is rotated about one end may be found by the equation:

I_{total} = m k^2 + m r^2

To find the I value of a body segment we rely on previous work on anthropometry where the radius of gyration (k) and the distance of the centre of mass from the proximal joint (r) and the mass of the body segment are found by studying the proportions of mass, height of an individual or by measurements of segment lengths.

Therefore, to find the internal moment all we need to do is find I_{total} from anthropometry and multiply the answer by the angular acceleration of the segment making sure we have converted to rads/s^2 first!

6.3.4 Inertial forces and inertial moment

Whenever we move there will be both linear and angular accelerations of our body segments. To be able to accelerate the body segments must overcome inertial forces (forces associated with the segment's unwillingness (inertia) to change linear and angular velocity). These inertial forces act in the opposite direction to the accelerations as they are resisting the object's motion. The inertial forces will affect joint forces and produce inertial moment about proximal joints. Inertial forces should be considered in all directions (x, y, z), and inertial moment should be considered in all planes (xy, xz, yz).

IF = m a

where: IF = inertial force, m = mass of body segment, a = linear acceleration of centre of mass (x, y, z).

IM = (mk^2 + mr^2) α

where: IM = inertial moment, m = mass of body segment, k = radius of gyration, r = position of centre of mass, α = angular acceleration of body segment (xy, xz, yz).

6.3.5 Weight of body segments

Every body segment has a mass (m), which has an acceleration due to gravity. Therefore, every body segment has a weight that will affect the joint forces and the moment about joints. The weight of the body segments will always be acting straight down, therefore, the position of the body segment will have an effect on the magnitude of the moment about the joint and the joint forces. The rotary component of the weight will always be acting perpendicular to the body segment. This force will cause a moment about the proximal joint (see Fig. 2.19):

Weight acting vertically = mg

Rotary component of weight = mg cos θ

where: m = mass of body segment, g = acceleration due to gravity, θ = angle of inclination of body segment from horizontal.

6.3.6 Centripetal force

When an object is moving in a circular path there has to be a force acting on it, otherwise it will move in a purely linear path. This force must be acting towards the centre of rotation. This force is known as the 'centripetal force'. If there is a force and the object has a mass, then from Newton's second law the object must also have an acceleration; again this must be acting towards the centre of rotation and this is known as the 'centripetal acceleration'.

Centripetal acceleration = $\omega^2 r$

where: ω = instantaneous angular velocity (radian/s), r = radius arm (distance from the centre of rotation to the centre of mass of the segment).

If we know the centripetal acceleration and the mass of the object, we can find the centripetal force.

F_{cen} = mass × centripetal acceleration

$F = m \times \omega^2 r$

During normal walking the angular velocity of the shank during swing phase can get up to 400°/s or 7 radians/s. If the centre of mass is 0.2 m from the knee joint and the mass of the shank is 4 kg, then the centripetal force will be 39 N. This force will be acting on the centre of mass and along the body segment, so it will produce no moment directly.

Students note : There has been some debate on whether this should be included in the calculation of joint forces in inverse dynamics. If measurements are taken from the inertial frame, i.e. the linear accelerations and the inertial forces acting on the centre of mass are calculated, this will automatically include centripetal acceleration and centripetal force, so they should not be included twice. However, if joint rotations are being studied exclusively in terms of rotational kinematic variables then centripetal force should be included separately, e.g. calculating the joint forces during an isokinetic exercise where the angular velocity and acceleration are known.

6.4 Joint forces

6.4.1 Terminology

Joint forces may be found by considering all the forces previously mentioned. Each force needs to be considered acting along a sensible frame of reference. In this case we consider the forces acting vertically and horizontally:

> **F y** = vertical joint force
> **F x** = horizontal joint force
> V_{GRF} = vertical ground reaction force
> H_{GRF} = horizontal ground reaction force
> **mg** = weight of body segment acting vertically
> IF_y = **m a_y** = inertial force acting vertically
> IF_x = **m a_x** = inertial force acting horizontally
> θ = angle of inclination of body segment from vertical.

6.4.2 Forces on the foot and ankle (Fig. 6.5)

$$F\,y_{\,ankle} = V_{GRF} - mg_{foot} + IF_y$$

$$F\,x_{\,ankle} = H_{GRF} + IF_x$$

6.4.3 Forces on the shank and knee (Fig. 6.6)

$$F\,y_{\,knee} = F\,y_{\,ankle} - mg_{shank} + IF_y$$

$$F\,x_{\,knee} = F\,x_{\,ankle} + IF_x$$

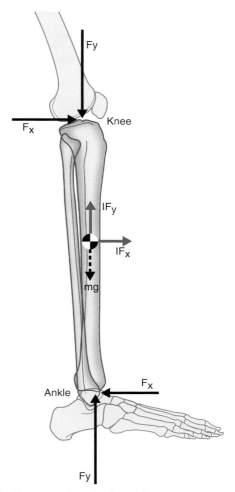

Figure 6.6   Forces on the shank and knee

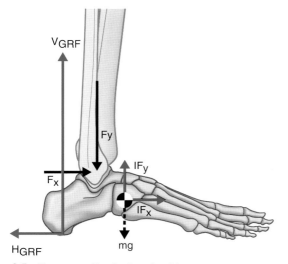

Figure 6.5   Forces on the foot and ankle

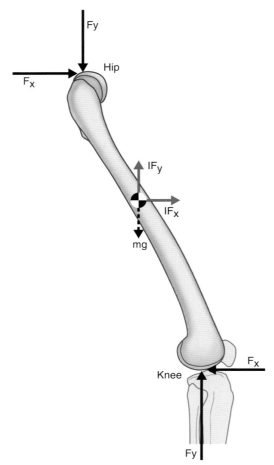

Figure 6.7   Forces on the thigh and hip

6.4.4 Forces on the thigh and hip (see Fig. 6.7)

$$F y_{hip} = F y_{knee} - mg_{thigh} + IF_y$$

$$F x_{hip} = F x_{knee} + IF_x$$

6.5 Joint moments

This requires the consideration of all the parameters mentioned in section 6.4: Joint forces. This leads us to the following general formula. Each component of the total moment can either be clockwise or anticlockwise, therefore, the symbol (±) has been used:

M = moment
V_{GRF} = vertical ground reaction force
H_{GRF} = horizontal ground reaction force
X_{ankle} = horizontal distance from ground to ankle joint centre
Y_{ankle} = vertical distance from ground to ankle joint centre
weight = component of weight acting perpendicular to body segment
X_{com} = distance to the centre of mass in X direction from the proximal joint

com = distance to the centre of mass from the proximal joint
I_{com} = moment of inertia about the centre of mass
α = angular acceleration of body segment
m = mass of body segment
IF = inertial force acting perpendicular to the body segment
segment length = length of body segment
joint force = rotational component of horizontal and vertical joint force.

6.5.1 Ankle joint moment (see Fig. 6.5)

$$M_{xy, ankle} = \pm (V_{GRF} \times X_{ankle}) \pm (H_{GRF} \times Y_{ankle}) \pm (\text{weight of foot} \times X_{com}) \pm I_{com}\, \alpha_{foot} \pm (IF \times com)_{foot}$$

6.5.2 Knee joint moment (see Fig. 6.6)

$$M_{xy, knee} = \pm (\text{joint force at ankle} \times \text{segment length}) \pm M_{ankle} \pm (\text{weight of shank} \times X_{com}) \pm I_{com}\, \alpha_{shank} \pm (IF \times com)_{shank}$$

6.5.3 Hip joint moment (see Fig. 6.7)

$$M_{xy, hip} = \pm (\text{joint force at knee} \times \text{seg length}) \pm M_{knee} \pm (\text{weight of thigh} \times X_{com}) \pm I_{com}\, \alpha_{thigh} \pm (IF \times com)_{thigh}$$

6.6 So why does it have to be so complex? A comparison of the simple and advanced models

6.6.1 Simplified model

If we know the magnitude, the direction and the point of application of the ground reaction force on the force platforms, the position of the force platforms relative to the position of the joints in the sagittal, coronal and transverse plane, then we can calculate the moment about each joint due to this force (see Chapter 2: Forces, moments and muscles) (Fig. 6.8).

If a ground reaction force of 600 N acts at 80° to the horizontal, and the point of application of the force and the distances to the joint centres are known, the moments about the joints can be estimated using the simple techniques covered in previous chapters.

$$M_a = (600 \sin 80 \times 0.02) + (600 \cos 80 \times 0.05)$$

$$M_a = 17\,\text{Nm}$$

$$M_k = -(600 \sin 80 \times 0.08) + (600 \cos 80 \times 0.38)$$

$$M_k = -7.7\,\text{Nm}$$

$$M_h = -(600 \sin 80 \times 0.3) + (600 \cos 80 \times 0.82)$$

$$M_h = -91.6\,\text{Nm}$$

However, this assumes that the body segments are not accelerating and decelerating during the activity.

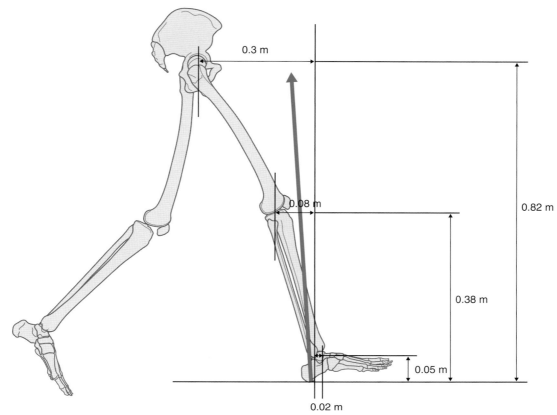

Figure 6.8   Simplified model

6.6.2 Advanced model

Previously we have simplified the method of calculating moment assuming the ground reaction force was the only force producing a moment. Although this is a useful technique to get a quick answer, it will only give an approximate answer, and can underestimate the true value; this is unacceptable for many applications.

Foot segment (Fig. 6.9a)
Acceleration of the com in x direction, $a_x = 0 \, \text{m/s}^2$
Acceleration of the com in y direction, $a_y = 0 \, \text{m/s}^2$
Angular acceleration, $\alpha = 2 \, \text{rad/s}^2$
Mass, m = 1 kg
Distance to centre of mass from joint, $X_{com} = 0.06 \, \text{m}$
Distance to centre of mass from joint, $Y_{com} = 0.03 \, \text{m}$
Moment of inertia, $I_{com} = 0.007 \, \text{kg/m}^2$
Ground reaction force = 600 N at 80°
Distances to ankle joint centre = as above.

Forces from foot to shank (joint forces at ankle)

$$F_{ay} = V_{GRF} - mg + ma_y$$

$$F_{ay} = 600 \sin 80 - 9.8 + 0$$

$$F_{ay} = 581 \, \text{N}$$

$$F_{ax} = -H_{GRF} + ma_x$$

$$F_{ax} = -104 \, \text{N}$$

Moments from foot to shank (moment at ankle)

$$Ma = -I\, \alpha + 600 \sin 80 \times 0.02 + 600 \cos 80 \times 0.05 + mg\, X_{com} + ma\, X_{com} + ma\, Y_{com}$$

$$Ma = -I\, \alpha + 600 \sin 80 \times 0.02 + 600 \cos 80 \times 0.05 + 10 \times 0.06 + 0 + 0 \quad Ma = -0.014 + 11.8 + 5.2 + 0.6$$

$$\mathbf{Ma = 17.6 \, Nm}$$

Shank segment (Fig. 6.9b)
The shank is beginning to move over the ankle joint. Therefore, its centre of mass will have a linear acceleration up and to the right. The angular acceleration will be in the clockwise direction:
Acceleration of the com in x direction, $a_x = 5 \, \text{m/s}^2$
Acceleration of the com in y direction, $a_y = 2 \, \text{m/s}^2$
Angular acceleration, $\alpha = 4 \, \text{rad/s}^2$
Mass, m = 4 kg
Distance to the centre of mass from proximal joint, com = 0.13 m
Moment of inertia, $I_{com} = 0.07 \, \text{kg/m}^2$
Length of body segment, l = 0.345 m
Angle of inclination from vertical, $\theta = 16.8°$.

$$F_{ky} = -mg - ma_y + F_{ay}$$

$$F_{ky} = -40 - 8 + 581$$

$$F_{ky} = 533 \, \text{N}$$

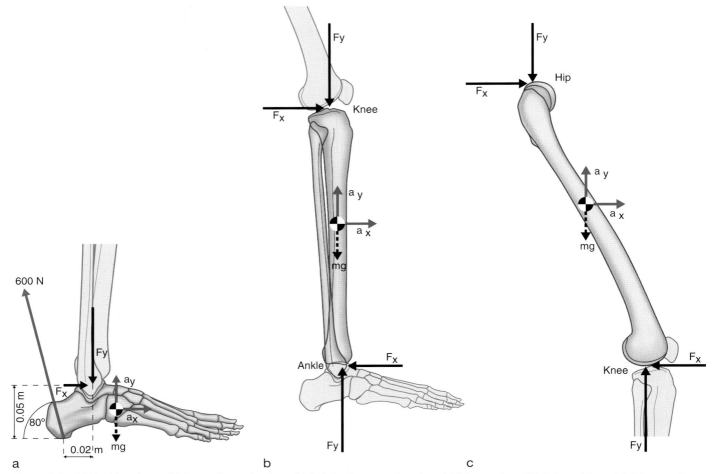

Figure 6.9 (a) Foot segment, (b) forces from shank to thigh (joint forces at knee) and (c) forces from thigh to pelvis or joint forces at hip

$$F_{kx} = -ma_x - F_{ax}$$

$$F_{kx} = -20 - 104$$

$$\mathbf{F_{kx} = -124\,N}$$

Moments from shank to thigh (moment at knee)

$$M_k = M_a - F_{ay}\,l\sin\theta + F_{ax}\,l\cos\theta - I\,\alpha + mg\,com\sin\theta + ma_y\,com\sin\theta + ma_x\,com\cos\theta$$

$$M_k = 17.6 - 581 \times 0.345\sin 16.8 + 104 \times 0.345\cos 16.8 - 0.07 \times 4 + 40 \times 0.13\sin 16.8 + 4 \times 2 \times 0.13\sin 16.8 + 4 \times 5 \times 0.13\cos 16.8 \; M_k = 17.6 - 58 + 34.3 - 0.28 + 1.5 + 0.3 + 2.5$$

$$\mathbf{M_k = -2.08\,Nm}$$

Thigh segment (Fig. 6.9c)

The thigh is beginning to move forward, however, the knee is also flexing. This causes the centre of mass to have a linear acceleration down and to the right. The angular acceleration will be in the clockwise direction:

Acceleration of the com in x direction, $a_x = 3\,m/s^2$
Acceleration of the com in y direction, $a_y = -2\,m/s^2$
Angular acceleration, $\alpha = 2.5\,rad/s^2$
Mass, $m = 6\,kg$

Distance to the centre of mass from proximal joint, com = 0.22 m
Length of body segment, $l = 0.46\,m$
Moment of inertia, $I_{com} = 0.18\,kg/m^2$
Angle of inclination from vertical, $\theta = 26.6°$.

$$F_{hy} = -mg + ma_y + F_{ky}$$

$$F_{hy} = -60 + 6 \times 2 + 533$$

$$\mathbf{F_{hy} = 485\,N}$$

$$F_{hx} = -ma_x - F_{kx}$$

$$F_{hx} = -6 \times 3 - 124$$

$$\mathbf{F_{hx} = -142\,N}$$

Moments from thigh to pelvis (moment at hip)

$$M_h = M_k - F_{ky}\,l\sin\theta + F_{kx}\,l\cos\theta - I\,\alpha + mg\,com\sin\theta + ma_y\,com\sin\theta + ma_x\,com\cos\theta$$

$$M_h = -2.08 - 533 \times 0.46\sin 26.6 + 124 \times 0.46\cos 26.6 - 0.18 \times 2.5 + 60 \times 0.22\sin 26.6 - 6 \times 2 \times 0.22\sin 26.6 + 6 \times 3 \times 0.22\cos 26.6 = 0$$

$$M_h = -2.08 - 109.8 + 51 - 0.45 + 5.9 - 1.18 + 3.54$$

$$\mathbf{M_h = -53.1\,Nm}$$

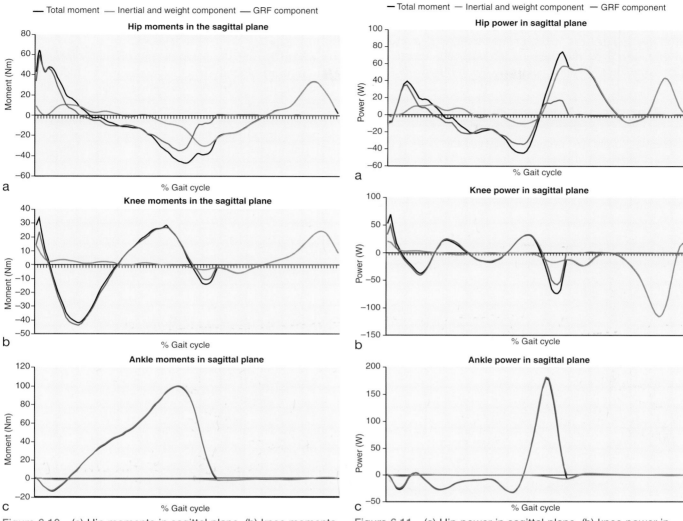

Figure 6.10   (a) Hip moments in sagittal plane, (b) knee moments in sagittal plane and (c) ankle moments in sagittal plane

Figure 6.11   (a) Hip power in sagittal plane, (b) knee power in sagittal plane and (c) ankle power in sagittal plane

6.7 So what effects do the simple and advanced methods have on moments and power calculated during gait?

6.7.1 The effect the simple and advanced methods have on moments

The graphs in Figure 6.10 show the relative effect of the moments caused by the ground reaction force and the inertial and weight components. These demonstrate that the moments about the ankle joint are not significantly affected by the inertia and the weight of the distal segment, the foot. This is not surprising as the mass, centre of mass and radius of gyration are comparably small and, therefore, have a minimal effect.

With the moments about the knee we begin to see some differences with the introduction of the inertial and weight components, although these appear to be only at heel strike, early loading and just before toe off.

The hip tells a different story, as the inertial and weight components have a significant effect, and can account for up to 25% of the moment during heel off to toe off. This

increase is not surprising, as the further proximal we travel, the greater the mass, centre of mass and radius of gyration distal to the joint of interest, and, therefore, the greater the inertial and weight moment components (Fig. 6.10a, b, c).

6.7.2 The effect the simple and advanced methods have on power

The graphs in Figure 6.11 above show the relative effect of the power caused by the ground reaction force and the inertial and weight components. These demonstrate that the power about the ankle joint is not significantly affected by the inertia and the weight of the distal segment, the foot. Again this is not surprising as the mass, centre of mass and radius of gyration are comparably small and therefore have minimal effect.

As with the moments the power about the knee shows some differences with the introduction of the inertial and weight components, again these differences only appear at heel strike and early loading and just before toe off.

As with the moments the hip power tells a different story with a much greater difference or error when only considering the effect of the ground reaction force. Again this increase is not surprising as the further proximal we travel the greater the mass, centre of mass and radius of gyration distal to the joint of interest, and therefore the greater the inertial and weight moment components.

Summary: Inverse dynamics theory

- Inertial forces are present whenever the body segments accelerate or decelerate during a movement. For slow movements the inertial forces will be minimal; however, for walking and running inertial forces can be considerable.

- Inertial forces have a direct effect on the joint forces, the moments acting around joints and the muscle power production.

- Inverse dynamics is one of the most complex methods used in movement analysis. However, in not including inertial forces, joint moments and power may be significantly underestimated.

- When conducting an analysis of joint moments and power it is important to consider inertial forces and moments wherever possible.

Measurement of Force and Pressure

Jim Richards and Dominic Thewlis

This chapter covers the measurement of force and pressure. This includes the different methods of assessing force and pressure, and the identification of measurements commonly used in research and clinical assessment.

Chapter 7: Aim

To consider the different methods of collecting and analysing force and pressure data, and to appreciate the different measures that may be taken.

Chapter 7: Objectives

- To summarize how force platforms work and distinguish what parameters can be measured
- To discuss the setting up of and use of force platforms in movement analysis laboratories
- To identify useful measures from force platforms
- To summarize how pressure-measuring devices work and distinguish what parameters can be measured
- To describe the different methods of assessing and measuring pressure
- To identify useful measures of pressure.

7.1 Methods of force measurement

Force platforms are considered as a basic but fundamentally important tool for gait analysis. The first force measurements date back as far as the late 19th century, when Marey used a wooden frame on rubber supports. Elftman (1939a) used a similar method with a platform on springs. However, it was not until the advancement of computers and electronic technology that the readings could be accurately measured. In 1965, Peterson and co-workers developed one of the first strain-gauge force platforms. A plethora of publications now exists on the applications of such devices in both clinical research and sports.

Since 1965 forces platforms have undergone considerable development by three internationally accepted manufacturers, Kistler Instruments, AMTI and the Bertec Corporation. Advances have been in the form of making the platforms more accurate (reducing crosstalk), increasing sensitivity (increasing the natural frequency), and making the platforms portable.

Force platforms measure and record the ground reaction forces (GRF) and their point of application (centre of pressure, COP). A ground reaction force is made up of three components acting at the centre of pressure. The three components can be categorized in an anatomical sense as: vertical forces (the weight of the body and how it progresses over the supporting limb), anterior–posterior forces (the accelerating and breaking forces), and medial–lateral forces (the force acting from side to side).

7.2 Force platform types

7.2.1 Frequency content and force platforms

Every mechanical system has a particular frequency at which it will vibrate when excited in the right way. A wine glass, for instance, may be made to make a tone by running a finger around the rim of the glass, equally an opera singer can break a glass by singing at the exact pitch or natural frequency of the glass, the glass then vibrates at this frequency and, according to the urban myth, breaks! The exact natural frequency will depend on the mass and the dimensions of the object. Force platforms are no exception and also have a natural frequency. This natural frequency should be avoided during testing as this would produce data which would not represent the task being studied; therefore, force platform's natural frequencies need to be considerably higher than the frequency content of the signal of interest.

Antonsson and Mann (1985) studied the frequency content of ground reaction forces during gait; it was found that in order to preserve 99% of the signal fidelity 15 Hz must be maintained. This requires a minimum sampling frequency of 30 Hz, although if we are interested in the transient effects at heel strike these are likely to fall in the 1% rather than the 99% of the signal fidelity. Therefore, higher sampling frequencies of 100 Hz and above are generally chosen. However, the frequency content of sporting tasks has been found to have much higher frequency during applications such as analysis of take-off and landing in jumping and running.

Generally force platforms come under two categories, strain gauge (AMTI, Bertec) or piezoelectric (Kistler) (Fig. 7.1a, b). It is accepted that piezoelectric force platforms are more sensitive and allow a larger range of force measurements.

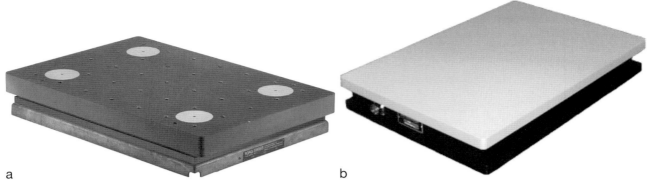

a   b

Figure 7.1   (a) Kistler and (b) AMTI Force platforms

They are also able to measure higher frequency content of up to 1000 Hz, their natural frequency, in all three directions, whereas strain gauge platforms generally have a natural frequency of 400–500 Hz, although strain gauge platforms are available up to 1000 Hz in the vertical and 500 Hz in the horizontal directions. However, piezoelectric force platforms are generally more expensive and offer no real advantage in clinical research. Therefore, for general use strain gauge platforms are more than adequate, however, for activities with a higher frequency content piezoelectric platforms are recommended.

7.2.2 Signal drift

Although piezoelectric platforms have the advantages of sensitivity, range and natural frequency, they do have the disadvantage of signal drift. Before each trial it is recommended that the platform is reset, this is a simple process of flicking a switch which drops all the signals to zero. However, if work is being carried out when the test subject is standing on the platform for more than 30 s, e.g. when looking at standing balance assessment or static measurements, piezoelectric platforms suffer from the signal drifting, which can introduce errors. Strain gauge platforms, however, are more stable due to the technology they use and are, therefore, better suited to these types of study.

7.2.3 How force platforms work

Strain gauge force platforms are based on the principle that when a force is applied to a structure, the structure changes in length. Strain is the ratio of changes between the original dimensions and the deformed dimensions. Strain gauges contain material which when distorted produces a resistance. So by measuring the resistance we can measure the strain. In order for the strain gauge to work correctly it must be wired up in what is known as a Wheatstone bridge arrangement, this simply arranges the gauges or resistors in an arrangement with four arms. For strain gauge platforms to work a power supply is required, as the strain is based on the resistance provided to the electrical current. The strain gauges are grouped in triplets in the pylons of the platform, situated in the corners. The resistance is normally relatively small so signals produced by strain gauge force platforms require amplification; this can either take place in the platform or in a separate amplifier.

Piezoelectric platforms are based on the use of piezoelectric crystals such as quartz. The basis for the generation of the signal is the same as strain gauges, in terms of the deformation of the crystal. However when piezoelectric crystals are deformed they generate what is known as an electric dipole moment, which in turn generates an electric current. As piezoelectric crystals generate their own current there is no need for a power supply. The coordinate system of the platform is determined by the alignment of the piezoelectric crystals on each pylon, which are aligned with the x, y and z axis of the platform (Fig. 7.4).

7.3 Force plate scaling

Piezoelectric and strain gauge force platforms essentially measure the same forces and moments; however, the ways in which they accomplish this are different. Strain gauge force platforms produce an output of 6 channels of analogue data. These are forces in the x, y and z directions (Fx, Fy, Fz) and the moments in the x, y and z (Mx, My, Mz). The moments and forces are calculated from readings taken at the four pylons situated at the corners of the force platform. So, strain gauge force platforms are relatively simple in their output with a single analogue channel representing a single force or moment that is then simply multiplied by a scaling factor to convert the raw voltage into forces and moments in newtons (N) and newton metres (Nm) respectively. Figures 7.2a and b show the raw voltage data and final output data from a typical strain gauge force platform.

Piezoelectric force platforms produce essentially the same data as strain gauge platforms, but the way in which they generate the data is different. Piezoelectric platforms generate 8 channels of analogue output, none of which contain any information about the moments acting on the platform (Mx, My or Mz). The channels are simply used to calculate the force data. Eight channels produce the following voltage data, which can then be used to calculate the force data in newton:

Fx

Ch1: fx12 – force in the x direction measured by pylons 1 and 2

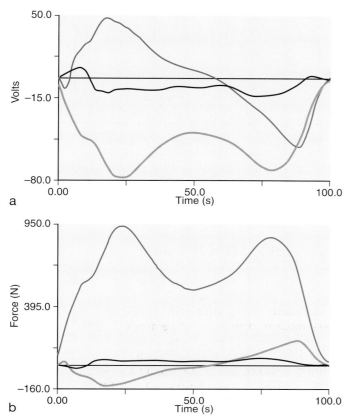

a

b

Figure 7.2   (a) Raw voltage and (b) final output data from a strain gauge platform

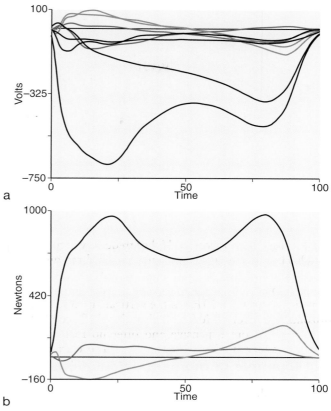

a

b

Figure 7.3   (a) Raw voltage and (b) final output data from a piezoelectric platform

Ch2: fx34 – force in the x direction measured by pylons 3 and 4

Fy

Ch3: fy12 – force in the y direction measured by pylons 1 and 2

Ch4: fy34 – force in the y direction measured by pylons 3 and 4

Fz

Ch5–8: fz1...fz4 – force in the z direction measured by pylons 1...4

The final force data are calculated by simply adding the x channels for the x data, the y channels for the y data and the z channels for the z data. Figure 7.3 shows the raw voltage data and the subsequent force data.

7.4 Calculating moments using a piezoelectric plate

Piezoelectric platforms do not provide a direct measurement of the moments about the platform, but these can be calculated if we know the location of the centre of the platform in the medial–lateral and anterior–posterior directions (Fig. 7.4).

$$Mx = b(fz1 + fz2 - fz3 - fz4)$$

$$My = a(-fz1 + fz2 + fz3 - fz4)$$

$$Mz = b(-fx12 + fx34) + a(fy14 - fy23)$$

We now know how to find the moments and forces produced from both piezoelectric and strain gauge force platforms, the next stage in the processing of force data is to calculate the centre of pressure. The following set of equations can be used with either type of force platform. The first stage we must address is the calculation of the moments about the platform (Mx' & My'), for this we need to know the moments about the platform axis, the forces and the offset between the vertical position of the centre of the platform and the top of the platform.

Moment in the sagittal plane (Mx') = Mx + Fy x az0

Moment in the coronal plane (My') = My + Fx x az0

We now know the force, the direction and the turning effect of the force, from these we can now calculate the centre of pressure by simply dividing the moment about the plate by the vertical force.

$$COPy = \frac{Mx'}{Fz}$$

$$COPx = \frac{My'}{Fz}$$

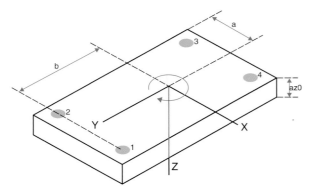

Figure 7.4 Dimensions needed for force and moment calculations

Finally, we can calculate the free moment about the platforms, or the vertical moment. These data along with the centre of pressure data are important to consider during the calculation of joint kinetics using inverse dynamics.

Moment in the transverse plane (Mz') = $Mz - Fy \times COPx + Fx \times COPy$

7.4.1 Example of moment calculations using a piezoelectric platform

We will now consider an example of an individual applying a known force of 800 N vertical force, 200 N posterior force and 50 N medial force. With moments of 150 Nm in the sagittal plane (X), 110 Nm in the coronal plane (Y), and 20 Nm in the transverse plane (Z). In this example a clockwise moment is considered as positive and anticlockwise negative.

Moments and CoP in the sagittal plane Mx' (Fig. 7.5a)

Moment in the sagittal plane (Mx')

$Mx + Fy \text{ x } az0 + Fz \text{ x } COPy = 0$

$150 - 200 \times 0.04 - 800 \times COPy = 0$

$142 - 800 \times COPy = 0$

$142 = 800 \times COPy$

$COPy = 142/800$

$COPy = 0.1775 \text{ m}$

Moments and CoP in the coronal plane My' (Fig. 7.5b)

Moment in the coronal plane (My')

$My + Fx \times az0 + Fz \times COPx = 0$

$110 - 50 \times 0.04 - 800 \times COPx = 0$

$108 - 800 \times COPx = 0$

$108 = 800 \times COPx$

$COPx = \dfrac{108}{800}$

$COPx = 0.135 \text{ m}$

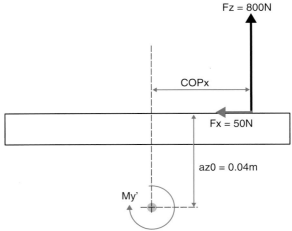

a   Platform centre of rotation

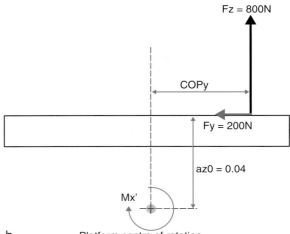

b   Platform centre of rotation

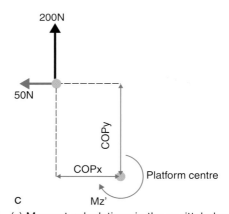

c

Figure 7.5 (a) Moment calculations in the sagittal plane, (b) moment calculations in the coronal plane and (c) moment calculations in the transverse plane

So the centre of pressure coordinates are:

$COPy = 0.1775 \text{ m}$

and

$COPx = 0.135 \text{ m}$

Moments in the transverse plane Mz' (Fig. 7.5c)
Finally, we can now calculate the moment in the transverse plane, which is sometimes referred to as the free moment (Mz').

$$Mz' = 20 + (200 \times 0.1775) + (-50 \times 0.135)$$

$$Mz' = 48.75 \, Nm$$

7.5 Considerations for force platform fitting and positioning

When a movement analysis laboratory is designed it is essential that consideration is given to future funding becoming available to expand equipment. So designs of a new movement analysis laboratory where two force platforms are available should leave sufficient space for an additional 2 platforms, otherwise fitting additional platforms in the future may become a very expensive job. For the different types of platforms the exact fitting differs, we will use an example of Kistler and AMTI platforms and how a laboratory can be future-proofed based around these platforms. Kistler platforms require a special frame to be fitted using specialist cement; each platform must be housed in its own pit. The solution for future-proofing is to incorporate two more pits in the desired configuration, then build blank platforms out of a thick board which can be used to fill the pits until the time comes when the funding becomes available to fit the new platform(s). This also can allow different configurations of platforms by moving them into the blank positions, in this way two platforms may be positioned to look at walking, running and gait initiation.

The fitting of AMTI platforms requires a set of rails which are resined or glued to the bottom of the pit. The platforms should not be within approximately 15 cm of each other; however, unlike Kistler platforms, they do not require an individual pit. So, within the laboratory specification a large pit can be included which meets the manufacturer's specification of platform size and separation distance. A

Figure 7.6 AMTI force platforms set for a step down task showing the 4 platform configuration

frame can then be designed to leave only the platforms exposed, and when additional monies become available, the correct size hole can be made in the frame and the platform fitted. Figure 7.6 shows the holes for the usual position of the force platforms, but with the platforms lifted to form a step. An alternative solution is to fit a false floor, this is a somewhat more expensive solution, however, it allows the platforms to be moved anywhere in the laboratory, provided the fixings are in place.

It is very important to note that all force platforms (besides some of the new USB platforms) have quite substantial cabling associated with them. This cable must run from the platform to the amplifier (normally situated by the control PC) so it is essential to either have the ability to pass these cables under a false floor or through a conduit with a large enough inner diameter to allow the cable and end connectors to pass.

7.6 Force platform location and configurations

In order to best use the space in your laboratory it is essential that the force platform pit(s) be located in a position that will allow for cameras to be easily positioned around the platforms and to ensure that steady-state gait can be achieved (in walking or running, dependent on the focus of the laboratory). It has been suggested in the past that labs that are near the smaller end of the spectrum should set up the force platforms in a way that runs diagonally across the laboratory. This works by creating a larger distance to achieve steady state gait. However, when using a multi camera system you may reduce the effectiveness of the cameras by forcing them into positions that may be less than ideal. Therefore, if your laboratory is of a smaller nature, concentrate on getting the best setup without reducing the accuracy of the movement analysis measurements. Perhaps the best configuration is to position the force platforms in the centre of the laboratory, allowing ample room either side to position cameras. If you plan on having doors at either end of the laboratory, try to line these up with the force platform pit. This will be useful if you ever want to investigate running gait, as it will allow the participant to start and finish outside of the laboratory, without having to stop by running in to a wall.

Once the position of the platform pit has been decided upon, it is essential that the possible configurations of platforms will maximize the number of foot contacts collected, or will allow the laboratory to be as adaptable as possible by considering all possible movement tasks that may be of interest. There have been many different configurations that have been suggested over the years; in the next section we will consider some of these. We will consider an example of four platforms, but highlight how these configurations can be used with fewer platforms as well.

7.6.1 Force platform configuration 1

The configuration shown in Figure 7.7 (bottom) is particularly suited to laboratories that are interested in gait, gait initiation, postural stability, child gait and running gait. The first two platforms are positioned next to each other to allow

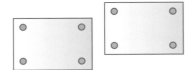

Figure 7.9   Force platform configuration 3

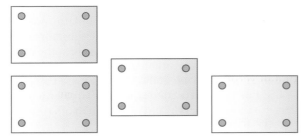

Figure 7.10   Force platform configuration 4

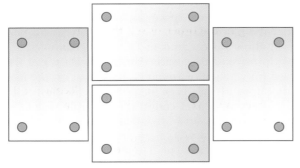

Figure 7.7   Force platform configuration 1

7.6.3 Force platform configuration 3

This configuration is particularly useful when working with larger systems, so typically four platforms would be the minimum. Normally this configuration would be used when dealing with children or pathologies where step length may be limited, as it increases the chance of a clean foot contact. With the platforms orientated in this manner it also allows for postural stability and gait initiation work; however, this will be limited to data from a single platform if the subsequent foot contacts are of interest (Fig. 7.9).

7.6.4 Force platform configuration 4

This configuration is very simple and is generally used for collecting walking and running gait data. We would not recommend this configuration as it very much limits the type of work by the relative spacing between the platforms (Fig. 7.10).

Force platforms are relatively expensive pieces of equipment; there are cheaper alternatives available such as walkmat systems. In the correct setting these types of systems may be more versatile (though they are less accurate), and will allow for multiple foot strikes to be recorded. They can be very useful in studies that concentrate on simpler gait variables, such as step time and gait velocity, as the heel-strike and toe-off phases of the gait cycle can be easily recorded.

Figure 7.8   Force platform configuration 2

the participant to have one foot on each platform during postural stability and gait initiation assessment where not only the force beneath each foot can be obtained but also the subsequent foot contacts.

In addition, if the two platforms are used along the x axis they will allow for child gait or individuals with a shorter step length. The subsequent two platforms are ideally positioned for normal gait collecting a total of three heel strikes. This is the current configuration we use at the University of Central Lancashire. A similar configuration which includes the inset second platform can be used if only two platforms are available; this again is particularly suited to gait (Fig. 7.7 (top)). We would recommend using this configuration as it is adaptable and covers a variety of activities.

7.6.2 Force platform configuration 2

This configuration position two platforms sideways at either end of two platforms that are orientated lengthways. This is particularly suited to gait analysis in children, as the relative distance between the platforms is small, which will increase the chance of getting a clean strike. Again two platforms can be removed from this configuration to provide one which still allows for child gait (Fig. 7.8).

7.7 Typical measurements from force platforms

7.7.1 The video vector generator

The video vector generator is a piece of equipment that combines the information from a force platform with a video image. The force platform information can be superimposed on top of the video information giving a picture of the action of the ground reaction forces with respect to the joints of the lower limb (Fig. 7.11). This information may be used to identify biomechanical pathologies and monitor changes due to treatment.

Before pathological gait can be studied using this technique, the patterns of 'normal' gait should be studied and related to function. Using this technique any deviation away from an expected gait pattern may be identified and related to a

Figure 7.11   Force vector generator

change in function. This information may be used to identify biomechanical pathologies and monitor changes due to treatment. One particular use that has found its way into clinical practice is using the video vector generator in the fine tuning of prosthetic legs, where adjustments can be made to the sagittal plane and coronal plane alignments of the socket and prosthetic joints.

Although this can be a very useful assessment tool on its own, it does not allow any measurements to be taken. However, some commercial software allows the visualization of the video vector whilst also recording the force data to allow more objective measurements to be taken. One example of such software is ProVec, by MIE Leeds UK, which can work with any commercial platform such as Kistler, AMTI or Bertec, and is capable of collecting data from multiple platforms, but also allows video data to be superimposed so that real-time video vectors can be displayed and recorded using a standard video recorder.

7.7.2 General description of graph shapes

From the force platform we can get a number of graphs and plots, these include: vertical, anterior–posterior and medio–lateral forces graphs, centre of pressure (or point of application) graphs, and Pedotti or butterfly diagrams. For each of these plots we can observe the shape by eye and look for differences between the plots obtained for a particular subject and a non-pathological gait pattern. Key points

in the gait cycle can then be identified on the traces and measurement taken. For each of these measurements the percentage difference can be studied between the left and right side, and between the subject tested and individuals who are pain and pathology free. This will not only identify what differences are present in the walking patterns, but also how big these differences are.

7.7.3 Vertical force measurements

Vertical force measurements are by far the most quoted in the literature as they may be measured using force platforms and pressure plates alike. In both cases a variety of useful measurements may be taken. These include: the first peak or maximum vertical loading force; the dip trough, which can give useful information about the movement of the body over the stance limb, and the second peak or maximum vertical thrusting force.

All the above measures may be reported in newton, but more usually these are reported with respect to body weight. This is where the value in newton is simply divided by the person's body weight. Normal values for the two peaks are in the order of 1.2 the value of body weight with the trough usually being in the order of 0.7 the value of body weight, although these are dependent on walking speed.

The timing at which these peaks and troughs occur can also be a very useful measure. So corresponding timing measures are: the time to the first and second peaks (the time to maximum vertical loading and maximum vertical thrusting force); the time to the trough, which is sometimes referred to as midstance, although we will consider this again when looking at the anterior–posterior forces; and the total contact time.

The usefulness of time in seconds is debatable as this will relate directly with walking speed; however, the time to each of these events in relation to the total stance time can be quite useful, especially when considering lower-limb amputee gait or individuals with an early heel lift or a leg length difference (Fig. 7.12a, b).

7.7.4 Anterior–posterior force measurements

As with the vertical force measurements, the anterior–posterior forces may also be studied. These include: the negative peak or maximum posterior loading force, and the positive peak or maximum anterior thrusting force. Again both of the above measures may be reported in newton or with respect to body weight. Normal values for the two peaks are in the order of 0.2 the value of body weight, but again these are dependent on walking speed.

The negative and positive aspect of these peaks can cause some confusion, as this depends on the direction of walking over the force platforms; for example, if an individual walked in exactly the same way to the right and then to the left then the results would show mirror image if the mirror were placed along the time axis. Therefore, the value of the maximum loading force and maximum thrusting forces would be the same, apart from in one direction; they would be negative and positive and in the other direction they would be positive and negative. There is no clear right and wrong to this, other than NEVER refer to them as positive

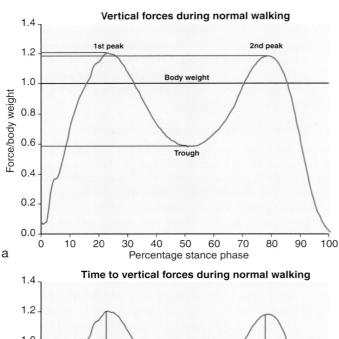

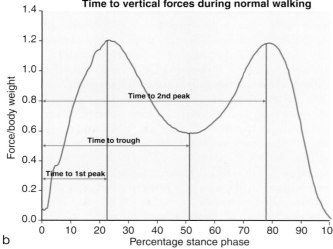

Figure 7.12   (a and b) Force in the vertical direction during normal walking

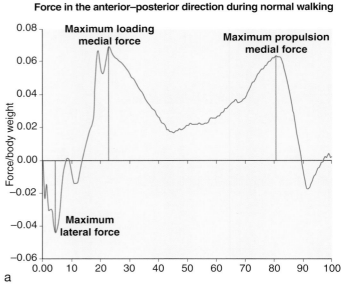

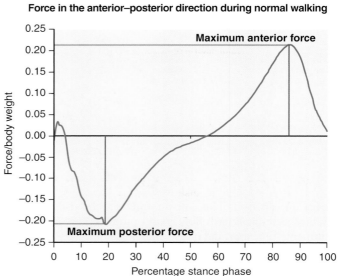

Figure 7.13   (a and b) Force in the anterior–posterior direction during normal walking

and negative forces and ALWAYS refer to them as posterior and anterior forces.

As with the vertical forces the timing at which these peaks occur can also be a very useful measure. So the corresponding timing measures are: the time to the maximum posterior loading force and maximum anterior thrusting force. A third timing measure may also be taken which is the time to cross over; this is where there is no anterior of posterior force acting. If this is the case then the body must be directly over the stance limb. Therefore, this would be a better measure of the point in time midstance occurs rather than the trough on the vertical force graph. It is interesting to note that in most people who are pain and pathology free these can be subtly different; however, during many pathological movement patterns these can in fact be very different (Fig. 7.13a, b and Fig. 7.14).

One final measurement that can be taken is the impulse, the area under the force–time graphs. These may be considered separately as posterior and anterior impulse in the same way as above (Fig. 7.15).

7.7.5 Medio–lateral force measurements

The same technique as before may also be applied to the maximum medial force and the maximum lateral force. And again these can be related to the person's body weight, with the maximum medial force being between 0.05 and 0.1 of body weight with the lateral force generally being less than the maximum medial force. This is particularly interesting when we consider the effect of foot orthoses, in particular the use of posting or wedging of the rearfoot, which can have substantial effects on these forces (Fig. 7.16).

7.7.6 Centre of pressure measurements

Independent measurements of 'centre of pressure' are not as common in force platform research, although the centre of pressure is used in conjunction with force data to create the Pedotti diagrams, and is vital when considering the moments

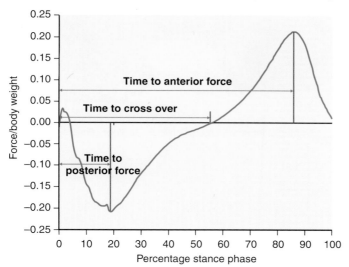

Figure 7.14   Force in the anterior–posterior direction during normal walking

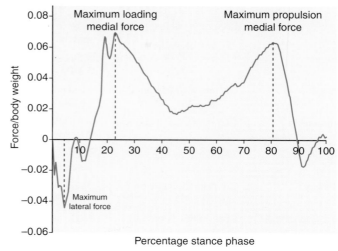

Figure 7.16   Force in the medial–lateral direction during normal walking

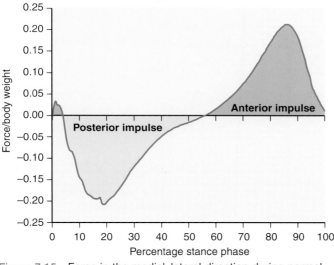

Figure 7.15   Force in the medial–lateral direction during normal walking

about joints. However, independent measurements of centre of pressure are frequently used with pressure plates. One of the reasons for this is that the force platforms do not record the shape of the contact between the foot and the ground, whereas pressure plates do. This leads to some difficulties in precisely identifying the movement of the centre of pressure with reference to known anatomical positions of the foot unless additional data are simultaneously collected from movement analysis. However, it is possible to measure the movement of centre of pressure away from a centre line and the movement of the centre of pressure in the anterior–posterior and medial–lateral directions (Fig. 7.17a, b).

7.8 Quantitative assessment of pressure

7.8.1 Why is pressure important to the foot?

Pressure is a very important measure as excessive pressures can cause tissue damage. This has been shown to be an

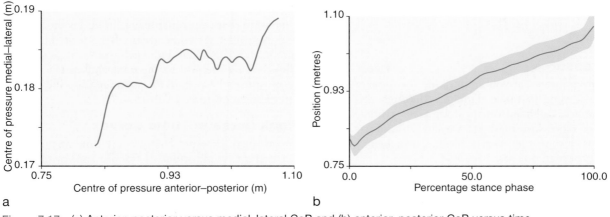

a   b

Figure 7.17   (a) Anterior–posterior versus medial–lateral CoP and (b) anterior–posterior CoP versus time

Table 7.1	Conversion of commonly used units of pressure into SI units	
Units commonly used	Corrected values	How to report results
N/mm²	1 N/mm² = 1 000 000 N/m²	1 MN/m² or 1 MPa
N/cm²	1 N/cm² = 10 000 N/m²	10 kN/m² or 10 kPa
kg/mm²	1 kg/mm² = 9 810 000 N/m²	9.81 MN/m² or 9.81 MPa
kg/cm²	1 kg/cm² = 98 100 N/m²	98.1 kN/m² or 98.1 kPa
mmHg	1 mmHg = 133.3 N/m²	133.3 N/m² or 133.3 Pa
psi (pounds per square inch)	1 psi = 6867 N/m²	6.867 kN/m² or 6.867 kPa

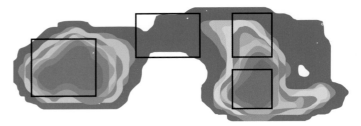

a

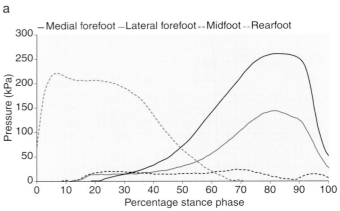

b

Figure 7.18   (a and b) Average pressures on a normal foot

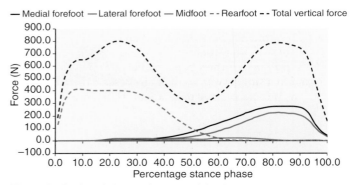

Figure 7.19   Loads beneath areas of the foot

important consideration in the prevention and treatment of ulceration, with the assessment of pressure being a possible early predictor of where ulceration might occur. This can lead to early treatment and can allow clinicians to prevent severe damage taking place. This section reviews measurements of pressure which are of particular value in the assessment of pathologies where the pressures on soft tissue may be excessive and lead to injury.

7.8.2 Units of pressure

Sometimes incorrect units are presented, e.g. N/mm² (which can easily be converted back to N/m² by multiplying by 1 000 000), worse still are units of pressure presented as kg/m² or kg/mm². These last two should be avoided as kg is the unit of mass and not force. Consider an astronaut on the moon; he will have less pressure beneath his feet than when he was standing on Earth. He will have the same mass in kg, but not the same weight (force on his feet) in newton.

7.8.3 Conversion of commonly used units of pressure into SI units
See Table 7.1.
7.8.4 Average pressure

The average pressure over the whole of the base of the foot tells us very little about what is going on under the structures of the foot. A better measure is the average pressure under specific areas of the foot (Fig. 7.18a, b).

7.8.5 Peak pressures

These are of far more interest if you are looking for signs of excessive pressure leading to tissue damage. Although this still uses the same areas defined on the foot as in average pressures, the largest pressure reading in each of the areas is now plotted rather than the averaged value, which may contain small areas of high pressure.

For normal subjects, typical pressures beneath the foot are 80–100 kPa in standing and 200–500 kPa in walking. In diabetic neuropathology pressures can be as high as 1000–3000 kPa. To put this in perspective, 3000 kPa is the same

pressure as 30.5 kg acting on 1 cm², half a 61 kg person's weight (610 N) acting on 1 cm² (*Ouch!*).

7.8.6 Load beneath areas of the foot

Another measure that can sometimes be found is the average load (force N) under different areas of the foot. However, much care needs to be taken with such measures as they are often influenced by the size of the area chosen (Fig. 7.19). Often the most useful aspect of this is to replicate the vertical force patterns seen on force platforms.

7.8.7 Peak pressure–time curves

How areas of peak pressure change over time at points on the foot is extremely important. If the pressure produced is only acting for a very short period of time then it has less time to cause tissue damage, if it acts for longer then there is a greater chance of tissue damage. To measure this, the area under the peak pressure–time or average pressure–time graph is taken for a particular area under the foot, usually under a particular anatomical landmark, this gives a single value for the pressure–time effect on that selected area. These measures are called a **pressure time integral** or a **peak pressure time integral**, depending on whether the average pressure or peak pressure data are used. The units are pascal seconds (Pas or kPas), or newton seconds per square metre (Ns/m^2 or kNs/m^2). Impulse force is also sometimes reported from the force–time graphs, although its usefulness is perhaps questionable for pressure analysis (Fig. 7.20).

7.8.8 Conversion of commonly used units of pressure time integrals (Table 7.2)

Currently it is only possible to measure the vertical forces using pressure-measuring devices, although work is being carried out by a number of companies to find a way of reliably measuring the shear pressures.

7.9 Methods of measuring pressure

7.9.1 Pressure-sensitive mats and film

Fuji Prescale Film is a pressure-sensitive film to assess the contact pressure between two surfaces. This has many uses in industry; however, it can be used to assess the average pressure under the foot. The film produces varying colours of red patches which instantly appear on the Prescale, which reveals the pressure distribution between the surfaces. Furthermore, the intensity of the red colours of the Prescale film is related to the amount of pressure applied to it.

The Shutrak uses carbon paper, which is laid out on top of paper, and in a similar way to the Fuji Prescale the amount of carbon on the under sheet depends on the pressure exerted

by the foot. The carbon paper records the impressions of the footfalls as the subject walks along.

The Harris-Beath mat is a thin rubber mat, the upper surface of which consists of a pattern of ridges at different heights filled with ink. The highest ridges compress under relative light pressures, and the lower ridges require progressively higher pressures, making the transfer of ink greater in some areas than others, depending on the amount of pressure exerted on the ridges.

All three of these give an indication of the pressure exerted; however, they cannot put a precise value to it. This is useful to get an impression of whether there are any areas of high pressures and abnormalities. However, they are limited as they cannot show how the pressure dynamically changes beneath the foot at different stages during stance phase.

7.9.2 Pedobarograph

The best known floor-mounted system for measuring pressure beneath the foot is the pedobarograph. This comprises an elastic mat laid on top of an edge lit glass plate (Fig. 7.21). When a subject walks on the mat it compresses and loses reflectivity, becoming progressively darker with increasing pressure. The amount of darkening gives a quantitative measurement. The underside of the plate is viewed by a camera, usually via a mirror set at 45°, the image from which may be processed to give a display of the different pressures experienced beneath the foot and to allow the dynamic changes in pressure to be assessed. Different areas under the foot can then be identified and the pressure-versus-time graphs plotted (Fig. 7.21).

The pedobarograph has the advantage of not relying on individual pressure sensors under the foot; therefore, the resolution of the pressure distribution is far better as

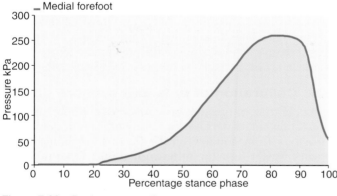

Figure 7.20   Peak pressure–time curves

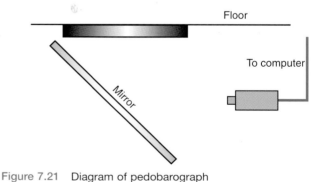

Figure 7.21   Diagram of pedobarograph

Table 7.2 Units commonly used/conversion factor			
Units commonly used	Conversion factor	Corrected values	How to report results
N.s/mm²	1 000 000	1 N.s/mm² = 1 000 000 N.s/m²	1 MN.s/m² or 1 MPa.s
N.s/cm²	10 000	1 N.s/cm² = 10 000 N.s/m²	10 kN.s/m² or 10 kPa.s
kg.s/mm²	9 810 000	1 kg.s/mm² = 9 810 000 N.s/m²	9.81 MN.s/m² or 9.81 MPa.s
kg.s/cm²	98 100	1 kg.s/cm² = 98 100 N.s/m²	98.1 kN.s/m² or 98.1 kPa.s

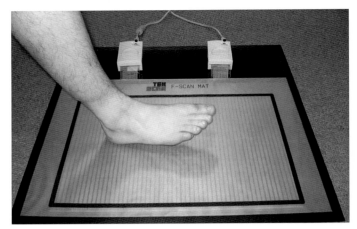

a

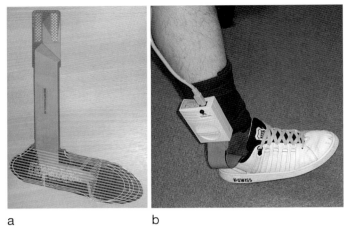

a   b

Figure 7.23   (a) In-shoe pressure sensor and (b) F-Scan system, Tekscan Inc, South Boston, MA

b

Figure 7.22   (a) Pressure mat system HRMat Tekscan Inc, South Boston, MA and (b) The RSscan 2 m plate

it is dependent on the camera resolution. However, most pedobarographs can only collect data at a frame rate of 25 Hz. This is only just fast enough to collect data from walking and is not suitable for faster activities. It also has the disadvantage of not being portable as it requires being set into the floor.

7.9.3 Pressure mats

Pressure mats use an array of load sensors which usually range from 1 to 4 sensors/cm² and vary in size from approximately 40 cm × 36 cm (Fig. 7.22a) to 2 m × 0.4 m (Fig. 7.22b), although mats with 15.5 sensors/cm² are now commercially available. These can record at a variety of different frequencies that vary from 40 Hz up to 500 Hz. These use a variety of technologies from capacitive sensor to resistive sensor technology. There is much debate on which is the best system; however, this generally comes down to sensor resolution (sensors/cm²), sampling frequency, stability of calibration and, perhaps the decisive factor for clinical use, the cost of the different systems. All systems offer valuable data for research and clinical assessment, although the majority of the scientific publications have previously been with the emed and Tekscan systems.

7.9.4 In-shoe pressure systems

So far we have looked at floor-mounted devices, but these have the major draw back in that they do not measure the

pressure directly acting on the foot, unless the subject is walking bare footed. In-shoe pressure systems are able to measure the interface pressures between the foot and the shoe or the foot and a foot orthosis. This gives important clinical data on the nature of pressure offloading and force distributions. The main difficulties which in-shoe devices face are: the curvature on the foot and the shape of foot orthoses, and the lack of space for the transducers. The transducers are therefore generally thin enough to fit in the shoe without affecting the very thing they are trying to measure. One example of this is the F-Scan system by Tekscan Inc (Fig. 7.23a, b).

7.9.5 Force sensors

There are many systems which use load cells, each of which measures vertical force beneath a particular area of the foot. Dividing the force by the area of the cell gives the mean pressure beneath the foot in that area. However, small load cells may also be individually placed under specific areas of interest to give an indication of the pressure under that area. One such sensor is the Flexi force sensor (Fig. 7.24).

7.9.6 Calibration of pressure sensors

The calibration of pressure systems varies considerably, and different manufacturers have a variety of ways of doing this. These vary from standing on the sensors and inputting the person's weight (usually in the wrong units of kg or worse lbs) this 'calibration' then relates to the subsequent measured readings, to calibration under a pressurized bladder.

The first method of standing on the sensors assumes that all the sensors have exactly the same properties, which is not an adequate basis upon which to undertake meaningful research. However, in its defense this technique is fast, and if the purpose is to look for approximate values of disproportionate pressures, say to predict possible site of ulceration, rather than accurate measurements, then it could be considered as fast and useful, and it is clearly better than walking over carbon paper. The counter argument, however, is 'when does a pressure become too high', in which case we need to know and be confident in the measurements taken.

Figure 7.24   Force sensors: Flexi force sensors, Tekscan Inc., South Boston, MA

The second method of calibration uses a pressurized bladder to provide an even distribution of pressure over all sensors. This is usually repeated at a number of pressures so a calibration curve is found for each sensor. Therefore, any variation in the sensors is taken into account and only then can the system be considered to be properly calibrated. Some manufacturers offer a service of recalibration where not only the magnitudes of the pressures, but also the speed of application of pressure is recorded. This is sometimes referred to as ramp loading. Ramp loading offers the advantage of also examining for any time dependence, or time lag, in the sensors.

Summary: Measurement of force and pressure

- Force platforms come in a variety of types. They are capable of measuring the ground reaction forces in the vertical, anterior–posterior, and medial–lateral directions.
- Separating the ground reaction force into the different body planes yields important information about the loading, propulsion and the stability of the body during different movement tasks.
- Pressure plates are only capable of measuring the vertical force; however, they are able to measure the distribution of the force, or pressure, beneath the foot or contact area. High pressures can cause tissue breakdown and injuries such as ulceration.
- Both force platforms and pressure plates can calculate the centre of pressure, although they do this in distinctly different ways. Force platforms give an overall position of the centre of pressure, whereas pressure plates give information as to the location of the centre of pressure in relation to the foot shape.
- Both types of system can measure distinctly different types of data. Force platforms are more useful in the assessment of the overall function during movement tasks, whereas pressure plates are better at determining variations in the loading or pressure patterns acting on specific areas of the foot.

Methods of Analysis of Movement

Chapter 8

Jim Richards, Dominic Thewlis and Sarah Jane Hobbs

This chapter covers the measurement of movement. This includes the different methods of assessing movement, the processes required to collect and analyse movement data, and the consideration of possible errors.

Chapter 8: Aim

To consider the different methods of collecting and analysing movement data, and to consider the different measures that may be taken.

Chapter 8: Objectives

- To describe the different methods of assessing movement data
- To summarize how movement analysis methods work
- To distinguish what parameters can be measured with different systems
- To describe the processing required when analysing movement data
- To identify possible sources of error and how these may be allowed for or controlled.

8.1 Early pioneers of movement analysis equipment

In the late 19th century the first motion picture cameras recorded patterns of locomotion for both humans and animals. In 1877 Muybridge demonstrated, using photographs, that when a horse is moving at a fast trot there is a moment when all of the animal's feet are off the ground and in 1887 published *Animal Locomotion*. Muybridge later used the same 24 cameras to study the movement patterns of a running man and in 1901 published *The Human Figure in Motion*. Marey, a French physiologist, used a photographic rifle (la fusil photographique) to photograph movement of animals in 1873, and in 1882 and 1885 to record displacements in human gait to produce a stick figure of a runner.

The 20th century saw the development of systems capable of automated and semi-automated computer-aided motion analysis. One of the first systems to become commercially available was the Ariel Performance Analysis System, which required the operator to manually identify the location of each marker used for each frame. Since then the problems of automatic marker identification have been at the forefront of computer-aided motion analysis development. In 1974 SELSPOT became commercially available, which allowed automatic tracking of active LED markers. Later Watsmart Optotrak and Codamotion used a similar technique. VICON, a television camera based system, became commercially available in 1982. Other systems based on television camera technology have followed, including the Motion Analysis Corporation system, Elite, and ProReflex by Qualysis.

The latter half of the 20th century has also seen the introduction of other methods of recording movement, including instrumented walkmats, accelerometers and electro-goniometers, which have all contributed to our current knowledge of normal and pathological movement.

8.2 Instrumented walkmat systems

Spatial parameters can be measured in a variety of simple ways, these include putting ink pads on the soles of the subject's shoes and walking on paper (Rafferty and Bell 1995, Rennie et al 1997), and using marker pens attached to shoes (Gerny 1983). Although very cheap, these systems can involve awkward and time-consuming analysis. Temporal parameters can be measured by timing how long it takes an individual to walk a set distance, and counting the number of steps it took to cover that distance. At best this will only give average velocity and cadence, and will give no value to the symmetry of these parameters. This technique is extremely susceptible to human error.

In the last two decades of the 20th century advances in computer technology led to the development of a number of instrumented walkmat systems. These allow fast collection of temporal and spatial gait data. Using a computer also allows easier, less time-consuming analysis. These systems can be found in work by: Al-Majali et al (1993), Arenson et al (1983), Crouse et al (1987), Durie and Farley (1980) and Hirokawa and Matsumura (1987).

8.2.1 Temporal and spatial parameters in clinical assessment

Wall et al (1987) applied a nomenclature for normal gait to abnormal walking patterns. This paper considered the basic definitions of 'step' and 'stride' and the temporal phases of the gait cycle using a walkmat system developed at Dalhousie University. A number of pathological gait patterns were also examined to test the universal clinical applicability of these definitions. As a result, this study by Wall and co-workers highlighted some of the major difficulties encountered in applying normal gait nomenclature in a precise and unequivocal manner to the description of some pathological gait patterns. Despite this, the authors concluded that the study of temporal and spatial parameters of gait is a quick and easy way of assessing many pathological gait patterns.

The relationship between length of stride, step frequency, time of swing and speed of walking for children and adults has been studied by many authors such as Andriacchi et al (1977), Grieve and Gear (1966), Hirokawa (1989) and Murray et al (1966). Hirokawa (1989) used the relationships between temporal and spatial parameters to investigate whether gait was modified under temporal and spatial constraints. These included: rhythm constraints, speed constraints, and walking up and down an incline of 5°. Hirokawa found that rhythm constraints resulted in no differences between male and female, but differences did appear between the two genders with speed constraints. The results from inclined walking showed that the ascent gave a longer step length and a lower cadence compared with the descent.

Gardner and Murray (1975) studied temporal parameters of gait from several pathologies including patients with unilateral hip pain, Parkinson's disease and hemoparesis, and compared the results with those obtained from normal walking. Wall and Ashburn (1979), and Mizahi et al (1982), used temporal and spatial parameters in the assessment of hemiplegic patients. Leiper and Craik (1991) studied the temporal and spatial parameters of gait in elderly women and investigated the relationship between physical activity, walking speed, cadence and relative step length.

Current uses of walkmat systems include: quantification of the difference in temporal and spatial parameters of gait between frail and non-frail elderly subjects, changes over time in patients with Peripheral Vascular Disease (PVD), and the recovery of persons following hip fracture. Lough (1995) used the temporal and spatial parameters of gait gathered from a walkmat system to quantify motor performance in patients with peripheral neuropathy undergoing treatment. Isakov et al (1996) used a 10 m conductive rubber walkway to gather temporal and spatial data, and to study symmetry in trans-tibial amputee gait.

8.2.2 Walkmat systems

One of the first computer-controlled walkmat systems was developed by Crouse, Wall, and Marble at the University of Dalhousie, Canada in 1984/5 and published in 1987. The system consisted of nine active mats and two dummy mats, each mat being 0.8 m long and 0.76 m wide. The original walkmat system developed by Wall and co-workers used metal rods running perpendicular to the direction of walking, but these sometimes interfered with the subject's walk.

This system was later modified by using printed circuit boards divided into a left and a right side with 87 copper tracks etched onto each side. Alternate tracks were connected by a 10 Ω resistor and both ends of the mat were connected to a constant current source of 1 mA. To record a walk

self-adhesive aluminium tape was placed on the soles of the subject's shoes. When the subject walked along the walk mat the metal tape created a potential divider and the constant current flowing through the resistors produced a voltage that was directly proportional to the position on the mat. Dummy mats were placed at the two ends of the walk mat to allow 0.8 m for the subject to start walking before reaching the active mats. The system was capable of measuring temporal and spatial parameters of gait, including: step and stride time, step and stride length, swing time, and double and single support time, but gave no indication of medial–lateral or transverse plane foot position.

Systems are now commercially available that do not require any modifications to the footwear. These offer far less interference with the gait cycle. One such system is the GAITRite™ system, which uses pressure sensor arrays to determine the foot positions (Fig. 8.1). These pressure sensors offer six levels of pressure assessment and give a rough guide to the pressures that determine the nature of the foot contact, i.e. heel striking or toe walking, as well as the temporal and spatial parameters. The resolution of the sensors also allows the measurement of medial–lateral and transverse plane foot position.

The design of this sensory array allows the system to be thin and light so it can be rolled up and transported easily (Fig. 8.2a, b). The validity and reliability of the GAITRite system's measurements were investigated and published by McDonough et al (2001) who concluded that the GAITRite system is a valid and reliable tool for measuring selected spatial and temporal parameters of gait. Since then, over 30 papers have been published using the system for a wide variety of pathologies including: Parkinson's, Alzheimer's, Huntington's disease; Stroke; Charcot-Marie-Tooth and, most recently, cerebellar- and basal-ganglia-related motor disorders.

It is clear that the study of the temporal and spatial parameters of foot contact in gait gives extremely valuable information for both research and clinical assessment; however, the movement of the different body segments in time and space reveals more detailed information about the nature of movement patterns and movement disorders.

Figure 8.1 Sensor Array of GAITRite™ system

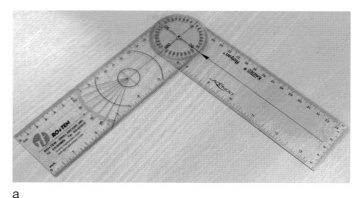

a

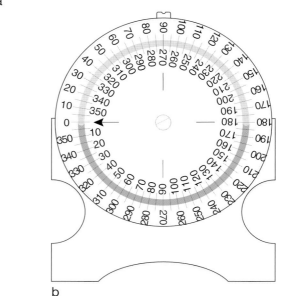

b

Figure 8.3   (a) 'Ruler' goniometer and (b) fluid-filled goniometer (MIE, UK)

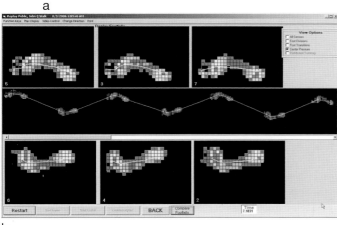

b

Figure 8.2   (a) GAITRite™ system and (b) typical output from GAITRite™

8.3 Electrogoniometers and accelerometers

8.3.1 Goniometers and electrogoniometers

What is a goniometer

A goniometer is a simple hand-held device for measuring joint angles. There are several types of goniometer, all giving a crude but useful measure of angles and range of motion. Clinically these allow a quick and useful assessment of static angles. However, these devices are of little use in measuring angles dynamically during different movement tasks. There are two main types of goniometer, the hinged 'ruler' and the fluid filled. The fluid-filled types are generally more versatile in the angles they can measure, but they measure relative to

gravity so if not used correctly can be prone to errors if the subject moves whilst taking readings (Fig. 8.3).

What is an electrogoniometer and a potentiometer

Potentiometers measure the change in linear or angular displacement by recording the change in voltage output. Angular displacement potentiometers allow movement about one plane to be measured, e.g. flexion extension of the knee. Potentiometers are generally a robust 'student proof' and low-cost method of collecting kinematic data, which can allow real-time data to be observed. However, if more than one joint is being assessed at one time then they may encumber the movement slightly, one example of potentiometer is produced by MIE (Leeds, UK) (Fig. 8.4a).

Electrogoniometers are very thin pieces of wire which are sensitive to bending. The amount of bending changes the output voltage. These can be sensitive to angular movement in up to three planes simultaneously, although biaxial and uniaxial electrogoniometers are more common, biaxial referring to the measure flexion–extension and abduction–adduction of a joint simultaneously. These are relatively inexpensive, accurate and reasonably unintrusive and so minimize any gait modification (Fig. 8.4b).

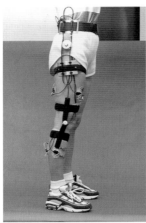
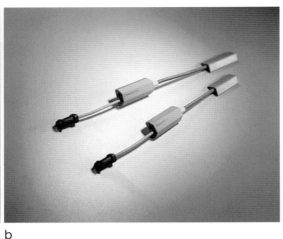

a   b

Figure 8.4   (a) Potentiometers, MIE, Leeds UK and (b) Electrogoniometers, Biometrics Ltd

8.3.2 Development of electrogoniometers

Electrogoniometers have been in development since the early 1970s (Marciniak 1973, Tata et al 1978). Early devices were bulky potentiometers, sometimes referred to as 'potentiometric goniometers', which were attached to the body segments with rigid bars. Various studies were carried out on normal subjects but they were cumbersome to wear especially if multiple joints were to be studied. For these reasons the clinical use of such devices was limited.

Nicol (1987) described a new flexible electrogoniometer which used strain gauge wire. This eliminated the use of rigid bars and made it possible for the electrogoniometers to be very light. This breakthrough in relatively cheap and unintrusive joint motion analysis gave rise to a plethora of publications on movement analysis of both normal subjects and patients on a variety of joints. These included studies of the hip and knee motion in pre- and postoperative hip-joint-replacement patients (Rowe et al 1989), dynamic analysis of wrist circumduction in normal subjects and subjects with wrist disorders (Ojima et al 1991); the assessment of subtalar motion (Ball & Johnson 1993) and active and passive ranges of movement of the ankle and knee motion in children with hemiplegic cerebral palsy (Hazlewood et al 1994).

8.3.3 Accuracy of electrogoniometers and potentiometers

It is not uncommon for the accuracy of angular displacement of video-based motion analysis to be assessed in comparison with electrogoniometric techniques (Batavia & Garcia 1996, Growney et al 1994, Klein et al 1992). However, for this to be useful the possible sources for error using electrogoniometers need to be considered. Possible sources of error when assessing human motion include:

- Movement of the end blocks of the electrogoniometer on soft tissue around a joint
- Placement of the electrogoniometer in the correct plane of interest to eliminate cross talk between two planes of motion, e.g. adduction and abduction, or rotation with sagittal plane movement

- The limiting mechanical properties of the strain gauge wire giving a finite accuracy of angular displacement measurements.

When used to study the accuracy of video-based motion analysis systems, if set up carefully, all but the last source of error should be eliminated. Nicol (1987, 1989) reported that the error in the measurement of angular displacements due to the mechanical properties of the strain gauge wire was within 1°. Therefore, accurate joint angular motion may be attained with careful placement of electrogoniometers.

8.3.4 Accelerometers

Accelerometers are devices that measure acceleration. These are usually force transducers designed to measure the reaction forces associated with a given acceleration. To measure, say, the acceleration experienced by the limb segments of the lower limb, an accelerometer would be needed on each limb segment.

Accelerometers allow a direct and immediate signal output which can provide real-time visualization and biofeedback. They tend to be relatively low cost; however, the acceleration measured is dependent on their position on the body segment, so when analysis of multiple segments is required the cost can become more significant. Some types are also sensitive to shock caused by large deceleration transients and can be broken easily. As the name suggests accelerometers record acceleration and, although they are very good when considering shock attenuation or the acceleration and deceleration of body segments, they do not give any direct information on segment angles and joint positions.

8.4 Movement analysis systems

Movement analysis systems use either a single camera or multiple cameras to reconstruct two- or three-dimensional movement data, which allows quantification of the kinematics of different movement tasks. To do this accurately and effectively it is important to consider the collection of the camera data, the processing methods to get two- or three-dimensional kinematic data, and, finally, the methods of analysis and modelling the data. These may be broken down into the following aspects that need to be considered when conducting any movement analysis:

- Camera positioning
- Camera speed, sampling frequency and shutter speed
- Synchronizing the cameras
- Calibrating image space
- Data capture
- Digitizing and transformation
- Data filtering
- Anatomical models and marker sets.

8.4.1 Camera positioning

Data collection consists of filming an activity using cameras. The number and position of the cameras dictates whether the study is two or three dimensional. For a two-dimensional study only one camera is needed, which has to be positioned in the plane of interest; for example, viewed from the side for sagittal plane analysis. For a three-dimensional study at least two cameras are needed. The position of the camera relative to the movement of interest should be orthogonal (90° apart) to obtain the greatest accuracy. Some variation is tolerable with the camera positions for a three-dimensional study and it is generally agreed that the cameras may be set between 60° and 120°, although the orthogonal positioning yields the best results (Woltring 1980). When using two cameras to study human-movement patterns, markers or points of interest on the body might not be in view from both cameras at all times. In this case these points cannot be tracked, as two cameras must see each marker at all times. For this reason it is common to see four or more cameras used for three-dimensional movement analysis, as this increases the chance of tracking markers or points of interest through the entire movement.

The number and positioning of cameras does not just affect the identification and tracking of markers, but also the accuracy of the calculation of the final coordinates of the markers or points of interest. Work has been carried out using different numbers of cameras to study the effect of reducing or increasing the number of cameras on the accuracy of the data produced. Woltring (1980) studied multicamera calibration and body marker trajectory reconstruction in three-dimensional gait studies. It was found that as the number of cameras was increased, the errors in the calculation of three-dimensional coordinates decreased. The most noticeable decrease in error was found when moving from two to three cameras. Subsequent increases in the numbers of cameras used yields a smaller reduction in error.

However, this finding should be treated with care as if a camera system consists of only three cameras then it is possible that not all the markers will be visible from all cameras. The number of cameras necessary, therefore, depends very much on the movement tasks being analysed, the anatomical models and marker set used (see Chapter 9). For instance, good gait data may be collected with a very simple marker set from four cameras; however, if you were to try the same with a more complex marker set the data quality would be poor. It is for these reasons that camera systems

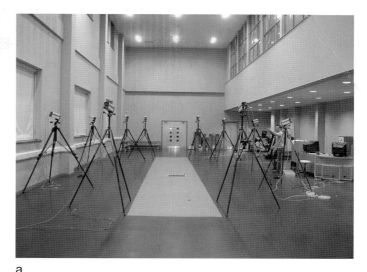

a

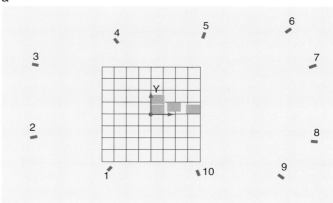

b

Figure 8.5   UCLan's movement analysis laboratory in the faculty of health. Picture of laboratory (a) and plan view of camera positions and force platforms (b)

containing 10 or more cameras are becoming more common in research laboratories (Fig. 8.5a, b). This raises rather important space considerations if more complex anatomical models and marker sets are required. So to determine the most appropriate camera system one has to look at cost, space and complexity of models likely to be needed.

8.4.2 Camera speed, sampling frequency and shutter speed

Standard video equipment with electronically shuttered video cameras has been used extensively in human movement analysis because of the price, immediacy and accessibility (Bartlett et al 1992). Frame rates from standard video cameras are often a limiting factor, as they operate at 25 to 30 frames per second providing a maximum sampling rate of 50 Hz for PAL (Phase Alternate Line) based systems and 60 Hz for NTSC (National Television Standards Committee) based systems. New developments in video technology include simple to operate, lower cost, high-speed cameras.

Faster camera systems are available to allow faster movement patterns, such as sprinting, to be recorded; the faster the activity the faster the sampling frequency or the camera speed must be. Cameras exist that can provide sampling frequencies up to 10 kHz, but it is well accepted that 50 Hz is adequate for studying many aspects of human walking. Nyquist's sampling criterion states that the sampling rate must be at least twice the maximum frequency of the signal, although this only gives the minimum usable sampling frequency (Antonsson & Mann 1985).

Shutter speed or shutter factor is also extremely important if a clear image is to be achieved. The shutter speed is the amount of time the camera shutter is open. If the shutter is open too long then the image will become blurred or smeared. For normal walking a shutter speed or shutter factor of 1/250 of a second or higher is required. If faster activities are being recorded, such as sprinting, a shutter speed of at least 1/1000 of a second is required.

8.4.3 Synchronizing the cameras

When filming an activity with more than one camera it is essential that all cameras record the event simultaneously, only then can the data from one view be combined with another to form a three-dimensional picture of the motion. The one requirement that must be met in order to combine simultaneous camera views is that all cameras must record a single distinct event called the synchronizing event. This event varies from system to system, a flash of light, an electronic beep and signals from a computer to start the cameras recording have all been used successfully. In addition to this, some systems synchronize the opening and closing of the shutter on each camera ensuring that precisely the same image is captured by each camera and not just an image during the same frame. This is usually achieved using a charged coupled device (CCD) on the cameras (Fig. 8.6).

8.4.4 Calibrating image space

The process by which three-dimensional coordinates are extrapolated from two-dimensional images requires information from two sources, inside the camera and outside the camera. These are generally referred to as the intrinsic and extrinsic properties of the camera. The intrinsic parameters refer to information such as the focal length and the centre of the image in relation to the lens, and importantly the distortion parameters of the lens. The extrinsic parameters refer to information such as the position and orientation of the camera and image in the coordinate system of the measurement, which is generally the laboratory coordinate system or global coordinate system (GCS). The intrinsic and extrinsic parameters are generally acquired using calibration techniques; the calibrations used for each parameter differ significantly. Essentially these calibrations are the calibration of the camera lens linearization and the calibration of the system.

Static calibration

The image space, the area in which the movement is to be recorded, must be calibrated to allow for the calculation of the positional information with respect to a known frame of reference. To calibrate the image space the location of fixed points within the area in which the movement is to be recorded must be known. These fixed points may be a calibration frame that is placed in the data collection area or points suspended from the ceiling. This information is recorded and the frame removed so data from the activity may then be collected.

The accuracy of the data produced from motion analysis systems depends considerably on the accuracy of the calibration procedure. It is important that the calibration frame fills a significant proportion of the image space of each camera view. The coordinates of the calibration frame must also be extremely accurate, for laboratory-based work ±0.1 mm is acceptable in all three planes. Any errors in the location of the calibration coordinates will affect the accuracy of the motion to be tracked.

The number of control points required depends on whether the study is two dimensional or three dimensional. For two dimensional, the position of at least four co-planar points must be known to define the measurements in one plane. When calibrating a two-dimensional system care must be taken to position the calibration frame correctly. Two-dimensional systems suffer from perspective error, which occurs when markers or points of interest move closer to or further away from the camera recording the activity. Because of this limitation it is extremely important that the calibration frame is in the same plane as the activity to be recorded. Even with this safe-guard, the segments on the near side of the body will seem longer than those on the far side.

For the calibration of three-dimensional movement analysis system at least six non-coplanar control points are needed (Woltring 1982) (Fig. 8.7). This means that there must be control points in all three planes. Many calibration frames for such systems have more than six calibration points so that they can cover a larger area for data collection and achieve greater accuracy.

When setting up the calibration the control points must be clearly visible from all the cameras. The accuracy of the calibration procedure can be seriously compromised if this is not the case, especially if the number of points visible

Figure 8.6   Qualisys ProReflex CCD camera

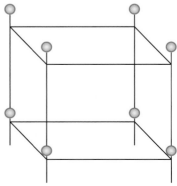

Figure 8.7   Calibration frame from an early motion analysis corporation system

falls below six. The area the control points cover should be approximately the same size as the event being filmed, as the accuracy of the measurements outside of the calibrated volume are compromised (Woltring 1982).

Dabnichki et al (1997) studied the accuracy and reliability of data collection with changes in calibration setup. A series of tests were conducted using the Elite motion analysis system. Dabnichki systematically varied five different factors: camera–object distance, distance from calibrated field, size of calibration field, position in the calibration field and rotation speed of segment. The results showed that the error is sensitive to relatively small changes of the first four factors.

Dynamic calibration

In order to define the extrinsic parameters of the camera, the position and orientation of the camera, the global coordinate system must be defined. Dynamic calibration can be achieved in a number of ways; however, the most common and reliable way is to use a static frame to define the origin, or zero position, and the direction of the positive x and y axis.

In addition to the static frame a wand is moved dynamically through the volume of the cameras. There are an incredibly large number of two-dimensional coordinates generated from the movement of the wand. To find the position and orientation of the cameras and the three-dimensional coordinates of the wand, a procedure known as bundle adjustment is used (Brown 1966). From this the position and orientation of the cameras and three-dimensional coordinates of the wand are calculated (Fig. 8.8a, b).

Norm of residuals

The determination of the coordinates for each marker is an approximation with errors. This error in each marker may be reported as a 'norm of residuals' (Nigg 1994), which is a summation of the errors present. This way of reporting on the errors involved in the calibration allows the user to determine whether there is any serious error. Typically, the 'norm of residuals' is found for the calibration frame for each trial digitized.

These residuals basically tell us what correction the movement analysis system will do; these are not the same as the errors in the data-collection volume. The standard deviation of the wand length or between static markers of the calibration frame may also be reported to give an idea of the potential errors in the calculation of marker positions.

Lens correction

The lens of all cameras is affected by distortions to some extent. These are caused by the material and imperfections produced during the manufacturing process. This introduces small errors into the system that, if not accounted for, can result in larger errors in the reconstruction of a two-dimensional image. If the error can be measured for the lens it can be accounted for during or post acquisition. To study lens distortion, points of known position, relative to one another, they are filmed. Tasi (1986) developed a method using 60 calibration points, Antonsson and Mann (1989) used over 12 000 points to obtain a far more detailed study. Ladin (1990) studied lens distortion in two dimensions by

a

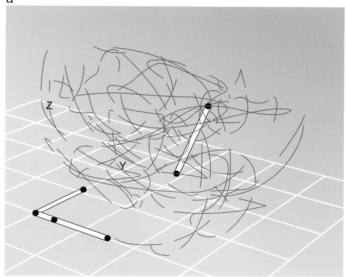

b

Figure 8.8   (a and b) Dynamic calibration

filming an area with known positions of equally spaced points. Ladin took measurements from film and compared them with the known values. The differences between these values were then plotted as vectors, the magnitude of the vector increasing as the lens distortion increased. In this way the lens distortion could be mapped. Ladin showed that substantial errors frequently occur due to lens distortion as the object being filmed moves away from the centre of the field of interest. To prevent such errors the centre of the field of view should be used, however this limits the user. With many movement-analysis systems the cameras are checked for lens distortion by the manufacturer and a lens correction matrix is incorporated into the software. This minimizes the effect of lens distortion. Alternatively information from the calibration frame can be used to correct for lens distortion, although this is not as accurate.

Dynamic methods for camera linearization can be used, such as the method used by Qualisys. The same principle can also be used in a static method. Markers or a checker

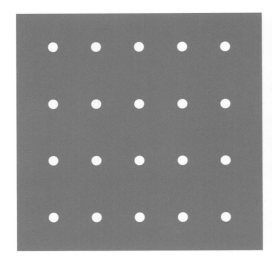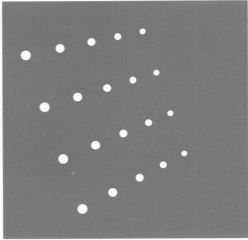

Figure 8.9 Typical data used to correct for lens distortion. The image shows the frame in an orientation with and without roll introduced

board grid are arranged on a frame so that the exact distance between each marker is known (Fig. 8.9). This is then either moved about directly in front of the camera whilst acquiring data, or a few frames of data are acquired whilst the frame is held in a static position. When the frame is moved it provides information about the depth characteristics of two-dimensional space or aspect. From these data the best-fit solution is then used to account for the errors associated with the camera lens.

8.4.5 Data capture

Once the camera set up is calibrated and the subject has had the marker set attached the movement can be recorded. After recording is complete the video data are transferred to the computer hard disk. This process is called capture or video collection. Many movement analysis systems, such as VICON (Jarrett et al 1974), Elite (Ferrigno & Pedotti 1985) and Qualisys capture the video image information straight to the hard disk. These are known as camera- or television-based systems. The second category are known as video-based systems, these collect the video information onto video tape first then transfer it to the hard disk. The use of video tape may decrease the resolution of the system slightly as the image is recorded onto analogue tape and then re-digitized. The introduction of digital video no longer has this drawback, although the format may need to be altered when the data are processed by the computer. Camera-based systems, such as Qualisys and VICON, record the direct output from the cameras, so the resolution is maintained.

The use of a video-based system does have an advantage as it keeps a valuable record on tape of the movement, which may be recollected should the transfer not be successful. However, the tracking of markers tends to be considerably more time consuming and file sizes tend to be larger than camera-based systems. Once the video information has been stored on the computer hard disk, the need for the video apparatus is eliminated and the information can be retrieved from the computer hard disk, one frame at a time, so that it may be digitized.

Clusters and markers

For many movement-analysis systems it is necessary to have markers placed on various anatomical landmarks to represent body segments. These markers are either described as passive or active. The use of markers should not significantly modify the movement pattern being measured; if this were the case then movement analysis with markers would fail the criteria set by Brand and Crowninshield (1981) 'the measurement technique must not significantly alter the performance of the evaluated activity.'

Markers may be singular to represent a joint or in the form of clusters which are positioned on the segment itself. Much work has been carried out determining the optimal configuration of marker clusters and it is now widely accepted that a rigid shell with a cluster of four markers is a good practical solution (Cappozzo & Cappello 1997, Manal et al 2000) (Fig. 8.10a).

Video-based systems tend to use either light-to-dark or dark-to-light contrast with the background. Whereas markers for camera-based systems are generally made of a retroreflective material called Scotchlite. This material is used to reflect light emitted from around the camera back to the camera lens. Some camera-based systems use a stroboscopic light while others use light from synchronized infra-red-light-emitting diodes mounted around the camera lens. Whichever technique is used the contrasting light markers on a dark background have the effect of showing the markers as bright spots (Fig. 8.10b).

In contrast, active markers produce light at a given frequency, so these systems do not require illumination and, as such, the markers are more easily identified and tracked (Chiari et al 2005). The most frequently used active markers are those that emit an infra-red signal such as light-emitting diodes (LED) (Woltring 1976). LEDs are attached to a body segment in the same way as passive markers, but with the addition of a power source and a control unit for each LED. Active markers can have their own specific frequency which allows them to be automatically detected. This leads to very stable real-time three-dimensional motion tracking as no markers can be misidentified as adjacent markers.

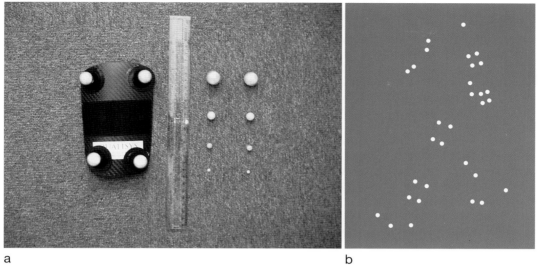

Figure 8.10   (a) Passive markers and marker clusters compared with a 30 cm ruler and (b) captured data from a camera-based system

Active markers also have the advantage that they can be used outside, as passive marker systems are usually confined to indoors as they are sensitive to incandescent light and sunlight. One example of an active system is CODA.

Errors involved with marker placement

The positions of markers are susceptible to two types of error, generally referred to as relative and absolute errors. Relative errors are defined as the relative movement between two or more markers that define a rigid segment. Absolute errors are defined as the movement of a marker with respect to the bony landmark it is representing. Collectively relative and absolute errors are often referred to as soft-tissue artefacts.

Markers are often placed on the skin over a specific anatomical landmark; however, this is not always acceptable to the subject being tested, especially on anatomical land-marks around the pelvis. Hazelwood et al (1997) compared marker placement on skin and lycra over the anterior superior iliac spine ASIS. It was reported that there was significantly more movement when the marker was placed directly on the skin than on lycra, which may lead to overestimation of the movement of the pelvis. Hazelwood and co-workers concluded that marker attachment may be preferable on close-fitting garments than directly on skin.

Relative and absolute errors are often caused by movement of the soft tissue on which the markers are placed (Cappozzo et al 1996, Ladin 1990, Lesh et al 1979). The magnitude of these errors has been studied by using pins secured directly into the bone and comparing the data collected from skin-mounted markers to markers attached to bone pins. These data give a direct measure of soft-tissue movement with respect to the skeletal system (Cappozzo 1991, Levens et al 1948, Reinschmidt 1996). Although this quantifies the errors involved and allows the development of corrective algorithms for skin movement it is not ethically acceptable to use bone pins for routine motion analysis purposes.

A large quantity of data are available describing the amount and the effects of soft-tissue artefacts from skin markers on human lower limb segments, but inconsistencies exist between the reported results. Differences can be accounted for by variation in marker placement and configuration, differences in techniques, inter-subject differences and differences in the task performed (Leardini et al 2005). Several studies (Alexander & Andriacchi 2001, Cappello et al 1997, Fuller et al 1997, Leardini et al 2005, Lucchetti et al 1998) found skin movement to occur because of skin sliding due to adjacent joint rotations or because of the transient response at impact or because of muscle contraction such as pre-activation of the quadriceps prior to touchdown (Reinschmidt et al 1997). Most of these studies assessed lower-limb motion and in particular knee kinematics and largely concluded that unacceptable inaccuracies in extrasagittal motions are present mainly because of soft-tissue artefacts at the thigh segment. Conversely, soft-tissue movement recorded using non-invasive markers on the shank have only a small effect on three-dimensional kinematics and moment estimates at the knee (Holden et al 1997, Manal et al 2002).

A number of techniques for minimizing soft-tissue arte-facts and compensating for their effects have been proposed. Again, these methods depend upon the marker configurations used in the analysis. Relative errors have been modelled using rigid body (Chéze et al 1995) and non-rigid body (Ball & Pierrynowski 1998) theory to best fit cluster marker trajectories during motion. However, as the cluster markers were fixed to a rigid plate these methods were not able to address absolute errors. Surface modelling also includes a point cluster technique, where an array of markers is used to estimate the position of the centre of mass and reference system orientation of a segment (Andriacchi et al 1998). Although an extended version of this method has reported improvements in estimation of the position of the underlying bones (Alexander & Andriacchi, 2001) it can only model skin deformations and has limited use in some applications due to the number of additional markers required.

A recent approach to compensate for skin sliding associated with joint flexion was proposed using an enhanced version of the calibrated anatomical system technique (CAST) (see Chapter 9), where static calibrations of the two extremes of motion of a specific task were recorded (Cappello et al 1997). From these calibrations a model was obtained that allowed for the change in relative position of each thigh marker between the flexed and extended positions. Improved femur orientation and position was achieved. The limitation of this method is that it should be designed specifically for the motor task under analysis; it may also be enhanced by using more sophisticated methods for characterizing skin deformation and sliding throughout the joint range of motion.

Another approach to this problem is known as global optimization. This involves simultaneous pose (position and orientation) estimation of multi-linked segmental models. These methods were originally developed by Kepple et al (1994) and Lu and O'Connor (2000) to minimize global measurement errors by taking into account known joint constraints. With these methods weighted sum of squares distances are minimized between simulated markers and markers determined by a constrained model with ball and socket joints between linked chains. Similar methods to compensate for false identification and occlusion of markers were also extended to include computation of local marker displacement due to skin movement artifacts (Cerveri et al 2005), but further validation is still required. Although advantages can be gained from global optimization, the constraints and/or complexity of the models limit their use for clinical assessment, particularly for patients with joint instabilities or deformities (Leardini et al 2005).

Future studies that are able to model the three independent contributions of inertia, skin sliding near the joints and segment deformation due to muscle contractions may reduce relative and absolute errors. Another approach would be to collect a large series of measurements from several populations that compare the movement of the soft tissues directly with the movements of the underlying bone (Leardini et al 2005). Until better compensation techniques become available, care must be taken in comparing movement data where different marker sets have been used.

8.4.6 Digitizing, transformation and filtering

Digitizing or tracking is the process of identifying points on the body using markers or a visual impression of the joint centres. There are two methods of digitizing, manual and automatic.

Manual digitizing

Using a computer cursor, the location of each of the subject's body joints, e.g. ankle, knee, hip, shoulder and elbow joints, can be selected and entered into the computer (Ariel 1974). Once this has been carried out for one frame the information stored on the hard disk can then be advanced one frame and the same points on the body identified. This needs to be carried out on each frame which builds up a stick figure of the movement. This allows movement with or without markers to be analyzed, but it can be very slow, especially if three-dimensional movement is being digitized using a number of cameras.

Automatic digitizing

Automatic digitizing uses markers that need to be identified once in the first frame but will be automatically tracked throughout all the remaining frames (Mann & Antonsson 1983) and (Keemink et al 1991). In all cases the centroid of the marker is calculated producing a point representing each marker for each camera view (Fig. 8.11a, b). This technique is much faster than manual digitizing, but it does rely on the use of markers that can encumber some movement patterns.

Transformation

Transformation is the computation of the two- or three-dimensional coordinates of the markers on chosen points on the body. Computation is performed based on or adapted from a direct linear transformation (DLT) method developed by Abdel-Aziz and Karara (1971). The DLT provides a relationship between the two-dimensional coordinates of a marker from each camera view and its three-dimensional location in space. The requirement of DLT is that all the data recorded from the different camera views are synchronized, i.e. simultaneous camera views of the activity.

Transformation can be used for two-dimensional or three-dimensional movement analyses. The calculation of the coordinates is carried out by the computer from the calibration, (section 8.4.4). The exact positions of the calibration points are stored in the computer, which can be used to calculate the exact position of a marker around the calibration area. The two-dimensional or three-dimensional coordinates of each marker can then be extracted from the system and used to represent the segment as a rigid body.

Data filtering

A smoothing or filtering operation is performed on the coordinates of each marker or position to remove small random digitizing errors. There are several smoothing algorithms or filters available; the most common are digital filters and spline techniques.

Spline techniques are described as piece-wise polynomials that are joined together at points called knots (Woltring 1985, Wood & Jennings 1979). These are usually based on cubic or quintic polynomials and are known as cubic spline or quintic spline techniques. Cubic spline is the most common smoothing technique in motion analysis as it balances closeness of fit with speed of calculation. Some motion analysis system's software allows the operator to choose the smoothing algorithm and the level of smoothing while others smooth automatically. The least squares spline approach requires the operator to input a smoothing parameter, which controls the smoothness and closeness of the fit. The general cross validation spline technique developed by Woltring (1985) involves an estimation of the smoothing parameter based on all the data points and prediction of a best fit curve, this subsequently does not require any input from the operator. The general cross validation is the technique favoured by many motion analysis systems' software.

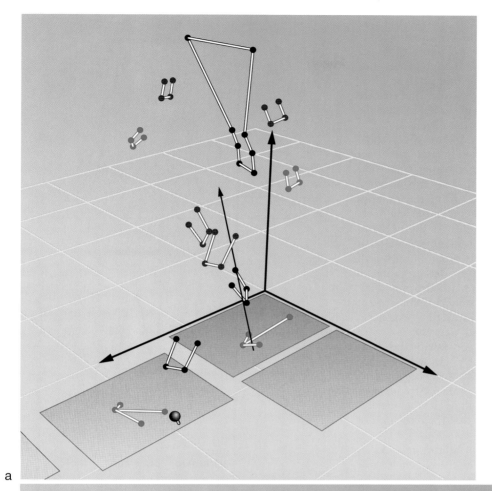

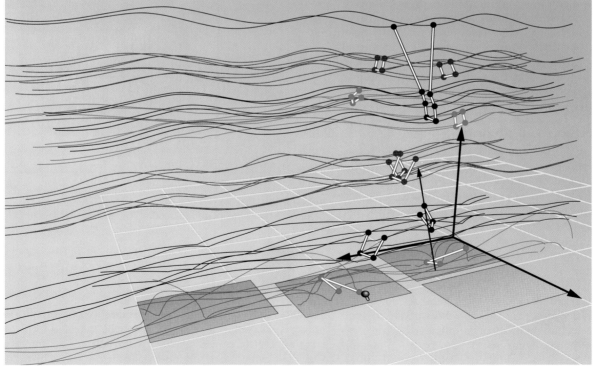

Figure 8.11   (a and b) Automatic digitizing using Qualisys Track Manager (QTM)

Low pass filters are also commonly used, typically 2nd or 4th order Butterworth filters with the cut off frequency set to 6 or 7 Hz for walking data. Low pass filters allow the low-frequency data through, but prevent the high-frequency data. The practical upshot of this is that the small random digitizing errors and some errors of soft-tissue artefacts are removed. However, much care needs to be taken so that the filtering does not change the movement data itself.

Figures 8.12a, b and c show an example of the vertical toe displacement, velocity and acceleration and the effect of no filtering, a 6 Hz 4th order Butterworth filter and a 4 Hz 4th order Butterworth filter. The unsmoothed data show the higher frequency 'noise' from the random digitizing errors causes a disproportionate error. The 6 Hz 4th order low pass Butterworth filter removes the peaks of the displacement graph, but allows a useable signal for velocity and acceleration. The 4 Hz 4th order Butterworth filter significantly affects the displacement data and causes an underestimation of the velocity and acceleration data. Therefore, not filtering will produce unsmooth displacement graphs and leave much of the velocity and all of the acceleration data unuseable. Filtering too aggressively with a 4 Hz cut off frequency will distort and falsify the data, but filtering at a cut-off frequency of 6–7 Hz will produce useable data for displacements, velocities and accelerations for walking. For faster activities higher cut-off frequencies are required. It is always worth looking at the marker velocity and acceleration data to check that the data are not over or under filtered.

Different time and frequency domain filtering techniques have been developed to remove these high-frequency error components, also Fourier series filtering and digital filtering are currently popular. However, these filters do not account for higher frequencies generated by impacts or rapid energy transfers. Alternative methods have more recently been proposed and results so far are encouraging (Chiari et al 2005), but irrespective of the processing technique, random errors must be minimized as data differentiation amplifies the noise to signal ratio, which results in considerable inaccuracies in derivative data.

8.4.7 Errors due to digitizing

We previously covered errors involved with marker placement; however, other sources include random errors in the form of electronic noise, digitizing errors, marker flickering or marker distortion (Chiari et al 2005). Two-dimensional video images using standard video cameras commonly suffer from marker distortion from higher speed distal segment movement. Pattern recognition algorithms and more advanced digitizing palettes or skilled manual digitizing can reduce errors in locating the centre of distorted markers, but inevitably notable errors may still remain. Camera-based systems use threshold detection algorithms to detect the two-dimensional coordinates of the brighter pixels covered by a marker. Detection may then be enhanced with a bi-dimensional cross-correlation template matching method provided that the markers are spherical (Chiari et al 2005). Errors in estimating the centre of a marker vary with technique, but can be improved with circle fitting using a least squares approach. Marker size can also influence centroid

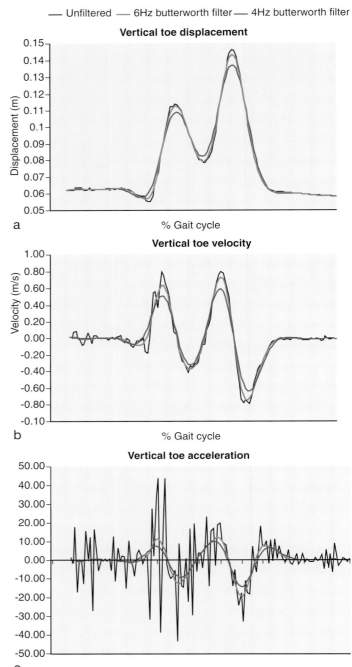

Figure 8.12 (a) Filtering of vertical toe displacement, (b) filtering of vertical toe velocity and (c) filtering of vertical toe acceleration

estimation as larger markers can merge with neighbouring markers and small markers may not be detected by a sufficient number of cameras, which will result in tracking errors. Optimal camera set up and calibration procedures may reduce errors resulting from marker merging and distortion, but further developments are still required to minimize these errors from the movement data.

8.5 Configurations for camera-based motion capture

Motion capture systems used in movement analysis laboratories can generally be grouped into two dimensional and three dimensional. The type of system used varies dependent on the requirements of the depth of analysis required. Two-dimensional systems are normally based on the use of simple video cameras positioned orthogonally to capture either the coronal or sagittal plane movement. Three-dimensional systems are normally made up of many cameras (generally between 4 and 10), these types of systems allow for a detailed three-dimensional analysis of human movement. Three-dimensional systems are generally much more expensive than two-dimensional systems. When purchasing a three-dimensional system one must be aware of the amount of cabling associated, so, if you have the opportunity to design your laboratory try to incorporate cabling in to the walls and floor wherever possible. This will allow for a much safer working environment for both you and any research participants/patients.

8.5.1 Configurations of two-dimensional motion analysis systems

Two-dimensional camera configurations comprise of a single video camera. These can give valuable information about single plane movements. A standard video camera will usually suffice, but this will not be able to pick up more complex multiplanar movements. The only additional cost associated with two-dimensional systems is the software to digitize and process the data. This software is produced by a number of manufacturers; these include HU-M-AN (HMA Technologies Inc.), APAS (Ariel Performance Analysis System) and Silicon coach. Some of these systems work on the basis of manual digitizing of markers, whereas others use colour and shape recognition to identify markers. When using systems of this type there are always a number of risks associated with the quality of the data, these include parallax error, perspective error, cross planar errors and digitizing errors. The use of two-dimensional systems relies on the placement of markers on the lateral aspect of the joint, which is used to identify the joint. This is not, in fact, the joint; however, the relative movements between the markers can provide some information with regards to the joint movement.

Camera configuration 1

Setting up the camera directly in the sagittal plane will allow for analysis of the joints of the lower limbs in the sagittal plane. Care must be taken to ensure the camera is exactly in the plane of movement (Fig. 8.13).

Camera configuration 2

This involves setting up the camera in the coronal plane; viewing the individual front on allows for the analysis of coronal plane variables. This can be of interest in the analysis of patients with known varus/valgus knee deformities. Care must be taken not to incorrectly identify internal rotation with flexion as valgus (Fig. 8.14).

Camera configuration 3

Using essentially the same setup as configuration 2, this time the camera is positioned posterior. This can be particularly useful when looking at rearfoot movement in the prescription of orthoses. Again care must be taken not to misinterpret cross planar motions in a single plane (Fig. 8.15).

8.5.2 Three-dimensional motion analysis systems

Three-dimensional systems remove much of the risk associated with two-dimensional systems; however, this can be directly related to the cost of the system. In general, the camera value can range from between £1000 and £12000 per camera. This can bring the overall cost of the hardware to well in excess of £100000. One must then account for support and software, which may be as much as another £2000 per year. However, the cost of such systems is generally matched by their performance. A three-dimensional system allows the user to take advantage of more advanced marker

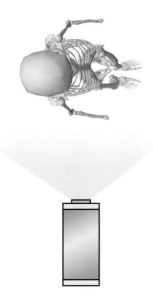

Figure 8.13   Camera set up for sagittal plane view

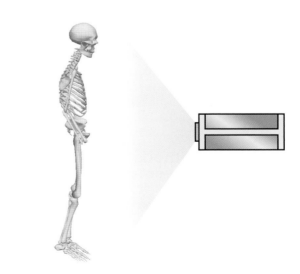

Figure 8.14   Camera set up for frontal plane view

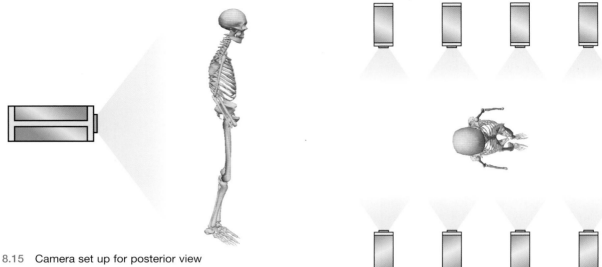

Figure 8.15   Camera set up for posterior view

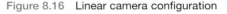

Figure 8.16   Linear camera configuration

configurations, as the system will generally automatically identify the markers and will not be affected by errors such as perspective and cross planar errors. As with two-dimensional systems, care must be taken when setting up three-dimensional systems. There are two main types of configuration, linear and umbrella. Linear refers to the cameras being positioned at set distances apart all running in two parallel lines. NB: this is only possible with certain systems which do not require all the cameras to track the calibration frame. Umbrella setups refer to those which use a bank of cameras round the front and rear.

Linear camera configuration

The linear camera configuration allows much greater data collection volume as not all of the cameras have to 'see' the reference frame. However, there is an increased risk of the cameras identifying one another as a camera due to cameras tracking the opposite camera. And there is increased risk of marker occlusion due to the limited number of cameras in a certain area (Fig. 8.16).

Umbrella camera configuration

This type of configuration is more suited to more advanced marker sets that exploit marker sets for multiple segment feet. The cameras are positioned in such a way that ensures at least three cameras are always tracking the data for each marker. This configuration will result in a slightly smaller calibrated volume (Fig. 8.17).

Figure 8.17   Umbrella camera configuration

Summary: Methods of analysis of movement

- Movement analysis systems can vary from the study of foot contact distances using ink pads to advance multicamera three-dimensional movement analysis.

- Each type of system can give very useful clinically relevant information about changes through rehabilitation and treatment.
- As the complexity of movement analysis systems increases so does the ability to look at the interactive effects between joints and body segments and the interaction between the different planes of the body.
- With an increase in complexity come longer setup times and the requirement for training for the users. Although with many systems now on the market the training requirements are reduced with improvements in the software.
- There are many systems currently on the market, however, the most important aspect for the user is having a clear idea of what measures will produce clinically useful data, without this investment in equipment is a folly.

Anatomical Models and Marker Sets

Chapter

9

Jim Richards and Dominic Thewlis

This chapter covers different marker sets commonly used in movement analysis. This includes modelling both of the lower limb and foot. The nature of six degrees of freedom measurement is considered and the associated errors encountered when considering different coordinate systems.

Chapter 9: Aim

To consider the different marker sets methods commonly used in movement analysis and consideration of errors associated with different techniques.

Chapter 9: Objectives

- To describe the different methods of marker placement in movement analysis
- To summarize the nature of six degrees of freedom analysis
- To contrast and compare the effect of using different anatomical landmarks on normal and pathological gait data
- To contrast and compare the effect of using different coordinate systems on normal and pathological gait data.

9.1 The simple marker set

The simplest marker set involves directly fixing markers on the skin over a bony anatomical landmark close to the centre of rotation of a joint. The position of the limb segment is then defined by the straight line between the two markers.

The first method requires less markers and so, theoretically, has less interference with the movement pattern, but does not allow the calculation of axial rotation of the body segment. The anatomical landmarks used are: head of the fifth metatarsal, lateral malleolus, lateral condyle of the femur, greater trochanter, anterior superior iliac spine, acromion process, lateral condyle of the humerus and styloid process at the wrist (Fig. 9.1).

9.2 Vaughan marker set

The Vaughan marker set consists of 15 markers on the lower limb and pelvis. This allows for more detail for the

location of the knee joint centre by including a marker in the coronal plane on the tibial tuberosity. The inclusion of the heel marker allows a more appropriate functional reference for the long axis of the foot to be determined between this and the metatarsal heads with the pivot point of the foot determined by the malleoli markers. The inclusion of the sacral marker also allows for a more functional reference for pelvis inclination in the sagittal plane and a meaningful measurement of pelvic tilt.

The anatomical landmarks used are: head of the fifth metatarsal, lateral malleoli, heel, tibial tuberosity, femoral epicondyle, greater trochanter, anterior superior iliac spine and sacrum (Fig. 9.2).

9.3 Helen Hayes marker set

As with the Vaughan marker set the inclusion of the heel marker and the sacral marker allows for a more appropriate functional reference for the foot and pelvis. However, the Helen Hayes marker set also includes tibial and femoral wands. These are markers on sticks that are attached to a pad fixed to the segment using tape or bandage. These are not placed on any anatomical position as such, and variations on the length of wand and positioning, anterior versus lateral, have been used. The inclusion of these wands allowed the femoral and tibial rotations to be quantified for the first time.

The anatomical landmarks used are: head of the second metatarsal, lateral malleoli, heel, tibial wand, femoral epicondyle, femoral wand, greater trochanter, anterior superior iliac spine and sacrum (Fig. 9.3).

9.4 The CAST marker set

The calibrated anatomical system technique (CAST) was first proposed by Cappozzo et al (1995) to contribute towards standardizing movement description in research labs and clinical centres for the pelvis and lower-limb segments. This method involves identifying an anatomical frame for each segment through the identification of anatomical landmarks and segment tracking markers, or marker clusters. Marker clusters can be directly attached to the skin or mounted on rigid fixtures, which are dependent upon the anatomy, the activity and the nature of the study.

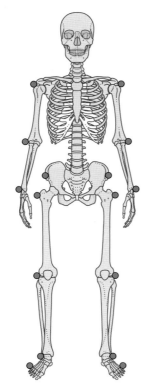

Figure 9.1   The simple marker set

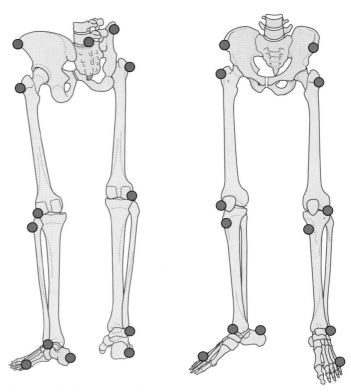

Figure 9.2   Vaughan marker set

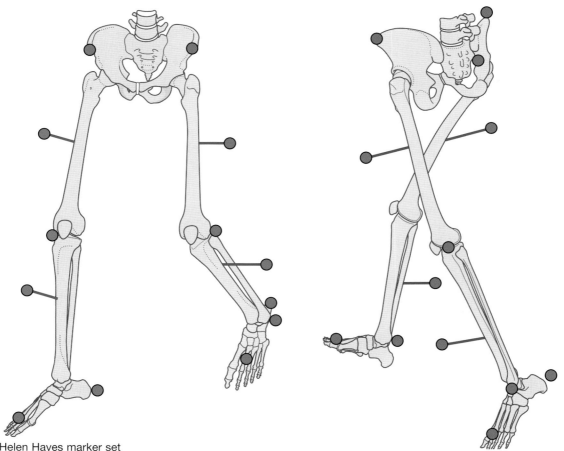

Figure 9.3   Helen Hayes marker set

These markers may be anatomical or arbitrary, individual or clusters and mounted on the skin, on wands or on rigid plates (Manal et al 2000).

9.4.1 Static 'anatomical calibration' markers

Markers are placed on lateral and medial aspects of joints on anatomical landmarks at the proximal and distal ends of the segment. This is similar to previous marker sets; however, with CAST an additional cluster of markers is also placed on each segment (Fig. 9.4). The anatomical landmark markers enable the proximal and distal ends of the segment to be identified in relation to the cluster of markers. For techniques using three-dimensional kinematics the coordinates in the laboratory or global coordinate system (GCS) defining the segment are transformed into a local coordinate system (LCS) or segment coordinate system (SCS) using coordinate transformation.

Different anatomical markers may be used to define the proximal and distal ends of a segment. For example the segments of the lower limb may be defined by:

- Foot segment: 1st and 5th metatarsal heads and the medial and lateral malleoli
- Tibial segment: medial and lateral malleoli and the femoral epicondyles
- Femoral segment: femoral epicondyles and the greater trochanter
- Pelvis segment: posterior superior iliac spines and anterior superior iliac spines.

9.4.2 Dynamic tracking markers

Marker clusters are placed on each body segment. These must be in place during the static 'anatomical calibration'. The exact placement of the clusters does not matter as the CAST technique uses the relative positions to the anatomical landmarks used in the static 'calibration'. These markers may be anatomical or arbitrary, individual or clusters and mounted on the skin, on wands or on rigid plates (Manal et al 2000). During placement we make sure that all markers on the clusters are positioned so they can be tracked effectively. To get the most effective tracking this usually requires the markers to be placed at an angle between the coronal and sagittal planes.

At least three non-collinear markers (markers that do not lie in a straight line) are required to track the segment position and orientation (the ensemble of position and orientation of a rigid body from any one frame relative to another in six degrees of freedom Cappozzo et al 2005); however, up to nine have been used. The usually accepted number is four or five markers per segment or cluster allowing for one or two markers to be lost at some stage during the movement tasks and still allow data in six degrees of freedom to be found (Fig. 9.5). This is sometimes referred to as marker redundancy (i.e. if you lose a marker during tracking the model will still work).

9.4.3 So what is the benefit of using CAST compared with other marker sets?

CAST offers the ability to model each body segment in six degrees of freedom. So as long as a segment has got an

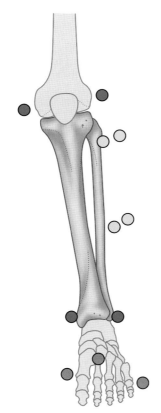

Figure 9.4 Anatomical markers and segment cluster

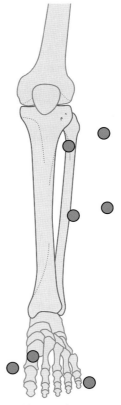

Figure 9.5 Dynamic tracking markers

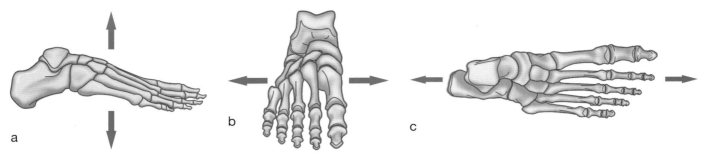

Figure 9.6 (a) Vertical movement, (b) medio–lateral movement and (c) anterior–posterior movement

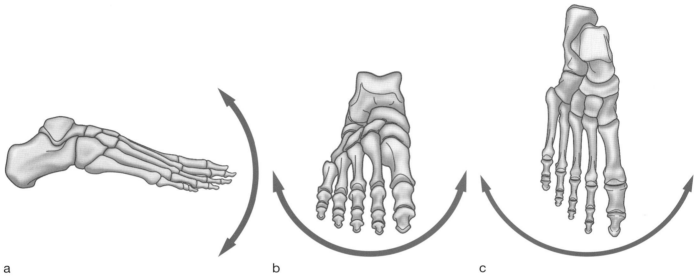

Figure 9.7 (a) Sagittal plane angular movement, plantar–dorsiflexion of the foot (engineers call pitch), (b) coronal (frontal) plane angular movement, pronation–supination of the foot (engineers call roll) and (c) transverse plane angular movement, inversion–eversion of the foot (engineers call yaw)

anatomical frame by using the 'static' markers and a cluster of 'dynamic' tracking markers, this further allows interactions and movements between the body segments again in six degrees of freedom, along the anatomical axis defined by either proximal or distal segment.

9.4.4 So what do we mean by 'six degrees of freedom' exactly?

Any body segment may move in six ways, independently, although in human movement all six ways often happen at the same time, this is good functionally as it allows a very adaptive mechanism; however, it makes understanding the function of each of these movements quite difficult.

The six ways a body segment can move are: three linear or translational movements, vertically, medio–laterally and anterior–posterior, and three rotational or angular movements in the sagittal, coronal and transverse planes. Figures 9.6 and 9.7 show these different movements on the foot, but these can be equally applied to any body segment.

However, if we are trying to look at the interaction of two segments about a joint then there are 12 degrees of freedom, six for each body segment. We can now start to get really complex when considering all the segments within, say, the foot, and this is where we need to listen to the clinical sense of what we are trying to quantify in terms of functional

anatomy before we tie ourselves in potentially unnecessary and unintelligible knots.

9.4.5 So why do we need 'six degrees of freedom'?

For many joints the use of six degrees of freedom is not strictly necessary to gain clinically useful information; therefore, more simple anatomical models are extremely useful for determining function changes due to surgical and conservative management, such as physiotherapy and orthotic management. However, more simple anatomical models do not give a full picture of the functioning and interaction of different joints in the body, and on occasions could give inaccurate measurements and misleading information.

Consider the measurement of knee valgus. With a simple marker setup what may appear as a valgus knee may, in fact, be nothing of the sort. If you were to stand, for instance with your knee flexed and your hip internally rotated then this would be presented as an extremely valgus knee, far beyond what the anatomy would in fact be capable of. If we now consider the same position using CAST and six degrees of freedom then we are able to isolate the angular movements in the three rotational planes independently and, therefore, gain the correct interpretation of the joint and segment positions and movement.

Much has been published on sagittal plane movements, but there has been far less attention on the interaction of coronal, transverse and sagittal movements. The question is how important are these extrasagittal movements; the answer is clear, VERY.

If we consider pretty much any foot orthotic management, clinicians will talk about pronation–supination, inversion–eversion, and pantar–dorsiflexion in terms of triplanar movement of the joints in the ankle foot complex. Therefore, any functional foot orthotic management is likely to be changing the foot mechanics in six degrees of freedom.

We will now consider patellofemoral bracing and taping in individuals with instability or pain in the patellofemoral joint. Most of the previous work has focused on the sagittal plane, although both of the above interventions are actually trying to change the coronal translational position of the patella, which in fact will change both the coronal and transverse plane rotational movements and probably have only a secondary effect in the sagittal plane.

Now the overriding aspect of these examples is the clinicians involved know what they are trying to achieve and the fault, if we can call it that, lies with the bioengineers not modelling the body in a complex enough way.

9.5 Methods of identifying anatomical landmarks

9.5.1 The CAST marker set with the Davis dynamic pointer (or pointy stick method)

CAST requires a medial and lateral, and proximal and distal segment reference. Previously we talked about the use of anatomical markers positioned on bony landmarks on the body. However, these anatomical landmarks may also be determined by using a wand of at least two coincident markers to point to the target anatomical landmark (Davis et al 1991). If the distance between these markers is known in relation to the end of the point of the wand, or stick, then the position of the end of the stick can be determined.

This method means that anatomical markers are not required to be stuck to the individual being tested. This method is now being incorporated into movement analysis software, such as Visual3D Motion Analysis Software by C-Motion, which allows this method of anatomical referencing to be applied simply and quickly. This method has certain advantages, for example, once the anatomical frame is defined and the cluster moves during a movement or becomes uncomfortable. It is possible to redefine the anatomical frame quickly without having to reapply markers, in addition a single anatomical frame, for example, the shank, can be redefined. This system may also be more accurate at defining the anatomical landmark as the pointer end is positioned directly on the location. This removes the need to account for marker diameter and marker centeroid calculation.

9.5.2 The CAST marker set with functional joint centre identification

Arguably the most reliable method for the calculation of the position of a joint centre and the ISB recommendation for identifying hip joint centre is the 'functional' approach validated by Leardini et al (1999) and Schwartz and Rozumalski (2005). The functional joint centre calculates the position between two moving body and defines the common point of rotation segments. Essentially this method examines the six degrees of freedom motion of two adjacent body segments defined using clusters. For the pair of body segments the axis of rotation is computed. From this information the most likely intersection of all axes for the two segments is found providing the position for the joint centre. This method can be used on all joints of the body; however, it is recommended that the shoulder joint is not attempted due to the complexity of the shoulder girdle. It is particularly useful for modelling the position of the hip-joint centre as this has generally been assumed to either lie in a line projected from the greater trochanter or based on a regression with respect to pelvis depth and width.

It has previously been suggested that the hip-joint centre may be represented by a simple projection 8 cm medial to the greater trochanter. This appears to be a simple and useful method for 'normal' individuals, however, this can cause quite a large error with individuals of different body shapes and body mass indices, and the author advises caution in using a simple projection from the greater trochanter when the hip and knee mechanics are key research objectives.

9.5.3 The effect of using different anatomical landmarks on gait data

In order to calculate accurate joint kinetics it is essential to locate the centre of rotation in a repeatable manner through the definition of an anatomical frame. This issue was highlighted by Della Croce et al (1999), who identified that the errors associated with incorrect anatomical frame definition are as, if not more, important than those caused by skin movement. Clinically, the definition of the joint centre is generally achieved by using palpable anatomical landmarks to define the medial–lateral axis of the joint. From these anatomical landmarks the centre of rotation is generally calculated in one of two ways: through the use of regression equations based on standard radiographic evidence or simply calculated as a percentage offset from the anatomical marker based on some kind of anatomical landmarks (Bell et al 1990, Cappozzo et al 1995, Davis et al 1991, Kadaba et al 1989).

The CAMARC (computer-aided movement analysis in a rehabilitation context) consortium proposed a standardized list of palpable anatomical landmarks in order to define the anatomical frame of the lower limbs; these were largely based on the work conducted by Cappozzo et al (1995). This work was designed to standardize methodology and resolve many of the historical issues found with modelling the segments of the lower limbs. The issue of hip joint identification is one that has been covered in much depth and there are still many debates around this area. However, the errors associated with knee joint location have received much less attention. Initially, it should appear a simple choice as to the correct landmark to use based on the CAMARC suggestions. However, traditionally there have been a number of landmarks used around the knee, which may not be a true representation of the knee joint centre of

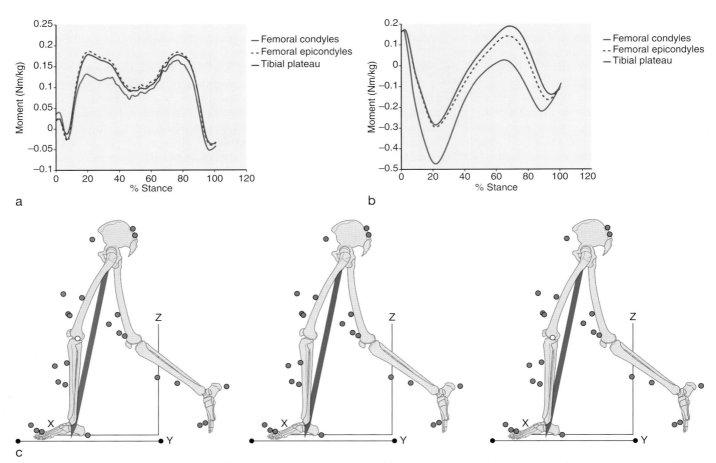

Figure 9.8   (a) Coronal knee movements (b) Sagittal knee movements (c) The change in the joint position using femoral epicondyle and tibial plateau.

rotation. Some of the anatomical landmarks may have an effect on anterior–posterior position of the centre of rotation, whereas some may affect the relative angle of the anatomical frame through a change in orientation. Holden and Stanhope (1998) examined the effect of changes in the anterior–posterior position of the knee joint centre on sagittal plane knee joint moments. Importantly, they identified that a displacement as small as 10 mm can result in a change in the functional interpretation of the moment. The methods used by Holden and Stanhope (1998) were to establish the anatomical frame based on a standard model and then to virtually reposition the anatomical landmarks to represent an anterior–posterior shift, rather than considering the effect of incorrect anatomical landmark identification. Manal et al (2002) examined the effect of expressing knee joint moments in two different orthogonal anatomical frames. The anatomical frames differed by approximately 15° throughout the transverse plane. It was noted that large differences were found in sagittal and coronal plane knee moments for what was deemed to be only a small change in the orientation of the anatomical frame.

Recent work by Thewlis et al (in press) has examined the common methods of identifying the knee with different anatomical landmarks. The different landmarks considered were: the femoral epicondyles, femoral condyles and tibial ridges. Each method was used to define the anatomical

frame, thus the segment end points of the distal femur and proximal tibia representing the knee joint centre. Gait data were then collected using CAST and the external net knee joint moments were calculated based upon the three different anatomical frames. The moments were analysed in the sagittal, coronal and transverse planes. The maximum deviation about the femoral epicondyle frame was found when using the femoral condyle frame with mean deviations of 30 mm anterior and 20 mm medial. This was found to have the effect of changing the peak knee moments by approximately 25% and 8% in the sagittal and coronal planes respectively (Fig. 9.8a, b, c).

From this work it is clear that anatomical frames need to be well defined and clearly reported to ensure clinically useable data. This study has identified that Holden and Stanhope (1998) and Manal et al (2002) both identified independent sources of discrepancy by changing the position and orientation of the segment respectively. Because of the relatively small distances between anatomical landmarks about the knee there is potential for misidentification. Although these errors may be small in terms of the distances between landmarks, the error is carried forward through all of the calculations, resulting in a much larger systematic error in the moment calculations. Therefore, the correct marker placement is of paramount importance in the reliability and repeatability of joint moment data.

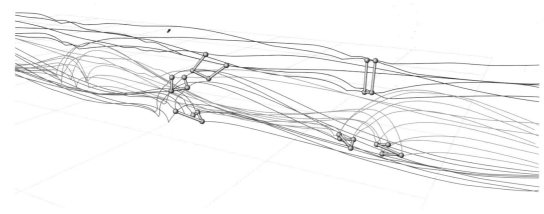

Figure 9.9   Tracked data for three-segment foot

9.6 Foot models

9.6.1 The multiple segment foot

In gait analysis the foot is nearly always considered as a single segment system with the ankle-joint complex considered as a simple hinge. However, it is becoming more widely accepted that the foot and ankle joint complex may be better described as rearfoot, midfoot and toes. This, interestingly enough, is what podiatrists have been telling us for years! It is also very interesting to note that modelling the foot as a deformable segment, rather than a rigid single segment has a significant effect on the accuracy of instantaneous power calculations between segments. It has also been suggested that modelling the metatarsal-phalangeal joint would improve the instantaneous power calculations. How the single segment foot came about was due to restrictions in the capability of biomechanical measurement to identify many small markers. However, now with careful marker placement and camera positioning, and with camera systems containing 8–12 cameras it is possible to track the movement of the tibia, the rearfoot, midfoot and the fore-foot as separate segments through multiple gait cycles in six degrees of freedom (Fig. 9.9).

9.6.2 Models for multiple segment foot

There are now a few foot models emerging from the literature (Carson et al 2001, MacWilliams et al 2003) where aspects of the rearfoot, midfoot and the forefoot are modelled as separate segments. Although this degree of measured kinematic detail is only in its infancy, it is quickly becoming apparent that many pathological conditions could benefit from this type of analysis. More recently, Woodburn et al (2004) considered the use of multisegment foot motion during gait in rheumatoid arthritis and concluded: 'This technique may be useful to evaluate functional changes in the foot and to help plan and assess logical, structurally based corrective interventions.' However, almost all studies so far have considered barefoot walking due to the nature of the marker placements on the feet, which makes the study of foot orthoses and the effect of footwear very difficult if not impossible.

The issue of putting markers on the shoe is an interesting one. It is questionable whether this gives us the same data

as on the foot itself; however, this is currently the only way we can look at shod walking and the effect of foot orthoses. It may be possible to modify the shoes to allow markers on the foot. However, this requires the structure of the footwear, which is an integral part of any orthotic management. Currently, the practice in our laboratory at UCLan, Preston is to look at orthotic management with a three segment foot model, but being mindful of the fact that markers are placed on the shoe and not the foot itself. The model shown in Figure 9.10 and 9.11 is an adaptation of the Carson foot model that may be appropriate to also attach to footwear, although care is required in the analysis as shoe-to-foot movement could produce substantial artefacts due to the small nature of some of the relative movements between foot segments. This adaptation allows analysis in six degrees of freedom between three segments of the foot. Instead of referring to rearfoot, midfoot and forefoot, I have chosen to call these the calcaneus, metatarsal and phalangeal segments to avoid any confusion of the definition of rearfoot, midfoot and forefoot.

The calcaneus may be defined with four markers, with two markers positioned on the rear of the calcaneus or on the rear of the shoes, and a further two markers on a line projected down from the medial and lateral malleoli. The calcaneus axis is then defined by the malleoli markers and the two markers projected down. All four markers are then used to track the movement of the calcaneus. The markers on the medial and lateral malleoli define the proximal end of the calcaneus, and the markers projected down from the distal. In this way the segment coordinate system of the calcaneus and tibia are similar, and allow data analysis with minimal cross planar measurement errors. The metatarsals may also be defined with four markers. To reduce the number of makers required on the foot or shoe, the two markers projected down from the medial and lateral malleoli define the proximal segment end, and markers on the lateral aspect of the 5th metatarsal, and medial aspect of the 1st metatarsal define the distal end. Additional tracking marker may be added on the dorsal surface between these proximal and distal anatomical landmarks. Again this allows a segment coordinate system similar to that of the rearfoot. The phalanges may be defined by the proximal markers on the lateral aspect of the 5th

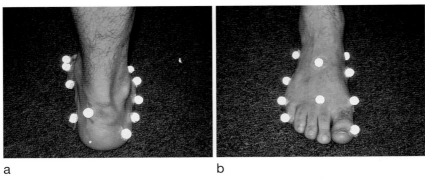

Figure 9.10   (a and b) Markers for a three-segment foot

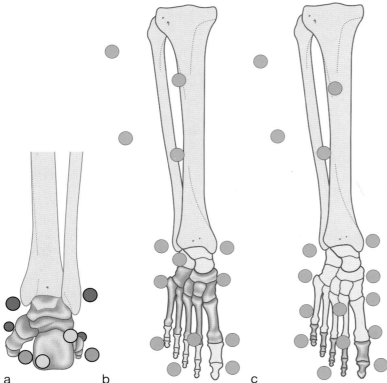

Figure 9.11   Anatomical calibration and tracking markers for a six degrees of freedom foot model

metatarsal and medial aspect of the 1st metatarsal, and the distal markers on the hallux or medial distal part of the shoe on one of the lateral phalanges or the lateral distal part of the shoe. An additional tracking marker may also be placed just anterior to the 2nd or 3rd metatarsal on the dorsal surface (Fig. 9.10a, b).

This model gives the ability to consider each section of the foot in six degrees of freedom as each segment is defined by at least four markers (Fig. 9.11).

A more extreme foot marker set involves putting pins in the different bones of the foot with trihedron marker clusters attached, a trihedron being a configuration of markers in all three planes and meeting at a single point. This enables the quantification of the relative movement between the different bones of the foot. This may well give very interesting data on the relative movement; however, it is questionable whether the person will walk exactly the same with pins fixed in the bones of the foot. It is also not ethically acceptable to use bone pins for routine motion analysis purposes.

9.7 Coordinate systems and joint angles

There are different ways in which we can define joints and segments. These vary from the simple method of using the global coordinate system and simple trigonometry to more advanced methods. Rather than delve into the mathematical manipulation we will look at what the terms mean and what effect these can have on the data. The most commonly found methods include: laboratory or global coordinate system (GCS), segment coordinate systems (SCS), and joint coordinate systems (JCS).

A GCS is were the segment angles are calculated from the x, y, z axis of the laboratory or global frame. A SCS uses the proximal and distal endpoints of the segment to determine an orientation of the x, y, z axis of the joint. A JCS is where the axis of two body segments (proximal and distal) is used to create a third floating axis, or agreeable axis, to the proximal and distal segments. Both the SCS and JCS are ways of identifying a local coordinate system at the joint which is more meaningful anatomically than the GCS. A third way of considering three-dimensional movement is with helical analysis. This does have some advantages over SCS and JCS; however, this does not consider rotations about the anatomical frame axes.

9.7.1 Calculation of joint angles in the global coordinate system

The segment angles can be calculated in GCS by knowing the coordinates of the proximal and distal end of a body segment in a particular plane. The segment angles can then be found by using simple trigonometry. If we assume that two segments are rigid in all other planes than the one we are interested in (i.e. do not move in the coronal and transverse when we are looking at the sagittal plane), and that they are aligned perfectly with the plane we are interested in, then the calculation of the joint angles is a simple matter of subtracting the two angles. This is the method relied upon for all two-dimensional movement analysis and this has been shown to have considerable errors.

Work conducted by McClay and Manal (1998) suggested that two-dimensional data are adequate to indicate peak rearfoot eversion displacement and velocity if foot placement is within normal limits. However, when the foot was not aligned in the sagittal plane, i.e. at heel strike or at toe off when the foot was plantarflexing, the two-dimensional and three-dimensional data did not agree. This was also apparent in the transverse plane, if the foot placement angle was excessively abducted it magnified any differences between the two-dimensional and three-dimensional data. Areblad et al (1990) also quantified the magnitude of this error. They compared data when the foot was abducted from 10° to 30° from the axis of the camera, and found that for every 2° of change in the alignment angle there was 1° of error introduced into the computed angle.

9.7.2 Errors between global and segment coordinate systems

The nature of these potential errors should be considered very carefully when interpreting any data where the GCS has been used. The examples below show the errors involved first for normal walking, and then for an individual with cerebral palsy who has significant internal rotation of the femoral segment (thigh). In introducing internal rotation of the thigh the GCS gives an enormous error in the coronal plane, suggesting the knee reaches 22° abduction or valgus deformity, when in fact this is mostly due to cross planar error from the knee flexion angle and the true abduction or valgus angle is only 8°. Such a large error could easily lead to incorrect management of this individual.

The nature of these errors means that if we are interested in movement in the extra-sagittal planes (i.e. coronal and transverse planes) we have to think about whether what we are measuring has been forced into a false anatomical frame rather than a true anatomical frame (Fig. 9.12a–d).

9.7.3 Cardan sequences and their effect on gait data

Girolamo Cardan (1501–1576) lectured and wrote on mathematics, medicine, astronomy, astrology, alchemy and physics. So it is in some ways appropriate that his contributions should be considered in a book on clinical biomechanics. Cardan's fame rests on his work in mathematics, and especially in algebra. In 1545 he published his 'Ars Magna', which was the first Latin treatise devoted solely to algebra and contained the solution of the cubic equation.

The Cardan sequence itself is a method where a series of three rotations, one about each of the coordinate axes is calculated that would place the joint in the same final orientation as the true movement. In other words they describe one local or segment coordinate system relative to another.

The Cardan sequences are characterized by the rotations about all three axes: xyz, xzy, yzx, yxz, zxy, zyx. Anatomical meaning has been given to one of the Cardan sequences, which is referred to as the JCS, by Grood and Suntay (1983). Assuming a segment coordinate system with z – up, y – anterior and x – lateral, the xyz sequence is the JCS; however, if a different definition of x,y,z directions is used the Cardan sequence for the JCS will change.

If we consider the Cardan sequence that assumes that the x axis is in the medial–lateral direction, the y axis is anterior–posterior (or the direction if travel), and the z axis is in the up and down or axial direction. Therefore, we can describe the JCS as x, y, and z as:

x = flexion–extension,
y = abduction–adduction,
z = longitudinal internal–external rotation

The JCS proposed by Grood and Suntay, for instance, usually relates to the Cardan sequence xyz, or flexion–extension, abduction–adduction, axial rotation. The JCS does have the advantage of relating to the commonly used clinical terms for lower-limb joint motion; however, the drawback is that an orthogonal coordinate system is not guaranteed, i.e. the coordinate systems of the different segments may not be correctly aligned, which can lead to cross talk between the different planes of movement.

So what effect does choosing different Cardan sequences actually have on joint kinematics? In the sagittal plane there is little or no effect in picking different sequences and the best would be xyz, where x is the flexion–extension axis for the reference segment, which would also be the default for most systems. This is due to the relatively large amount of movement that occurs in the sagittal plane, the graphs below show the knee flexion–extension patterns for a normal individual and an individual with cerebral palsy (Fig. 9.13a and b).

However, when we look in the coronal and transverse planes where far less movement occurs we should be far more careful Figure 9.14a–d. Much of the published research does not state which Cardan sequence is used; therefore, we must assume that the 'default' xyz has been used.

The black lines for all graphs show the Cardan sequence xyz (flexion–extension, abduction–adduction, internal–external rotation) and xzy (flexion–extension, internal–external rotation, abduction–adduction). It is very interesting to note that both these sequences produce very similar results. It is also interesting to note that the peaks occur at peak knee flexion, which would imply that cross talk between the planes is occurring. When a flexion–extension is placed second in the

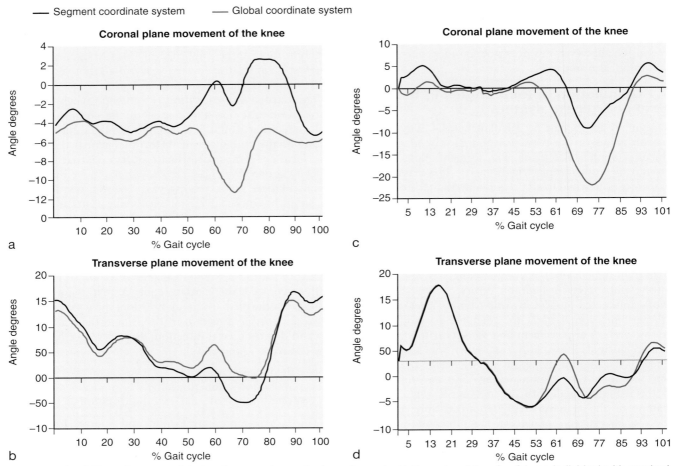

Figure 9.12   (a–d) Errors between global and segment coordinate systems. (a, b) Normal walking, (c, d) in an individual with cerebral palsy

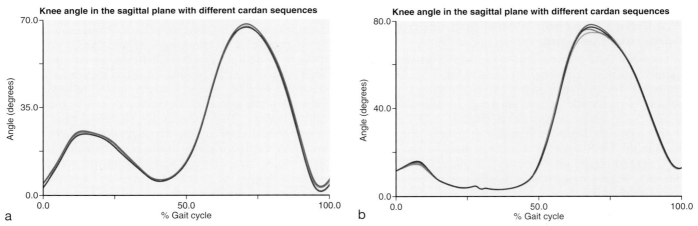

Figure 9.13   (a) Knee motion with the different Cardan sequences for the same gait trial for normal walking and (b) knee motion with the different Cardan sequences for the same gait trial for an individual with cerebral palsy

order of rotations yxz and zxy, two very different patterns are produced which seem to increase the cross talk between planes. When x is placed last in the order of rotations (yzx, zyx) then x or the flexion–extension has least effect and the patterns for the coronal and transverse planes look independent to the movement in the sagittal plane (i.e. no planar cross talk) and show near identical results. The reason

for the difference is an effect due to the dependence in the sequence order, which is orientated to the movement in the anatomical plane being considered.

So if we now think about the implications of this to clinical research. Much has been talked about regarding the three-dimensional movement of the foot, ankle and knee joints and the effect of orthoses. It is quite likely that all,

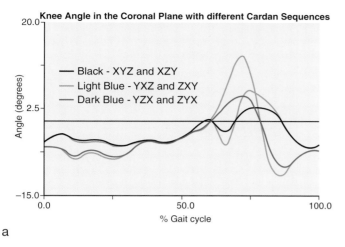

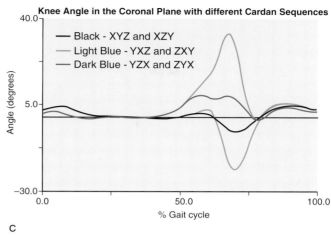

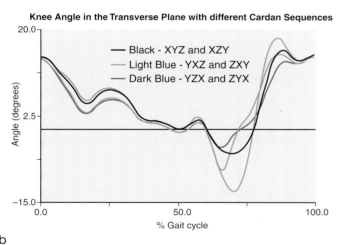

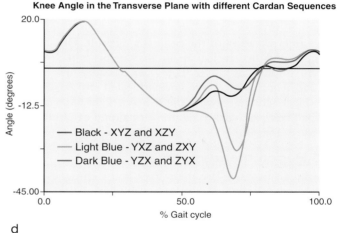

a

c

b

d

Figure 9.14   (a–d) Knee motion in the coronal and transverse planes when using the different Cardan Sequences. (a, b) Normal walking, (c, d) in an individual with cerebral palsy

or most, of the results found with research to date are true effects. However, when we are trying to determine very small changes in the coronal and transverse planes that may still be clinically significant, we need to be clear in our reporting to allow comparison and replication of appropriate data analysis.

Schache et al (2001) studied the effect of the different Cardan angle sequences on the three-dimensional lumbo-pelvic angular kinematics during running. They concluded that different Cardan angle sequences were not found to substantially effect typical three-dimensional lumbo-pelvic angular kinematic patterns during running. However, Nguyen and Baker (2004) found clinically significant differences between the different sequences of rotation for subjects with pathological thoracic motion, and concluded that the conventional sequence (flexion, lateral bending, axial rotation) is preferable for the thorax.

Clearly the issue of the order of Cardan sequence is coming to the fore. One suggestion for a possible way forward is to look at the 'principal axis' where a Cardan sequence is picked based on the plane being considered, e.g. to analyse the transverse plane (z) the Cardan sequence will be zyx and to analyse the coronal plane (y) the sequence will be yzx.

In both these cases I have placed the sagittal plane (x) last to reduce its weighting to avoid possible cross talk, as the knee flexion contained by far the most significant movement during walking. However, if we are dealing with a joint where this is not the case different Cardan sequences may be required.

These are far from being recommendations as there are currently very few published papers on the effect of Cardan sequences, and the best mathematical conventions have yet to be universally agreed for all joints. However, it is clear that the different Cardan sequences do yield significantly different data.

9.7.4 Helical angles

Helical angles are often included in movement analysis software. A helical angle, finite helical axes, or screw axis can be described as a three-dimensional angle of one segment to another in terms of a rotation about and translation along a single axis; this was first suggested by Woltring (1985). This does have some advantages over SCS and JCS as it allows for a combined effect of all three planes and, therefore, does not suffer from planar cross talk. However, helical angles do not consider rotations about the anatomical frame, so the

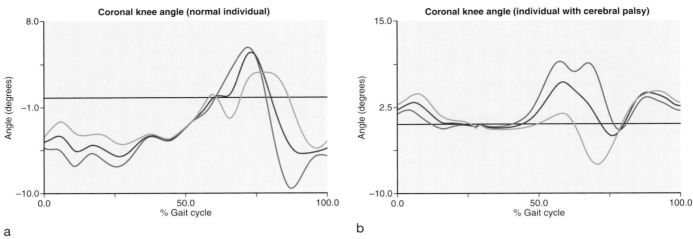

Figure 9.15   (a and b) Helical angle of the knee projected into the coronal plane (black), jcs xyz (light blue) and the principal axis yzx (dark blue)

clinical interpretation of the results is difficult. One further development is that helical angles may be projected into the different anatomical frames. Below we consider the effect of using the helical angle of the knee projected into the coronal plane (black) compared with the JCS xyz (light blue) and the principal axis yzx (dark blue) in normal and cerebral palsy gait (Fig. 9.15a, b).

9.7.5 Recommendations

In the literature there are many reported techniques, most notable is the original JCS proposed by Grood and Suntay (1983), finite helical axes (Woltring 1985) and, more recently, a comparison of different techniques by Cappozzo et al (2005).

Although it may appear a daunting task to pick the correct mathematical technique, it should be noted that the majority of work, unless stated, has used the JCS, which is equivalent to the Cardan sequence (xyz), which is recommended by the International Society of Biomechanics (ISB) for the lower limb (Wu et al 2002). Therefore, to enable comparison to previously published data the JCS (xyz) should be used unless there is a VERY good reason not to. And whichever sequence or method is used, make sure it is reported clearly to allow comparison of data, as without comparison of data we have no way of sharing knowledge.

One other recommendation comes from the International Shoulder Group who state that the shoulder angle (upper arm relative to torso) should be described by Euler sequences (zyz, zxz, yxy, yzy). 'The ISB recommendation on definitions of joint coordinate systems of various joints for the reporting of human joint motion – Part II: shoulder, elbow, wrist and hand' (Wu et al 2005), considered the use of different sequences for the different relative movements between segments. This produced the recommendation of the sequence yxy for the movement between the humerus and the scapula, and between the humerus and the thorax, which are thought to be more appropriate for shoulder movement than the 'traditional' Cardan sequences. However, this does not seem to work for all movements during different tasks and, therefore, great care must be taken to ensure that sequence gives clinically and anatomically meaningful data.

Summary: Anatomical models and marker sets

- There are many anatomical models and marker sets reported in the literature. From these it is possible to plot an increase in complexity over time.
- The increase in complexity in the models relates to the ability of movement analysis systems to track more and more markers, but also the increase in the knowledge of modelling human movement.
- Simple marker sets or models have the advantage of requiring only a few cameras, whereas the more advanced models often require more than eight cameras to track the markers. However, simple models are not able to look at the more complex movements between joints and the different planes of the body.
- With more advanced models we are now able to quantify foot movement by considering the foot in multiple segments. This will lead to more clinically relevant research to find the nature of the interactions between the foot segments and the efficacy of foot orthotic management.
- With an increase in the complexity also come questions on how we define the orientation of body segments and joints. The use of simple joint geometry can lead to misinterpretation of data, especially when the movement of the joints occurs in multiple planes of body simultaneously. Therefore, great care must be taken when describing and reporting clinical data.

Measurement of Muscle Function and Physiological Cost

Chapter 10

Jim Richards, Dominic Thewlis and James Selfe

This chapter covers the methods commonly used to assess muscle function and physiological cost. This includes the use of EMG, isokinetic and isometric testing, and physiological measurement. This chapter also covers common measurements that may be found and how these can relate to different aspects of muscle function and physiological cost.

Chapter 10: Aim

To compare the different methods of assessing muscle function and physiological cost, and distinguish what information can be drawn from their use.

Chapter 10: Objectives

- To describe the nature of EMG signals
- To explain the different methods of processing EMG
- To compare the different methods of processing and what information they can give
- To describe what parameters may be measured by isokinetic and isometric testing
- To describe what information may be found when measuring physiological cost.

10.1 EMG – Electromyography

10.1.1 So what is the link between electricity and muscle activity?

The early work on the link between muscles and electricity was conducted in the 1600–1700s. Swammerdam (1637–1680) discovered that stroking the innervating nerve of the frog's gastrocnemius generated a contraction and the first connection between muscles and electricity was made. Alessandro Volta (1745–1827) developed a device that produced electricity, which could be used to stimulate muscles and subsequently invented the first electric battery. Luigi Galvani, who is often credited as the father of neurophysiology, conducted similar work with frogs' legs in 1791. Galvani showed that electrical stimulation of muscular tissue produces contraction and generates a force.

So why can't we pick on someone our own size? Guillaume Duchenne (1850) applied electric stimulation to intact skeletal muscles in humans. Duchenne was one of the first to investigate electricity for therapeutic purposes, and is considered to be the father of electrotherapy. *The Mechanisms of Human Facial Expression*, first published in French in 1862, included work carried out with The Old Man who was afflicted with almost total facial anaesthesia and showed that scientists have ways of making you smile (Fig. 10.1a, b).

So what causes an EMG signal?

Nerve impulses cause twitch responses in muscle fibres, these combined cause the bulk contractions of a muscle. The EMG signal itself is the electrical signal associated with the contraction of a muscle and the signal is produced by the depolarizing of motor units, often referred to as motor unit action potential (MUAP). The muscle membrane is the electrical source which has a potential of about $-70\,mV$, although the measured potentials often range between $50\,\mu V$ and 20–$30\,mV$. This electrical signal is usually proportional to the level of the muscle activity, or motor unit activity, although this does not obey the same relationship for the different types of contraction. An EMG is sometimes also referred to as a myogram. EMGs can be used to detect abnormal muscle electrical activity that can occur in many diseases and conditions. An electromyogram (EMG) is a record of the electrical activity of muscles.

10.1.2 Muscles and fibre types

Muscles are often grouped into type I (slow oxidative fibres or slow twitch), type IIA (fast oxidative fibres or fast and fatigue resistant) and type IIB (fast glycolytic fibres or fast twitch). Type I fibres have a slow contraction velocity and can produce a moderate force and are very resistant to fatigue. Type IIA fibres have a fast contraction velocity and are resistant to fatigue. Type IIB fibres have a fast contraction velocity and are able to produce much higher forces, but they fatigue easily. The terms slow and fast twitch can be a little misleading. A better description is low and high activation thresholds. Type I fibres have a low activation threshold, whereas Type II fibres have a higher activation threshold. As the speed or force of contraction is increased there is a sequential recruitment of the type I, IIA and IIB muscle fibres. Although the types of muscle fibres may well have an effect on EMG signal, EMG analysis cannot currently discern between the signals from the different fibre types.

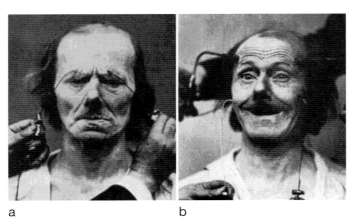

Figure 10.1   (a and b) The mechanisms of human facial expression (Duchenne 1850)

10.1.3 Frequency and amplitude of EMG

EMG signals have both a magnitude and a frequency response. Frequency range of the usable EMG signal is between 1 Hz and 500 Hz and the amplitude of the EMG signal varies between 1 μV and 1 mV. The concept of magnitude and frequency can be applied to any signal, but the best way to think about this is the parallel with sound waves. The magnitude of a sound wave is how loud the signal is, and the frequency is the pitch, e.g. Mendelssohn's Violin Concerto will have a good proportion of higher frequencies, whereas the heavy metal band 'Motorhead' will have a large proportion of lower frequencies, and is usually played at significantly greater amplitude!

The EMG signal may be displayed in a number of ways. Clinical EMG biofeedback devices may display the magnitude of the signal by how many lights can be illuminated with a contraction. However, for more scientific study the EMG signal is either displayed as a continuous line which oscillates up and down (Fig. 10.2a), or as a signal power to frequency plot (Fig. 10.2b). The latter may be considered in the same way as a graphic equalizer display on a stereo shows the sound wave. Figures 10.3a and b show a music signal from Pink Floyd's 'Shine on you crazy diamond'.

10.1.4 Methods of recording EMG

There are two main methods of collecting EMG: surface EMG (EMG) and intramuscular EMG. EMG involves placing the electrodes on the skin overlying the muscle to detect the electrical activity of the muscle. Intramuscular EMG involves pushing an electrode into the muscle itself.

Surface EMG

Surface EMG uses electrodes that are positioned on the skin above the muscle of interest. There are various electrode configurations that can be used including monopolar, bipolar (single differential) and double differential.

The monopolar arrangement (Fig. 10.4) is the simplest configuration. This requires one electrode to be placed over the muscle and a second reference electrode on a bony prominence. This arrangement is rarely used in systems that record EMG signals as the fidelity of the signal is questionable for detailed

analysis, although this is sometimes used in clinical EMG biofeedback devices.

The bipolar or single differential arrangement of electrodes (Fig. 10.5) is where two electrodes are used to measure the EMG signal, these are placed between 1 and 2 cm apart along the orientation of the muscle fibres and a third reference electrode on a bony prominence. The single differential arrangement detects signals from both sites, this allows the signal that is common to both electrodes to be removed and the difference or differential to be amplified. This has the advantage of removing external noise more effectively and, therefore, produces a much cleaner signal of the 'true' EMG activity.

The shape and size of the electrodes used determines the area of muscle tissue being examined and, therefore, the number of motor units that may be detected within this area. However, if electrodes are too large then they are more susceptible to collecting data for surrounding muscles and not just the target muscle, this is referred to as cross talk, which can cause problems by misleading the identification of the action of a particular muscle. There are several ways to try to reduce the effect of cross talk; these include using double differential electrodes.

The double differential arrangement (Fig. 10.6) requires the use of three electrodes, usually in one single solid unit. These electrodes work in much the same way as the single differential, only now the signals from three electrodes are compared, causing an even greater reduction in noise; however, this has the added benefit of reducing the pick up volume and, therefore, reducing the possible effect of surrounding muscles and, thus, the cross talk. These may not be appropriate when considering large muscles close to the surface, or when cross talk is unlikely, as the reduction on the pick up volume will also reduce the number of motor units being investigated.

For all three electrode arrangements, a good firmly secured ground electrode is essential. This ground or reference electrode should be placed on the body on a bony prominence and should be sufficiently large to create a very good electrical contact. The purpose of this electrode is to give an electrical reference of the surrounding electrical activity; this can include electrical noise from surrounding equipment or internal electrical activity such as the heart beating.

Electrodes are either of solid reusable construction with either bar or circular electrode configurations (Figs 10.7a, b and 10.8a, b), reusable nickel-plated discs (Fig. 10.9) or disposable silver/silver chloride (Ag/AgCl) (Fig. 10.10a, b).

The position of the electrodes with respect to the motor points and myotendonous junction can also significantly affect the results, with the best location being in the midline of the belly of the muscle between the nearest innervation zone and the myotendonous junction.

To successfully measure EMG activity the electrical resistance of the skin should be below a certain level; this has the effect of improving the signal-to-noise ratio. If skin resistance is too high then the fidelity of the signal will be reduced. If the skin resistance is too low the electrical shorting can occur between the electrodes and will produce a poor signal. For a good EMG, a skin resistance of less than 10 kΩ is sometimes recommended. A skin resistance

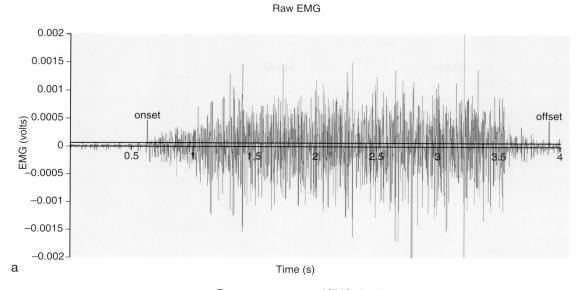

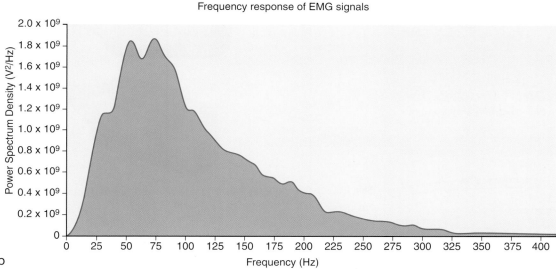

Figure 10.2   (a) EMG signal of biceps isometric contraction and (b) EMG signal power to frequency plot

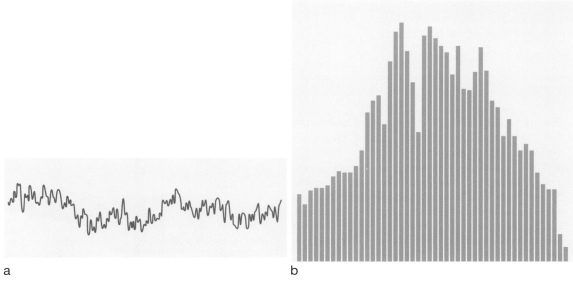

Figure 10.3   (a) Music signal from Pink Floyd's 'Shine on you crazy diamond' and (b) signal power-to-frequency plot (graphic equalizer display) from same

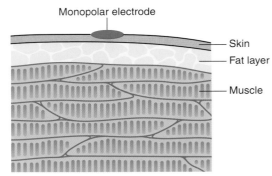

Figure 10.4   Monopolar electrode

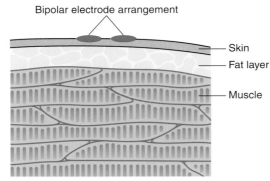

Figure 10.5   Bipolar electrode arrangement

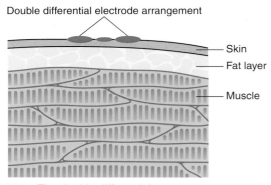

Figure 10.6   The double differential arrangement

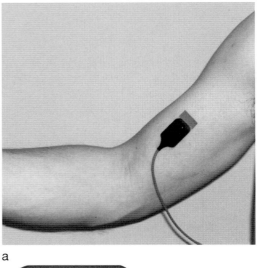

a

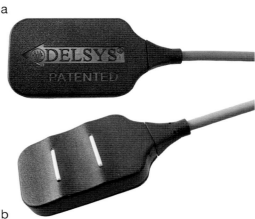

b

Figure 10.7   (a and b) Fixed bar reusable single differential electrodes by Delsys

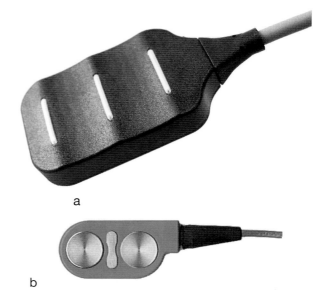

a

b

Figure 10.8   (a) Double differential electrodes by Delsys and (b) double differential electrodes preamplified by Motion Lab Systems, Inc

of greater than $100\,k\Omega$ has been shown to significantly reduce the fidelity of the EMG signal under a frequency of $100\,Hz$, although not all authors agree on the best skin resistance for EMG collection. However, all authors agree that keeping skin resistance constant or the same (within reason) on different test days improves the repeatability and usefulness of the data collected. The smaller the electrodes, the more critical the skin resistance becomes. Skin resistance depends on the number of dead cells on the skin surface, children have low skin resistance (fewer dead skin cells); older people have higher skin resistance (more dead skin cells). Good skin preparation gives better EMG results and the usual recommendations are to remove hair and dead

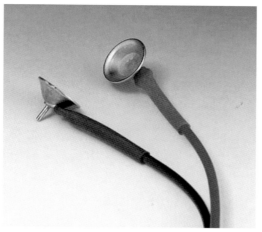

Figure 10.9   Reusable nickel-plated discs electrodes, Axon Systems, Inc.

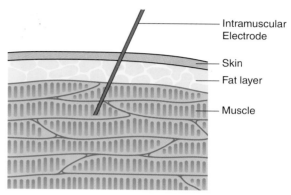

Figure 10.11   Intramuscular EMG electrode arrangement

skin cells with a process of abrading the skin, cleaning with alcohol, drying and then applying the electrodes.

Whenever we measure muscle activity when movement occurs, the muscle will move its position in relation to the skin above, which changes the relative position of the electrode with respect to the muscle and this could lead to signals from a different area of the muscle being recorded. There is little way round this problem; however, it is possible to check by observation that the electrode is above the muscle bulk throughout the range of motion to be studied and does not move over the innervation zone or the myotendonous junction.

Another drawback is that when using surface EMG electrodes it is only possible to pick up signals from the muscles located close to the skin. Signals from deeper muscles cannot be recorded reliably. This is further confounded by the effect of the thickness of the fatty tissue between the electrode and the muscle, which acts as an insulator and can affect both the magnitude and frequency response of

the EMG signal recorded. In these cases there is little option other than using intramuscular EMG.

Intramuscular EMG
Needle electron

Needle electrodes (Fig. 10.11 and 10.12) are pushed through the skin and fat layers and into the muscle beneath. The needle is quite thin, varying between 0.30 and 0.65 mm, and can be made from a variety of materials including: a bipolar arrangement gold-plated needle with a platinum-iridium electrode wire or a monopolar arrangement made from Teflon-coated surgical-grade stainless steel. These can record much higher frequencies of EMG than surface EMG, and can be positioned to record much deeper muscles than surface EMG and suffer from little or no cross talk, they are also capable of identifying individual motor unit recruitment. However, several needle electrodes may be needed at various points in the muscle tissue to obtain a picture of the EMG activity in larger muscles. There is discomfort when needle electrodes are inserted; this is a similar feeling to an injection, although nothing is injected during an EMG investigation. After testing the muscle often feels slightly sore. Needle electrodes have also been used extensively for studying neuropathy and myopathy.

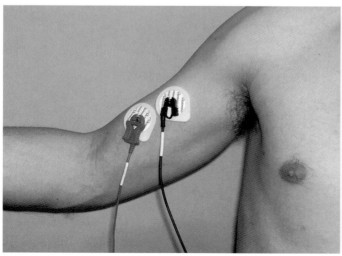

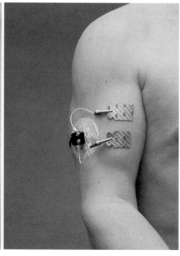

a

b

Figure 10.10   (a and b) Ag/AgCl disposable electrodes

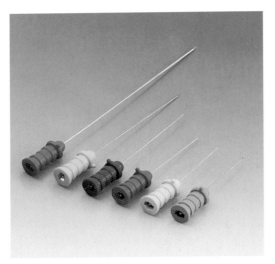

Figure 10.12   Needle electrodes, Axon Systems, Inc.

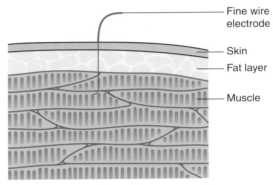

Fine wire electrode

Skin

Fat layer

Muscle

Figure 10.13   Fine wire electrode arrangement

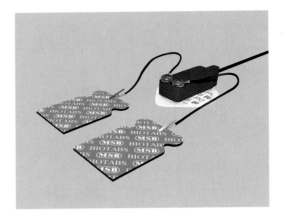

a

b

Figure 10.14   (a and b) MIE Telemetry EMG System: Preamplifier, Transmitter and MT8

Figure 10.15   Delsys Bagnoli EMG System

Fine-wire electrodes

Fine-wire electrodes can also be used (Fig. 10.13). As with needle electrodes these are pushed through the skin and fat layers into the muscle. However, fine-wire electrodes are implanted using a hypodermic needle, usually of diameter around 0.5 mm depending on the diameter of the electrode. The needle is then withdrawn leaving the electrode positioned in the muscle. Fine-wire electrodes can be made from a number of combinations of materials including: bi-filament Teflon-coated silver wire, nickel chromium alloy or surgical-grade stainless steel wire; the diameters used vary between 0.025 and 0.125 mm, with the bi-filament allowing for a bipolar arrangement. The end 2 mm of the coating is removed or bared to form the electrodes. The electrodes are often barbed to ensure they remain fixed in position when the hypodermic needle is removed. The wire is flexible so it doesn't change its position in the muscle and causes less micro-trauma to the muscle. As with needle electrodes these allow recording of deeper muscles and little or no cross talk, and get round some of the problems caused by the fat layer, therefore, they are able to record higher frequencies of EMG signals. However, only the area in the immediate vicinity of the bared tips collects motor unit activity, which may not represent the activity over the whole muscle bulk,

so electrodes have to be very carefully placed and, as with needle electrodes, several may be required in a muscle to obtain a full picture of the motor unit activity.

EMG systems

There are a variety of types of EMG system available, these can be categorized as telemetry (Fig. 10.14a, b) and 'hard wired' (Fig. 10.15). The different types of system have advantages and disadvantages. Telemetry systems require no wires connecting the subject to the data collection/processing unit, although they do have to wear a small transmitter, which sends signals to the receiver. This means the subject is free to move with little restriction; however, it is possible to pick up small radio frequencies, which can sometimes contaminate the signal. It is possible to sample at fairly high frequencies with such systems; however, as the number of channels increases the maximum frequency that may be transmitted reduces, therefore, to record high-fidelity EMG the number of channels is usually restricted to 4 or 8. The hard-wired type allows for any number of channels of EMG with 16 being a typical number of channels. Systems do exist with 32 and even 64 channels, although the time it would take to attach electrodes to 64 muscles would be considerable! However, hard-wired systems do require an 'umbilical' wire to be attached to the system, this means that much higher frequencies may be recorded; the cable has to be well shielded against electrical noise, but the use of an umbilical wire can limit the size of the test area. Cable lengths vary with the different systems, but these are usually no more than 15 m. Due to the pros and cons of the different systems research laboratories may have two systems: one telemetry and one hard wired.

Although the above considerations are important for the different types of EMG system and system configurations, the most important factor is the quality or fidelity of the EMG signal. This is usually reported in the following terms: common mode rejection ratio (CMRR), signal-to-noise ratio, bandwidth and sampling frequency.

A commonly accepted value for CMRR is above 90 db with a bandwidth usually between 10 and 500 Hz. Most EMG systems are capable of measuring at sampling frequencies of above 1000 Hz. A sampling frequency of 1000 Hz is considered the minimum required to analyse the frequency component of surface EMG signals. However, a sampling frequency of 2000 Hz, four times the maximum signal of EMG, is considered best practice as this improves the fidelity of the EMG signal. For intramuscular EMG where the motor unit action potentials are being investigated, then up to 10 000 Hz (10 kHz) is often recommended.

10.1.5 Processing of EMG signals

Raw EMG (Fig. 10.16)

EMG signals are low voltage, and the signal can be hidden by other electrical noise. Therefore, EMG signals have to be amplified to reduce the effect of this noise, typically between 1000 and 10 000 times to give a measurable signal. To reduce electrical interference the amplifiers are often positioned close to or are part of the electrodes, reducing the length of wire, which can pick up interference.

Often the EMG signal will oscillate either side of a floating reference; this is referred to as low-voltage offset or bias. The way to remove bias is to find the mean value of the entire signal and then subtract this from the original signal, therefore, pulling the data to a 'zeroed' position. The threshold of the signal can then be set to give information as to whether the muscle is firing or not. This gives an on/off measurement of whether the muscle is active or not, or muscle activity onset and offset. The threshold is often determined by measuring the noise amplitude and finding the value of 2 or 3 standard deviations of the noise, this will include 95% or 99.7% of the noise amplitude respectively. There are other methods of determining a threshold; however, in all cases if the signal passes above or below the threshold value it may be considered as an onset or offset respectively.

The size of the raw EMG signal indicates the amount of muscle activity. An increase in the signal indicates a larger amount of motor unit activity, although there is no precise relationship to relate this to exact numbers of motor units that are active. Although the motor unit activity relates to the magnitude of the force produced by a muscle, this EMG signal is **not** directionally proportional to the force in the muscle.

Rectification (Fig. 10.17)

Rectification is required because the raw EMG signal (when the low voltage offset has been removed) oscillates positive and negative either side of the zero line, therefore, if we

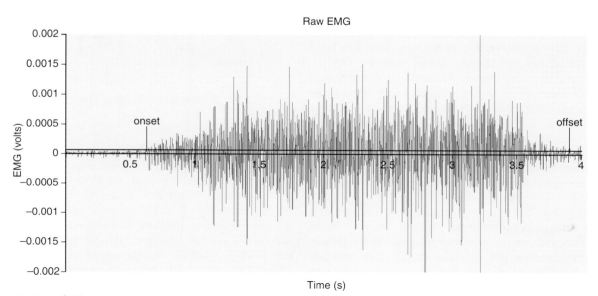

Figure 10.16   Raw EMG

Rectified EMG

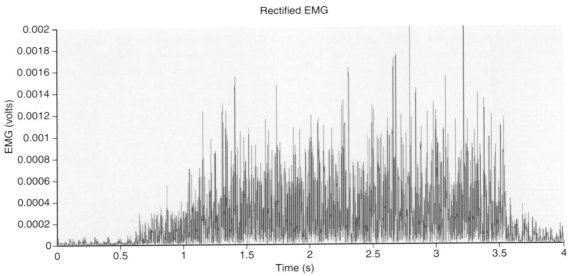

Figure 10.17   Rectified EMG Signal

were to try to find the mean value we would end up with zero. Rectification takes the entire signal and makes all the negative values in the signal positive. This can be achieved by first squaring the signal then taking the square root. This is sometimes preferred when determining the threshold for the onset or offset of the muscle.

Filtering and enveloped EMG

Enveloped EMG is a common method of showing the level of muscle activity which involves 'filtering' or 'processing' the EMG signal. Common processing includes the filtering of the full wave rectified signal using a low pass filter. The low pass filter lets the lower frequencies through while stopping the higher frequencies. The practical upshot of this is a smoothing effect similar to that used in movement analysis. There is much debate as to how much this should be filtered; typical amounts of filtering used in the literature vary between 6 and 25 Hz cut off frequencies for a low pass filter, Figures 10.18, 10.19 and 10.20 show the effect of these two filtering amounts. A 6 Hz filtering produces a smoother pattern that shows a closer agreement with the pattern for muscle force during isometric contractions. This has been used in many papers and textbooks as it shows a smooth pattern and is, therefore, easier to obtain a mean value; however, this does remove most of the frequency component and reduces the magnitude of the peaks of the signal that may be of interest. For example, when studying the control of postural stability the muscle firing pattern will not be constant, but will, in fact, comprise of a series of spikes of activity. For these reasons a 25 Hz cut off frequency is becoming more popular in the research literature (Figs 10.18 and 10.19).

Another method of filtering popular in the research literature is using RMS (root mean square). The root mean square is calculated using a moving window. The root mean square calculation consists of three steps: squaring each data point in the signal, determining an average value over a specified window length, e.g. 0.125 s, and then taking the square root (Fig. 10.20).

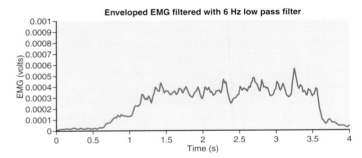

Figure 10.18   Enveloped EMG signal filtered with a 6 Hz low pass filter

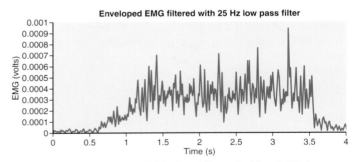

Figure 10.19   Enveloped EMG signal filtered with a 25 Hz low pass filter

Many EMG systems often limit the bandwidth to, for example, 20–500 Hz; this is the range of signals that the system lets through. This may be changed in some systems, as some authors feel this is a little too aggressive with 10–500 Hz being used. The purpose of the bandwidth is to remove movement artefacts which appear as low-frequency signals. Movement artefacts usually appear as large low-frequency oscillations, which are caused by the movement of the connecting cable or by movement of the electrode on the skin. If movement artefacts do occur, they can also be removed by passing the collected data through a high pass

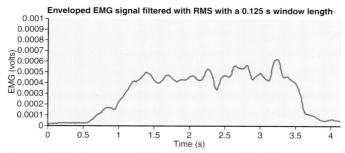

Figure 10.20 Enveloped EMG signal filtered with RMS with a 0.125 s window length

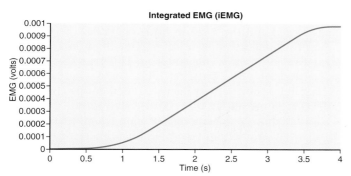

Figure 10.21 Integrated EMG (iEMG)

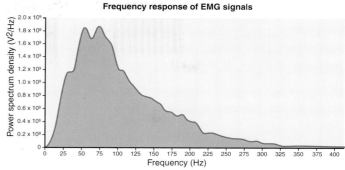

Figure 10.22 Frequency response of EMG

filter, usually set at 10 Hz, which removes the movement artefacts without affecting the EMG signal greatly.

Another filtering method is 'notch' filtering. This is where a narrow band of frequencies is removed. The practical upshot of this is that if EMG signals are contaminated with electrical noise this can be removed. For this reason notch filters between 59 and 61 Hz are used when the resident electrical signal is 60 Hz, and 49–51 Hz when the resident electrical signal is 50 Hz. However, it should be noted that notch filters do not just remove the electrical noise, they remove both the EMG and electric noise indiscriminately between these frequencies. This can cause a small distortion of the data, in particular the median frequency (see Fig. 10.22), and should only be used as a very last resort. Although in some situations, where a larger amount of electrical interference is present, this may be necessary.

Integrated EMG (iEMG)

Integrated EMG (iEMG) refers to the area under the full rectified EMG trace. This has been used as an indicator of work done by the muscle, although this term is contentious as during an isometric contraction no mechanical work is done! However, if, for example, we wished to examine the amount of work done by a muscle group during push off during walking, events at the start and end of the push off would need to be identified and the area under the rectified EMG trace found. Therefore, iEMG would give us a single value for the muscle "Work Done" for this period. In Figure 10.21 we see the area under the graph increasing during the contraction and then levelling off as the muscle action reduces and stops. The value when this graph levels off is the iEMG value for that contraction, although for a

continuous activity the timing of the start and stop events or onset/offset needs to be very carefully defined.

Frequency response of EMG

The frequency of the EMG signal is the rate at which the signal oscillates up and down. These oscillations are produced from the twitching of the muscle fibres. In any EMG signal there is a range of frequencies of these twitches. A reconstruction of these frequency components allows us to find out which frequencies are present in a particular signal. These frequencies can then be plotted against the magnitudes. This process is carried out by a mathematical algorithm called a fast Fourier transformation (FFT). Two parameters that are often reported as measures of fatigue are the central (median) frequency or the mean (average) frequency (see section 10.1.6) (Fig. 10.22).

The number of zero crossings, or zero crossing rate (ZCR), in the raw EMG has been previously used as an indicator of the rate of firing, or the number of action potentials generated. This has also been used to assess spectral changes in EMG signals. It has been shown that there is excellent agreement between the median frequency and ZCR in normal muscles under a variety of muscle length tension and fatigue conditions.

Normalizing of EMG

Comparison of the amplitude of EMG signals between individuals and even between different test days can be difficult, although this is frequently what we are trying to achieve when assessing the effect of different conditions and treatments. This is due to the number of confounding variables that can affect EMG. If we are looking for immediate changes this presents less challenges than when we are monitoring possible change over a period of time; however, in most cases some form of normalizing is advised.

One way of normalizing, which has been used extensively, is the maximal voluntary contraction (MVC). This involves recording a maximal isometric contraction and relating the subsequent EMG data to this. This has the drawback of: how do you know that the subject has given a maximal contraction and can they give a maximal contraction if there is neurological involvement or joint pathology that may cause inhibition? The other issue is relating anisometric contraction, i.e. concentric and eccentric, to isometric which produce different EMG signals (see section 10.2.5).

These problems aside, we still require some experimentally reproducible method of normalizing EMG.

Another method is using the maximum observed EMG signal during an activity. This is best carried out using an averaged value of at least three, but preferably five trials. This is particularly useful when looking for immediate changes, for instance, different conditions, as it shows proportional changes in muscle activity to the reference average value. This, therefore, allows comparison of the proportional effects of the conditions being considered for different individuals, as each individual will have their own reference average value. This technique may also be applied to iEMG in the same way.

10.1.6 What information can be gain from EMG

Isometric EMG and muscle force

The 'link' between the magnitude of the EMG signal and muscle force has caused many debates in the literature. There is undeniably a similarity in the pattern of the isometric force generated by a muscle and the enveloped EMG signal; however, to get to this similarity in pattern we have to pass the EMG data through a low pass filter with a cut off frequency of 3 Hz.

This can be demonstrated easily by measuring the EMG signal from biceps brachii and increasing the load being held at the distal end (hand), making sure the contraction is isometric. The graph below shows how the average enveloped EMG signal increases as the load being held at the distal end (hand) increases. This produces a relationship or correlation coefficient of r = 0.96 and a coefficient of determination $R^2 = 0.92$, indicating that 92% of the enveloped signals represent a straight line relationship with the force being held. Although the values below only go to a load on the distal end of 6 kg, similar relationships have been seen up to 80% of maximal voluntary contraction (Fig. 10.23).

However, there are several problems in relating the EMG signal with joint moment data. These problems include the fact that a single muscle or muscle group may not be solely responsible for the internal moments that relate to the external moments. This can include more than one muscle supporting the moment, leading to a lower EMG signal, or the action of antagonistic muscle activity, which would lead to a greater EMG signal in relation to the joint moment. But perhaps a more confounding and confusing factor is that a shortening of the muscle would also lead to a greater EMG signal in relation to the joint moment (see section 12.6.5). Another important factor in the relationship between internal muscle action and external moments is the effect of different types and speed of muscle contractions. Next we consider the effect of concentric and eccentric contractions on the magnitude of the EMG signal.

Variations in concentric and eccentric EMG

Concentric contractions are where the muscle shortens during the activity. These are generally the weakest muscle contractions, requiring more motor unit activity than isometric and eccentric for a particular load. Eccentric contractions are where the muscle lengthens during the activity; these are generally the strongest muscle contractions, requiring less motor unit activity for a particular load.

Isometric contractions are stabilizing contractions where the muscle length remains virtually constant.

Moritani et al (1987) investigated in the biceps brachii of 12 men during concentric and eccentric contractions. Results demonstrated that RMS amplitude and mean power frequency of the surface EMG were significantly higher during concentric contractions than eccentric contractions. Intramuscular recordings showed greater motor unit activities during concentric contractions. Grabiner and Owings (2002) demonstrated that the EMG during knee extensor eccentric contractions is significantly smaller than that during the knee extensor concentric contractions for a constant rate of change of joint moment.

One way of demonstrating this difference is by using surface EMG and recording the signal from biceps first with the elbow flexed and the forearm horizontal, and then flexing (concentric) and extending (eccentric) the elbow at a constant angular velocity with a constant load. This generates the raw and enveloped EMG patterns (Figs. 10.24 a,b), with the greatest motor unit activity being required during concentric and less required during the eccentric activation.

This variation of the amounts of motor unit activity with the different contraction types, although interesting, causes one of the most difficult problems for EMG. We saw previously that a reasonable relationship exists between muscle force and isometric EMG; however, if we now consider the dynamic relationship between EMG signal, muscle force, joint speed and type of contraction, we quickly move away from being able to describe the changes in the loads in the muscles in such a simple way. This is not to say that this is not currently being investigated; however, to do this requires a combination of inverse dynamics and EMG in what are often referred to as 'EMG assisted models'.

EMG changes during fatigue

FFT analysis of the frequency response gives important information about endurance and fatigue. If the median or mean frequency remains the same or similar through a test then the muscle has shown good endurance. If the median frequency response decreases then the muscle is fatiguing. This frequency shift is due to the sodium and potassium movement slowing down through the channels in the muscle, decreasing the rate at which the motor units are firing. If the contraction is submaximal an increase in the magnitude

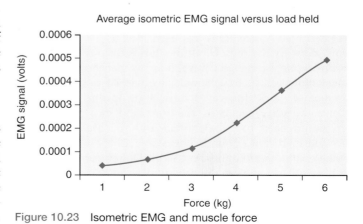

Figure 10.23   Isometric EMG and muscle force

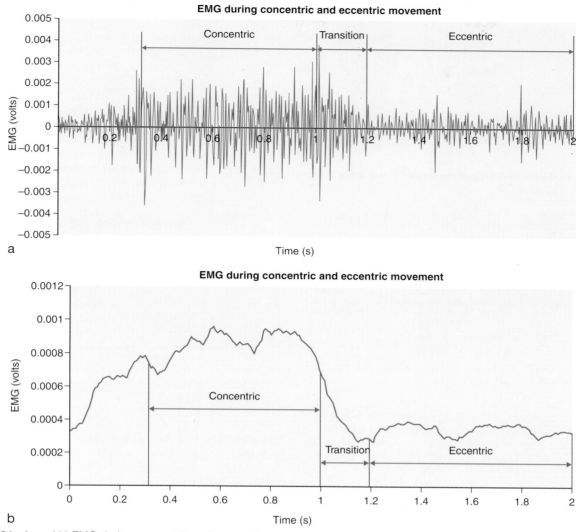

Figure 10.24   (a and b) EMG during concentric and eccentric movement

of the signal may also be seen as the muscle fatigues, this relates to an increase in the number of motor units active.

The graphs in Figure 10.25 show the frequency response and magnitude of the EMG signal from the biceps when the subject holds a mass of 10 kg for 1 min. These show a frequency shift to the left and an increase in the magnitude of the signal, both indicate a substantial amount of fatigue.

The amount of fatigue can be quantified by considering the median frequency. The median frequency is the middle frequency of the magnitude versus frequency graph, or the power versus frequency graph. This may be calculated by finding the sum of all the magnitudes up to each frequency and dividing by the total sum. This expresses the contributions up to a given frequency as a percentage of the total magnitude, e.g. the percentage of the power spectrum up to a frequency of 80 Hz is the sum of all the power magnitudes from 0 to 80 Hz divided by the total power present in all frequencies.

The median frequency is the frequency when 50% of the sum of the magnitudes is below and above, i.e. at 50% of the percentage of the total magnitude. The graph (Fig. 10.26) shows how we can measure the frequency shift from the data presented above.

The median frequency may be found during each second of an exercise, which then may be plotted against time. This can inform about the rate of fatigue the muscle is experiencing throughout the exercise. Figure 10.27 shows a graph of the rate of fatigue over a 30 s period while holding a 10 kg weight. During the 30 s period there is a steady decrease in the median frequency, which relates to the decreasing rate at which the motor units are firing and therefore the muscular fatigue.

10.1.7 Clinical EMG and biofeedback

The term biofeedback was first coined in 1969 by a group of workers who went on to found the Biofeedback Society of America. They defined biofeedback as 'the use of appropriate instrumentation to bring covert physiological processes to the conscious awareness of one or more individuals' (Wolff 1978). In practical terms this means converting a physiological event into auditory and visual signals that are proportional to the size of the events and then using that

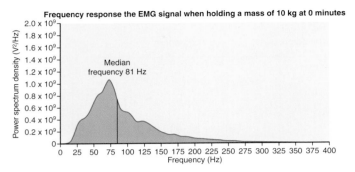

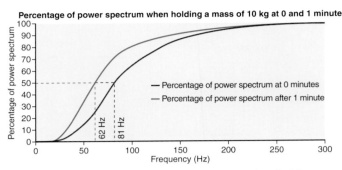

Figure 10.26 Percentage of power spectrum when holding a mass of 10 kg at 0 and 1 minute

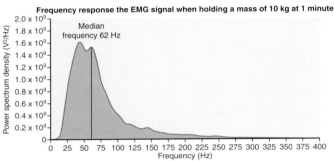

Figure 10.25 EMG changes during fatigue

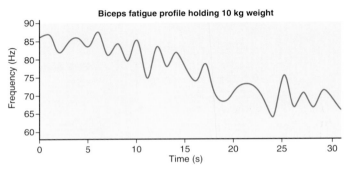

Figure 10.27 Biceps fatigue profile holding 10 kg weight

information to modify that physiological event (Nelson & Currier 1991). Biofeedback is a tool that is used in many clinical fields, although broadly its use can be divided into two principal areas (Low & Reid 1992):

1. For the control of stress-related conditions, particularly those in which the autonomic nervous system is involved, e.g. blood pressure, heart rate, peripheral blood flow
2. Conditions where there are movement abnormalities or muscle imbalances either in neurological or musculoskeletal conditions.

Intramuscular EMG work tends to be reserved for research activity, whilst surface EMG can be used clinically as a rehabilitation tool. For insertion in the muscle, needle electrodes are often used. The advantages of needle electrodes are that the activity that they detect can be localized much more accurately than in the case of electrodes placed on the skin surface and they allow the activity of even single motor units to be recorded. Their disadvantages are that they require to be sterilized before use, and they inevitably involve discomfort to the patient during insertion. The advantages of surface electrodes are that they are simple and painless to apply, and they provide a composite picture of the activity of underlying motor units. Their disadvantages are that they are not particularly suitable for recording single MUAPs and they do not permit such precise localization of the signal source as needle electrodes.

Despite the fact that surface EMG is only a close approximation of the actual level of electrical activity occurring in the muscle, and there may be contamination of the signal by cross talk and electrical interference, it is fair to say that an increase in EMG signal reflects an increase in muscle

tension and, conversely, a decrease in EMG signal reflects a relaxation of the muscle.

Types of feedback
Feedback which varies continuously as a function of changes in muscle activity is termed analogue feedback and is the type that has been used most extensively in the clinical use of EMG feedback.

Regarding the merits of auditory versus visual feedback, auditory feedback has the advantage that the patient does not need to concentrate on a visual display, and can use the feedback even whilst the eyes are closed, which may be found helpful whilst the patient's attention is focused on internal, proprioceptive cues. Also, visual feedback is not particularly suitable in gait training or throwing activities. However, very small changes in activity levels may be more sensitively indicated using visual feedback. Musculoskeletal uses of biofeedback tend to be dominated by three areas that target superficial muscles:

- Spinal scanning
- Shoulder instabilities
- Knee problems especially concerning the extensor mechanism.

Clinical benefits of using biofeedback
Instant feedback
Biofeedback provides instant feedback as to whether the exercise is performed correctly. This is particularly useful when the exercises are not particularly easy to perform. With the use of biofeedback the patient can be taught much

more quickly what a particular muscle contraction feels like. This is particularly important as it enables them to take that sensation away with them out of the clinic, so when they perform the exercise at home they know exactly what it feels like. This instant feedback is especially useful in the early stages of rehabilitation.

Shaping

This is achieved by adjusting the threshold setting of the machine. If in neurological or stress rehabilitation programmes you require the patient to relax more you turn the threshold of the machine down, this makes it more sensitive. In this way it becomes harder for the patient; this is called negative shaping. More commonly used in musculoskeletal work is positive shaping, whereby the threshold of the machine is turned up as the patient progresses. This will help to elicit a stronger contraction in order to reach the required level of feedback. Patients can be made to work extremely hard using this process.

Identification of poor phases of contraction

Biofeedback enables the therapist to determine whether the contraction is being sustained over the chosen time period during isometric exercises and that the contraction is sustained during both concentric and eccentric phases of an isotonic exercise.

Objective measurement

Quantitative scoring of EMG activity is desirable for two main reasons. Firstly, it allows the therapist to evaluate the patient's progress over a number of training sessions and to decide whether or not further training is likely to produce worthwhile gains in function. Secondly, it is helpful to the patient to know what progress he/she has made relative to other training sessions as well as receiving feedback during the session. This information is itself a form of feedback and knowledge of results has been shown to be an effective way of maintaining a high level of motivation.

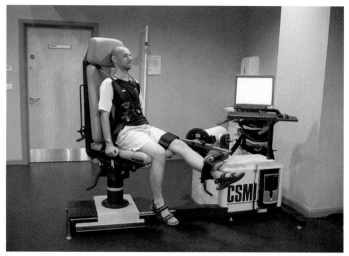

Figure 10.28   Isokinetic machine

10.2 Muscle strength and power assessment

10.2.1 Simple clinical methods

The Oxford scale aims to assess the functional ability of an individual. Scores 0–3 give a very useful functional progression by assessing if the individual can support against gravity; however, care must be taken that the body segments are constantly placed to ensure a consistent and 'correct' effect due to the weight of the body segment and associated muscle action. Scores 3–5, however, are open to considerable variability as the exact definition of light resistance and strong resistance will vary from clinician to clinician. Also the position of the applied load on the body segments, or the length of the body segment, will vary the moment arm which will have a significant effect on the muscle force needed to resist. This leads to difficulties in the comparison of assessments using Oxford scale between clinicians doing the testing and the individuals being tested.

One method of improving the measurements taken in clinical assessment is using a device called a myometer, which measures force and can be attached to different body segments using a sling. One example of a myometer is the Nottingham mecmesin myometer, which is a force gauge that has been used to assess muscle strength component of the Constant Score to evaluate shoulder function. Although this does have the drawback of assessing isometrics and not dynamic tasks and care must still be taken in the positioning the sling on the body segments to ensure repeatable and useful measurements.

10.2.2 Isokinetic and isometric testing machines

The use of isokinetics allows for a standardized assessment by controlling, or presetting the angular velocity and measuring the resistance that can be produced by an individual. In controlling the angular velocity and measuring the resistance, the muscle power produced becomes very easy to find. Isokinetics machines also allow concentric, eccentric and isometric moments (commonly referred to as torque in isokinetics) and concentric and eccentric power to be found separately. Many isokinetic machines are also capable of isotonic assessment, isotonic referring to constant load, or torque, throughout the range of motion. Isotonic testing is a simulating of free weights, although isokinetic machines also have the ability to allow for the weight of the segment through the range of motion being tested, therefore giving a closer representation of the torque and power provided by the muscles (Fig. 10.28).

10.2.3 Measurements taken in isometric testing

The term Isometric refers to exercise where a force is applied, but no movement occurs. Therefore, the type of contraction being tested is always isometric. Variables that have been used in research include:

- Maximum torque during a contraction
- Maximum torque at different joint angles

- Ratio of maximum torque of antagonistic muscle
- Maximum torque-to-bodyweight ratio
- Impulse torque.

Torque measures during a contraction

A single value of peak torque may be recorded during a contraction. This does not tell us how the torque is produced over time, but just the maximum value observed. The peak torque at various time points may also be considered, this gives a measure of the endurance or fatigue, i.e. the ability to not only produce, but also maintain a particular force. This is often carried out at a percentage of the maximum force, or torque, which can be generated.

The peak torque at different joint angles can also be assessed. This is a series of measures of peak torque that are taken at different joint angles. This showns the effect of the angle of pull of the muscle relative to the body segment and the muscle length. Both of these factors affect the maximum amount of torque that can be produced. Figure 10.29 shows how the peak torque during a knee extension exercise changes as the knee is moved from 90° of flexion to 0° of flexion.

Figure 10.30 shows the relationship between the peak torque produced and the joint angles. From this second figure we can see that near to full extension much less force can be produced, and as the knee flexion angle gets over 60°

the extensor torque begins to plateau, although increases in isometric torque are seen up to a knee flexion angle of 90°.

Ratio of maximum torque of antagonistic muscle

The maximum torque of antagonistic pairs of muscles and the ratio between them may be found. However, care is advised as this does not relate to work done or power production as no movement is occurring during isometrics. Although the study of different antagonistic pairs of muscles can produce interesting data of the maximum torque values at different joint angles.

Maximum torque-to-bodyweight ratio

Sometimes it is necessary to compare results from different individuals. Therefore, the maximum torque values may be divided by bodyweight. This is an attempt to allow for larger subjects having larger muscle bulk and, therefore, should be able to produce larger torque values. By normalizing in this way we are measuring the maximum torque that can be produced for a given muscle bulk. This allows different individuals to be compared, although this can be susceptible to errors due to anthropometric variations.

Impulse torque

The impulse torque is the area under the torque-versus-time graph. This relates to the maximum torque produced and how long it may be sustained. This has been erroneously

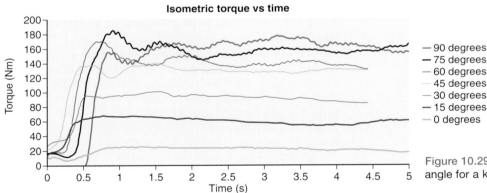

Figure 10.29   Maximum torque at different joint angle for a knee extension exercise

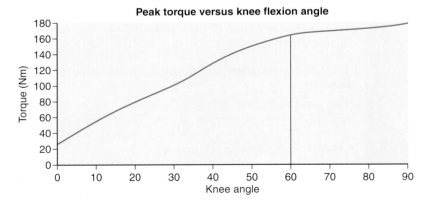

Figure 10.30   The relationship between the peak torque and joint angles

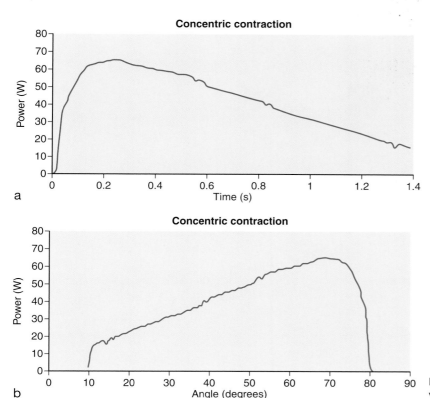

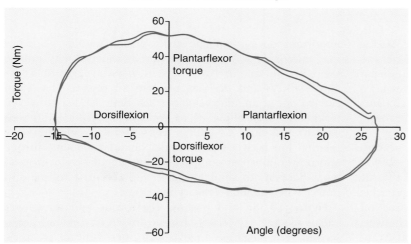

Figure 10.34   (a) Power versus time and (b) power versus angle

Figure 10.35   Plantar/dorsiflexor torque versus angle

to the kicking of the ball but more due to the deceleration of the tibia by the hamstrings after the ball has left the foot. A more functional assessment, therefore, would be to examine the antagonistic pair of muscles by testing the extensors concentrically and the flexors eccentrically, or visa versa depending on the antagonistic pair being assessed or the activity being replicated.

So should the concentric power and torque be more balanced with the eccentric? Previously we considered that concentric muscle action was the weakest, then isometric, with eccentric muscle action being the strongest. The data in Figure 10.37 shows that greater power may be obtained by

working a particular muscle eccentrically when compared to concentrically at the same angular velocity.

$$\text{ratio} = \frac{\text{Concentric}}{\text{Eccentric}} = 65:78$$

$$\text{ratio} = \frac{\text{Concentric}}{\text{Eccentric}} = 0.83:1$$

This increase in strength and power of eccentric muscle action when compared to concentric is also supported by the EMG data we saw in the previous section (see section 10.1). This demonstrates that eccentric contractions are stronger

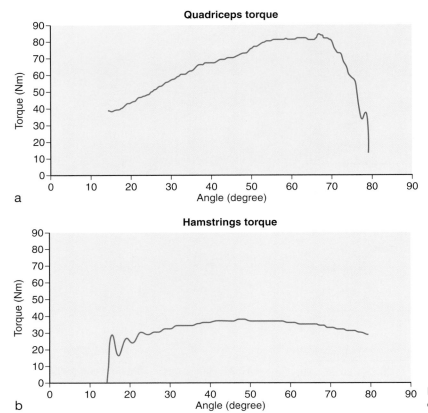

Figure 10.36   (a and b) Concentric torque of quadriceps and hamstrings at 30°/s

than concentric contractions. This would, therefore, lead us to the conclusion that eccentric flexors/concentric extensors should indeed be more balanced; however, this relationship will also depend on the angular velocity being tested, i.e. as the speed increases do we get a greater discrepancy between concentric, eccentric and isometric muscle torque and power.

Aagaard et al (1995) found that the eccentric/concentric hamstrings/quadriceps ratio approached 1:1 at 240°/s, whereas other authors (Osternig et al 1996) found that the eccentric/concentric hamstrings/quadriceps ratio approached 1:1 at 60°/s post anterior cruciate ligament reconstruction. Both of which support the differences in the balance between concentric/concentric ratio and the eccentric/concentric ratio of the antagonistic pair of muscles with the latter considered as being more functionally relevant.

The effect of angular velocity on concentric and eccentric torque and power

When considering the effect of angular velocity on concentric and eccentric torque and power we have to be very careful what we mean by torque (moment) and power, as power is a product of both moment and angular velocity. If we are testing at a set angular velocity then this becomes less important, however, the big question is whether flexion and extension velocities will be the same during functional tasks and whether we need the torque or the power to be balanced at the different stages of acceleration and deceleration during the functional tasks. This is particularly

important during ballistic tasks where angular velocities may exceed 1000°/s. At this point isokinetics may not be the best tool as currently most devices struggle to assess above 400°/s and the vast majority of research has been carried out at angular velocities less than 300°/s. However, isokinetics does allow us to control and isolate different angular velocities to gain a very useful insight into the relationship between joint angles, angular velocity, torque and power, albeit at comparably low angular velocities. So what happens to the concentric and eccentric torque and power when angular velocity increases?

Figures 10.38a and b show the torque and the power versus the angular velocity for the ankle evertors in degrees/second. The negative angular velocities indicate eccentric and the positive concentric. These data show a number of relationships, perhaps the most noticeable is the difference in the torque produced concentrically and eccentrically. At 60°/s this shows that the concentric torque is 70% of the eccentric value, with the eccentric torque increasing from the isometric state up to 120°/s, which is in agreement with Hortobagyi and Katch (1990), and the concentric torque decreasing from the isometric state.

As the concentric angular velocity increases, the torque significantly reduces; however, at the same time the power continues to rise, this is due to power being a product of both the torque and the angular velocity: $P = M\omega$ (see section 5.3: Angular work, energy and power). At 240°/s the power plateaus, which indicates the maximum concentric power available occurs at around 240°/s. However, a different

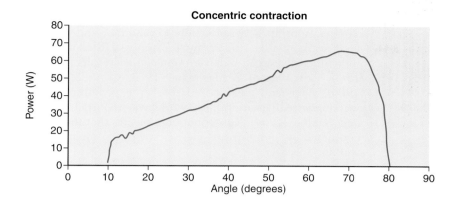

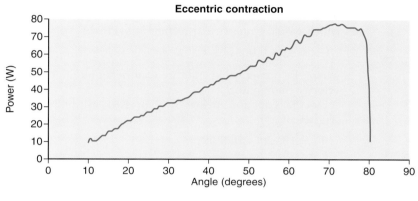

Peak concentric power = 65W   Peak eccentric power = 78W

Figure 10.37   Concentric eccentric power (peak concentric power = 65 W, peak eccentric power = 78 W)

pattern is seen during eccentric power with the torque initially increasing before decreasing more slowly leading to higher values for eccentric power.

At this point we have to be very careful about stating 'the maximum amount of power a muscle can produce about a joint'. For instance, in most amateur sprinters a concentric power can often be produced about the ankle in excess of 1000 W. However, isokinetic testing of the ankle would be unlikely to reach half this value. There are a number of reasons for this discrepancy. Firstly, during sprinting the power is generated in a stretch shorting cycle or plyometric effect, where rapid eccentric activity is followed by rapid concentric activity, which generates more power and is very hard to replicate meaningfully using isokinetics. Secondly, the ankle angular velocities involved during sprinting are in the order of 500°/s for stance phase and 1000°/s during swing phase. The power absorption and generation which occurs during stance phase at similar speeds attainable by isokinetic testing. However this potential for a discrepancy in the angular velocities between isokinetic and functional sporting tasks can cause problems in interpretation and has lead to subsequent criticism. There has been much debate on the nature of the results obtained from isokinetics versus functional tasks; much of this has focused on the nature of power production. However, the ability to measure in a controlled environment, such as isokinetics, is invaluable in the assessment of improvement through both sports training and rehabilitation, whereas more functional tasks may be susceptible to variations but

give a better understanding of how useful the power is, after all power is nothing without control!

10.3 The physiological cost of walking

Inman (1967) stated that nature does not care how individuals walk, but they should walk as efficiently as possible. This is an important point in rehabilitation, subjects undergoing rehabilitation may not walk as efficiently if they try to imitate a normal gait pattern. However this will vary from condition to condition.

Relative efficiency may be studied by measuring physiological cost to determine if efficiency increases or decreases. Many parameters may affect this, such as walking speed, level of disability and the type of surface. There are several ways to measure this, including oxygen consumption, heart rate and mechanical energies.

10.3.1 Oxygen consumption and energy expenditure

Passmore and Durnin (1955) reviewed results obtained from previous studies of human energy expenditure determined by oxygen uptake. This included the energy expenditure of activities such as sleeping, walking, climbing and running. An equation was found which stated that energy expenditure was linearly proportional to walking speed, between 3 and 6.5 km/h, for level walking. Passmore and co-workers stated

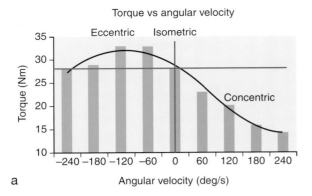

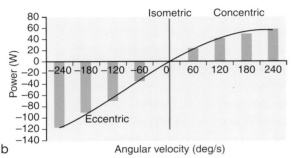

Figure 10.38 (a) Concentric eccentric torque of the ankle evertors and (b) concentric eccentric power of the ankle evertors

that age, sex and race had no statistically significant effect on the metabolic cost of the work done or energy. Passmore also stated the type of surface may have an effect on the energy cost of walking, although, unless the surface is markedly rough, the effect will probably not exceed 10%.

Measures of energy expenditure have been used to compare normal and pathological gait patterns for many years. Simonson and Keys (1947) studied the energetics and motor co-ordination of two poliomyelitis patients and two normal subjects. The study required the subjects to walk on a driven treadmill at various speeds and grades while a measure of oxygen consumption was taken. Motor co-ordination was investigated using high-speed motion pictures to record the subject's locomotion. This study included a comparison between the use of braces and unaided locomotion. Oxygen consumption was found to be a good index for the level of energy expenditure and that relief was obtained from the use of braces.

Passmore and Draper (1965) recommended the use of the following equation to calculate the energy expenditure from the oxygen percentage concentration of expired air:

Oxygen uptake and energy expenditure

$$E = \frac{4.92 \, V \, (20.93 - O_e)}{100}$$

where: E = energy expenditure in calorie/minute, V = volume of expired air per minute and O_e = percentage oxygen concentration of expired air.

Or the equation below if considered in joules/min:

$$E = \frac{20.59 \, V \, (20.93 - O_e)}{100}$$

10.3.2 Energy expenditure during walking

The relationship between energy expenditure and speed in level walking was studied by Ralston (1958). Since that time other investigators have found similar results (Bobbert 1960, Corcoran & Brengelmann 1970, Cotes & Meade 1960). A general equation for energy expenditure versus walking speed based on these works was reported by Rose and Gamble (1994). This equation indicates that the energy consumed by an individual increases with the square of the walking speed.

The equation for energy expenditure during walking reports energy expenditure in calorie/kg/minute rather than calorie/minute as reported by Passmore and Draper (1965). Controlling for body mass allows comparison of the energy expenditure per minute per kilogram between individuals of different mass, rather than the total energy consumed, which would be particular to that individual:

$$E_w = 32 + 0.005v^2$$

where: E_w = energy expenditure (calorie/kg/minute) and v = velocity (m/minute).

Or the equation below if expressed in joules/kg/min (Fig. 10.39):

$$E_w = 133.95 + 0.0209v^2$$

Imms et al (1976) studied oxygen consumption of normal subjects and of patients recovering from fractures of the leg with plaster of Paris casts. It was found that walking with a cast almost doubled the energy expenditure at 1.5 m/s. The subjects who walked with crutches without plaster of Paris casts also showed an increase in energy expenditure at all speeds of walking, the gap widened with increased walking speed, but the levels were not as high as when they walked with the plaster of Paris casts on. Imms and co-workers showed that walking with the aid of sticks required more energy than walking with crutches. It was also reported that unequal stride lengths, i.e. a change in symmetry of spatial parameters of gait, induced by pain, stiffness of joints or muscular weakness may contribute to the elevation of the energy expenditure in walking. This was due to interference with the normal patterns of kinetic and potential energy changes during vertical and horizontal oscillations of the body. Patients who retained slight asymmetries of gait at the end of rehabilitation also had the persistence of increased energy expenditure when all walking aids had been discarded. This supports the link between mechanical energies and physiological energy expenditure, and implies that a change in the kinematics of a movement will affect the physiological cost of that movement.

Crouse et al (1990) used measures of oxygen consumption and cardiac response of ambulation with short leg and long leg prostheses in a patient with bilateral above-knee amputation, and compared the performance with three 'able-bodied men'. Oxygen uptake (VO_2), minute ventilation (VE), and heart rate (HR) were measured for the amputee and the able-bodied controls during progressive treadmill exercise to maximum capacity.

Olree et al (1996) studied the effort required in 11 children with cerebral palsy during treadmill walking. Oxygen uptake was measured directly at varying walking speeds. The authors

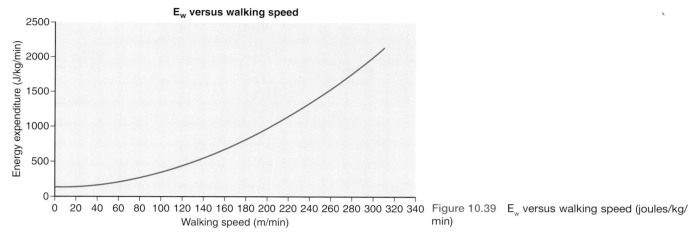

Figure 10.39 E_w versus walking speed (joules/kg/min)

concluded that oxygen uptake was the best method of assessing effort and stated that the assessment of effort in children with cerebral palsy is a vital determinant of the efficacy of any given treatment.

It is clear from these studies that the use of oxygen uptake as a measure of physiological cost is well established and in use in research and clinical practice. However, in all these studies the subjects were required to walk on a treadmill and breathe through a mouth piece.

10.3.3 Energy expenditure with respect to distance walked

The measurement of energy per unit distance walked provides a quantitative measure of energy economy. This has been viewed in the same way as fuel economy in a motor car:

$$E_m = \frac{E_w}{v} = \frac{32}{v} + 0.005v$$

where: E_m = energy expenditure (calorie/kg/m) and v = velocity (m/minute).

Or the equation below if expressed in joules/kg/m:

$$E_m = \frac{E_w}{v} = \frac{133.95}{v} + 0.0209v$$

where: E_m = energy expenditure per metre (calorie/kg/m or joule/kg/m), E_w = energy expenditure (calorie/kg/minute or joule/kg/min) and v = walking speed (m/minute).

Figure 10.40 shows how the energy expenditure per metre walked varies with walking speed. When this value is at a minimum the individual is walking at their most efficient speed for that condition. Therefore, from this relationship we can determine that the most efficient walking speed, which is 80 m/min or 4.8 km/h (3 miles/h) for normal able-bodied walking. Any increase or decrease in walking speed will cause an increase in the energy expenditure per metre walked and a reduction in efficiency (Corcoran & Brengelmann 1970, Ralston 1958). In this way the most efficient walking speed can be found for a particular individual. Such work has been carried out on many pathological gait patterns, including amputee gait (Crouse et al 1990).

10.3.4 Heart rate and physiological cost

Astrand and Ryhming (1954) investigated the relationship between oxygen uptake and heart rate, and subsequently formed a nomogram for the calculation of aerobic capacity from pulse rate during submaximal work. This accounted for pulse rate, maximal oxygen uptake, bodyweight, oxygen intake, work level and sex. Using the nomogram they claimed that maximal attainable oxygen intake (aerobic capacity) can be calculated from the heart rate and oxygen intake (or work level) reached during a test of the submaximal rate of work in a treadmill test, cycle test or step test. It was suggested that the individual's aerobic capacity/kg bodyweight/min would give a good measure of physical fitness.

Rowell et al (1964) used the nomogram developed by Astrand and Ryhming to predict the maximum VO_2 from the pulse rate and VO_2 at a single submaximal workload. Rowell and co-workers studied the limitations to the prediction of maximal oxygen intake when using heart rate. The problems with using heart rate were identified, these included: pulse rate varying independently of the O_2 uptake but directly with the emotional state or degree of excitement of the subject, the degree of physical conditioning, the elapsed time after the previous meal, total circulating haemoglobin, the degree of hydration of the subject, alterations in ambient temperature and hydrostatically induced changes resulting from prolonged erect posture.

It was found that the ambient temperature can alter the relationship of the submaximal pulse rate to the VO_2 in such a fashion that estimates of the maximal VO_2 in high environmental temperature are seriously in error. It was found that an ambient temperature of 62°F (16.6°C) provided the most favourable condition for prediction. With the factors that affect heart rate as a predictive tool for oxygen uptake identified, it is possible to use heart rate as a measure of physiological cost. However, the factors reported by Rowell et al (1964) should be controlled for as strictly as possible.

10.3.5 Heart rate and walking speed

MacGregor (1979) used the heart rate as an index of physiological cost. This suffers from two principal disadvantages:

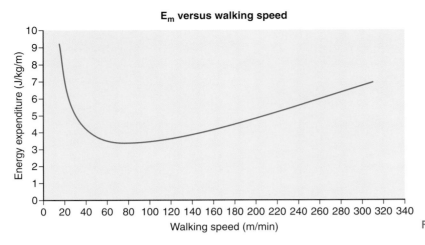

Figure 10.40 E_m versus walking speed

the relationship is non-linear and the variations in physical fitness; reciprocating heart beat interval (RHI) at rest, shows considerable inter-individual variation such that the RHIs under specified work rates are not directly comparable. MacGregor stated that if this function is divided by walking speed it gives a physiological cost index (PCI).

$$PCI = \frac{\text{heart rate during walking} - \text{heart rate during rest}}{\text{walking speed}}$$

It was found after a large number of tests that the PCI tends to be lowest at that walking speed self-selected by the patient to give optimum performance or minimal effort. This is true of normal subjects as well as a wide variety of patient groups. Confidence limits were found for PCI at preferred walking speed and a number of patient groups were compared with the results for the normal subjects.

MacGregor (1979) described a method of long-term ambulatory physiological surveillance using a modified tape recorder. The equipment recorded patterns of postural changes using accelerometers as well as heart rate throughout a 24-hour period. This made it possible to determine the time spent in each posture, this enabled subjects' physiological cost to be studied in relation to activities throughout a 24-hour period. It was found that the long-term ambulatory physiological surveillance equipment or LAPSE provided a non-invasive, relatively non-obtrusive system for physiological and biomechanical surveillance. This allowed the possibility of repetition of test protocols virtually without ethical restriction, and gave objective measures of physical handicap in a non-laboratory environment.

MacGregor (1981) evaluated patient performance using LAPSE. A patient with polio was used and compared with a normal subject in a laboratory test. This gave values for the normal limits at the 99% level of the physiological cost index and walking speed for normal male and female subjects. Data were also obtained from 10 patients with rheumatoid arthritis and the effect of placebo tablets and a non-steroidal anti-rheumatic agent was studied with respect to PCI. This investigation demonstrated the potential of studying the relationship of physiological cost versus walking performance in subjects with gait pathologies.

Nene and Patrick (1989) used PCI to evaluate locomotion with the ORLAU Parawalker. Prior to this paper few studies had been published on energy expenditure with the use of these devices. ORLAU had, in the past, used the physiological cost index (PCI) as an indicator of energy expenditure of handicapped gait. However, in cases of traumatic paraplegia with a high thoracic level injury, absence or incomplete function of the sympathetic nervous system can result in an unpredictable heart rate response; consequently for greater accuracy evaluation of the energy cost of the Parawalker gait was performed by direct measurement of the oxygen consumption. This demonstrates that PCI is not always an adequate measure of the energy expenditure, and that care should be taken when using PCI to make sure the conditions are correct to use this method of physiological measurement.

Nene (1993) studied the physiological cost index of walking in adolescents and adults. The subjects walked in a figure-of-eight path during which walking speed and heart rate were measured. It was found that both heart rate and walking speed were higher in adolescent subjects than in adults. It should be noted that Nene, when reviewing previous work carried out on treadmills, stated that the artificial contrasts of treadmill walking do not represent the energy expenditure of normal walking adequately, although no reference was provided to back up this statement.

Gussoni et al (1990) used PCI as an indicator of the energy cost of walking in subjects with total hip joint replacement. This study reported confidence limits for healthy controls, which allowed the results from the patient testing to be plotted and compared with normal.

Haskell et al (1993) described the conceptual basis and preliminary evaluation of a procedure using simultaneous recording of heart rate and two motion sensors to provide an accurate profile of physical activity. When heart rate is used as a measure of physical activity, it has to be noted that the slope of the relationship between heart rate and oxygen uptake varies between subjects, depending on their endurance capacity or fitness. The relationship between heart rate and oxygen uptake for a particular subject will vary depending on the level of activity. Haskell stated that heart rate can be influenced by the emotional status of the subject and environmental conditions, such as temperature and humidity. As a result it has been generally accepted that heart rate alone is not an accurate method of assessing physical activity, although it can be used as an indicator.

Summary: Measurement of muscle function and physiological cost

- The EMG signal is an electrical signal associated with the contraction of a muscle and the signal is produced by the depolarizing of motor units, often referred to as motor unit action potential (MUAP).
- EMG can be collected using a variety of techniques. The most common is surface EMG as this does not require electrodes to be pushed through the skin as with intramuscular EMG.
- EMG signals may be processed in a number of ways. These can give information about the amount of motor unit activity and also information about the fatigue within a muscle.
- Muscle function may be assessed using isokinetic and isometric testing. This allows the joint moments and power to be assessed in a controlled environment.
- Whole-body physiological cost may be assessed using expired air and heart rate. These can be used to determine the amount of internal energy used during a particular task in relation to a resting state.

Biomechanics of Direct and Indirect Orthotic Management

Jim Richards

Chapter

11

This chapter covers the biomechanics of orthotic management of the lower limb. This includes the theoretical mechanics of indirect and direct orthotic management and clinical case study data of the use of the devices covered.

Chapter 11: Aim
To compare the different theoretical methods of controlling and supporting the lower limb with orthotic management and their effect on signal case studies.

Chapter 11: Objectives
- To describe the theoretical function and the clinical effect of different configurations of ankle foot orthoses
- To describe the theoretical function and the clinical effect of different configurations of knee orthoses
- To explain how moments can be altered about a joint
- To explain how shear and axial forces can be altered about a joint
- To describe the theoretical function and the clinical effect of different configurations of foot orthoses
- To explain how the line of action of the ground reaction forces can be altered about a joint.

11.1 Mechanics of direct orthotic management

Direct orthotic management can be considered to work by three mechanisms: changing the moments directly at a joint, changing shear forces and changing axial forces. In all cases this involves a device being placed around the joint which applies an external system of forces. Most orthoses aim to affect joints and segments directly; however, many orthoses also have additional or secondary effects on a proximal segment or joints, without having any direct contact. In this chapter we will cover both the direct effects of each of these mechanisms, the effects on the joint being targeted and also the additional indirect effects on joints not directly targeted by the orthoses.

11.2 Modification of joint moments with orthoses

Modification of moments about joints is by far the most common method of direct orthotic management. These devices are varied and aimed to support and/or control the movement of one or more planes of movement of different joints. In this section we will cover the theory of the direct orthotic management of the ankle and knee joints with examples of their use on single clinical cases.

11.3 Biomechanics of ankle foot orthoses

Plastic ankle foot orthoses have been used to manage weakness and spasticity about the ankle joint for over 40 years. However, the basic design has not changed significantly. The different design options consist of rigid, posterior leaf spring and hinged, although other variations have been tried including the plastic spiral ankle foot orthoses and, more recently, the introduction of carbon-fibre posterior leaf spring ankle foot orthoses.

11.3.1 Rigid ankle foot orthoses
Rigid ankle foot orthoses, as the name suggests, are of a completely rigid design which aims to block all movement about the ankle joint and foot in all planes. These are usually made from moulded plastic that extends up the back of the shank and under the foot to the metatarsal-phalangeal joint, although sometimes this is extended over the whole length of the foot (Fig. 11.1a, b).

The rigid design of the orthoses has the effect of supporting a dorsiflexion moment produced by the ground reaction force about the ankle by providing a posteriorly directed force on the anterior tibial strap, which prevents or controls tibial movement over the foot. In this way, the stiffness of the rigid ankle foot orthosis produces a plantarflexion moment that opposes the moment about the ankle from the ground reaction force. Rigid ankle foot orthoses can also be used to resist knee flexion by setting them into slight plantarflexion; however, if excessive knee flexion needs to be managed knee orthoses may give more direct control, or if there is ankle involvement using knee ankle foot orthoses may be a better option (section 11.5) (Fig. 11.2a, b).

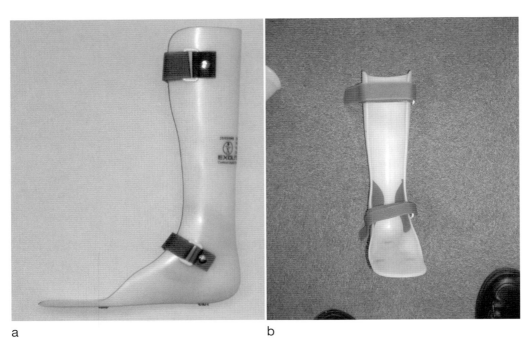

a   b

Figure 11.1   (a and b) Rigid ankle foot orthosis

The clinical guidelines for the use of rigid ankle foot orthoses are when an individual has: weakness or absence of ankle dorsiflexors and plantarflexors, severe spasticity resulting in equinovarus of the foot during swing and stance phase, weak knee extensors and proprioceptive sensory loss.

If the plantarflexors are weak, the ankle dorsiflexes too rapidly and results in poor control. This has the additional effect of a rapid movement of the tibia forwards causing excessive knee flexion and subsequently a crouch gait pattern. If the dorsiflexors are weak then this can lead to foot drop during swing phase and foot slap at heel strike. In blocking ankle movement this has the effect of supporting plantar/dorsiflexion, pronation/supination and inversion/eversion movement between the metatarsals, cuboid, calcaneus and tibia; so these move as a single segment. In reality movement of the metatarsal-phalangeal joints still occurs due to reduction in the rigidity of most devices under the forefoot. This blocking effect of the ankle movement can generate problems for the users forcing them into an early heel lift and the indirect effect of hyperextension of the knee joint. This hyperextension of the knee joint, or at least the movement of the knee away from the flexed position, is one of the key reasons for fitting rigid ankle foot orthoses, as this aims to reduce the crouch gait position that can be present in cerebral palsy. However, the blocking of the ankle can also make progression on the tibia forward over the stance limb difficult, in essence blocking second rocker of the ankle.

There are several options in the casting and fitting of rigid ankle foot orthoses, as the orthosis may be set in neutral, plantarflexion or dorsiflexion. If the ankle foot orthosis is set into plantarflexion then the tibia will be inclined posteriorly during second rocker at the ankle. This will have the effect of reducing the knee flexion moment that may be desirable in crouch gait; however, too much plantarflexion may not be desirable as this will make the progression of the body over the stance limb difficult and can force the knee

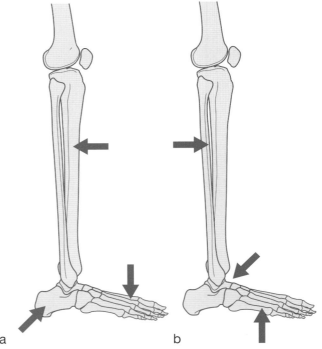

a   b

Figure 11.2   Force system on a rigid ankle foot orthosis. Stance phase (a), swing phase (b)

into hyperextension. The setting into plantarflexion will also have the effect of reducing ground clearance as the foot will also be in a plantarflexed position during swing phase. If the ankle is set into dorsiflexion then this will increase the moment about the knee during second rocker at the ankle, but would allow for greater ground clearance during swing phase. Therefore, the most important consideration for the amount of plantarflexion or dorsiflexion provided by the orthosis is the degree of knee control the individual patient has.

11.3.2 The effect of rigid ankle foot orthoses

The effect of setting a rigid ankle foot orthoses into dorsiflexion allows the tibia to assume a position in front of the ankle joint. This can cause problems for the control of the movement from heel strike to the foot flat position. This is usually achieved by eccentric control into plantarflexion by the ankle dorsiflexors. In particular this can cause problems when walking down slopes. Restrictions in the plantarflexion during loading and dorsiflexion during the progression of the body over the stance limb can be demonstrated by examining what happens to individuals who are pain and pathology free when wearing a rigid ankle foot orthosis.

Figure 11.3a and b shows the initial movement into plantarflexion is reduced while wearing a rigid ankle foot orthoses, although some movement is possible. The movement into dorsiflexion is delayed and does not reach the values without the orthosis, although nearly 10° is attained. The nature of where this movement occurs is a point of debate, as most data, including the data presented below, consider the foot as a single segment including the calcaneal, cuboid and metatarsal segments. This does not necessarily tell us the ankle-joint movement, however, the fact that movement can occur between the foot and tibia in an individual who is pain and pathology free when wearing a rigid ankle foot orthosis is interesting and raises the question: exactly how rigid is rigid?

Notwithstanding that some movement can occur, some individuals who wear rigid ankle foot orthoses do have difficulty in moving their tibia over the foot and subsequently have difficulty in moving the body forward. To aid the progression of the body over the stance limb, or roll over action, a rocker profile is often added to the shoe. This has the effect of allowing the progression of the tibia forwards over the foot without necessarily requiring movement of the ankle joint itself. In fact, this may have the additional benefit of reducing the eccentric work done by the ankle plantarflexors, if this is the intention of the orthosis.

Richardson (1991) reported on the use of rocker-soled shoes in the treatment of subjects with calf claudication. Rocker-soled shoes are believed to reduce the force required at heel off and toe off and, therefore, should reduce the work done by the gastrocnemius and soleus. Richardson found that walking distance was significantly improved as well as the distance covered before the onset of pain referred to as 'bothered distance'. The closing comments of this study are of value. Richardson stated that the clinical value of the use of rocker-soled shoes will not be fully realized until the optimal shoe design and the safety of this shoe have been established. Hullin et al (1992) reported on the kinetics and kinematics during walking with the use of heel raises and rocker soles in subjects with spina bifida. Hullin and co-workers observed that heel raises alter the tibial floor angle, but do not allow tibial progression or heel lift. Rocker soles, however, control the progression of the centre of pressure and allow heel lift and, therefore, permit tibial progression in the absence of ankle dorsiflexion. It should at this point be highlighted that little work has been carried out to determine the interaction of rocker soles in conjunction with AFOs, although this is common clinical practice in many countries.

The largest effect is in the restriction of movement into plantarflexion during the power production phase of the ankle motion. This restriction will make it almost impossible for the individual to produce any power about the ankle. This blocking of movement is often used to prevent spastic reactions in the plantarflexors; however, it is now being brought into question whether this is entirely a good thing in the majority of cases, and many clinics are now considering posterior leaf spring ankle foot orthoses and hinged ankle foot orthoses as a viable treatment for cerebral palsy and stroke where spasticity is not so severe.

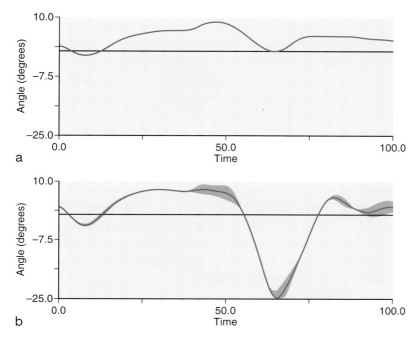

Figure 11.3   (a) Normal subject with rigid ankle foot orthosis and (b) normal subject without ankle foot orthosis

11.3.3 Posterior leaf spring ankle foot orthoses

Posterior leaf spring ankle foot orthoses, sometimes referred to as flexible plastic shell orthoses, aim to provide dorsiflexion assistance during swing phase, while giving some stability for inversion–eversion of the ankle joint. The clinical guidelines for the use of posterior leaf spring ankle foot orthoses are for: weakness or absence of dorsiflexors, good pronation–supination stability, absence of foot varus ot valgus, absence of to moderate spasticity and good knee stability.

Posterior leaf spring ankle foot orthoses are usually too flexible to give support in the transverse plane movement of the foot to the tibia, which has been related to pronation and supination (Nester 2003), although this will in part depend on the 'trim lines', i.e. the width and thickness of the material of the posterior leaf spring.

The trim lines of posterior leaf spring ankle foot orthoses are critical to what these orthoses are capable of. Traditionally these have been primarily used for dorsiflexion assistance during swing phase to prevent foot drop, in which case not much material will be required to stop the foot plantarflexing as this will have to support the weight of the foot, or at most resist spastic muscle activity of the plantarflexors. However, clinically posterior leaf spring ankle foot orthoses may also be used to assist the eccentric action of plantarflexors during stance phase. This may be achieved by having wider trim lines. This will provide some resistance to movement into dorsiflexion and, therefore, theoretically improving the control of the movement over the stance limb. This sounds very good; however, the amount of material that should be left will depend on the person's body weight and their available eccentric control of the plantarflexors. This

requires the balancing, or tuning, of the orthosis to the individual's needs, which clinically may be difficult to assess; however, the benefits to the individual can be considerable as this allows muscle activity that may reduce muscle atrophy compared with rigid designs. There are a number of different designs of posterior leaf spring ankle foot orthoses, these vary from moulded plastic (Fig. 11.4) to carbon fibre (Fig. 11.5).

11.3.4 The effect of posterior leaf spring ankle foot orthoses

The clinical case study of the use of posterior leaf spring ankle foot orthosis shows a 60-year-old patient who had been suffering from problems with his walking for several years. The patient had got to the point where walking to the local shops was no longer possible.

When the patient walked without the orthosis the ankle motion on the left side showed movement starting from a dorsiflexed position and then moving into further dorsiflexion indicating poor foot placement and poor control by the posterior muscles of the calf. Poor propulsion was also seen on both left and right, again indicating a deficit in function in the calf group. The knee movement during swing phase showed normal values; however, during stance phase the knee assumed a flexed position on both left and right sides with the left side never dropping below 40° of flexion. The movement of the thigh on the left and right sides was also reduced. The left side showing a deficit in flexion during the beginning of stance phase indicating the limb was not being advanced forwards and, therefore, step length was reduced (Fig. 11.6).

The force patterns seen on both left and right showed similar deficits in the first and second peaks and the trough, indicating poor loading and push off and a poor movement of the body over the stance limb, particularly on the left side (Fig. 11.7a, b).

A posterior leaf spring ankle foot orthosis was fitted to the left side. The aim of the orthosis was to improve the ankle and knee movement, and the progression of the body over the stance limb. This would theoretically offer some

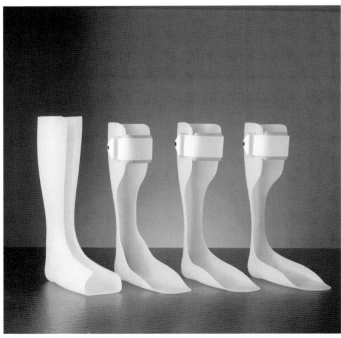

Figure 11.4 Otto Bock moulded plastic ankle foot orthoses. Far left: rigid; middle: alternative trim lines; far right: posterior leaf spring

Figure 11.5 Otto Bock WalkOn™ carbon composite posterior leaf spring ankle foot orthoses for plantarflexion/dorsiflexion assistance

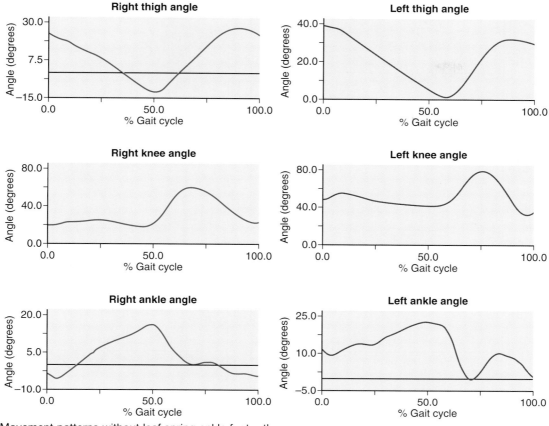

Figure 11.6   Movement patterns without leaf spring ankle foot orthoses

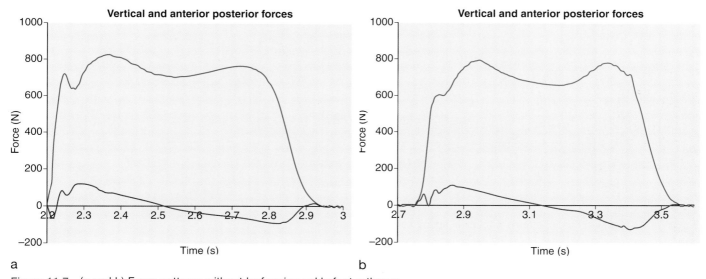

a

b

Figure 11.7   (a and b) Force patterns without leaf spring ankle foot orthoses

resistance to the ankle joint to ensure the ankle was held in neutral position at heel strike, while also giving some resistance into dorsiflexion to offer more control of the tibia over the ankle and to have an indirect effect of reducing the knee flexion.

With the posterior leaf spring ankle foot orthosis fitted to the ankle, motion for the left and right sides showed a much improved position at heel strike, which enabled the ankle to move into plantarflexion during first rocker. The orthosis also allowed an improved control of the tibial movement over the ankle joint and a reduced knee flexion angle during stance phase. The thigh motion also showed an improved movement pattern with symmetry between the left and right sides (Fig. 11.8).

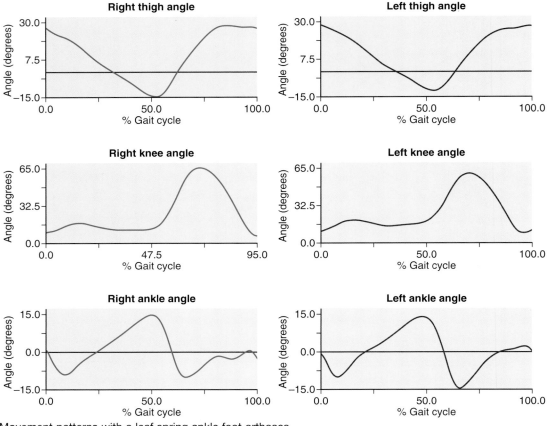

Figure 11.8   Movement patterns with a leaf spring ankle foot orthoses

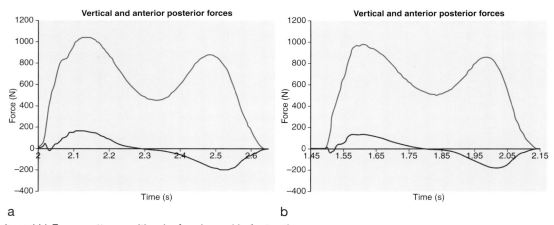

a   b

Figure 11.9   (a and b) Force patterns with a leaf spring ankle foot orthoses

The force patterns showed a significant improvement in the loading and propulsion forces, but perhaps most significant was the improvement in the trough, which supports the improvements seen in the movement of the body over the stance limb in the ankle and knee movement patterns (Fig. 11.9a, b).

With a posterior leaf spring ankle foot orthosis fitted, the patient's foot position at heel strike was controlled and he was able to move his body over the stance limb, but with a small amount of resistance from the orthosis. This resistance not only improved the ankle dorsiflexion control, but also allowed the femur to move forwards over the tibia and move the knee towards extension. Although the position of the ankle could have been set using a rigid ankle foot orthosis, this would not have allowed the same control of the movement of the tibia forwards. The most important aspect in all of this was the patient was again able to walk reasonable distances and his quality of life was much improved and he often joked about the springs in his heels.

11.3.5 Hinged ankle foot orthoses

Hinged ankle foot orthoses allow free movement of the ankle in plantar flexion and dorsiflexion, but aim to provide a block of ankle movement in the coronal and transverse

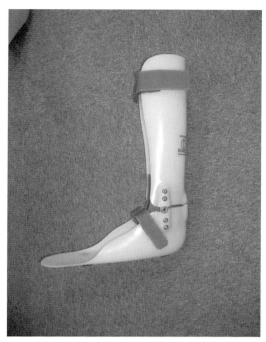

Figure 11.10 Metal hinged ankle foot orthoses

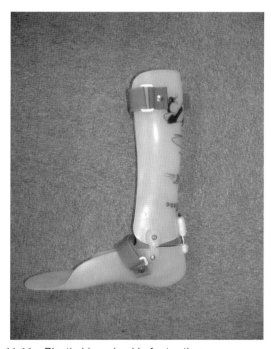

Figure 11.11 Plastic hinged ankle foot orthoses

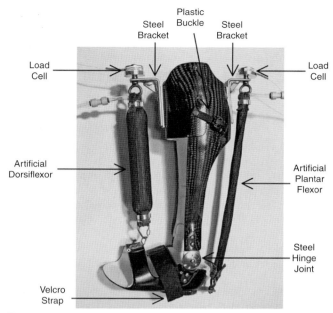

Figure 11.12 Pneumatically powered ankle foot orthosis

planes, pronation–supination and inversion–eversion. Although the movement is apparently free in the sagittal plane, the range of motion available is often controlled with plantarflexion and/or dorsiflexion stops. These plantarflexion and dorsiflexion stops are set depending on the restrictions a particular patient requires. A dorsiflexion stop may be set to stop the tibia collapsing over the foot, but yet still allowing a degree of movement of the tibia forwards over the foot. This may be used if the patient has a degree of

eccentric control during second rocker, but the prevention of too much movement is required. A plantarflexion stop may be set to prevent foot drop during swing phase or foot slap (uncontrolled movement into the foot flat position) at heel strike. In this way particular limits can be set to give similar benefits as the casting options in rigid ankle foot orthoses, but the hinge has the benefit of giving some control to the patient.

Two common hinged ankle foot orthosis designs are metal hinged (Fig. 11.10) and plastic hinged (Fig. 11.11). The metal hinged giving a good degree of rigidity and the plastic giving some support, but not as much as the metal in the coronal and transverse planes. The plastic hinges also offer a small amount of resistance in the sagittal plane in plantarflexion and dorsiflexion.

One reasonably recent development is in the realms of powered ankle foot orthoses (Fig. 11.12). Ferris et al (2005, 2006) designed and further developed a pneumatically powered ankle foot orthosis with myoelectric (low pass filtered EMG) control, allowing the artificial muscles to be theoretically controlled from residual muscle activity. Robotic exoskeletons and powered orthoses are a very interesting development for the future; however, there is still much to do to improve the portable power supplies, the artificial muscle control systems and the aesthetics to make them a clinical viable option.

11.3.6 The effect of hinged ankle foot orthoses

The clinical case study of the use of hinged ankle foot orthoses shows a young adult with cerebral palsy. This individual was fitted with a metal hinged ankle foot orthosis to assist his walking. The hinged ankle foot orthosis provided had a dorsiflexor stop at 20°.

When the patient walked without the ankle foot orthosis the ankle begins in dorsiflexion and quickly collapsed into further dorsiflexion and internal rotation. This movement of the tibia forward coupled with internal rotation of the foot forces the knee into flexed and apparently valgus position, before eventually moving into extension as the body moves over the stance limb (Fig. 11.13a, b).

With a hinged ankle foot orthoses fitted, the foot started in slight plantarflexion before then moving into dorsiflexion in a more controlled manner. This had the effect of allowing the knee to be in a more normal position, although the knee moved into a slightly hyperextended position at mid-stance.

So how can the sagittal plane movement improve when the orthosis allowed movement into plantarflexion and dorsiflexion? The restriction of the dorsiflexion to 20° prevented the collapse into excessive dorsiflexion during second rocker; however, the orthosis also restricted movement in the coronal and transverse planes. This gave added stability and prevented tibial and femoral internal rotation and, therefore, offered a more stable knee position (Fig. 11.14a, b).

11.3.7 Fine tuning ankle foot orthoses

Singerman et al (1999) investigated the effect of mechanically loading four different designs of ankle foot orthoses. Perhaps the most notable aspect of this work was the loading and recording of the plantarflexion and dorsiflexion moments in relation to the amount of deflection. Although this did not consider the effect of the moments on patients, it gives tantalizing evidence to the concept of fine tuning ankle foot orthoses to individual patient's needs and the effect of the different designs currently available.

The solid design showed that a dorsiflexion of 5° produced a resistive moment of approximately 35 Nm into both plantarflexion and dorsiflexion. This is very interesting if we put this in the context of the physiological moment produced in normal adult gait, where at 10° of dorsiflexion, maximum dorsiflexion during second rocker, we would be expecting approximately 80 Nm. Therefore, rigid ankle foot orthoses produce a similar physiological moment. It is also interesting to note the maximum dorsiflexion attained by a normal subject wearing a rigid ankle foot orthosis was nearly 10° with a moment at this point of 85 Nm. This link between the mechanical and biomechanical testing would imply that the eccentric work done by the plantarflexors would be significantly reduced as this is now being controlled almost entirely by the orthosis.

Singerman et al (1999) found that the posterior leaf spring ankle foot orthosis produced a moment of 15 Nm in plantarflexion and dorsiflexion with a deflection of 10°.

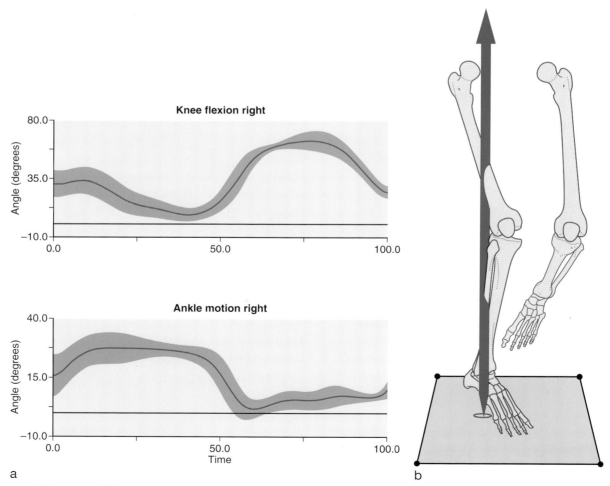

a   b

Figure 11.13   Movement without a hinged ankle foot orthosis. (a) Sagittal plane movement of the ankle and knee joint. (b) The coronal plane position of the ankle and knee

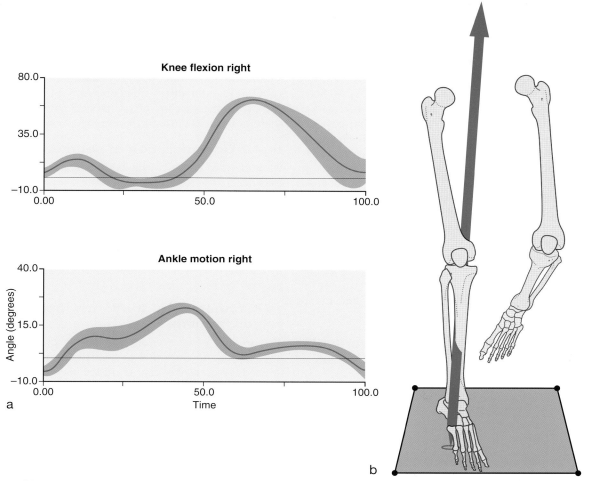

Figure 11.14 Movement with a hinged ankle foot orthosis. (a) Sagittal plane movement of the ankle and knee joint. (b) The coronal plane position of the ankle and knee

This is approximately 20% of the maximum physiological moment during second rocker of ankle movement. This would imply wearing a posterior leaf spring ankle foot orthosis would assist, but not support, the moment about the ankle independently. The flexible plastic hinged design also offered a resistance of 10 Nm over a deflection of 12°, which is in the order of 10% of the physiological moment.

There are a number of points of caution to these findings. All the above comparisons are with normal adult walking and, therefore, the balance between the orthoses and pathological movement and moments will be very different for patients. Therefore, if we consider the use of ankle foot orthoses in children the dorsiflexion moments will be substantially different due to their weight, foot length and a variety of other anthropometric factors. So this brings us back to the importance of clinical assessment and the balancing and tuning of orthoses to achieve the maximum functional benefits, with the minimum of risk of other clinical considerations, such as whether spastic reactions are induced by merely the movement of the joint or by the moments and loads in the muscles, and also the effect of joint contractures on available joint positions. One thing is certain, work into the balance between the mechanics and biomechanics of ankle foot orthoses, and the link between

this and clinical assessment requires further interdisciplinary research.

11.4 Biomechanics of knee orthoses

The biomechanics of knee orthoses will be considered in relation to their ability to control or change the biomechanics of the knee in the sagittal, coronal and transverse planes. The use of knee orthoses to change the biomechanics of the knee will be examined with examples of varus moments at the knee, shear forces across the knee and the torsional stability of the knee.

11.4.1 Knee orthoses to correct moments

The use of knee orthoses to correct and to support moments about joints is one of the most common uses of direct orthotic management. The theory covered in this section could be applied to many different types of orthotic management including; prevention of knee flexion, prevention of hyperextension or genu recurvatum, and knee valgus and varus instability and deformity although the exact arrangement of the forces needs to be specific to each condition. These use a variety of types of hinges, joints and locks; however, the example that we will consider is the use of valgus bracing in the management of knee varus in medial compartment osteoarthritis.

The aims of knee valgus braces are to unload the painful compartment, through bending moments applied proximally and distally to the knee joint, and reducing the varus deformity (Pollo 1998). Several studies have been conducted into the use of valgus knee braces for medial compartment osteoarthritis and have reported that patients experience significant pain relief and an improvement in physical function (Hewett et al 1998, Kirkley et al 1999, Lindenfeld et al 1997, Matsumo et al 1997, Richards et al 2005) and also a reduction in medial compartment load (Pollo et al 2002, Richards 2006a). But how can a valgus brace reduce the load on the medial compartment of the knee? The answer is that this is a very hard thing to measure directly; however, measures that give an indirect indication of the loading on the medial compartment are a reduction in the knee adduction moments and the varus angle of the knee. We will now consider the biomechanical theory of how knee bracing may be used to change the moments at the knee joint.

11.4.2 Consideration of individual segments

When investigating the action of knee bracing to reduce moments we first need to consider the distal (tibial) and proximal (femoral) segments separately. If we first consider

the proximal segment. This requires a medial force acting away from the knee joint to deliver a corrective moment, and a lateral force is also required that should act as close to the knee as possible. The lateral force does not create a moment about the knee; however, it is essential as the brace requires an equal and opposite reaction force (Fig. 11.15). In a similar way the distal segment also requires a medial force away from the knee joint to deliver a corrective moment and a lateral force as close to the knee as possible (Fig. 11.16).

11.4.3 Consideration of segments together

We can now consider the body segments together. When considering the forces on both body segments we now have two lateral forces acting at the knee. The two lateral forces' optimum position is at the joint centre, therefore, producing no moment. Whereas the medial forces theoretically need to be as far away from the joint as possible (Fig. 11.17). The lateral forces can be provided by one point of application, which gives us what is often referred to as a three-point-pressure or force system (Fig. 11.18).

11.4.4 Analysis of the forces acting on valgus bracing

The amount of correction that can be placed on the knee will depend on the bone and cartilage profiles within the joint. However, we can consider the supportable angle by considering the mechanics of the orthosis, and the interaction with the body segments. We will first consider the system of forces required to totally support a 5° knee varus angle with no involvement of internal structures and tissues.

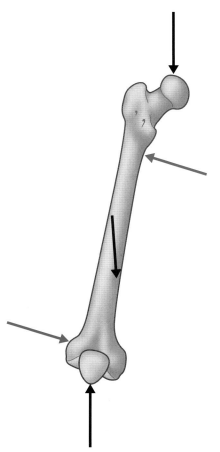

Figure 11.15   Proximal segment

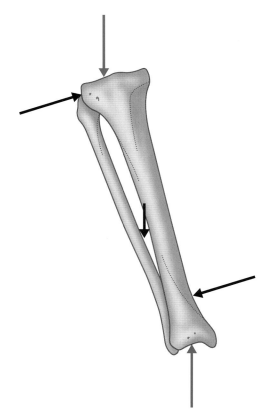

Figure 11.16   Distal segment

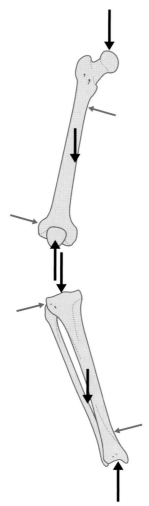

Figure 11.17   Combined segments

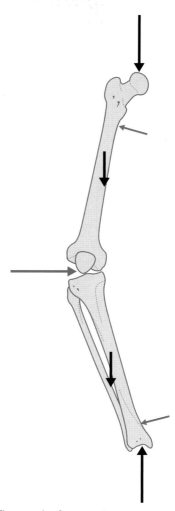

Figure 11.18   Three-point force system

To do this we again have to consider the proximal and distal segments separately.

Distal segment

If the total varus angle is 5°, we will consider this to be partly due to the positioning of the proximal and distal segments. Therefore, we will consider the proximal segment is aligned 2.5° to the vertical:

The length of the shank is 0.45 m
The weight and centre of mass of the shank from the knee are 4.05 kg and 0.25 m
The $F_{orthosis\ medial}$ is placed 0.25 m away from the knee joint
Angle of inclination 2.5° to the vertical.

The force on the ankle joint will depend on the ground reaction force and the weight of the foot. If the subject is 90 kg and the mass of the foot is 1.26 kg then the force on from the ankle on the tibia will be or 870.54 N:

$-(F_{Ankle}$ sin 2.5 × length of shank) + (weight of shank × sin 2.5 × centre of mass)

$+(F_{orthosis\ medial}$ × point of application of orthosis) = 0

$-$ (870.54 × sin 2.5 × 0.45) + (4.05 × 9.81 × sin 2.5 ×

0.25) + ($F_{orthosis\ medial}$ × 0.25) = 0

$-17.09 + 0.43 + (F_{orthosis\ medial}$ × 0.25) = 0

$F_{orthosis\ medial}$ × 0.25 = 16.66

$$F_{orthosis\ medial} = \frac{16.66}{0.25}$$

$F_{orthosis\ medial}$ = 66.64 N

Therefore, $F_{orthosis\ lateral}$ must also be 66.64 N, which will be acting at the knee joint centre and, therefore, will not provide a moment (Fig. 11.19).

Proximal segment

In the same way we can now consider the distal segment. The total angle at the knee was 5°, with the tibia segment being 2.5° away from the vertical. Therefore the thigh segment will also be 2.5° away from the vertical.

If we consider the moments acting around the knee joint then the vertical forces at the hip F_{Hip} and the weight of the thigh segment will provide an adduction moment, whereas force of the orthosis on the thigh segment $F_{orthosis\ medial}$ will provide an abduction moment. Therefore, if we know the information below then we can find the $F_{orthosis\ medial}$ force:
The length of the thigh is 0.5 m

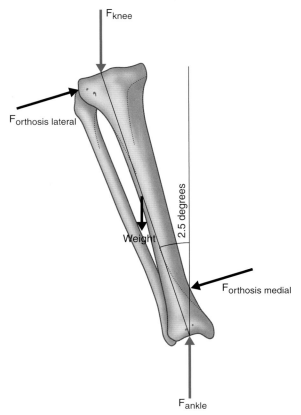

Figure 11.19   Distal segment

So to support the thigh angulation a force of 57.4 N will be required from the orthosis. This also means that an equal and opposite force will be required from $F_{orthosis\ lateral}$ to maintain the balance of forces on the orthosis, although $F_{orthosis\ lateral}$ will not provide a moment about the knee.

However, the largest force will, in fact, be at the knee joint as this must comprise of the horizontal components of the lateral forces from **both** the proximal and distal segments as both act on the knee. Therefore, the total lateral knee force may be found by:

Lateral knee force = $F_{orthosis\ lateral}$ (femoral) × cos 2.5 + $F_{orthosis\ lateral}$ (tibial) × cos 2.5

Lateral knee force = 57.4 × cos 2.5 + 66.64 × cos 2.5

Lateral knee force = 123.92 N

The magnitude of this force and the size of the contact area produce a contact pressure that is the limiting factor of the angle, which may be supported solely by the orthosis.

11.4.5 Is there a maximum supportable angle using valgus brace?

To find the maximum theoretical angle that may be solely supported by a valgus brace we need first to consider the maximum tolerable contact pressure on the knee.

The weight and centre of mass of the thigh from the knee are
    8.64 kg and 0.26 m
The $F_{orthosis\ medial}$ is placed 0.3 m away from the knee joint
Angle of inclination 2.5° to the vertical.

The force on the hip joint will depend on the ground reaction force and the weight of the foot, shank and thigh. If the subject is 90 kg and the mass of the foot is 1.26 kg, the mass of the shank is 4.05 kg and the mass of the thigh is 8.64 kg, then the force from the hip onto the head of the femur will be 746.05 N.

Both $F_{orthosis\ lateral}$ and F_{Knee} are considered to be acting at the knee joint centre and, therefore, will not provide a moment (Fig. 11.20).

Therefore, if the orthosis is to support the femur then:

(F_{Hip} sin 2.5 × length of thigh) + (mg_{thigh} × sin 2.5 × centre of mass) − ($F_{orthosis\ medial}$ × point of application of orthosis) = 0

(746.05 × sin 2.5 × 0.5) + (8.64 × 9.81 × sin 2.5 × 0.26) − ($F_{orthosis\ medial}$ × 0.3) = 0

16.27 + 0.96 − ($F_{orthosis\ medial}$ × 0.3) = 0

17.23 = $F_{orthosis\ medial}$ × 0.3

17.23/0.3 = $F_{orthosis\ medial}$

57.43 N = $F_{orthosis\ medial}$

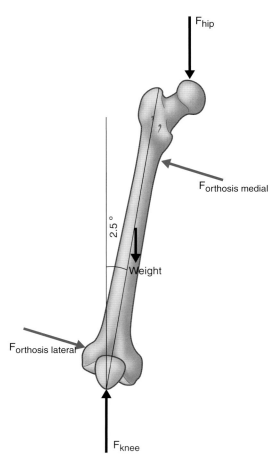

Figure 11.20   Proximal segment

We now need to consider the maximum size of pad, which may be applied to the knee joint in order to find the maximum force that can be applied. A pressure of greater than 32 mmHg or 4.3 kPa has been shown to cause interruption of arteriolar-capillary blood flow (Berjian et al 1983). However, this is based on long-term pressure application and not intermittent application of pressure that occurs during walking, for instance pressures on the foot often exceed 250 kPa and stump socket maximum pressure in lower-limb prosthetics have been recorded at 34 kPa for standing and 95 kPa for walking (Lee et al 1997).

We now need to consider the maximum size of pad, which may be applied to the knee joint in order to find the maximum force that can be applied. If we, therefore, consider a pressure of 95 kPa on the proximal and distal pads of the valgus brace, and contact area of 2 cm by 5 cm, then the maximum force that can be applied to the knee may be estimated:

$$Pressure = \frac{Force}{Area}$$

$$Pressure \times Area = Force$$

$$95\,000\,\frac{N}{m^2} \times 0.001\,m^2 = Force$$

$$95\,N = Maximum\ pad\ force$$

If we consider this as the maximum force on both the proximal and distal pads we can find the maximum supportable joint angle may be found.

Distal segment

$-(F_{Ankle} \sin \theta \times length\ of\ shank) + (mg_{shank} \times \sin \theta \times centre\ of\ mass) + (F_{orthosis\ medial} \times point\ of\ application\ of\ orthosis) = 0$

$-(888.29 \times \sin \theta \times 0.45) + (4 \times 9.81 \times \sin \theta \times 0.25) + (95 \times 0.25) = 0$

$-399.73 \times \sin \theta + 9.81 \sin \theta + 23.75 = 0$

$389.92 \times \sin \theta = 23.75$

$$\sin \theta = \frac{23.75}{389.92}$$

$\theta = \sin^{-1} 0.0609$

$\theta = 3.49°$

Proximal segment

$(F_{Hip} \sin \theta \times length\ of\ thigh) + (mg_{thigh} \times \sin \theta \times centre\ of\ mass) - (F_{orthosis\ medial} \times point\ of\ application\ of\ orthosis) = 0$

$(800 \times \sin \theta \times 0.5) + (5 \times 9.81 \times \sin \theta \times 0.26) - (95 \times 0.3) = 0$

$400 \sin \theta + 12.75 \sin \theta - 28.5 = 0$

$412.75 \sin \theta = 28.5$

$$\sin \theta = \frac{28.5}{412.75}$$

$\theta = \sin^{-1} 0.0690$

$\theta = 3.96°$

However, as before, the largest force will be at the knee joint as this must comprise of the horizontal components of the lateral forces from both the proximal and distal segments as both act on the knee. Therefore, the total lateral knee force will be:

$Lateral\ knee\ force = F_{orthosis\ lateral}\ (femoral) \times \cos 3.96 + F_{orthosis\ lateral}\ (tibial) \times \cos 3.49$

$Lateral\ knee\ force = 95 \times \cos 3.96 + 95 \times \cos 3.49$

$Lateral\ knee\ force = 189.6\,N$

If the maximum sustainable pressure is 95 kPa then the lateral knee pad size may be found:

$$Pressure = \frac{Force}{Area}$$

$$Area = \frac{Force}{Pressure}$$

$$Area = \frac{189.6}{95\,000}$$

$$Area = 0.001996\,m^2$$

This equates to a circular pad size of radius 0.0252 m or diameter 5.04 cm.

Therefore, the maximum angle that may be solely supported by a valgus brace with a 5.04 cm diameter lateral knee pad is 7.45°. In reality valgus bracing is useful at much larger knee varus angle as it is very unlikely that the entire load will be supported by the brace. This supportive element of valgus braces is responsible for the alleviation of pain and the improvement of function often seen with patients suffering from medial compartment osteoarthritis. In the next section we will consider the biomechanical effects of valgus bracing on individuals with medial compartment osteoarthritis This angle is specific to this length of brace. Any increase or decrease in the length of the arms of the brace will increase and decrease the maximum angle that can be supported effectively. However as the length of the brace increases patient compliance to wear it is likely to decrease.

11.4.6 Valgus bracing in medial compartment osteoarthritis

It is widely known that knee osteoarthritis is more prevalent in the medial compartment of the knee joint than the lateral compartment and it has been estimated that during normal gait approximately 60–80% of the load across the knee joint is transmitted to the medial compartment (Prodromos et al 1985). During walking, individuals have an almost continuous large, external varus moment about their knees throughout stance phase, with the exception of a small valgus moment at initial contact (Johnson et al 1980, Matsumo et al 1997). It has been suggested that this varus or adduction moment and the increased loads are a causation factor for the incidence of medial compartment osteoarthritis (Goh et al 1993). These increasing loads have a degenerative effect on the cartilage in the medial compartment with a narrowing in the joint space between the medial femur and medial tibial plateau. This causes a moment arm increased over that of the unaffected side in a control population (Wang et al

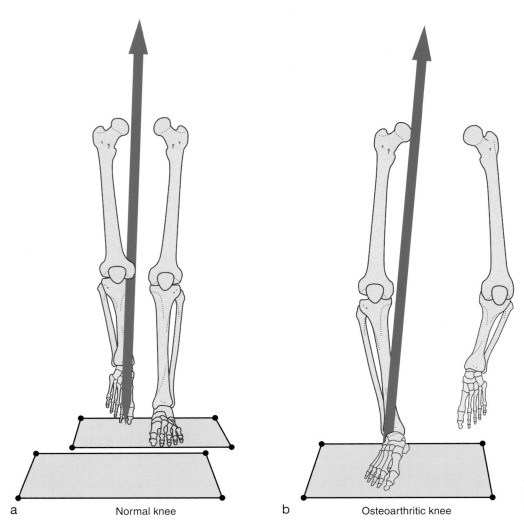

a   Normal knee   b   Osteoarthritic knee

Figure 11.21   Ground reaction forces and adduction moment: (a) normal knee and (b) osteoarthritic knee

1990). Increasing disability will arise from the increased moment arm with pain and functional impairment being the principal complaints of knee osteoarthritis sufferers (Kim et al 2004), ultimately leading to a reduced quality of life (Fig. 11.21a, b).

Treatment options available to the sufferer are aimed at minimizing these forces at the medial compartment of the knee (Pollo 1998). Surgical options such as high tibial osteotomy (HTO) and unicompartmental arthroplasty attempt to unload the medial compartment by removing a portion (wedge) of the tibia, and decrease the loading at the medial compartment by transferring the load to the less affected lateral compartment (Maly et al 2002, Noyes et al 1992). However, these types of surgery may not be appropriate for many individuals, such as the younger population, and, therefore, conservative treatment modalities have been introduced in an attempt to reduce this excessive compartmental loading without the need for surgical intervention, and increase the individual's functional independence.

One form of conservative treatment for medial compartment osteoarthritis of the knee is valgus bracing. Valgus braces often claim more than just the ability to support and often claim to offload the painful compartment, correct the varus alignment of the knee and improve quality of life. Various studies have investigated the biomechanical effects and the pain reduction using such devices. This section will consider case study data on the use of valgus bracing in medial compartment osteoarthritis.

Varus knee angle

The effect of valgus bracing on knee varus has been a point of debate for some time; however, recent research (Pollo et al 2002, Richards 2006) has shown that bracing can have a direct effect on the knee angulation in the coronal plane. The data below show the immediate effect of an individual walking with and without a valgus brace. The brace fitted in this instance was an OAdjuster (DJO), which allows the clinician to dial in a 'correction'. In this case the brace was adjusted until contact was made with the lateral aspect of the knee joint, and then a further 5° was dialled in. This was to first take up the slack in the brace, and then to try to correct by a further 5°. The greatest effect in the varus angle is during loading response from 0 to 20% of the gait cycle (Figs 11.22 and 11.23). At approximately 10% of the gait cycle, the point of greatest loading, the difference between the braced and unbraced conditions was 4°, indicating that actual correction is in a similar order to the dial in correction, which in turn will reduce the moment arm of the ground reaction force in the coronal plane.

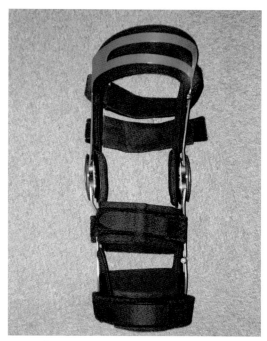

Figure 11.22   OA Adjuster, DJO Inc.

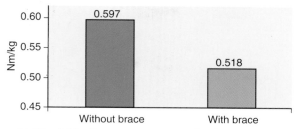

Figure 11.24   Adduction moments normalized to bodyweight (Richards et al 2006a)

Knee adduction moments

Kim et al (2004) looked at the adduction moment in individuals with and without medial compartment knee osteoarthritis. They found a significant difference in the adduction moment between the osteoarthritis group and an age and gender matched normal group; the osteoarthritis group having on average a 50% increase in their adduction moments. Kim also found a correlation between knee adduction moments with the WOMAC Score. This supports the comments by Goh et al (1993), who suggested that the adduction moment and the increased loads are a causation factor for the incidence of medial compartment osteoarthritis.

The reduction in the moment arm seen above with the reduction in the varus deformity during loading, should in turn lead to a reduction in the adduction moment about the knee joint. Below we see that this is, indeed, the case, with the braced condition reducing the adduction moment by 13% (Fig. 11.24) (Richards et al 2006a).

Ground reaction forces

Ground reaction forces give useful information about the loading and propulsion during walking. For both the vertical and anterior posterior forces, increases in the loading and propulsive forces are seen (Fig. 11.25). But isn't an increase in force bad? The ground reaction forces do not tell us much about the loading patterns within the knee; however, they are useful in determining how well an individual can load and push off during walking.

These results show improvements in the knee angle in the coronal plane during stance phase, which is supported by a significant reduction in the adduction moments about the knee. Larger vertical loading and propulsive forces were also seen indicating an improved weight acceptance and reduction in pain; however, the force values did not achieve values in the normal range. Overall, these findings show that valgus bracing can give a degree of correction to the varus position of the knee and reduced adduction moments, which gives the subject substantial functional improvements during gait.

Although this appears to be very clear evidence for the mechanical effect of valgus bracing, further research is needed on the effect of different designs and different amounts of correction. Can we, for instance, get the same amount of correction using a smaller brace, and what is the

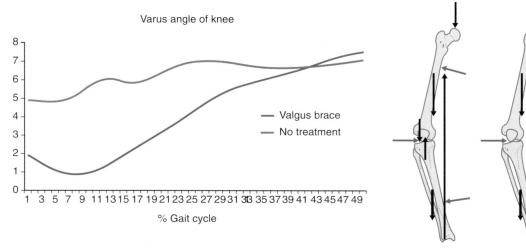

Figure 11.23   Varus angle from 0 to 50% of the gait cycle

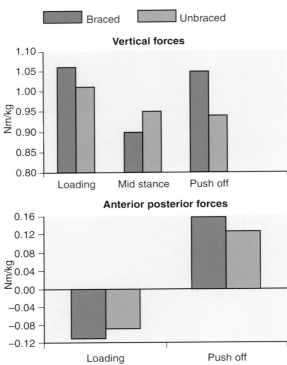

Figure 11.25   Vertical and anterior posterior forces with and without bracing (Richards et al 2006a)

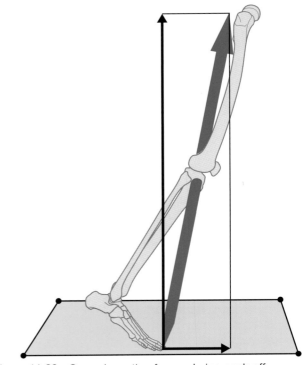

Figure 11.26   Ground reaction forces during push off

limit of correction we can achieve either by building the correction into the brace or by dialling the correction into the brace?

11.4.7 Modification of translational forces at the knee with orthoses

Much has been written on the use of anterior draw testing to determine deficits in the Anterior Cruciate Ligament (ACL). This test looks for translational movement between the tibia and femur.

One treatment that aims to regain translational stability is ACL bracing. ACL braces are sometimes confused with other types of bracing, e.g. valgus bracing in osteoarthritis, which aim to change the moment in the coronal plane; however, the theoretical action of ACL bracing is entirely different. With osteoarthritis bracing we considered that the force system could be reduced to a three-point force system; however, this is not the case with ACL bracing. When walking we have both vertical and anterior–posterior forces. The anterior–posterior forces will cause shear forces at the ankle and knee joints, which the ACL will, in part, resist and support; however, when the ACL becomes damaged it can no longer support these forces (Fig. 11.26).

To consider the theoretical action of ACL bracing we first need to consider the ground reaction forces and the action of these forces on the ankle, knee and hip joints. If we consider the forces acting on the tibial and femoral segment separately during late stance phase, at the ankle joint there will be a vertical and anterior force from the foot onto the tibia, which will be resisted by an equal and opposite posterior force at the knee. This posterior force at the knee will subsequently be transmitted to the femoral

segment, partly by the action of the ACL, this force will then be balanced by an equal and opposite posterior force at the hip (Fig. 11.27).

Therefore, the anterior force acting on the femur, and the equal and opposite posterior force acting on the tibia, will come from a tensile force in the ACL. So what happens when the ACL does not function correctly? To consider this we will imagine a complete absence of the ACL and any other structures that may be able to support these forces in part. Therefore, if these shear forces at the knee are not supported, the anterior force at the ankle will be unopposed and the tibial segment will move in an anterior direction, but at the same time the posterior force from the hip on the femoral segment will try to move in a posterior direction. This demonstrates the nature of the anterior draw test and how it relates to ACL dysfunction (Fig. 11.28a, b).

Surgical reconstruction of the ACL aims to replace the ligament with either an artificial ligament, sometimes made from Gore-Tex, or a graft harvested from the central third of the patella tendon or a hamstring tendon. This rebalances the internal forces in the knee and gives translational stability back to the knee. ACL bracing has a similar end functional goal; however, this is achieved by applying an external system of forces, which aims to replace the forces from the ACL and to return translational stability to the knee.

To achieve translational stability to the knee, the brace needs to provide a posteriorly directed force on the anterior proximal aspect of the tibia and an anteriorly directed force acting on the posterior distal aspect of the femur, which will stop its translation posteriorly (Fig. 11.29).

Additional forces are also required to give the brace stability. An anteriorly directed force is also required further

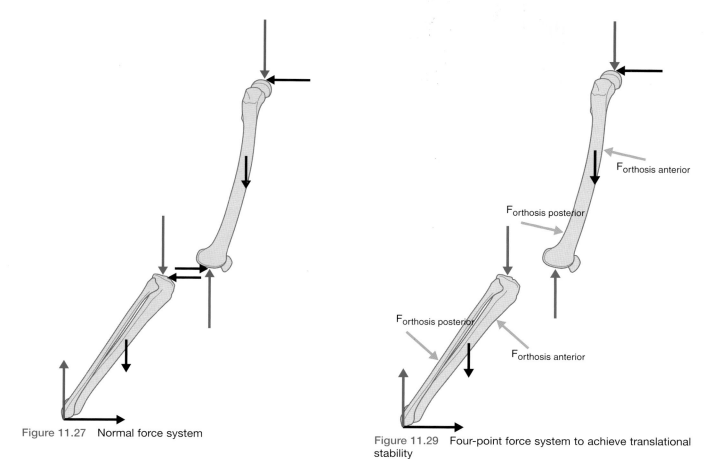

Figure 11.27 Normal force system

Figure 11.29 Four-point force system to achieve translational stability

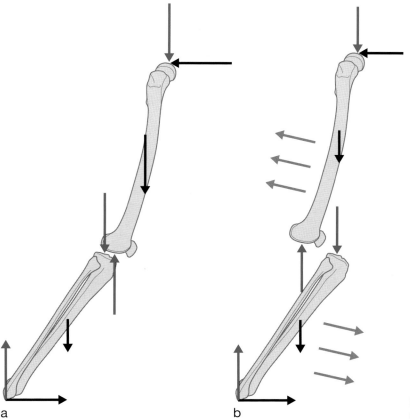

a

b

Figure 11.28 (a and b) Force system with anterior cruciate ligament deficient knee distal on the tibia, and a posteriorly directed force acting on the anterior proximal aspect of the femur.

To reduce the turning effect, the forces either side of the knee should be placed as close to the joint centre as possible, therefore, minimizing the moment required from the additional forces. Previously we considered braces that can control the moments about a joint where we could use a three-point force system; however, the nature of the direction of the forces required for translational stability is different and a three-point force system would not give support in the correct way. Therefore, a different load system and a different design of brace are required to control shear forces with four forces now being required to prevent translational movement between body segments. This is sometimes referred to as a four-point fixation brace or a four-point force system. Movement is possible with such an orthosis if the brace is hinged to allow flexion in the sagittal plane, one example of a hinged four point ACL brace is the 4Titude Ligament Knee Brace (Fig. 11.30).

11.4.8 The 'mechanics' of soft bracing of the knee

The focus of many studies on patellofemoral pain has been on the loading limb rather than on the eccentrically controlling limb, although clinically it is most often the eccentrically controlling limb that has most pain. One of the aims of the different treatments is to improve the control of the knee joint; both patellofemoral bracing and taping attempt to do this by realigning the patella. If the patella is being re-aligned then this should have greater implications to the coronal and transverse plane mechanics of the knee. Research to date has mainly focused on the sagittal plane with the mechanics of the torsional and coronal planes attracting very little attention.

Since McConnell's landmark paper in 1986 there has been considerable clinical and research interest in taping techniques for the patellofemoral joint. Patellofemoral taping techniques are now considered as part of standard clinical practice. Although a consensus view that tape is effective at relieving pain is emerging in the literature, there is still an ongoing debate about the mechanism of effect of taping. Recent work has highlighted the importance of the potential proprioceptive effects of taping (Baker et al 2002, Callaghan et al 2002).

Compared to taping there has been much less research on the effect of braces in the management of patellofemoral problems, with only 7% of the recent research literature focusing on this modality (Selfe 2004). The pain-relieving effects of bracing are reported as occurring through an increased stabilization of the joint, which reduces the force of muscular contraction (Nadler & Nadler 2001). In particular patellofemoral braces are designed to 'reduce compression of the patella as well as to prevent excessive lateral shifting' (Nadler & Nadler 2001). Although the results tend to be positive, because of the small number of studies the usefulness of braces remains controversial. The fact that soft braces, by definition, have no rigid structures has caused much debate over their function. This is highlighted by the fact that in some European countries soft braces are not considered therapeutic and, therefore, cannot be prescribed,

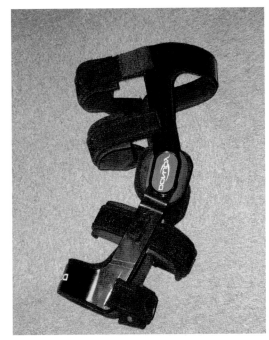

Figure 11.30   4Titude Ligament Knee Brace, DJO Inc

whereas their hinged counterparts can be. So what are the 'mechanics' behind soft patellofemoral bracing and what effect can these have on joint loading and stability?

The system of forces in patellofemoral bracing

The purpose of patellofemoral bracing is to allow full flexion movement but to provide medial–lateral and rotational stability to the knee by realigning the patella. To achieve this the brace is of soft design, which allows the middle section of the brace to move independently of the proximal and distal aspects; therefore, a torsional 'correction' may be produced by tensioning the straps either medially or laterally depending on the patella correction required. On some designs of brace a semicircular buttress is fitted to the brace to ensure the force is directed onto the patella (Fig. 11.31).

The effect of patellofemoral bracing on joint stability

The vast majority of research into stair climbing has focused on the sagittal plane, however, according to Kowalk et al (1996), although the knee abduction–adduction moment is not in the primary plane of motion, its magnitude should not be ignored when trying to understand the stability and function of the knee during stair climbing activities. Powers (2003) adds that the knee is designed to absorb rotary forces through its transverse plane motion. Powers also goes on to state that motion of the tibia and femur in the frontal and transverse planes can influence patellofemoral mechanics. The comparison of patella bracing and taping during functional tasks is beginning to attract attention. As the reported purpose of these treatments is to realign the patella, the largest effects should be on the coronal and transverse planes of the knee.

The study of the effect of patellofemoral bracing on joint stability (Selfe et al in press) involved the testing of 12

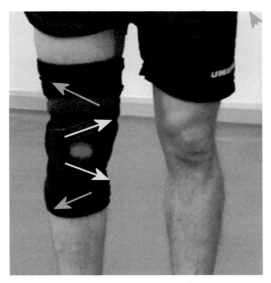

Figure 11.31   The system of forces in patellofemoral bracing

healthy subjects who were asked to conduct a slow step-down exercise to assess the control of the knee during a slow eccentric controlled exercise. The step down was conducted under three randomized conditions a) no intervention, b) neutral patella taping and c) a patellofemoral brace. A step was designed to accommodate one of the plates; the other plate was embedded in the floor, this arrangement produced a standard step height of 20 cm. The force platforms allowed for the measurement kinetics in the sagittal, coronal and transverse planes. Reflective markers were placed on the foot, shank and thigh using the CAST technique (Chapter 9). The purpose of the step-down exercise was to assess the control of the knee as the body was lowered as slowly as possible from the step. The kinematic and kinetic data about the knee were then quantified from toe off, of the contralateral limb to contact of the supporting, eccentrically controlling limb.

The results from the coronal plane movement and moments show that the patellofemoral brace is having a controlling effect on the mechanics of the knee. This is supported by the results from the transverse plane, which show a reduction in the range of motion and moments experienced at the knee with the patellofemoral brace. Interestingly, the taping also showed an improvement in the torsional stability of the knee. These results suggest that both taping and bracing are, indeed, having an effect on the coronal and torsional mechanics of the knee, allowing an eccentric descent with considerably more control, with the brace having the largest effect. Although not presented below, the sagittal plane did not show any change in the two interventions (Figs 11.32a, b and 11.33a, b).

The nature of these results raises the question: how exactly do 'soft' orthoses work? Do they have a direct effect on the mechanics or do they improve proprioception and, therefore, aid joint control? It is at this point we have to say that we do not yet know the answers to this. However, one message that is clear is that to investigate the effects of such orthoses we need to examine the three-dimensional mechanics rather than considering a single plane.

11.5 Biomechanics of knee ankle foot orthoses

11.5.1 Use of knee ankle foot orthoses

Knee ankle foot orthoses (KAFOs) combine the benefits of ankle foot orthoses and knee orthoses. They are generally used when larger moments are required to control the knee and when there is both substantial lack of control and stability of the ankle and knee joints. The designs of knee ankle foot orthoses can be divided into two categories, conventional and cosmetic. Conventional knee ankle foot orthoses are constructed using leather and metal, with the leather forming the straps and pads, and the metal forming side steels. Cosmetic, contemporary, or plastic knee ankle

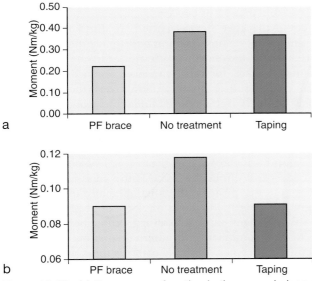

Figure 11.32   (a) Knee range of motion in the coronal plane and (b) transverse plane

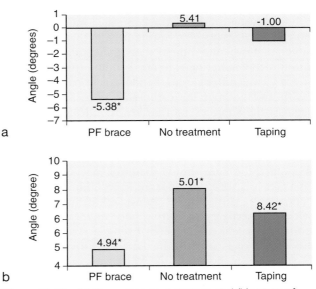

Figure 11.33   (a) Coronal knee moments and (b) range of torsional moments

foot orthoses are constructed in a similar way to plastic ankle foot orthoses, with metal hinges joining the sections (Fig. 11.34a, b).

11.5.2 Common force systems for knee ankle foot orthoses

Knee ankle foot orthoses can use a three-point force system to offer either resistance to knee flexion moments or knee extension or hyperextension moments (Fig. 11.35a, b, c). However, the nature of the resistive forces will vary with the external moments due to the position of the ground reaction forces with respect to the joints at different stages during the gait cycle.

Knee ankle foot orthoses can come in many configurations with completely rigid joints, to free moving hinges with hyperextension stops and hinged or leaf spring designed ankle component. The configurations of flexion and extension stops allow different controlling forces at the different stages of the gait cycle by preventing further movement. A similar effect can be achieved by locking the knee, which may be necessary; however, this of course prevents any functional movement.

11.5.3 Clinical case study of the use of knee ankle foot orthoses

The clinical case study of the use of a knee ankle foot orthosis shows a teenager with spina bifida. The orthotic intervention comprised of a pair of stock orthopaedic boots with a compensatory raise to the left, a unilateral cosmetic knee ankle foot orthosis, and a rigid ankle foot orthoses section with high lateral walls. The orthotic knee joint provided free motion in the sagittal plane, but was designed to provide lateral stability by the addition of a cosmetic thigh-corset top section.

Without the knee ankle foot orthosis fitted, the subject's ankle joint collapsed into a huge amount of dorsiflexion. This will cause the muscles in the posterior compartment of the ankle joint to stretch considerably, which would be very uncomfortable and dangerous as the subject would also be very unstable. With the orthosis fitted this movement was held effectively allowing a much more controlled movement over the stance limb. It is also interesting to note that the subject was able to move into dorsiflexion indicating the 'rigid' ankle foot orthosis section is in fact bending (Fig. 11.36).

There is a large difference in the movement patterns at the knee with and without the orthosis (Fig. 11.37). Without the orthosis the subject's foot strikes the ground with the knee in 28° of knee flexion. With the knee in this position the stride length was significantly reduced and also forced the ankle into the excessive dorsiflexion seen above. After initial contact, the knee should then flex and extend as the load is taken on the front foot and the body moves over the stance limb. However, the subject's knee continued to flex with little recovery indicating poor quadriceps control and poor movement of the thigh over the tibia. With the orthosis the knee is initially flexed to 3°, giving a much longer step length; however, the knee was still collapsing into further flexion, but not to the same degree, giving better movement of the body over the stance limb than without the orthosis. During swing phase the knee flexion without the

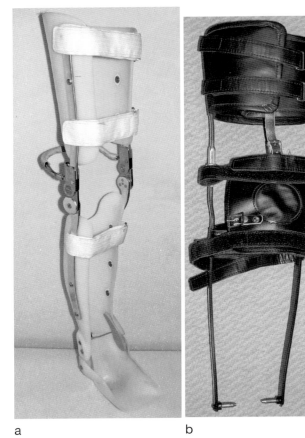

a   b

Figure 11.34   Knee ankle foot orthoses: (a) cosmetic KAFO and (b) conventional KAFO

orthosis was greater than normal, whereas with the orthosis it is slightly lower than expected. This could be due to the orthosis restricting some motion of the knee during swing phase. The orthosis was clearly offering support and the increase in step length was of considerable benefit to the subject; however, the movement of the body over the knee joint was still an area of concern.

So could the knee flexion pattern be further improved? If the ankle foot orthosis section were made more rigid this may reduce the movement of the tibia forwards and bring the femur further forward, therefore, reducing the knee flexion during stance phase. Alternatively the ankle foot orthosis could be set into slight plantarflexion offering a greater resistance to knee flexion, although this may have a detrimental effect of the foot clearance during the swing phase.

The motion of the knee in the coronal plane was of the most concern. Without the orthosis the knee collapses into internal rotation pushing the knee medially into a valgus position. Without the orthosis the knee appears to collapse into 30° of valgus during loading, although this is more likely to be a combination of internal rotation, flexion and abduction of the knee. With the orthosis this was reduced to 18° valgus (Fig. 11.38).

Although improved, this movement will be extremely detrimental for the patient and to prevent any further

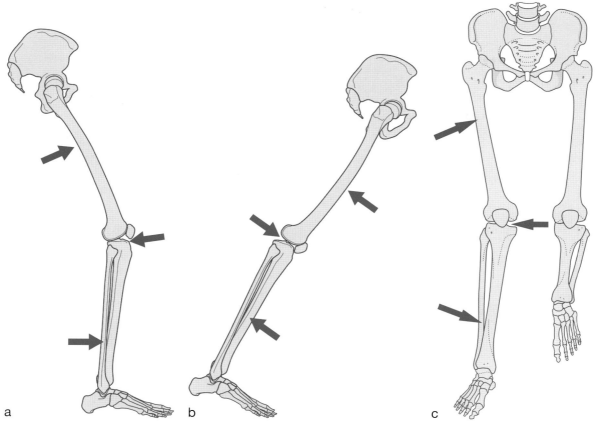

Figure 11.35   Three-point force system with a knee ankle foot orthoses: (a) knee flexion, (b) knee extension and (c) knee valgus

damage/deformity at the knee this motion needs to be reduced whilst still allowing the knee to move freely in the sagittal plane. This may be achieved by the strengthening of the hinge and side steels, and by applying a force on the medial side of the knee, although the amount of correction needed would require a substantial pressure that may not be tolerable.

11.6 Foot orthoses

So what are foot orthoses? These are shaped or moulded inserts for the shoe which aim to hold the foot in position, change the foot position, or change the range of motion of either the whole foot or between the different segments of the foot. Foot orthoses can have a direct effect on the segments of the foot, but they can also have significant clinical effects indirectly much further up the body to the pelvis, lower back and, arguably, as far up as the shoulders and neck.

Foot orthoses come in many shapes and forms, the most basic form is a simple ethyl vinyl acetate (EVA) wedge, while some are pre-made contoured devices, which may or may not need some form of modification to the patient's prescription. Lockard (1988) highlighted the fact there are many classification systems used to describe shoe inserts. These range from the description of the properties of the

materials used, i.e. soft, semi-rigid or rigid, to the type of procedure used to construct the appliance, i.e. moulded and non-moulded. Anthony (1991) defines an orthoses as 'an orthopaedic device which is designed to promote the structural integrity of the joints of the foot and lower limb, by resisting ground reaction forces that cause abnormal skeletal motion to occur during the stance phase of gait'. Root et al (1977) suggests they 'assist in controlling foot geometry and force direction, stabilising joints and reducing muscle contractions'.

The foot is an extremely complex system of articulating segments. Therefore, the movements of the foot and ankle cannot be completely explained by rotations about a single plane, but by a combination of movements in all three planes. This makes the assessment of the foot and the action of foot orthoses one of the most complex biomechanical systems in the body. This fact is compounded by the fact that the analysis of the foot, up until fairly recently, has been only considered as a single segment due to restrictions in movement analysis technology.

It is highly likely that in the coming years our knowledge of foot function and the effects of foot orthotic management will be greatly expanded. These next sections consider both the direct action of several types of commonly used foot orthoses on the foot and also their indirect action on the lower limb and pelvis. This section includes summaries from

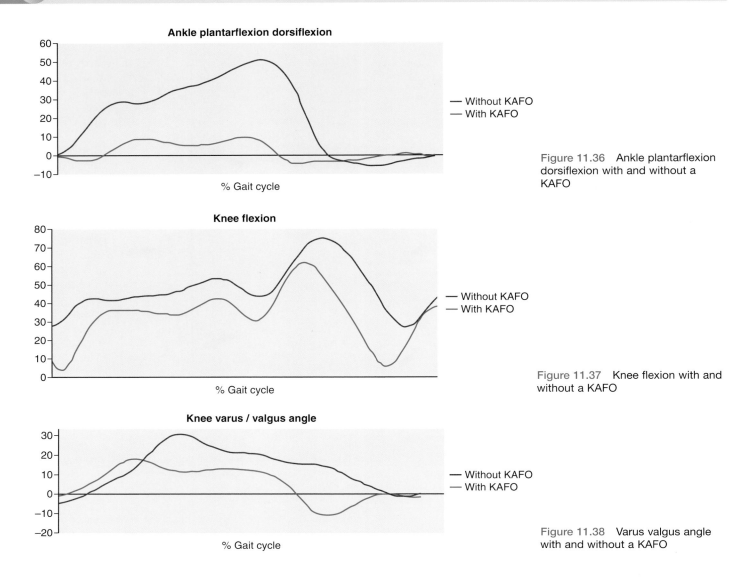

Figure 11.36 Ankle plantarflexion dorsiflexion with and without a KAFO

Figure 11.37 Knee flexion with and without a KAFO

Figure 11.38 Varus valgus angle with and without a KAFO

key papers and clinical case studies; however, I would advise any reader to remain up to date with advances, in this field in particular, by looking at the current research literature.

11.6.1 The assessment of leg-length discrepancy

Leg-length discrepancies of 2 cm or less are very common. Inequalities in leg length greater than 1.5 cm have been linked with low back pain and abnormal gait with higher energy consumption and early fatigue. And undetected leg-length discrepancy can often contribute to chronic pain and biomechanical adaptations of the lower limb and pelvis.

If the presence of a leg-length discrepancy needs to be assessed then this may be conducted by examining for both real and apparent leg-length discrepancy. Real leg-length discrepancies may be assessed with the patient lying supine from a point on the upper pelvis (anterior superior iliac spine) to the medial maleolus, or from the greater trochanter to the lateral maleolus. Leg-length discrepancies may also be apparent. This is where the legs will actually measure the same length, but will function as though they are different because of pelvic obliquity or curvature in the back.

Apparent leg-length discrepancy may be measured with the patient lying supine, and a measurement from the navel or sternum to the medial maleolli.

A number of visual clues can be present with individuals with a leg-length discrepancy. These can include the dropping the hip on the shorter side, head and shoulder tilting or bending the knee excessively on the contralateral side. There may be also an appearance of vaulting or stepping into a hole, or other gait asymmetries such as unequal step lengths.

11.6.2 Treatment of leg-length discrepancy

With leg-length discrepancies we are confronted with 'to treat or not to treat?' that is the question. There are a variety of schools of thought; some clinicians will not treat discrepancies less than 1 cm while others would not treat discrepancies less than 2 cm. Some clinicians would not measure the discrepancy and only treat if there are the associated adaptations of the lower limb and pelvis. These can include hip hiking, where the patient raises the hip on the longer side with associated head and shoulder tilting in the coronal plane. However, most clinicians would agree that treatment should not be considered unless there are associated symptoms of lower back pain.

We will now consider a patient in her mid 20s with chronic lower back pain. The patient was referred for gait analysis after having been found to have a leg-length discrepancy with the left side being 2 cm shorter than the right. An assessment was carried out looking in particular at the movement of the lower limb and pelvis, but also the ground reaction forces. The subject was then fitted with a simple 1 cm heel raise to allow for the leg-length discrepancy and then immediately re-tested with the device.

Ground reaction forces with and without the heel raise

The results with no heel raise show the shorter side had a marked reduction in the loading response forces in comparison to normal. The movement over the body, the stance limb during mid-stance and the vertical propulsive force were also affected, with the trough occurring much earlier than normal. The longer limb showed a less smooth and reduced loading response on the right side, a shallow trough indicating a poor progression of the body over the stance limb and the lower propulsive force (Fig. 11.39a, b).

With the heel raise the sorter limb showed significant improvement in the loading response. The movement of

the body over the stance limb shown by the trough and the vertical propulsive peak are also improved. The longer limb showed improved movement of the body over the stance limb on the left side; also the smoothness and magnitude of the loading response forces on the unaffected side were improved. The magnitudes of the vertical forces show a much better balance between left and right with the heel raise inserted (11.40a, b).

Perttunen et al (2004) investigated the gait asymmetries in 25 patients with limb-length discrepancy. Perttunen found that the duration of the stance phase was reduced in the short limb and the vertical ground reaction force during the push-off phase was greater in the long limb. The push-off phase was also initiated earlier in the short leg. These results support this clinical case study where the loading of the longer limb is greater than that of the shorter limb.

But what accounts for this change in ground reaction forces? If we consider the analogy of the patient 'stepping into a hole' then we might expect the forces on the shorter side to, in fact, be greater than the longer, as the foot hits the ground, but this clearly does not happen. It is at this point we need to consider the action of the pelvis. Although the shorter side is descending for longer, the pelvis reaction is to try to adapt to the difference, which has the effect of gently lowering the leg until contact is made. This offers an additional method of deceleration of the shorter limb before the foot reaches the ground, so the foot hits the ground with a lower velocity than normal. If we now consider that this patient was referred for lower back pain, the pelvic involvement becomes very important.

Movement of the pelvis with and without the heel raise

As mentioned previously, some clinicians will examine an individual walking from the coronal plane and examine pelvic, shoulder or head tilting as indicators of functional asymmetry in individuals with suspected or measured leg-length discrepancy. We will now consider the differences in pelvic movement with and without the 1 cm heel raise using movement analysis.

The graphs (Fig. 11.41a, b) show a marked difference in the pelvic movement with and without the heel raise. Without the heel raise we see an asymmetrical movement pattern, with all the movement being on one side. This relates to the pelvis dropping down on the shorter side, which at no point drops down on the contralateral side. With the heel raise, the pelvic movement shows a good balance of alternation of pelvic drop during the gait cycle and a more normal pattern.

The improvements in the balance of the forces and the pelvic movement should reduce the strain on the pelvis and lower back, as less compensation will have to be made. In this particular case the patient's lower back pain did, indeed, reduce when wearing the heel raise. This sounds very good, although whether the use of heel raises for long-term management produces its own compensations and secondary effects is not clear. We also have to be careful with the use of pelvic obliquity as a measure of the efficacy of heel raises. This is highlighted by comments from Wagner (1990) who stated that pelvic tilt (obliquity) is often the consequence

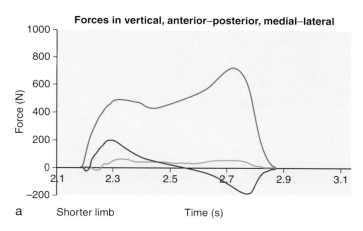

Forces in vertical, anterior–posterior, medial–lateral

a   Shorter limb

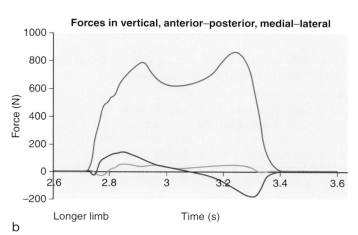

Forces in vertical, anterior–posterior, medial–lateral

b   Longer limb

Figure 11.39   Ground reaction forces with no heel raise: (a) shorter limb and (b) longer limb

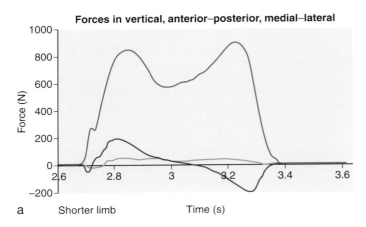

a Shorter limb

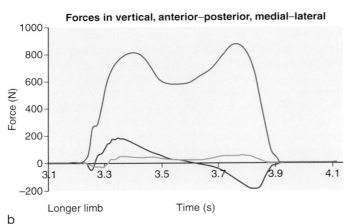

b

Figure 11.40 Ground reaction forces with heel raise: (a) shorter limb and (b) longer limb

the kinematics and kinetics of normal walking gait. This considered not only the effects on the foot and ankle, but also the effects at the knee of both medial and lateral wedging. Branthwaite et al (2004) studied the effect of simple insoles on three-dimensional foot motion during normal walking. They found significantly reduced maximum eversion angle between wearing orthoses and no orthoses.

The underlying theme of all these papers is that they were carried out on normal individuals who did not require foot orthoses; yet these may be considered as real effects. But are individuals going to respond in the same way if they have a lack of control in pronation or supination, or have a different foot type, or are either currently suffering or have previously suffered from overuse running injuries? And what amounts of pronation or supination instability are controllable by such devices? What are the limiting factors to their use clinically? We must also consider the modelling of the foot, which is predominantly modelled as a single segment, whereas podiatrists will consider the action of an orthosis on at least three segments of the foot. It as at this point that we still do not have enough literature to refer to when considering the true clinical action of wedging on the foot.

11.6.4 Control of the line of forces

The technique of wedging inside the shoe is sometimes referred to as posting or wedging by a podiatrist. The principal effect of the wedge is to change the orientation of the calcaneus, and, therefore, the subtalar joint when the plantar surface of the heel of the shoe is flat on the ground. A wedge would, therefore, be used if there is some structural deformity that results in the calcaneus not being vertical when the subtalar joint is in neutral. It is assumed clinically that posting the foot induces either a supinatory or pronatory moment on the subtalar joint, and, therefore, will limit the amount of foot pronation.

The action of the orthosis to alter the supinatory or pronatory moments will depend on the point of application and direction of the ground reaction force during the various stages of stance phase. This changes the moments in the coronal plane about the subtalar joint, but may also alter the moments about the knee and hip joint. The diagrams (Figs. 11.44a, b & c) show a somewhat exaggerated theoretical effect of medial and lateral posting of the rearfoot on the moments about the subtalar joint.

11.6.5 The effect of wedging or posting the rearfoot during normal walking

Rearfoot motion

The graph in Figure 11.45 shows how the rearfoot kinematics are changed with the introduction of a medial and lateral rearfoot wedge. These graphs indicate the medial wedging reduces pronation during contact phase, while the lateral wedging increases pronation during contact phase (Fig. 11.45).

Medial and lateral forces

One way to objectively assess the function of the wedge is to study the ground reaction forces in the frontal plane, with particular attention to the medial–lateral force. This

of a discrepancy in leg length and can be corrected either with orthotic devices or by operative equalization of the leg length. However, pelvic tilt (obliquity) can also occur independently of the leg length in cases of asymmetry of the pelvis, malposition of the hip joint or contracted scoliotic deviation of the spine. In such cases with complex deformities correction of the pelvis should aim at a balanced body posture rather than necessarily a symmetric level of the iliac crests.

11.6.3 Wedging or posting of the rearfoot

The prescription and fitting of medial wedges is commonplace in podiatric practice (Figs 11.42 and 11.43). Wedging aims to control rearfoot motion, which can be responsible for ankle instability and abnormal moments about proximal joints. Foot orthoses have been shown to reduce excessive pronation of the foot. Nester et al (2003) stated that despite their wide clinical application and success, our understanding of the biomechanical effects of foot orthoses is relatively limited.

Wedging or posting the orthoses can be carried out on both the medial and lateral sides of the foot. There have been many papers considering the biomechanical effect of foot orthoses to control or change rearfoot motion. Nester et al (2003) studied the effect of foot orthoses on

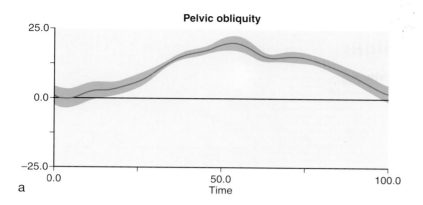

Pelvic obliquity

a

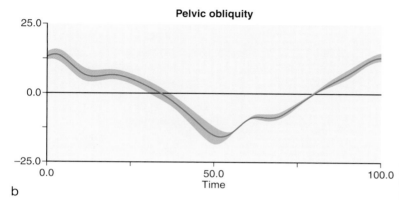

Pelvic obliquity

b

Figure 11.41   Pelvic movement in the coronal plane (pelvic obliquity): (a) without heel raise and (b) with heel raise

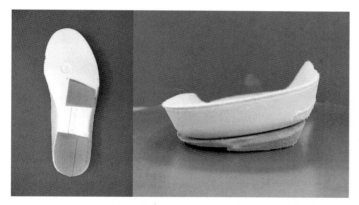

Figure 11.42   Medial wedge on a preformed full length foot orthosis

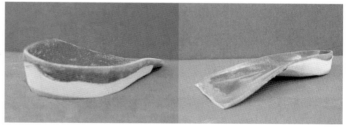

Figure 11.43   Bespoke cast orthosis with built in medial wedge

can cause difficulties, as few podiatrists have access to force platforms at this time. Those that do carry out objective analysis of force often rely on pressure plate systems that cannot yet measure the forces in any direction other than vertically and are, therefore, not suitable to assess the effect of wedging. The graphs below show that the introduction of a medial rearfoot wedge increases the lateral thrust during loading, whereas a lateral wedge decreases the lateral thrust during loading. In late stance the medial forces are also slightly affected, with the medial wedge reducing the medial force and the lateral wedge increasing the medial force (Fig. 11.46).

Nester et al found that medially wedged orthoses decreased rearfoot pronation and increased the laterally directed ground reaction force during the contact phase, suggesting a decrease in the ability to absorb shock and, therefore, a greater shock loading or shock attenuation; whereas laterally wedged orthoses increased rearfoot pronation and decreased the laterally directed ground reaction force during the contact phase, suggesting decreased shock attenuation.

Moments about the knee joint
The moments about the knee joint in the coronal plane may also be affected by wedging the rearfoot. This is due

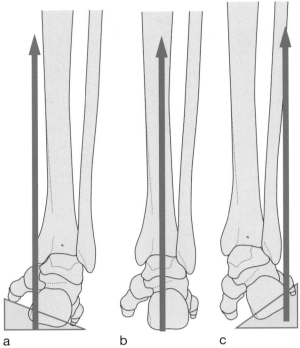

a   b   c

Figure 11.44   (a) Medial posting, (b) no posting and (c) lateral posting

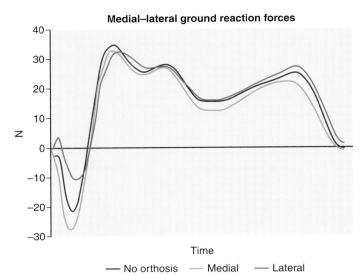

Figure 11.46   Medial and lateral forces. Adapted from Nester et al 2003

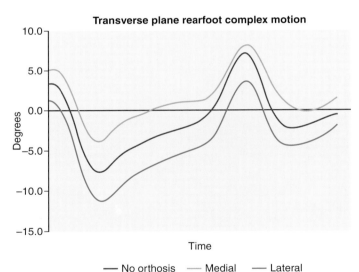

Figure 11.45   Rearfoot motion. Adapted from Nester et al 2003

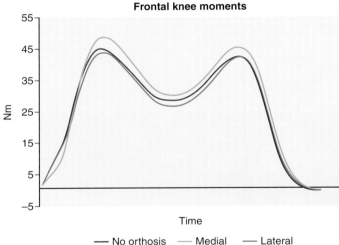

Figure 11.47   Moments and the knee joint. Adapted from Nester et al 2003

to changes in the alignment of the rearfoot in relation to the tibia and changes in the medial–lateral forces acting. The graphs (Fig. 11.47) show an increase in the moments about the knee in the coronal plane with the medial wedge. However, the lateral wedge does not appear to affect the moments about the knee.

11.6.6 The effect of lateral wedging in medial compartment osteoarthritis

We considered the importance of varus or adduction moments in the progession and management of medial compartment osteoarthritis previously when considering the use of valgus brace to reduce the varus deformity and, therefore, reduce the adduction moments. However, another treatment that has been suggested is the use of lateral wedging of the foot. In the previous section we saw how in the application of the ground reaction force, the centre of pressure may be theoretically changed; but can this really be used as an effective way of reducing the adduction moments at the knee? A lateral wedged insole has a thicker lateral border and applies a valgus moment to the heel, attempting to move it into an everted position. It is theorized that by changing the position of the ankle and subtalar joints during weight-bearing (Pollo 1998) the lateral wedges may apply a valgus moment across the knee as well as the rearfoot.

The knee adduction moment has been shown to be significantly decreased in subjects with medial compartment osteoarthritis using laterally wedged insoles (Jones et al 2006). Jones et al found that the use of lateral wedging significantly reduced the adduction moments at the knee by 23%, which should, in turn, reduce the loading on the medial compartment. It is also clear that such devices give some patients functional improvements during gait, such as improved ground reaction force patterns; however, it is still unclear if the knee varus angulation is improved with such devices. With such indirect management of the knee many biomechanical factors come into play including: the position of the centre of pressure, the medial ground reaction force, the foot type and also foot contact area.

Summary: Biomechanics of direct and indirect orthotic management

- Different configurations of ankle foot orthoses can be used to block movement about the ankle joint, assist with muscle function present, or allow free movement within 'safe' limits. The use of ankle foot orthoses can have clinical effects at the ankle, knee, hip and pelvis.
- Different configurations of knee orthoses or knee brace are required to support moments about a joint, shear and axial forces. Each configuration when correctly prescribed can improve joint function, stability and quality of life.
- Foot orthoses can have a direct effect on the foot and ankle movement, and the ground reaction forces. Foot orthoses can have a clinically significant effect on the control and function of the knee, hip and pelvis.
- The nature of each individual's muscle and joint function dictates which would be the most effective orthotic management.

Common Movement Tasks in Clinical Assessment

James Selfe, Jim Richards and Dominic Thewlis

This chapter covers the biomechanics of common movement tasks used in clinical assessment of the lower limb. This includes step and stair ascent and descent, sit to stand, timed up and go, gait initiation and squats and dips.

Chapter 12: Aim

To consider the biomechanics of common movement tasks used in clinical assessment of the lower limb.

Chapter 12: Objectives

- To consider the concept of kinetic chains in the clinical assessment of lower limb tasks
- To explain the theoretical aspects of the different movement tasks used in clinical assessment
- To describe the movement patterns during the different movement tasks
- To critically evaluate the different movement tasks in relation to joint function and control.

12.1 Kinetic chains

Useful terminology has been borrowed from mechanical engineering to describe this concept; this is the concept of kinetic chains, which can be open or closed. In mechanical engineering the link concept considers rigid overlapping bars that are connected in series by pin joints. The system is considered closed if both ends are connected to an immovable framework, thus preventing translation of either the distal or proximal joint centre. This creates a system where movement at one joint produces movement at all other joints in a predictable manner (Palmitier et al 1991).

When applied to human movement it is apparent that there can never be a situation where there is a truly closed kinetic chain and certainly the movement of the knee joint is more complex than that occurring around a pin joint. However, a closed kinetic chain is said to occur in the lower limb when the foot meets considerable resistance, e.g. the ground. An open kinetic chain occurs when the foot is free to move in space with little or no resistance (Palmitier et al 1991).

There are a number of important biomechanical differences between these two states. Firstly, the pattern of muscle activity is quite different, in the open chain movement the quadriceps

work is predominantly concentrically to produce knee extension. In the closed chain movement the quadriceps work is predominantly eccentrically to decelerate the flexing knee (Doucette & Child 1996). Secondly, the forces applied to the knee joint are quite different with greater compressive forces and lower shearing forces in the closed chain position compared to the open chain (Palmitier et al 1991). Finally, the patella is optimally aligned with the femur in the closed chain compared to the open chain, this leads to greater patellofemoral joint congruence and, therefore, stability (Doucette & Child 1996).

Closed kinetic chain (CKC) exercises are assumed to be more functional than open kinetic chain (OKC) exercises because they produce a muscle recruitment pattern that simulates functional activities. During CKC exercise simultaneous hip and knee extension occur when rising from the flexed position causing rectus femoris to simultaneously eccentrically lengthen across the hip, but concentrically shorten across the knee. Conversely, the hamstrings lengthen across the hip but shorten at the knee. This form of pseudoisometric muscle contraction has been labelled as the concurrent shift (Palmitier et al 1991).

12.2 Steps and stairs

Steps and stairs are an important aspect of daily life whether we are at home or out in the community. Access to many buildings and internally within buildings is often determined by our ability to negotiate steps and stairs. In many parts of the world legislation is in place to ensure alternative access arrangements are in place. However, there are also a number of recommendations for and regulations governing stair design. For example, the international building code states that the maximum riser height on a stair should be no more than 21 cm (International Code Council 2003), in the UK the guidelines for inclusive mobility recommend a maximum riser height of 17 cm (Department for Transport 2004). The reason for this focus on stairs is that going up and down stairs from a mechanical view point is quite different to level walking.

That stairs are much more challenging than level walking is evidenced by the inclusion of step and stair activities in the assessment of lower-limb functional status (Cowan et al 2000, Salsich et al 2002, Selfe et al 2001b) and their inclusion in rehabilitation regimes (Cook et al 1992, McConnell 2002, McGinty et al 2000). Patients with conditions where muscle function is impaired may be particularly prone to difficulties with stair climbing and, in fact, in some populations negotiating stairs can be quite hazardous. In the UK in 1992 one-quarter of non-fatal falls in older people, living in ordinary housing, were from stairs (Wright 1994). Fatal falls on or from steps or stairs demonstrate an increased incidence with increased age. Older adults aged 65 or over accounted for 68% of the total of deaths in this category of fall in England and Wales in 1994 /1995 (Dowswell et al 1999). Whilst it is acknowledged that the cause of falls from steps or stairs is likely to be multifactorial, this section will focus on reviewing the biomechanics of step and stair climbing. In the context of this chapter step or stair climbing refers to both ascent and descent (Table 12.1).

12.2.1 Step and stair ascent

When ascending subjects are required to raise their centre of gravity during the pull up and then actively carry it forward to the next step. This is achieved through concentric muscular contraction, which displaces the centre of gravity vertically, a by product of which is the generation of potential energy.

Clinically, it is important to note that McFadyen and Winter (1988) identified toe off during the pull up phase as the greatest point of instability in the ascent of stairs. There are two explanations for this: firstly, the effect of the external flexion moments and secondly, the articular geometry of the joints, in particular the knee joint.

At toe off, all the body weight is transferred onto the stance limb, where the hip, knee and ankle joints are all in a flexed position. In this position all the external moments applied to the major lower limb joints are flexion moments, subjects, therefore, require the generation of considerable concentric muscle activity to overcome the collapsing effect of these external moments. As pull up continues, stability increases due to the decreased effect of these external flexion moments.

When ascending the stance knee starts from a relatively unstable position of semi-flexion, with the ligaments lax and little congruence between the articular surfaces of the femur and tibia. As the pull up takes place, the stance knee moves towards a more extended position approximating to the close pack position of the joint (the most stable joint posture) with the ligaments tightening and the articular surfaces becoming more congruent (Shinno 1971) (Table 12.2).

12.2.2 Step and stair descent

Stair descent is more challenging than stair ascent. From a clinical perspective Shinno (1971) suggests that during descent stability is more dependent on quadriceps function; therefore, any weakness in the quadriceps may show up as an impaired ability to descend stairs compared with ascending stairs. McFadyen and Winter (1988) support this view and state that the hip musculature contributes little to the work of lowering the body; this is accomplished predominantly by eccentric contraction of the quadriceps.

When descending subjects must actively carry their centre of gravity forwards and then resist gravity during the controlled lowering phase. This is achieved through eccentric muscular contraction, which controls the rate of lowering of the centre of gravity by absorbing kinetic energy.

If strong eccentric contractions were not employed, the centre of gravity would accelerate under the influence of the gravitational pull of the Earth (Jevsevar et al 1993).

From biomechanical and anatomical points of view, stair descent is the reverse of ascent; interestingly, this is partly what makes stair descent more challenging than ascent. During the controlled lowering phase the hip and knee joints start from a relatively extended position and then flex, which causes a progressive increase in the external flexion moments which, in order to prevent collapse, have to be matched by the generation of progressively higher levels of eccentric muscle contraction. In a study of 10 healthy males, analysing the motions, forces and moments of the major joints of the lower limb, it was found that the mean flexion–extension moment at the knee for stair ascent was 57.1 newton-metres (N-m). For stair descent the mean flexion–extension moment was nearly three times greater at 146.6 N-m (Andriacchi et al 1980). Anatomically, the stance knee starts in a relatively stable extended position and progressively moves into a more unstable position of flexion as controlled lowering takes place. This also causes a progressive demand for increased muscular control.

In addition to the reasons outlined above, there is another factor that contributes to the explanation as to why step descent is more challenging compared to step ascent, this is related to the quadriceps extensor mechanism, in particular to the role of the patellofemoral joint.

Some confusion on the role of the patella occurs in the literature with some authors referring to the patella as the fulcrum for the extensor mechanism of the knee and others referring to the patella as a balancing beam for the patella tendon force and quadriceps force.

For clarity it is worth listing the components of a lever:

- Balance beam
- Fulcrum (pivot)
- Load
- Effort.

It is important to consider the patella as the balance beam for the extensor mechanism and the patella contact zone as the fulcrum. When moving from full extension to full flexion discrete parts of the patella articulate with the femur, these

Table 12.1	Phases of stair climbing (McFadyen & Winter 1988)	
Ascent		**Descent**
Weight acceptance		Weight acceptance
Pull up		Forward continuance
Forward continuance		Controlled lowering

Table 12.2	Key muscles involved in stair climbing (McFadyen & Winter 1988)	
Ascent		**Descent**
Vastus lateralis		Vastus lateralis and medialis
Gluteus medius and soleus		Gastrocnemius and soleus

are referred to as contact zones. Patellar contact zones have a horizontal orientation and spread over approximately one-third of the articular surface of the patella. Wiberg (1941) was the first to attempt a systematic study of patellofemoral contact zones. These studies showed that a band of contact moved proximally from the pole towards the base of the patella, as the knee moved from extension towards flexion (Fig. 12.1).

The proximal migration of the contact zone during knee flexion occurs due to the cam shape of the femoral condyles and the constant position the patella holds relative to the tibia due to the inelastic patellar tendon (Fig. 12.2).

During stair descent as knee flexion occurs, because of the proximal shift of the patella contact zone, the patella tendon lever lengthens and the quadriceps lever shortens. The effect of the moving contact zone is quite significant; at angles of less than 60° knee flexion the quadriceps lever arm works with a mechanical advantage, however, at angles of greater than 60° knee flexion the quadriceps work at a mechanical disadvantage (Gill & O'Connor 1996, Nissel & Ekholm 1985). An interesting paradox is, therefore, created; as the external moment increases with progressive knee flexion, the demand for higher levels of eccentric quadriceps activity increases at the same time as the quadriceps are becoming progressively less efficient.

Clinically, Selfe (2000) confirmed that in a group of healthy volunteers a critical angle occurred, where there was a sudden reduction in eccentric control, during a slow step descent at 61° knee flexion. In a later study on a group of patients with patellofemoral pain syndrome, the critical angle was observed to occur earlier at 58° knee flexion (Selfe et al 2001a). This helps to confirm that patients with impairment in their extensor mechanism function may have particular problems with stair descent.

Although the focus of this section has been predominantly on the knee, a number of authors have also described the effects of stair climbing on the other joints of the lower limb (Tables 12.3a, b).

When comparing the effects of loading between the hip and the knee in the same subjects, dramatic changes occur depending on activity. The knee is exposed to 33% higher compressive force than the hip during level walking and 116% higher compressive force than the hip during stair climbing (Taylor et al 2004). Having an insight into the differential magnitude of the loads applied to the joints of the lower limb is important for a number of reasons. Coupling anatomical knowledge about the positions in which joints are inherently either stable or unstable along with understanding the magnitude of loading helps to present a clearer picture as to why joints get injured. Having this understanding should in turn help clinicians to plan logical progression through rehabilitation programmes incrementally loading joint structures during different functional activities.

Finally, using stair climbing as an example gives us a useful biomechanical insight into the importance of weight

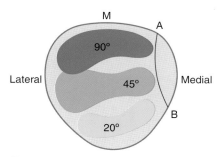

Figure 12.1   Posterior aspect of the patella showing size and orientation of patellar contact zones at three different angles of knee joint flexion (Fulkerson & Hungerford 1990)

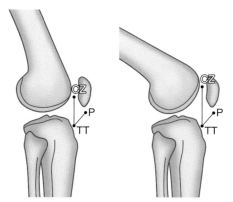

Figure 12.2   The proximal migration of the contact zone during knee flexion – where TT to P is a constant length due to the patella tendon and TT to CZ lengthens due to the cam shape of the femoral condyles (Selfe 2000)

Table 12.3a   Range of motion required at the lower limb joints for stair climbing

	Ascending			Descending		
	Hip	Knee	Ankle	Hip	Knee	Ankle
Andriacchi et al 1980	41.9°	83°	13.6° DF 25.3° PF	28.2°	87.9°	27.0° DF 25.6° PF
Laubenthal et al 1972		83°			83°	
Jevsevar et al 1993		98.6° young 88.1° old			90.3° young 84.1° old	

DF: dorsiflexion; PF: plantarflexion

Table 12.3b   Joint loading, expressed as multiple of bodyweight (BW), during stair climbing activities

	Joint	Amount of loading
Taylor et al 2004	Hip Tibifemoral joint Compression Tibiofemoral joint Shear	2.5 × BW 5.4 × BW 1.3 × BW
Reilly and Martens 1972	Patellofemoral joint	3.0 × BW
Seedhom et al 1979	Patellofemoral joint	2.5 – 3.0 × BW
Morrison 1970	Tibiofemoral joint	3.0 × BW

control and the changes in loading in the lower limb joints that can occur with fairly small, but clinically significant, changes in bodyweight. Reilly and Martens (1972) report that the patellofemoral joint compression force (PJF) is in the region of three times the bodyweight when involved in stair climbing. If we then apply these data to a very simple example of a patient who is 2 kg over their optimum bodyweight going up a flight of stairs that has 10 steps, we can see what a disproportionate and potentially detrimental effect the extra weight has on the patellofemoral joint (Table 12.3c).

There are two groups of patients that this knowledge is particularly pertinent to: the obese and the intensive sports player. When considering the obese patient the magnitude of these forces is going to be very large. It is therefore, important to consider weight loss strategies as part of the rehabilitation. There often emerges a 'catch 22' situation as one of the keys to weight loss is exercise; however, this may aggravate joint problems. Clinicians need to be sensitive to this issue and plan rehabilitation activities carefully in order not to provoke the very problem that the patient is seeking help for.

The intensive sports player presents a slightly different rehabilitation challenge. The problem is often that they have a very high calorie intake, which is fine while they are playing a lot of sport. When they have an injury they are unable to use as many calories, but often their appetite is undiminished and they maintain a very high calorie intake, which means that their weight increases. In terms of rehabilitation this can be problematic. Another reason that weight may increase is due to 'comfort eating', which occurs due to depressed mood because of being unable to play sport and because of boredom as 'there is nothing else to do!' The subject of weight control is a very sensitive one and problems associated with weight control can be associated with other underlying emotional problems so clinicians have to proceed carefully in this area.

Finally, in this section it is also worth considering the work of Nissel and Ekholm (1985) who reported significant gender differences in the loading across the patellofemoral joint. They found that women compared to men had shorter patellar tendon moment arms, which lead to a 20% increase in patellar force. They argue that females are, therefore, exposed to higher patellofemoral joint stress than men of the same weight. This may account for the higher reported prevalence of patellofemoral disorders in females.

12.2.3 Motion of the lower limbs during stair descent

We will now consider the functional movement of the ankle and knee joints during stair decent. These will be described by angle against time graphs and angular velocity graphs to gain an understanding of not only the range of the motion of the different phases of joint motion but also control of the joint motion.

Ankle-joint motion

The ankle joint starts off in slight dorsiflexion during initial standing. The ankle then moves into dorsiflexion slowly as the body moves over the foot to take the first step. The toe then comes off the ground, and a second smaller movement into dorsiflexion ensures foot clearance of the step. The

ankle joint then plantarflexes to prepare for the contact with the next step down. At contact with the next step the ankle rapidly dorsiflexes as the foot takes the load and the body moves the tibia over the ankle joint. The foot then comes off the ground and the ankle joint plantarflexes to prepare for the next step. The angular velocity graph shows the rate at which the ankle joint is plantarflexing (negative) and dorsiflexing (positive) (Fig. 12.3a, b).

Knee joint motion

The knee joint starts off flexed as the subject prepares to take a step. The knee then flexes to clear the step then extends to move the tibia forwards and down to the next step. At contact with the next step the knee flexes to take the load and to control the descent of the centre of mass

Table 12.3c	Effect of changing bodyweight on patellofemoral loading	
Patient = 70 kg	Patient = 72 kg
×1 step PJF = 210 kg	×1 step PJF = 216 kg
Total PJF for 10 steps = 2100 kg	Total PJF for 10 steps = 2160 kg Extra PJF applied during one flight of 10 stairs = 60 kg

PJF: patellofemoral joint compression force.

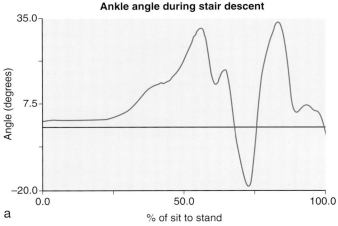

a

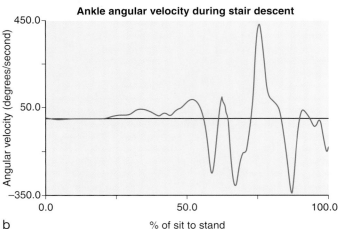

b

Figure 12.3   (a and b) Ankle-joint motion

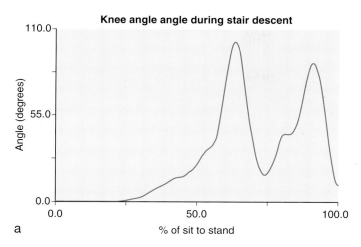

Knee angle angle during stair descent

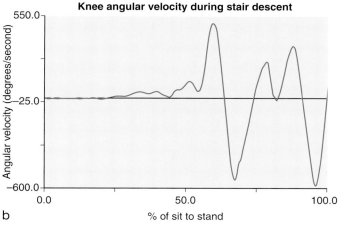

Knee angular velocity during stair descent

Figure 12.4   (a and b) Knee-joint motion

Table 12.4	Knee flexion angle/height of chair seat	
	Knee flexion angle	Height of chair seat
Laubenthal et al 1972	93°	45 cm
Jevsevar et al 1993	96.9° young 84.4° old	Adjusted to each subject's medial tibiofemoral joint line in standing

- Initial phase – used to generate upper-body momentum. Centre of mass predominantly translates horizontally forwards
- Transitional phase – momentum from upper body is transferred to the whole body as the centre of mass changes from horizontal to vertical translation
- Extension phase – vertical ascent of body takes place.

In this study they investigated the effects of four different chair heights on a group of healthy young adults (25–36 years) and a group of healthy older adults (61–79 years). All subjects increased trunk flexion velocity by nearly 50% to overcome the mechanical difficulty associated with lower chair height. The authors explain that due to conservation of momentum, this allows the upper body momentum to be harnessed to assist the hip and knee extension required to initiate lift off from the seat, the authors refer to this as momentum transfer.

If chair height is lower the starting position of the centre of gravity is lower making lift off from the seat more demanding. Older subjects tend to move more slowly, therefore, they generate less upper body momentum during the first phase, which leads to difficulties actually getting out of the chair.

to the lower level. The knee then moves towards extension once again to move the tibia forwards and down to the next step. The angular velocity graph shows the rate at which the knee joint is flexing (positive) and extending (negative) (Fig. 12.4a, b).

12.3 Sitting to standing

12.3.1 Introduction

Rising from a seated position is a significant mechanical challenge and in particular requires considerable quadriceps activity. Quadriceps demand is increased in two ways: firstly, the quadriceps are required to generate enough concentric moment to extend the knee against the combined effects of gravity and body weight; secondly, they have to resist the antagonistic action of the hamstrings. In order to rise from a chair, trunk flexion with associated hip flexion occurs. Excessive hip flexion is resisted by contraction in the hamstrings, which simultaneously induces knee flexion; this 'unwanted' knee flexion then has to be overcome by additional quadriceps activity (Ellis et al 1980).

12.3.2 Amount of knee flexion required for sitting (Table 12.4)

Schenkman et al (1996) described three phases of sit-to-stand activity:

12.3.3 Biomechanics of sit to stand

The motion of the ankle, knee and hip joints may be studied during sit to stand activities by considering the angle against time and the angular velocity of each joint. All three movement patterns are distinctly different and the interaction of these joints gives a very detailed means of assessment of the sit-to-stand task.

Ankle-joint motion during sit-to-stand task
The ankle motion is initially in slight dorsiflexion, although this will vary slightly with different initial foot positions. The ankle then moves smoothly into an increasing dorsiflexed position. As the person leaves the chair the ankle moves back towards the ankle neutral position. The angular velocity graph shows an initial dorsiflexion velocity (positive) followed by a plantarflexion velocity (negative) (Fig. 12.5a, b).

Knee-joint motion during sit-to-stand task
The knee joint is initially flexed at 90°, then after a short delay smoothly extends to near full extension when the person is upright. The angular velocity graph shows a smooth increase and decrease in the extension velocity (negative) demonstrating a controlled movement into extension (Fig. 12.6a, b).

Hip-joint motion during sit-to-stand task
The hip joint is initially flexed at 90° at the onset there is an immediate movement into further flexion as the trunk

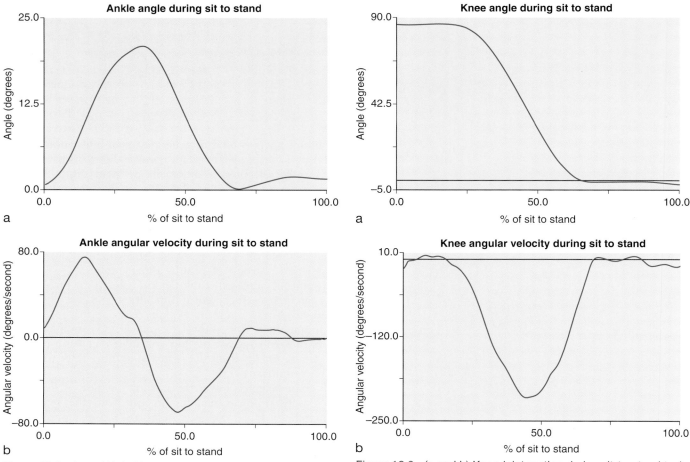

Figure 12.5   (a and b) Ankle-joint motion during sit-to-stand task

Figure 12.6   (a and b) Knee-joint motion during sit-to-stand task

is moved forward over the feet. Then at approximately the same time as the onset of knee extension the hip starts to extend until the upright position is attained. The velocity graph shows an initial flexion angular velocity (positive) as the trunk is inclined forwards, followed by an extension velocity (negative) until the upright position is attained (Fig. 12.7a, b).

12.4 The timed up and go test

The timed up and go test (TUG) is commonly used to measure functional mobility in older adults. As the name implies the time taken to rise from a chair, walk 3 m turn and return to the chair and sit down is measured. Subjects who are able to complete the test in less than 20 s have been shown to be independent in activities of daily living and walk at speeds that are sufficient for community mobility. Those subjects requiring greater than 30 s to complete the test tend to be more dependent in activities of daily living and often require gait aids (Podsiadlo & Richardson 1991). The test has also been shown to be a sensitive and specific measure for identifying community-dwelling adults who are at risk for falls (Shumway-Cook et al 2000).

The advantages of using a functional test of this type are many. For example, it has excellent face validity, as

subjects can relate to the activity and easily see the relevance of the test to their own mobility. It is easy and simple for clinicians to extract the relevant data, i.e. time from the test. Although from a clinical point of view it is an excellent test, as it provides a number of highly relevant challenges listed below, biomechanical analysis of the whole task is a challenge, although the different activities may be studied in isolation:

- Rising from the seat
- Attaining balance
- Gait initiation and acceleration away from the seat
- Steady state gait
- Deceleration and preparation for turning
- Turning through 180°
- Acceleration
- Steady state gait
- Deceleration and preparation for turning
- Turning through 180°
- Gait cessation
- Descent to the seat.

12.5 Gait initiation

Gait initiation is the mechanical and neurological process by which the body's centre of mass (CoM) decouples or

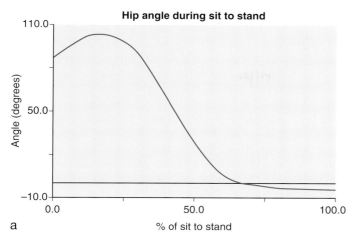

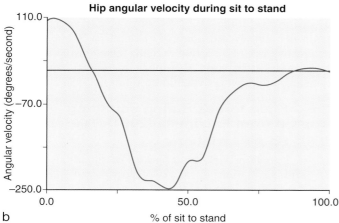

Figure 12.7 (a and b) Hip-joint motion during sit-to-stand task

beyond support limb toe off to the time when the swinging limb becomes the stance limb and toe off occurs. Therefore, gait initiation was broken down into preparatory phase, take off phase and stabilizing period. Elble et al (1994) described gait initiation as movement from a steady state to the point up to and including when the swinging toe left the ground. Brunt et al (1999) defined gait initiation as the transition from quiet stance to steady state gait. These events have generally been identified based on either force platform data or electromyography data. Force analysis has identified events based on the projected centre of pressure during contact phases of gait initiation. The process of gait initiation has therefore been generally accepted to consist of two main phases, the preparatory (postural) phase and stepping (monopodal) phase (Fiolkowski et al 2002, Mickelborough et al 2004, Viton et al 2000), with the preparatory and a stepping phases being of similar duration.

The preparatory phase is when the body begins the decoupling process, shifting the centre of pressure initially in the direction of the swinging limb and then in the direction of the stance limb (Halliday et al 1998). The preparatory phase lasts from onset until the toe off of the stepping foot and is divided into two sub-phases: a release phase and an unloading phase (Archer 1994). During the release sub-phase the centre of pressure is moved towards the swing foot which has the effect of increasing the horizontal ground reaction force components that accelerate the centre of mass in the opposite direction (Polcyn 1998). This release sub-phase lasts until the furthest point of posterolateral centre of pressure movement, when the centre of pressure abruptly changes direction marking the start of the unloading sub-phase. During the unloading sub-phase, the centre of pressure moves rapidly across to the stance foot, unloading the swing foot for toe off.

The second main phase of gait initiation is the stepping phase; this is the point at which the swinging leg is no longer in contact with the floor and lasts until the swinging limb makes its first initial contact. The stepping-foot toe off marks the start of the stepping phase of gait initiation, which is subdivided into single and double support sub-phases. The single support sub-phase lasts from toe off on the stepping foot until initial contact of the stepping foot, with double support sub-phase lasting from initial contact of the stepping foot until the toe off of the original supporting foot.

Figure 12.8 shows the movement of the centre of pressure (black line) and centre of mass (blue line) during gait initiation. This shows the direction of walking from left to right with the right foot being the initial swing foot. Onset is

separates from the centre of pressure (CoP) causing the body to fall forward about the ankle joint (Halliday et al 1998, Henriksson & Hirschfeld 2005, Martin et al 2002, Viton et al 2000). Gait initiation is normally a stereotypical and unconsidered transition from stance into walking, with a consistent pattern of muscle activity (Mann et al 1979, Mickelborough et al 2004). In the absence of external forces, muscle activity is required to initiate gait from a standstill. An appropriate horizontal ground reaction force component must be generated to accelerate the centre of mass forwards and towards the stance side. To achieve this coordinated muscle activity initially moves the centre of pressure towards the swing leg. Jian et al (1993) extended gait initiation

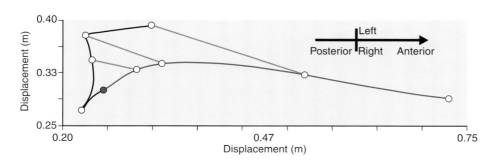

Figure 12.8 The characteristic pattern of horizontal centre of pressure and centre of mass displacement during gait initiation

marked with a blue circle and the major foot contact events are shown as open circles on each curve. During the release phase the centre of pressure moves from onset to its furthest point in the posterolateral direction with little movement of the centre of mass. During the unloading phase the centre of pressure moves across to the stance limb while the centre of mass moves towards the midline between the two feet. The stepping phase sees a movement of the centre of pressure forwards from heel to toe on the stance foot, at the same time the centre of mass moves forward as the swing limb is no longer in contact with the floor and as the body moves forward. This decoupling of the centre of mass and centre of pressure generates an acceleration vector which can be shown as a line between the centre of pressure and centre of mass.

12.6 Squats and dips

Squatting is a fundamental human movement and resting postural activity. It is a basic component of many sporting activities and is, therefore, found in many training and rehabilitation regimes in various altered formats. Although not so common in Western societies, it is a very common resting posture adopted regularly by millions of people worldwide. During squatting a number of significant biomechanical events take place.

12.6.1 Quadriceps wrap

Quadriceps wrap (tendo-femoral wrap or wrap around effect) is the term coined to describe the point at which the quadriceps tendon comes into contact with the femur and starts to bear some of the load. Quadriceps wrap is considered to be a protective mechanism for the patella, by causing an unloading of the patellofemoral joint. The greatest rate of loading of the patellofemoral joint occurs just before quadriceps wrap. After quadriceps wrap has occurred, the rate of patellofemoral joint loading plateaus (Gill & O'Connor 1996). There is no consensus as to the precise knee angle at which quadriceps wrap occurs (Table 12.5).

To date, no references to quadriceps wrap have appeared in the rehabilitation literature, this may be because the functional range that is of primary interest in rehabilitation is the first 30° of flexion. However, many athletic and occupational activities require the knee to be flexed beyond the point at which quadriceps wrap occurs and it may be relevant to consider this phenomenon when rehabilitating these patients.

12.6.2 Quadriceps neutral

The quadriceps neutral angle is defined as 'the knee flexion angle for which quadriceps contraction results in no anteroposterior shear on the tibia' (Singerman et al 1999). At low flexion angles, due to the anterior orientation of the patella tendon, the effect of the quadriceps is to shear the tibia in an anterior direction. At high angles of flexion, due to the posterior orientation of the patella tendon, the effect of the quadriceps is to shear the tibia in a posterior direction. The changing direction of pull of the patellar

tendon is due to articular geometry of the femoral condyles, which are cam shaped. It is interesting to consider that, although quadriceps neutral appears to be quite a significant biomechanical event of the knee, no references to the effect it has on the patellofemoral joint have been found (Table 12.6).

It is interesting to reflect that, although quadriceps wrap and quadriceps neutral appear to be quite significant biomechanical events of the patellofemoral joint, neither event is referred to in mainstream rehabilitation literature. Future researchers should consider whether quadriceps wrap and/or quadriceps neutral are important phenomena when investigating patient populations.

In a study analysing the joint and muscle forces of deep squatting, differences between descent and ascent were found. During a slow descent, both the patellofemoral joint reaction force (PFJRF) (7.41 × bodyweight) and the quadriceps force (5.27 × body weight) were greater than when slowly ascending, PFJRF (4.73 × bodyweight) quadriceps force (4.94 × bodyweight) (Dahlkvist et al 1982). The authors attributed this phenomenon to the larger momentum that occurs when descending.

12.6.3 Knee forces during squatting adapted from Escamilla (2001) (Table 12.7)
12.6.4 Squat variations

As stated previously many variations of squat exist (Tables 12.7 and 12.8). Earl et al (2001) performed mini squats with simultaneous hip adduction, this increased quadriceps activity by 25%. Stuart et al (1996) compared power squat, front squat and lunge. They found that during the lunge quadriceps activity was significantly increased and hamstring activity was significantly decreased.

Purdam et al (2004) compared two groups of patients performing eccentric squats for chronic patellar tendinopathy. One group with foot flat the other with foot inclined down (plantar flexed) at an angle of 25°. The group on the decline board improved significantly more than the flat group. This effect was considered to be due to decreased calf muscle tension allowing a greater isolation of the knee extensor mechanism.

12.6.5 Joint moments and EMG activity during a single limb dip

The use of eccentric activities for rehabilitation associated with tendinopathy has been well documented (Cook &

Table 12.5	Angle at which quadriceps wrap occurs
Ellis et al 1980	80°–105°
Nissel and Ekholm 1985	60°

Table 12.6	Angle at which quadriceps neutral occurs
Escamilla 2001	50°–60°
Singerman et al 1999	50°–55°

Table 12.7 Knee forces during squatting

	Mean body weight (N)	Mean load lifted (N)	Normalized peak tibiofemoral shear % (BW+load)	Normalized mean peak tibiofemoral compression % (BW+load)	Normalized mean peak patellofemoral compression % (BW+load)
Stuart et al 1996	798	223	29	54	
Ariel 1974	888	1982	56	276	
Escamilla et al 1998	912	1437	80	133	194
Escamilla et al 2001	917	1309	99	154	210
Wilk et al 1996	912	1442	76	261	
Toutoungi et al 2000	765	0	353		
Nissell and Ekholm 1985	932	2453		198	191
Hattin et al 1989	790	339		367	
Wretenberg et al 1996		650			324
Reilly and Martens 1972	834	0			765

N: newtons; BW: bodyweight
Adapted from Escamilla 2001

Table 12.8 Muscle activity during squatting

	Muscle	Peak activity knee flexion angle
Escamilla et al 1998	Quadriceps	80°–90°
	Hamstrings	10°–60° (ascent)
	Gastrocnemius	60°–90°
Stuart et al 1996	Hamstrings	30°

Khan 2001, Panni et al 2000, Roos et al 2004). A number of authors (Alfredson et al 1998, Jonsson & Alfredson 2005, Khan et al 1998, Purdam et al 2004) have suggested that a 25° decline squat in comparison to a flat squat produces a significant improvement in the ability of the individual to participate in sports and a reduction in pain. There is, however, no scientific justification given as to why 25° was chosen for the decline. The suggested depth of squat based on the angle of knee flexion varies between 50° and 90° (Alfredson et al 1998, Onishi al 2000, Young et al 2005). Initially, Purdam et al (2004) proposed 50°, with the basis for this being that the force in the patellar tendon is equal to that of the quadriceps tendon when in this particular orientation. However, subsequently Purdam et al (2004) proposed 90° of flexion, with Jonsson and Alfredson (2005) using 70° of flexion. Based on this variation in the range of flexion, within the literature there is no consensus within contemporary research. However, clinically there can be considerable differences in the amount of knee flexion different individuals are able to achieve during eccentric squat activities, so the relevance of controlling the amount of knee flexion is debatable.

To investigate the optimum angle of decline Richards et al (2006) considered four angles: 0°, 8°, 16° and 24°. The subjects were instructed to perform the squat as slowly as possible to approximately 90°. Whilst performing the squat movement, force and analysis data electromyography (EMG) were collected from rectus femoris and gastrocnemius. External joint moments were calculated using inverse dynamics methods. The enveloped EMG magnitudes at maximum knee flexion (Figs 12.9 and 12.10), the iEMG (integrated EMG) during the squat, and the ankle and knee moments at maximum knee flexion were recorded (Figs 12.11 and 12.12). EMG and iEMG were normalized to the maximal dynamic contraction (Kellis & Baltzopoulos 1996).

The ankle moments during a squat showed a significant decrease with the introduction of a declined angle. It is interesting to note that the ankle moment is not significantly different between 0° and 8°, but for all subsequent increases a significant difference was seen in the pairwise comparisons. This can be explained by examining the nature of the change in ankle angle in relation to the base of support from the foot. As the decline increases so the base of support decreases; however, the further away from the horizontal, the larger the effect of the angular changes on the base of support. The reduction of the base of support has the effect of reducing the moment arm between the ground reaction force and the joint and thus the moment.

The knee moments during a squat also showed significant increase with the introduction of a declined angle. However, knee moments showed significant changes in the comparisons for all angles apart from between 16° and 24°. Although the moment about the ankle is significantly reduced, this does not correspond to the level of muscle activity seen in the gastrocnemius. This, in effect, requires an increase in stability leading to an increase in the activity of the gastrocnemius to stabilize the ankle in this position; an alternative explanation is the shortening of the muscle, which would also lead to a greater EMG signal in relation to the joint moment. This would suggest that increasing the angle of decline to 24° increases the activity of the gastrocnemius,

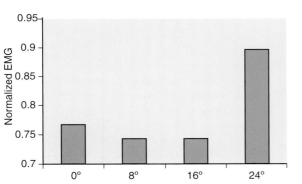

Figure 12.9   Electromyography (EMG) from Gastrocnemius

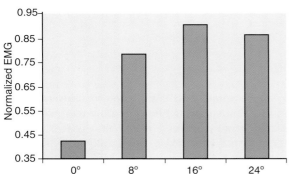

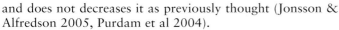

Figure 12.10   Electromyography (EMG) from Rectus Femoris

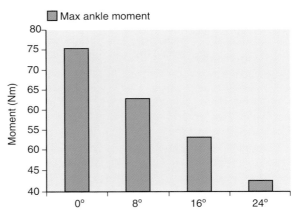

Figure 12.11   Ankle Joint Moment at different decline angles

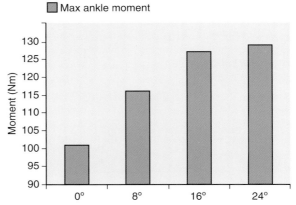

Figure 12.12   Knee Joint Moment at different decline angles

and does not decreases it as previously thought (Jonsson & Alfredson 2005, Purdam et al 2004).

The effectiveness of different angles of decline has been established for targeting the knee extensors, concluding that a 16° decline produces an exercise that specifically targets the knee extensors with minimum effect about the ankle. At 24° of decline an increase in gastrocnemius activity is evident, which implies that the increased angle challenges the stability of the ankle. However, further studies are required to establish the effectiveness in specific exercises used in clinical practice.

Summary: Common movement tasks in clinical assessment

- A closed kinetic chain is said to occur in the lower limb when the foot meets considerable resistance, e.g. the ground. An open kinetic chain occurs when the foot is free to move in space with little or no resistance.
- The majority of research literature has been on walking. The study of the movement patterns during different functional tasks is equally important to individuals' participation and quality of life.
- There are many clinical tests that may be investigated using biomechanics. This allows the critical evaluation of the different tasks used in clinical assessment to be analysed in detail in relation to joint function and control. Investigating these will help to explain the theoretical aspects of the different movement tasks used in clinical assessment.

References

Aagaard P, Simonsen EB, Trolle M, Bangsbo J, Klausen K. Isokinetic hamstring/quadriceps strength ratio: influence from joint angular velocity, gravity correction and contraction mode. Acta Physiologica Scandinavia 1995;154(4):421–427.

Abdel-Aziz YI, Karara HM. Direct linear transformation from comparator coordinates into object space coordinates in close range photogrammetry. In: ASP symposium on close range photogrammetry. American Society of Photogrammetry, Urbana, IL, 1971; pp. 1–18.

Alexander EJ, Andriacchi TP. Correcting for deformation in skin-based marker systems. Journal of Biomechanics 2001;34:355–361.

Alfredson H, Pietila T, Jonsson P, Lorentzon R. Heavy-load eccentric calf muscle training for the treatment of chronic achilles tendinosis. The American Journal of Sports Medicine. 1998;26(3):360–366.

Al-Majali M, Solomonidis SE, Spence W, Bell F, Rafferty D. Design specification of a walk mat system for the measurement of temporal and distance parameters of gait. Gait and Posture 1993;1:119–120.

Andriacchi TP, Ogle JA, Galante JO. Walking speed as a basis for normal and abnormal gait measurements. Journal of Biomechanics 1977;10:261–268.

Andriacchi TP, Anderson G, Fermier RW, Stern D, Galante JO. A study of lower limb mechanics during stair climbing. Journal of Bone and Joint Surgery America 1980;62:5–749.

Andriacchi TP, Alexander EJ, Toney MK, Dyrby C, Sum J. A point cluster method for in vivo motion analysis: applied to a study of knee kinematics. Journal of Biomechanics England 1998;120(6):743–749.

Andriacchi TP, Koo S, Dyrby C, Chaudhari A. Rotational changes at the kenn during walking are associated with cartilage thinning following ACL injury. In: 9th International Conference on Orthopaedics, Biomechanics, Sports Rehabilitation. Assisi 2005(Nov 11–13); pp. 99–100.

Anthony RJ. The manufacture and use of functional foot orthosis. Karger, Basal, Switzerland, 1991.

Antonsson EK, Mann RW. The frequency of gait. Journal of Biomechanics 1985;18(1):39–47.

Antonsson EK, Mann RW. Automatic 6 DOF kinematic trajectory acquisition and analysis. Journal of Dynamic Systems, Measurement and Control 1989;111:34–35.

Archer SE, Winter DA, Prince F. Initiation of gait: a comparison between young, elderly and Parkinson's disease subjects (abstract). Gait and Posture 1994;2.

Areblad M, Nigg BM, Ekstrand J, Olsson KO, Ekstrom H. Three-dimensional measurement of rearfoot motion during running. Journal of Biomechanics 1990;23(9):933–940.

Arenson JS, Ishai G, Bar A. A system for monitoring the position and time of feet contact during walking. Journal of Medical Engineering and Technology 1983;7(6):280–284.

Ariel G. Method for biomechanical analysis of human performance. Research Quarterly 1974;45 (1):72–79.

Astrand P, Ryhming I. A nomogram for calculation of aerobic capacity (physical fitness) from pulse rate during submaximal work. Journal of Applied Physiology 1954;7:218–221.

Baker V, Bennell K, Stillman, B, Cowan S, Crossley K. Abnormal joint position sense in individuals with patellofemroal pain syndrome. Journal of Orthopaedic Research 2002;20:208–214.

Ball P, Johnson GR. Reliability of hindfoot goniometry when using a flexible electrogoniometer. Clinical Biomechanics 1993;8:13–19.

Ball KA, Pierrynowski MR. Modelling of the pliant surfaces of the thigh and leg during gait. In: Proceedings of the SPIE – The International Society for Optical Engineering, BIOS '98 – International Biomedical Optics Symposium 1998;3254:435–446.

Bartlett RM, Challis JH, Yeadon MR. Cine/video analysis. In: Bartlett RM (ed.) Biomechanical Analysis of Performance in Sport. British Association of Sports Sciences, Leeds, 1992; pp. 8–23.

Batavia M, Garcia RK. The concurrent validity of a dynamic movement measured by the Ariel Performance Analysis System, the Qualysis MacReflex motion analysis system, and an electrogoniometer (abstract). Physical Therapy 1996;76:S75.

Bell A, Pederson D, Brand R. A comparison of the accuracy of several hip centre location predication methods. Journal of Biomechanics 1990;23(6):617–621.

Bell F, Ghasemi M, Rafferty D, Richards J, Weir E. An holistic approach to gait analysis: Glasgow Caledonian University's CRC. Gait and Posture 1995;3:185.

Bell F, Shaw L, Rafferty D, Rennie J, Richards J. Movement analysis technology in clinical practice. Physical Therapy Review 1996;1:13–22.

Berjian RA, Douglass HO Jr, Holyoke ED, Goodwin PM, Priore RL. Skin pressure measurements on various mattress surfaces in cancer patients. American Journal of Physical Medicine 1983;62(5):217–226.

Bobbert AC. Energy expenditure in level and grade walking. Journal of Applied Physiology 1960;15:1015–1021.

Brand RA, Crowninshield RD. Locomotion studies–caves to computers (abstract). Journal of Biomechanics 1981;14(7):497.

Branthwaite HR, Payton CJ, Chockalingam N. The effect of simple insoles on three-dimensional foot motion during normal walking. Clinical Biomechanics 2004;19(9):972–977.

Braune W, Fischer O. Uber den Schwerpunkt des menschlichen Korpers, mit Rucksicht auf die Ausrustung des deutschen Infanteristen. Abhandlungen der mathematisch-physischen classe der Konigl, Sachsischen Gesellschaften der Wissenschaften 1889;26:561–672.

Bresler B, Frankel J. The forces and moments in the leg during level walking. Transactions of the ASME 1950;27–36.

Brown DC. Decentering distortion of lenses. Photometric Engineering 1966;32(3):444–462.

Bruckner J. The gait workbook: a practical guide to clinical gait analysis. SLACK Incorporated, 1998.

Brunt D, Liu SM, Trimble M, Bauer J, Short M. Principles underlying the organization of movement initiation from quiet stance. Gait and Posture 1999;10(2):121–128.

Burgess-Limerick R, Abernethy B, Neal J. Relative phase quantifies interjoint co-ordination. Journal of Biomechanics 1993;26(1):91–94.

Callaghan M, Selfe J, Bagley P, Oldham J. Effect of patellar taping on knee joint proprioception. Journal of Athletic Training 2002;37(1):19–24.

Cappello A, Cappozzo A, La Palombara PF, Lucchetti L, Leardini A. Multiple anatomical landmark calibration for optimal bone pose estimation. Human Movement Science. 1997;16:259–274.

Cappozzo A. Three dimensional analysis of human walking: experimental methods and associated artefacts. Human Movement Science 1991;10:589–602.

Cappozzo A, Catani F, Croce UD, Leardini A. Position and orientation in space of bones during movement: anatomical frame definition and determination. Clinical Biomechanics 1995;10(4):171–178.

Cappozzo A, Catani F, Leardini A, Benedetti MG, Della Croce U. Position and orientation in space of bones during movement: experimental artefacts. Clinical Biomechanics 1996;11(2): 90–100.

Cappozzo A, Cappello A. Surface-marker cluster design criteria for 3-d bone movement reconstruction. IEEE Transactions on Biomedical Engineering 1997;40(12): 1165–1174.

Cappozzo A, Della Croce U, Leardini A, Chiari L. Human movement analysis using photogrammetry. Part 1: theoretical background. Gait and Posture 2005;21:186–196.

Carson MC, Harrington ME, Thompson N, O'Connor JJ, Theologis TN. Kinematic analysis of a multi-segment foot model for research and clinical applications: a repeatability analysis. 2001

Cavagna GA, Saibene FP, Margaria R. External work in walking. Journal of Applied Physiology 1963;18:1–9.

Cerveri P, Pedotti A, Ferrigno G. Kinematical models to reduce the effect of skin artifacts on marker-based human motion estimation. Journal of Biomechanics 2005;38(11):2228–2236.

Chandler RF et al. Tech. Report AMRL-TR-74-137. Wright-Patterson Air Force Base, Aerospace Medical Research Laboratories, 1975.

Charteris J, Taves C. The process of habituation to treadmill walking: a kinematic analysis. Perceptual Motor Skills 1978;47:659–666.

Chéze L, Fregly BJ, Dimnet J. A solidification procedure to facilitate kinematic analyses based on video system data. Journal of Biomechanics 1995;28:879–884.

Chiari L, Della Croce U, Leardini A, Cappozzo A. Human movement analysis using stereophotogrammetry. Part 2: instrumental errors. Gait and Posture 2005;21:197–211.

Chou LS, Draganich LF. Placing the trailing foot closer to an obstacle reduces flexion of the hip, knee, and ankle to increase the risk of tripping. Journal of Biomechanics 1998;31(8):685–691.

Clauser CE, McConville JT, Young JW. Weight, volume, and centre of mass of segments of the human body. AMRL technical report. Wright-Patterson Air Force Base, Ohio, 1969.

Cook J, Khan K. What is the most appropriate treatment for patellar tendinopathy. British Journal of Sports Medicine 2001;35(5):291–294.

Cook TM, Zimmermann CL, Lux KM, Neubrand KM, Nicolson TD. EMG comparison of lateral step up and stepping machine exercise. Journal of Orthopaedic and Sports Physical Therapy 1992;16(3):108–113.

Corcoran, Brengelmann. Oxygen uptake in normal and handicapped subjects, in relation to speed of walking beside velocity controlled cart. Archives of Physical Medicine and Rehabilitation 1970;51:78–87.

Cotes JE, Meade F. The energy expenditure and mechanical energy demand in walking. Ergonomics 1960;3:97–119.

Cowan SM, Bennell K, Hodges PW. The test-retest reliability of the onset of concentric and eccentric vastus medialis obliquus and vastus lateralis electromyographic activity in a stair stepping task. Physical Therapy in Sport 2000;1:129–136.

Craik RL, Oatis CA. Gait analysis theory and action, 1 edn. Mosby, St Louis, 1995.

Crouse J, Wall JC, Marble AE. Measurement of temporal and spatial parameters of gait using a microcomputer based system. Journal of Biomedical Engineering 1987;9(1):64–68.

Crouse S, Lessard C, Rhodes J, Lowe R. Oxygen consumption and cardiac response of short-leg and long-leg prosthetic ambulation in a patient with bilateral above knee amputation: comparisons with able-bodied men. Archives of Physical Medicine and Rehabilitation 1990;71:313–317.

Dabnichki P, Lauder M, Aritan S, Tsirakos D. Accuracy evaluation of an on-line kinematic system via dynamic tests. Journal Medical Engineering Technology 1997;2:53–66.

Dahlkvist NJ, Mayo P, Seedhom BB. Forces during squatting and rising from a deep squat. Engineering in Medicine 1982;11(68):76.

Davids JR, Holland WC, Sutherland DH. Significance of the confusion test in cerebral palsy. Journal of Pediatric Orthopaedics 1993;13(6):717–721.

Davis R, Ounpuu S, Tyburski D, Gage J. A gait data collection and reduction technique. Human Movement Sciences 1991:10:575–587.

De Bruin H, Russell DJ, Latter JE, Sadler JT. Angle-angle diagrams in monitoring and quantification of gait patterns for children with cerebral palsy. American Journal of Physical Medicine 1982;61(4):176–192.

de Leva P. Adjustments to Zatsiorsky-Seluyanov's segment inertia parameters. Journal of Biomechanics 1996;29(9):1223–1230.

della Croce U, Cappozzo A, Kerrigan DC. Pelvis and lower limb anatomical landmark calibration precision and its propagation to bone geometry and joint angles. Medical and Biological Engineering and Computing 1999;37(2):155–161.

della Croce U, Camomilla V, Leardini A, Cappozzo A. Femoral anatomical frame: assessment of various definitions. Medical Engineering and Physics 2003;25(5):425–431.

Dempster WT. Space requirements of the seated operator. WADC Technical Report 55–159. Wright-Patterson Air Force Base, Ohio, 1955.

Dempster WT, Gabel WC, Felts WJL. The anthropometry of manual work space for the seated subject. American Journal of Physical Anthropology 1959;17:289–317.

Doucette SA, Child DD. The effect of open and closed chain exercise and knee joint position on patellar tracking in lateral patellar compression syndrome. British Journal of Orthopaedic and Sports Physical Therapy 1996;23(2):104–110.

Dowswell T, Towner E, Cryer C, Jarvis S, Edwards P, Lowe P. Accidental falls: fatalities and injuries ad examination of the data sources and review of the literature on preventive strategies. Department of Trade and Industry, London, URN 99/805, 1999.

Drezner J, Staudt L, Fowler E. Examination of intersegmental coordination in spastic cerebral palsy patients before and after selective posterior rhizotomy. Gait and Posture 1994;2:61.

Drillis R, Contini R. Body segment parameters. Report no.1163–03, Office of Vocational Rehabilitation, Department of health, Education and Welfare, New York, 1966.

Durie ND, Farley RL. An apparatus for step length measurement. Journal of Biomedical Engineering 1980;2(1):38–40.

Earl JE, Schmitz RJ, Arnold BL. Activation of the VMO and VL during dynamic mini-squat exercises with and without isometic hip adduction. Journal of Electromyography and Kiniesiology 2001;11:381–386.

Elble RJ, Moody C, Leffler K, Sinha R. The initiation of normal walking. Movement Disorders 1994;9:139–146.

Elftman H. Forces and energy changes in the leg during walking. American Journal of Physiology 1939;125:339–356.

Elftman HO. The force exerted by the ground in walking. Arbeitsphysiologie 1939;10:485–491.

Ellis M, Seedhom BB, Wright V, Dowson D. An evaluation of the ratio between the tension along the quadriceps tendon and the patellar ligament. Engineering in Medicine 1980;9(4):189–194.

Escamilla RF. Knee biomechanics of the dynamic squat. Medicine and Science in Sports and Exercise 2001;33(1):127–141.

Escamilla RF, Fleisig GS, Zheng N, Barrentine SW, Wilk KE, Andrews JR. Biomechanics of the knee during closed kinetic chain and open kinetic chain exercises. Medicine and Science in Sports and Exercise 1998;30(4):556–569.

Escamilla RF, Fleisig GS, Zheng N, Lander JE, Barrentine SW, Andrews JR, Bergemann BW, Moorman CT. Effects of technique variations on knee biomechanics during the squat and leg press. Medicine and Science in Sports and Exercise 2001;33(9):1552–1566.

JAMA. Evidence Based Practice or Evidenced Based Medicine. The users' guides to evidence-based medicine. Journal of the American Medical Association, 1992.

Ferrigno G, Pedotti A. ELITE: a digital dedicated hardware system for movement analysis via real-time TV signal processing. IEEE Transactions on Biomedical Engineering 1985;32(11):943–950.

Ferris DP, Czerniecki JM, Hannaford B. An ankle-foot orthosis powered by artificial pneumatic muscles. Journal of Applied Biomechanics 2005;21(2):189–197.

Ferris DP, Gordon KE, Sawicki GS, Peethambaran A. An improved powered ankle-foot orthosis using proportional myoelectric control. Gait and Posture 2006;23(4):425–428.

Fiolkowski P, Brunt D, Bishop M, Woo R. Does postural instability affect the initiation of human gait? Neuroscience Letters 2002;323(3):167–170. *Links*

Fulkerson JP, Hungerford DS. Disorders of the Patellofemoral Joint, 2 edn. Williams and Wilkins, Baltimore, 1990.

Fuller J, Liu L-J, Murphy MC, Mann RW. A comparison of lower-extremity skeletal kinematics measured using skin- and pin-mounted markers. Human Movement Science 1997;16:219–242.

Gage JR. The clinical use of kinetics for evaluation of pathological gait in cerebral palsy. Journal of Bone & Joint Surgery (Am) 1994;76(4):622–631.

Gage JR. The role of gait analysis in the treatment of cerebral palsy. Journal of Pediatric Orthopedics 1994;4(6):701–702.

Gardner GM, Murray MP. A method of measuring the duration of foot–floor contact during walking. Physical Therapy 1975;55(7):751–756.

Gerny K. A clinical method of quantitative gait analysis. Physical Therapy 1983;63:1125–1126.

Gill HS, O'Connor JJ. Biarticulating two-dimensional computer model of the human patellofemoral joint. Clinical Biomechanics 1996;11(2):81–89.

Goh JC, Bose K, Khoo BC. Gait analysis study on patients with varus osteoarthrosis of the knee. Clinical Orthopaedics and Related Research 1993;(294):223–231.

Grabiner M, Owings T. EMG differences between concentric and eccentric maximum voluntary contractions are evident prior to movement onset. Journal Experimental Brain Research 2002;145(4):505–511.

Grieve DW. Gait patterns and the speed of walking. Biomedical Engineering 1968;3:119–122.

Grieve D, Gear J. The relationship between length of stride, step frequency, time of swing and speed of walking for children and adults. Ergonomics 1966;5(9):379–399.

Grood ES, Suntay WJ. A joint coordinate system for the clinical description of three-dimensional motions: application to the knee. ASME Journal of Biomedical Engineering 1983;105:136–144.

Growney E, Cahalan T, Meglan D. Comparison of goniometry and video motion analysis for gait analysis. Journal of Biomechanics 1994;27:624.

Gussoni M, Margonato V, Ventura R, Veicsteinas A. Energy cost of walking with hip joint imparement. Physical Therapy 1990;70:195–301.

Hallen LG, Lindahl O. The 'screw-home' movement in the knee-joint. Acta Orthopaedica Scandinavica 1966;37(1):97–106.

Halliday SE, Winter DA, Frank JS, Patla AE, Prince F. The initiation of gait in young, elderly, and Parkinson's disease subjects. Gait and Posture 1998;8(1):8–14.

Haskell W, Yee M, Evans A, Irby P. Simultaneous measurement of heart rate and body motion to quantitate physical activity. Medicine and Science in Sports and Exercise 1993;25(1):109–115.

Hattin HC, Pierrynowski MR, Ball KA. Effect of load cadence and fatigue on tibiofemoral joint force during a half squat. Medicine and Science in Sports and Exercise 1989;21:613–618.

Hazlewood ME, Brown JK, Rowe PJ, Salter PM. The use of therapeutic electrical stimulation in the treatment of hemiplegic cerebral palsy. Developmental Medicine and Child Neurology, 1994;36(8):661–673.

Hazlewood ME, Hillman SJ, Lawson AM, Robb JE. Marker attachment in gait analysis: on skin or lycra? Gait and Posture 1997;6:265.

Henriksson M, Hirschfeld H. Physically active older adults display alterations in gait initiation. Gait and Posture 2005;21(3):289–296.

Hershler C, Milner M. Angle–angle diagrams in above-knee amputee and cerebral palsy gait. American Journal of Physical Medicine 1980;59(4):165–183.

Hewett TE, Noyes FR, Barber-Westin SD, Heckmann T. Decrease in knee joint pain and increase in function in patients with medial compartment arthrosis: a prospective analysis of valgus bracing. Orthopedics 1998;21:131–138.

Hirokawa S. Normal gait characteristics under temporal and distance constraints. Journal of Biomedical Engineering 1989;11:449–456.

Hirokawa S, Matsumura K. Gait analysis using a measuring walkway for temporal and distance factors. Medical and Biological Engineering and Computing 1987:25:577–582.

Holden JP, Stanhope SJ. The effect of variation in knee center location estimates on net knee joint moments. Gait and Posture 1998;7(1):1–6.

Holden JP, Orsini JA, Lohmann Siegel K, Kepple TM, Gerber LH, Stanhope SJ. Surface movement errors in shank kinematics and knee kinetics during gait. Gait and Posture 1997;5: 217–227.

Hortobagyi T, Katch FI. Eccentric and concentric torque-velocity relationships during arm flexion and extension. Influence of strength level. European Journal of Applied Physiology and Occupational Physiology 1990;60(5):395–401.

Hullin MG, Robb JE, Loudon IR. Ankle-foot orthosis function in low-level myelomeningocele. Journal of Pediatric Orthopaedics 1992;12:518–521.

Hurley GR, McKenney R, Robinson M, Zadravec M, Pierrynowski MR. The role of the contralateral limb in below-knee amputee gait. Prosthetics and Orthotics International 1990;14(1):33–42.

Hurmuzlu Y, Basdogan C, Carollo JJ. Presenting joint kinematics of human locomotion using phase plane portraits and Poincare maps. Journal of Biomechanics 1994;27(12):1495–1499.

Hurmuzlu Y, Basdogan C, Stoianovici D. Kinematics and dynamic stability of the locomotion of post-polio patients. Journal of Biomedical Engineering 1996;118(3):405–411.

Imms F, MacDonald I, Prestidge S. Energy expenditure during walking in patients recovering from fractures of the leg. Scandinavian Journal of Rehabilitation Medicine 1976;8:1–9.

Inman VT. Human locomotion. Canadian Medical Association Journal 1966;94:1047–1054.

Inman VT. Conservation of energy in ambulation. Archives of Physical Medicine and Rehabilitation 1967;48.

Inman VT, Ralston HJ, Todd F. Human Walking. Williams and Wilkins Company, Baltimore, MD, 1981.

Isaac Newton. Philosophiae Naturalis Principia Mathematica. 1687.

Isakov E, Burger H, Krajnik J, Gregoric M, Marincek C. Influence of speed on gait parameters and on symmetry in trans-tibial amputees. Prosthetics and Orthotics International 1996;20(3):153–158.

Jarret MO, Andrews BJ, Paul JP. Quantitative analysis of locomotion using television. ISPO World Congress, Montreux, Switzerland, 1974.

Jevsevar DS, Riley PO, Hodge WA, Krebs DE. Knee kinematics and kinetics during locomotor activities of daily living in subjects with knee arthroplasty and in healthy control subjects. Physical Therapy 1993;73(4):229–242.

Jian Y, Winter DA, Ishac MG, Gilchrist L. Trajectory of the body COG and COP during initiation and termination of gait. Gait and Posture 1993;1:9–22.

Johnson F, Leitl S, Waugh W. The distribution of load across the knee. A comparison of static and dynamic measurements. British Journal of Bone and Joint Surgery 1980;62(3):346–349.

Jones RK, Nester CJ, Kim WY, Tyson S, Laxton P, Jari S, Johnson D, Richards JD. Direct and indirect orthotic management of medial compartment osteoarthritis of the knee, ESMAC & GCMAS meeting, Amsterdam, 25–30 September, 2006.

Jonsson P, Alfredson H. Superior results with eccentric compared to concentric quadriceps training in patients with jumper's knee: a prospective randomised study. British Journal of Sports Medicine 2005;39:847–850.

Kadaba MP, Ramakrishnan HK, Wootten ME, Gainey J, Gorton G, Cochran GV. Repeatability of kinematic, kinetic, and electromyographic data in normal adult gait. Journal of Orthopaedic Research 1989;7(6):849–860.

Keemink CJ, Hoek van Dijke GA, Snijders CJ. Upgrading of efficiency in the tracking of body markers with video techniques. Medical and Biological Engineering and Computing 1991;29(1):70–74.

Kellis E, Baltzopoulos V. The effects of normalization on antagonistic activity patterns during eccentric and concentric isokinetic knee extension and flexion. Journal of Electromyography and Kinesiology 1996;6(4):235.

Kepple TM, Arnold AS, Stanhope SJ, Siegel KL. Assessment of a method to estimate muscle attachments from surface landmarks: a 3D computer graphics approach. Journal of Biomechanics 1994;27(3):365–371.

Khan K, Maffulli N, Coleman B, Cook J, Taunton J. Patellar tendinopathy: some basic aspects of science and clinical management. British Journal of Sports Medicine 1998;32: 346–355.

Kim WY, Richards JD, Jones RK, Hegab A. Single limb stance adduction moment in medial compartment osteoarthritis of the knee. The Knee 2004;11:225–231.

Kingma I, Toussaint HM, Commissaris DACM, Hoozemans MJM, Ober MJ. Optimising the determination of the body centre of mass. Journal of Biomechanics 1995;28(9):1137–1142.

Kirkley A, Webster-Bogaert S, Litchfield R, Amendola A, MacDonald S, McCalden R, Fowler P. The effect of bracing on varus gonarthrosis. American Journal of Bone and Joint Surgery 1999;81–A:539–548.

Klein PJ, Gabusi CA, Brinn MB. Validation of linear and angular displacement estimation by computer-assisted motion analysis. Physical Therapy 1992;72:s11(abstract).

Kowalk DL, Duncan JA, Vaughan CL. Abduction-adduction moments at the knee during stair ascent and descent. Journal of Biomechanics 1996;29(3):383–388.

Ladin Z, Mansfield PK, Murphy MC, Mann RW. Segmental analysis in kinesiological measurements. Image-based motion measurements, SPIE 1990;1356:110–120.

Laubenthal KN, Smidt GL, Kettlekamp DB. A quantitative analysis of knee motion during activities of daily living. Physical Therapy 1972;52(1):34–43.

Leardini A, Cappozzo A, Catani F, Toksvig-Larsen S, Petitto A, Sforza V, Cassanelli G, Giannini S. Validation of a functional method for the estimation of hip joint centre location. Journal of Biomechanics 1999;32(1):99–103.

Leardini A, Chiari L, Della Croce U, Cappozzo A. Human movement analysis using stereophotogrammetry. Part 3. Soft tissue artifact assessment and compensation. Gait and Posture 2005;21: 212–225.

Lee VS, Solomonidis SE, Spence WD. Stump-socket interface pressure as an aid to socket design in prostheses for trans-femoral amputees–a preliminary study. Proceeding from the Institute of Mechanical Engineering [H] 1997;211(2):167–180.

Leiper CI, Craik RL. Relationship between physical activity and temporal-distance characteristics of walking in elderly women. Physical Therapy 1991;71(11):791–803.

Lesh MD, Mansour JM, Simon SR. A gait analysis subsystem for smoothing and differentiation of human motion data. Journal of Biomechanical Engineering 1979;101:205–212.

Levens AS, Inman VT, Blosser JA. Transverse rotation of the segments of the lower extremity in locomotion. American Journal of Bone and Joint Surgery 1948;30A:859–872.

Lindenfeld TN, Hewett TE, Andriacchi TP. Joint loading with valgus bracing in patients with varus gonarthrosis. Clinical Orthopaedics 1997; 344:290–297.

Lockard MA. Foot orthoses. Physical Therapy 1988;68(12): 1866–1873.

Lough J. Quantifying motor performance in patients with peripheral neuropathy undergoing treatment (abstract). Physiotherapy 1995;81:745.

Low J, Reid A. Electrotherapy explained. Buterworth Heinemann. Oxford, 1992.

Lu TW, O'Connor JJ. Three dimensional computer graphics based modelling and mechanical analysis of the human locomotor system. In: Sixth International Symposium on the 3D Analysis of Human Movement. 1–4 May, 2000.

Lucchetti L, Cappozzo A, Cappello A, Della Croce U. Skin movement artefact assessment and compensation in the estimation of knee-joint kinematics. Journal of Biomechanics 1998;31:977–984.

MacGregor J. Rehabilitation ambulatory monitoring. Disability, Strathclyde Bioengineering Seminars, MacMillan, London, 1979;159–172.

MacGregor J. The evaluation of patient performance using long-term ambulatory monitoring technique in the domiciliary environment. Physiotherapy 1981;67(2):30–33.

MacWilliams BA, Cowley M, Nicholson DE. Foot kinematics and kinetics during adolescent gait. Gait and Posture 2003;17(3):214–224.

Maly MR, Culham EG, Costigan PA. Static and dynamic biomechanics of foot orthoses in people with medial compartment knee osteoarthritis. Clinical Biomechanics (Bristol, Avon) 2002;17(8):603–610.

Manal K, McClay I, Stanhope S, Richards J, Galinat B. Comparison of surface mounted markers and attachment methods in estimating tibial rotations during walking: an in vivo study. Gait and Posture 2000;11:38–45.

Manal K, McClay I, Richards J, Galinat B, Stanhope S. Knee moment profiles during walking: errors due to soft tissue movement of the shank and the influence of the reference coordinate system. Gait and Posture 2002;15: 10–17.

Mann RA, Hagey JL, White V, Liddell D. The initiation of gait. Journal of Bone and Joint Surgery 1979;61–a:232–239.

Mann RA, Antonsson EK. Gait analysis–precise, rapid, automatic, 3-D position and orientation kinematics and dynamics. Bulletin of the Hospital for Joint Diseases Orthopedic Institution 1983;43(2):137–146.

Mansour JM, Lesh MD, Nowak MD, Simon SR. A three dimensional multi-segmental analysis of the energetics of normal and pathological gait. Journal of Biomechanics 1982;15(1):51–59.

Marciniak W. Design of an electrogoniometer for the examination of the movements of the knee and foot during walking. Chirurgia Narzadow Ruchu i Ortopedia Polska 1973;38(5):573–579.

Marey EJ. Animal mechanism: a treatise on terrestrial and aerial locomotion. New York: Appleton. Republished as Vol. XI of the International Scientific Series. 1873.

Martin M, Shinberg M, Kuchibhatla M, Ray L, Carollo JJ, Schenkman ML. Gait initiation in community-dwelling adults with Parkinson disease: comparison with older and younger adults without the disease. Physical Therapy 2002;82(6):566–577.

Matsumo H, Kadowaki K, Tsuji H. Generation II knee bracing for severe medial compartment osteoarthritis of the knee. Archives of Physical Medicine and Rehabilitation 1997;78:745–749.

McClay I, Manal K. A comparison of 3D lower extremity kinematics during running between excessive pronators and normals. Clinical Biomechanics 1998;13(3):195–203.

McConnell J. The physical therapist's approach to patellofemoral disorders. Clinical Sports Medicine 2002;21(3):363–387.

McDonough AL, Batavia M, Chen FC, Kwon S, Ziai J. The validity and reliability of the GAITRite system's measurements: a preliminary evaluation. Archives of Physical Medicine and Rehabilitation 2001;82(3):419–425.

McFadyen B, Winter DA. An integrated biomechanical analysis of normal stair ascent and descent. Journal of Biomechanics 1988;21(9):733–744.

McGinty G, Irrgang JJ, Pezullo D. Biomechanical considerations for rehabilitation of the knee, Clinical Biomechanics 2000:15:160–166.

Messier SP, Loeser RF, Hoover JL, Semble EL, Wise CM. Osteoarthritis of the knee: effects on gait, strength, and flexibility. Archives of Physical Medicine and Rehabilitation 1992;73(1):29–36.

Mickelborough J, van der Linden ML, Tallis RC, Ennos AR. Muscle activity during gait initiation in normal elderly people. Gait and Posture 2004;19(1):50–57.

Miller C, Verstraete M. Determination of the step duration of gait ignition using a mechanical energy analysis. Journal of Biomechanics 1996;29(9):1195–1199.

Mizahi J, Suzak Z, Heller L, Najenson T. Variation of the time distance parameters of the stride as related to clinical gait improvement in hemiplegics. Scandinavian Journal of Rehabilitation Medicine 1982;14:133–140.

Moritani T, Muramatsu S, Muro M. Activity of motor units during concentric and eccentric contractions. American Journal of Physical Medicine 1987;66(6):338–350.

Morrison JB. The mechanics of the knee joint in relation to normal walking. Journal of Biomechanics 1970;3:51–61.

Murray MP. Gait as a total pattern of movement. American Journal of Physical Medicine 1967;40:290–333.

Murray MP, Drought AB, Kory RC. Walking patterns of normal men. American Journal of Bone and Joint Surgery 1964;46A:335–360.

Murray MP, Kory RC, Clarkson BH, Sepic SB. Comparison of free and fast speed walking patterns of normal men. American Journal of Physical Medicine 1966;45:8–25.

Murray MP, Sepic SB, Barnard EJ. Patterns of sagittal rotation of the upper limbs in walking. Physical Therapy 1967;47(4):272–284.

Murray MP, Kory RC, Sepic SB. Walking patterns of normal women. Archives of Physical Medicine and Rehabilitation 1970;51(11):637–650.

Muybridge E. Animal locomotion. Reprinted In: Brown LS (ed.) (1957). Animal in motion. Dover, New York, 1887.

Muybridge E. The human figure in motion. Chapman and Hall, London, 1901.

Nadler R, Nadler S. Assistive devices and lower extremity orthotics in the treatment of osteoarthritis. Physical medicine and rehabilitation. State of the Art Reviews 2001;15(1): 57–64.

Nelson RM, Currier DP. Clinical electrotherapy, 2nd ed. Appleton & Lange, Conneticut, 1991.

Nene AV. Physiological cost index of walking in able-bodied adolescents and adults. Clinical Rehabilitation 1993;7(4): 319–326.

Nene AV, Patrick J. Energy cost of paraplegic locomotion with the ORLAU parawalker. Paraplegia 1989;27:5–18.

Nester CJ, van der Linden ML, Bowker P. Effect of foot orthoses on the kinematics and kinetics of normal walking gait. Gait and Posture 2003;17(2):180–187.

Nguyen TC, Baker R. Two methods of calculating thorax kinematics in children with myelomeningocele. Clinical Biomechanics (Bristol, Avon) 2004;19(10):1060–1065.

Nicol AC. A flexible electrogoniometer with widespread applications. In: Jonsson B (ed.) Biomechanics XB. Human Kinetics Pub, Illinois, 1987; 1029–1033.

Nicol AC. Measurement of joint motion. Clinical Rehabilitation 1989;3:1–9.

Nigg BM, Herzog W. Biomechanics of the musculo-skeletal system. John Wiley & Sons Ltd, 1994.

Nissel R, Ekholm J. Patellar forces during knee extension. Scandinavian Journal of Rehabilitation Medicine 1985;17:74.

Noyes FR, Schipplein OD, Andriacchi TP, Saddemi SR, Weise M. The anterior cruciate ligament-deficient knee with varus alignment. An analysis of gait adaptations and dynamic joint loadings. American Journal of Sports Medicine 1992;20(6):707–716.

Ojima H, Miyake S, Kumashiro M, Togami H, Suzuki K. Dynamic analysis of wrist circumduction: a new application of the biaxial flexible electrogoniometer. Clinical Biomechanics 1991;6(4):221–229.

Olney SJ, Monga TN, Costigan PA. Mechanical energy of walking of stroke patients. Archives of Physical Medicine and Rehabilitation 1986;67:92–98.

Olney, Costigan, Hedden. Mechanical energy patterns in gait of cerebral palsied children with hemiplegia. Physical Therapy 1987;67:1348–1354.

Olney SJ, Grondin RC, McBride ID. Energy and power considerations in slow walking (abstract). Journal of Biomechanics 1989;22:1066.

Olree KS, Engsberg JR, White DK. Indices of effort and oxygen uptake in children with cerebral palsy. Developmental Medicine and Child Neurology 1996;38(S74):49–50.

Onishi H, Yagi R, Akasaka K, Momose K, Ihashi K, Handa Y. Relationship between signals and force in human vastus lateralis muscle using multipolar wire electrodes. Journal of Electromyography and Kinesiology 2000;10:59–67.

Osternig LR, James CR, Bercades DT. Eccentric knee flexor torque following anterior cruciate ligament surgery. Medicine and Science in Sports and Exercise 1996;28(10):1229–1234.

Palmitier RA, An KN, Scott SG, Chao EY. Kinetic chain exercise in knee rehabilitation. Sports Medicine 1991;11(6):402–413.

Panni A, Tartarone M, Maffulli N. Tendinopathy in athletes. Outcome of nonoperative and operative management. American Journal of Sports Medicine 2000;28(3):392–379.

Passmore R, Draper MH. Energy metabolism. In: Albance A (ed.) Newer methods of nutritional biochemistry. Academic, New York, 1965.

Passmore R, Durnin J. Human energy expenditure. Physiology Review 1955;35:801–840.

Patrick J. Gait laboratory investigations to assist decision making. British Journal of Hospital Medicine 1991;45:35–37.

Paul JP. Forces transmitted by joints in the human body. Proceedings of the Institute of Mechanical Engineering 1967;181(3J):8–15.

Perry J. Gait analysis: Normal and pathological function. SLACK Incorporated, Thorofare, NJ, 1992.

Perttunen JR, Anttila E, Sodergard J, Merikanto J, Komi PV. Gait asymmetry in patients with limb length discrepancy. Scandinavian Journal of Medicine and Science in Sports. 2004;14(1):49–56.

Petersen WA, Brookhart JM, Stone SA. A strain-gage platform for force measurements. Journal of Applied Physiology 1965;20:1095–1097, 8750–7587.

Pierrynowski M, Winter D, and Norman R. Transfers of mechanical energy within the total body and mechanical efficiency during treadmill walking. Ergonomics 1980;23.

Pierrynowski MR, Norman RW, Winter DA. Mechanical energy analyses of the human during local carriage on a treadmill. Ergonomics 1981;24(1):1–14.

Podsiadlo D, Richardson S. The timed up and go: a test of basic functional mobility for frail elderly persons. Journal of the American Geriatric Society 1991;39:142–148.

Polcyn AF, Lipsitz LA, Kerrigan C, Collins JJ. Age-related changes in the initiation of gait: degredation of central mechanisms for momentum generation. Archives of Physical Medicine and Rehabilitation 1998;79:1582–1589.

Pollo FE. Bracing and heel wedging for unicompartmental osteoarthritis of the knee. American Journal of Knee Surgery 1998;11:47–50.

Pollo FE, Otis JC, Backus SI, Warren RF, Wickiewicz TL. Reduction of medial compartment loads with valgus bracing of the osteoarthritis knee. American Journal of Sports Medicine 2002;30:414–421.

Powers CM. The influence of altered lower extremity kinematics on patellofemoral joint dysfunction: a theoretical perspective. Journal of Orthopaedics and Sports Physical Therapy 2003;33:639–646.

Prodromos CC, Andriacchi TP, Galante JO. A relationship between gait and clinical changes following high tibial osteotomy. American Journal of Bone and Joint Surgery 1985;67(8):1188–1194.

Purdam CR, Johnson P, Alfredson H, Lorentzon R, Cook JL, Khan KM. A pilot study of the eccentric decline squat in the management of painful chronic patellar tendinopathy. British Journal of Sports Medicine 2004;38:395–397.

Quanbury A, Winter D, Reimer G. Instantaneous power and power flow in body segments during walking. Journal Human Movement Studies 1975;1:59–67.

Rafferty D, Bell F. Gait analysis – a semiautomated approach. Gait and Posture 1995;3(3):184.

Ralston HJ. Energy speed relation and optimal speed during level walking. Internationale Zeitschrift für Angewandte Physiologie Einschliesslich Arbeitsphysiologie 1958;17:277.

Ralston H, Lukin L. Energy levels of human body segments during level walking. Ergonomics 1969;12(1):39–46.

Reilly DT, Martens M. Experimental analysis of the quadriceps muscle force and patellofemoral joint reaction force for various activities. Acta Orthopaedica Scandinavica 1972;43:126–137.

Reinschmidt C. Three-dimensional tibiocalcaneal and tibiofemoral kinematics during human locomotion – measured with external and bone markers. Ph.D. thesis. University of Calgary, Calgary, Alberta, 1996.

Reinschmidt C, van den Bogert T, Nigg BM, Lundberg A, Murphy N. Effect of skin movement on the analysis of skeletal knee joint motion during running. Journal of Biomechanics 1997;30(7): 729–732.

Rennie J, Bell F, Rafferty D, Robb J. Measurement of spatial parameters of gait and velocity in schools and centres for young adults with learning disabilities. Physiotherapy 1997;83(7):364.

Richards JD, Pramanik A, Sykes L, Pomeroy VM. A comparison of knee kinematic characteristics of stroke patients and age-matched healthy volunteers. Clinical Rehabilitation 2003;7(5):565–571.

Richards J, Selfe J, Kilmurray S. The biomechanics of step descent under different treatment modalities used in patellofemoral pain. 9th International conference of Orthopaedics, Biomechanics and Sports Rehabilitation edn, University of Perugia, 2005.

Richards J, Jones R, Kim W. Biomechanical changes in the conservative treatment of medial compartment osteoarthritis of the knee using valgus bracing. International Cartilage Repair Society, 2006a.

Richards J, Thewlis D, Selfe J, Cunningham A, Hayes C. The biomechanics of single limb squats at different decline angles Enkle de Enkle congress 2006b. 2006b.

Richardson JK. Rocker-soled shoes and walking distance in patients with calf claudication. Archives of Physical Medicine and Rehabilitation 1991;72(8):554–558.

Rigas C. Spatial parameters of gait related to the position of the foot on the ground. Prosthetics and Orthotics International 1984;8(3):130–134.

Rine RM, Ward J, Lindeblad. Use of angle–angle diagrams to analyze effects of lower extremity in children with cerebral palsy. Physical Therapy 1992;72(Suppl):S57–S58.

Roos E, Engstrom M, Lagerquist A, Soderberg B. Clinical improvement after 6 weeks of eccentric exercise in patients with mid – portion Achilles tendinopathy – a randomized trial with 1-year follow up. Scandinavian Journal of Medicine and Science in Sports 2004;14:286–295.

Root ML, Orien WP, Weed JH. Normal and Abnormal Function of the Foot: Clinical Biomechanics, Vol. 2. Clinical Biomechanics Co, Los Angeles, 1977.

Rose J, Gamble JG. Human walking. Williams and Wilkins, Baltimore, 1994.

Rowe PJ, Nicol AC, Kelly IG. Flexible goniometer computer system for the assessment of hip function. Clinical Biomechanics 1989;4:68–72.

Rowell L, Taylor H, Wang Y. Limitatiions to prediction of maximal oxygen intake. Journal of Applied Physiology 1964;19(5):919–927.

Rydell NW. Forces acting on the femoral head-prosthesis. A study on strain gauge supplied prostheses in living persons. Acta Orthopaedica Scandinavica 1966;37(Suppl 88):1–32.

Salsich GB, Brechter JH, Farwell D, Powers CM. The effects of patellar taping on knee kinetics, kinematics, and vastus lateralis muscle activity during stair ambulation in individuals with patellofemoral pain. Journal of Orthopaedic and Sports Physical Therapy 2002;32(1):3–10.

Saunders JBDM, Inman VT, Eberhart HS. The major determinants in normal and pathological gait. Journal of Bone and Joint Surgery 1953;35A:543–558.

Schache AG, Wrigley TV, Blanch PD, Starr R, Rath DA, Bennell KL. The effect of differing Cardan angle sequences on three dimensional lumbo-pelvic angular kinematics during running. Medical Engineering in Physiotherapy 2001;23(7):493–501.

Schenkman M, Riley PO, Pieper C. Sit to stand from progressively lower seat heights – alterations in angular velocity. Clinical Biomechanics 1996;11(3):153–158.

Schwartz MH, Rozumalski A. A new method for estimating joint parameters from motion data. Journal of Biomechanics 2005;38(1):107–116.

Seedhom BB, Takeda T, Tsubuku M, Wright V. Mechanical factors and patellofemoral osteoarthrosis. Annals of Rheumatic Diseases 1979;38:307–316.

Selfe J. Peak 5 motion analysis of an eccentric step test performed by 100 normal subjects. Physiotherapy 2000;86(5):241–247.

Selfe J. The Patellofemoral joint: a review of primary research. Critical Reviews in Physical and Rehabilitation Medicine 2004;16(1):1–30.

Selfe J, Harper L, Pedersen I, Breen-Turner J, Waring J. Four outcome measures for patellofemoral joint problems: part 1 development and validity. Physiotherapy 2001a;87(10):507–515.

Selfe J, Harper L, Pedersen I, Breen-Turner J, Waring J. Four outcome measures for patellofemoral joint problems: Part 2 reliability and clinical sensitivity. Physiotherapy 2001b;87(10):516–522.

Shinno N. Analysis of knee function in ascending and descending stairs. Medicine and Sport 1971;6:202–207.

Shumway-Cook A, Brauer S, Woollacott M. Predicting the probability for falls in community dwelling older adults using the timed up and go test. Physical Therapy 2000;80(9):896–903.

Sidway B, Heise G, Schoenfelder-Zohdi B. Quantifying the variability of angle–angle plots. Journal of Human Movement Studies 1995;29:181–197.

Simonson E, Keys A. Working capacity in patients with orthopaedic handicaps from poliomyelitis, 1947.

Singerman R, Berilla J, Archdeacon M, Peyser A. In vitro forces in the normal and cruciate deficient knee during simulated squatting motion. Transactions of ASME 1999;121:234–242.

Sojka AM, Stuberg WA, Knutson LM, Karst GM. Kinematic and electromyographic characteristics of children with cerebral palsy who exhibit genu recurvatum. Archives of Physical Medicine and Rehabilitation 1995;76(6):558–565.

Stuart MJ, Meglan DA, Lutz GE, Growney ES, An KN. Comparison of intersegmental tibiofemoral joint forces and muscle activity during various closed kinetic chain exercise. American Journal of Sports Medicine 1996;24:792–799.

Sutherland DH, Cooper L. The pathomechanics of progressive crouch gait in spastic diplegia. Orthopedic Clinics of North America 1978;9:143–154.

Tasi RY. An efficient and accurate camera calibration technique for 3D machine vision. Proceedings of the 1986 IEEE Computer Society Conference on Computer Vision and Pattern Recognition, 1986; pp. 364–374.

Tata JA, Quanbury AO, Steinke TG, Grahame RE. A variable axis electrogoniometer for the measurement of simple plane movement. Journal of Biomechanics 1978;11:421–425.

Taylor WR, Heller M, Bergmann G, Duda GN. Tibio femoral loading during human gait and stair climbing. Journal of Orthopaedic Research 2004;22(3):625–632.

Thewlis D, Richards J, Bower J. Discrepancies in knee joint moments using common anatomical frames defined by different palpable landmarks. Journal of Applied Biomechanics (in press).

Toutoungi DE, Lu TW, Leardini A, Catani F, O'Connor JJ. Cruciate ligament forces in the human knee during rehabilitation exercises. Clinical Biomechanics 2000;15:176–187.

Viton JM, Timsit M, Mesure S, Massion J, Franceschi JP, Delarque A. Asymmetry of gait initiation in patients with unilateral knee arthritis. Archives of Physical Medicine and Rehabilitation 2000;81(2):194–200.

Wagner H. Pelvic tilt and leg length correction. Orthopaedics 1990;19(5):273–277.

Wall JC, Ashburn A. Assessment of gait disability in hemiplegics. Scandinavian Journal of Rehabilitation Medicine 1979;11;95–103.

Wall JC, Charteris J, Turnbull G. Two steps equals one stride equals what? Clinical Biomechanics 1987;2:119–125.

Wang JW, Kuo KN, Andriacchi TP, Galante JO. The influence of walking mechanics and time on the results of proximal tibial osteotomy. American Journal of Bone and Joint Surgery 1990;72(6):905–909.

Wiberg G. Roentgenographic and anatomic studies on the femoropatellar joint. Acta Orthopaedica Scandinavica 1941;12:319–410.

Wilk KE, Escamilla RF, Fleisig GS, Barrentine SW, Andrews JR, Boyd ML. A comparison of tibiofemoral joint forces and electromyographic activity during open and closed kinetic chain exercises. American Journal of Sports Medicine 1996;24:518–527.

Winter DA. Energy assessment in pathological gait. Physiotherapy Canada 1978;30:183–191.

Winter DA. Knowledge base for diagnostic gait assessments. Medical Progress Through Technology 1993;19(2):61–81.

Winter DA. A. B. C. (Anatomy, Biomechanics, Control) of Balance during Standing and Walking. ISBN : 0-9699420-0-1, 1995.

Winter DA, Quanbury AO, Reimer GD. Analysis of instantaneous energy of normal gait. Journal of Biomechanics 1976;9(4):253–257.

Wolff SL. Essential considerations in the use of EMG Biofeedback. Physical Therapy 1978;58:25.

Woltring HJ. Calibration and measurement in 3-dimensional monitoring of human motion by optoelectronic means. II. Experimental results and discussion. Biotelemetry 1976;3(2):65–97.

Woltring HJ. Planar control in multi-camera calibration for three-dimensional gait studies. Journal of Biomechanics 1980;13(1):39–48.

Woltring HJ. Estimation and precision of 3D kinematics by analytical photogrametery. Computing in Medicine 1982;232–241.

Woltring HJ, Huiskes R, de Lange A. Finite centroid and helical axis estimation from noisy landmark measurements in the study of human joint kinematics. Journal of Biomechanics 1985;18(5): 379–389.

Wood GA, Jennings LS. On the use of spline functions for data smoothing. Journal of Biomechaincs 1979;12:477–479.

Woodburn J, Nelson KM, Siegel KL, Kepple TM, Gerber LH. Multisegment foot motion during gait: proof of concept in rheumatoid arthritis. Journal of Rheumatology 2004;31(10):1918–1927.

Wretenberg P, Feng Y, Arborelius UP. High and low bar squatting techniques during weight training. Medicine and Science in Sports and Exercise 1996;22:218–224.

Wright F. Accident prevention and risk taking by elderly people: The need for advice. Age Concern, London, 1994.

Wu G, Siegler S, Allard P et al. Standardization and Terminology Committee of the International Society of Biomechanics. ISB recommendation on definitions of joint coordinate system of various joints for the reporting of human joint motion – part I: ankle, hip, and spine. International Society of Biomechanics. Journal of Biomechanics 2002;35(4):543–548.

Wu G, van der Helm FC, Veeger HE et al. International Society of Biomechanics. ISB recommendation on definitions of joint coordinate systems of various joints for the reporting of human joint motion – part II: shoulder, elbow, wrist and hand. Journal of Biomechanics 2005;38(5):981–992.

Young M, Cook J, Purdam C, Kiss Z, Alfredson H. Eccentric decline squat protocol offers superior results at 12 months compared with traditional eccentric protocol for patellar tendinopathy in volleyball players. British Journal of Sports Medicine 2005;39:102–105.

Zatsiorsky V, Seluyanov V. The mass and inertia characteristics of the main segments of the body. In: Matsui H, Kobayashi K (eds). Biomechanics VIII–B. Human Kinetics Publishers, Champaign, IL, 1983; pp. 1152–1159.

Index